JOHN PREBBLE

John Prebble is an Englishman who spent his boyhood in a Scots township in Canada where, he believes, he was first inspired by thoughts of Scotland and its history. He began his writing career as a journalist and is now a novelist, historian, film-writer, and the author of many highly praised plays and dramatised documentaries for television. His great tetralogy on the destruction of the clans – *The Highland Clearances*, *Culloden*, *Glencoe* and *Mutiny* – has been described in the Scottish Historical Review as 'a major achievement in Scottish historical writing . . . probably one of the most important influences setting the historical framework of the Scottish people today'. A less enthusiastic Professor of Scottish History has said that Prebble has 'contributed a great deal to the state of mind of left-wing agitation in Scotland.' John Prebble believes that both statements are certainly exaggerated. His other books include an account of the seventeenth century Scots colony on Panama, *The Darien Disaster*, and *The Lion in the North*, which he called 'a personal history' of Scotland.

THE KING'S JAUNT

'By giving us back our history, John Prebble has helped to restore our sense of worth. For that we owe him a great deal.'

JAMES HUNTER, *Scotsman*

'His passionate, partisan and beautifully re-searched books are the product of a lifelong preoccupation with the Highlands' sad, violent history.'

NICHOLAS PHILLIPSON, *Sunday Telegraph*

'Almost unnoticed, except by the thousands who read his books, John Prebble has eased himself into the position of one of our leading historians, whose works are as scholarly as they are readable.'

PROFESSOR JOHN KENYON, *Observer*

'All his books are as excitingly readable as good novels, yet they are firmly based on first-hand research.'　HUGH MACDIARMID

'The author is quite probably one of the most important influences in setting the historical framework for the debate on the condition of the Scottish people today. Many historians share his generous sympathies with the fate of Highland society and he has no need for empty academic praise.'

ERIC RICHARDS, *Scottish Historical Review*

by the same author

THE KING'S JAUNT

George IV in Scotland, August 1822
'One and twenty daft days'

JOHN PREBBLE

FONTANA/Collins

First published by Collins Publishers, 1988
First published in 1989 by Fontana Paperbacks,
8 Grafton Street, London W1

Copyright © 1988 by John Prebble

Fontana Paperbacks is a part of the Collins Publishing Group

Printed and bound in Great Britain by
William Collins Sons and Co. Ltd, Glasgow

For Jonathan Clark
my grandson

CONTENTS

ILLUSTRATIONS

ILLUSTRATIONS

Alasdair Ranaldson MacDonell of Glengarry from a drawing by
    Denis Dighton *On loan to the Clan Donald Museum, Skye*
Ranald MacDonell, henchman to Glengarry, from a drawing by
    Denis Dighton *On loan to the Clan Donald Museum, Skye*

John Campbell, Earl of Breadalbane by Henry Raeburn
    The Scottish National Portrait Gallery
Mrs Grant of Laggan by James Tannock
    The Scottish National Portrait Gallery
39 Castle Street, Edinburgh by J. W. M. Turner
    The Pierpont Morgan Library, New York
John Townsend 'One of the Most Famous Runners' by Denis
    Dighton
George IV entering the Palace of Holyrood House by David
    Wilkie *Scottish National Portrait Gallery*
George IV in St Giles Cathedral by J. W. M. Turner
    The Tate Gallery, London
George IV at the Provost's Banquet by J. W. M. Turner
    The Tate Gallery, London

The Theatre Royal, Edinburgh, 1830, a drawing by Thomas
    Shepherd
George IV at Edinburgh Castle by James Skene
    By courtesy of Edinburgh City Libraries
A View of Edinburgh from Calton Hill, 1819 by George Vincent
    The Fine Art Society, London
George IV on the steps of Hopetoun House by Denis Dighton
    Hopetoun House Preservation Trust
Willie Duff, from a painting by Kenneth MacLeay
    Windsor Castle, the Royal Library © Her Majesty the Queen
A contemporary photograph of Willie Duff
    By courtesy of Edinburgh City Libraries

PART ONE

The Journey or the Jaunt?

'He is bent on going to Vienna, God knows why,
but if the Ministers possibly can,
they will put a spoke in his wheel.'

– Lord Montagu to Sir Walter Scott

> *'My suffering countrymen! I remain under the firm conviction that I die a Martyr in the Cause of Truth and Justice, and in the hope that you will soon succeed in the cause which I took up arms to defend.'*
>
> – ANDREW HARDIE, August 1820

John Baird was dead, and so was Andrew Hardie, hanged and then beheaded before the Court House in Stirling. The scaffold had been erected during the night, and the weavers were brought to it on an afternoon of September sunlight, seated on a hurdle and soberly dressed, their Bibles held in white-gloved hands. The headsman sat with them, his axe between his knees. He wore a boy's fur cap, a black gown, and black crape masking all but his eyes. He was a young man, or so thought Hardie who remarked upon his age to one of the accompanying clergymen. When the minister agreed and added that it was a painful duty for one so youthful, Hardie shook his head. 'I'm not certain of that,' he said. 'He seemed to look us *stern* in the face.'

The shops in Broad Street, leading immediately to the scaffold were all closed, but the windows above were crowded and the air was noisy with shouts and screams and sometimes laughter. The sympathy of the people was with the condemned Radicals, and this unsettled the English soldiers of the 13th Foot who lined the route from the Castle and guarded the square before the Court House. More redcoat Englishmen of the 7th Dragoons, having entered the town discreetly by its back streets that morning, now rode in close escort to the hurdle, each bobbing helmet of glazed leather surmounted by an absurd roach of bearskin. Some of these soldiers would later weep when the weavers died.

Released from the hurdle the two men looked about them, and Baird was disappointed in the size of the crowd, having believed, he said, that at least six thousand would come to witness their martyrdom. He was the older of the two by ten years and he kept his eyes

3

from the gallows above, but Hardie looked at it boldly, placing his right hand on his breast and crying, 'Hail harbinger of eternal rest!' Yet each needed the steadying arm of a minister as they went up the steps and into the Court House. There they stayed for half an hour, occupied in a slow and customary ritual – the adjustment of their clothes for the convenience of the hangman and the headsman, an impassioned recital of prayers by all present, and the singing of the 130th Psalm, *Lord, from the depths to thee I cry'd.* When this was done, and both men had taken a little wine and eaten a small biscuit, their hands were bound behind them.

Before they went out into the square again the Sheriff of Stirling, Ranald MacDonald, asked for their word that they would make no political statements from the gallows. They agreed, saying they would speak for no more than eight or ten minutes, and that upon the Bible only. Outside in the sunlight, however, and perhaps encouraged by the warm welcome they were given by the crowd, Baird bowed in response and began to speak of Truth and Justice, of the Radical cause for which he was dying. Aware of MacDonald's angry frown, he stopped, and then spoke of God the Judge of all mankind and Christ its Saviour. He was appealing to the crowd to set aside all folly and observe the Sabbath when again he stopped, uncertain and confused, walking to the edge of the scaffold to consult a minister's watch and asking if he had exceeded his allotted time. Hardie, who had been kneeling in prayer, now rose hastily. With an opening cry of 'Countrymen!', he said he too was dying a martyr in the cause of Truth and Justice. A loud and ambiguous shout of *'Amen!'* (from a pickpocket hoping for a diversion, it was said) provoked cheers, applause, and a brief scuffle quickly suppressed by men of the 13th. 'Hardie . . .' warned MacDonald, 'remember, Sir, your solemn promise.' The weaver now addressed the crowd as 'Friends . . . !', asking them to go home quietly to their devotions when all was done, to avoid taverns and resist the temptation to drink a toast to John Baird and Andrew Hardie.

Standing close to each other now, and almost back to back, both men prayed fervently as the hangman arranged the ropes about their necks and pulled caps over their heads. Baird held his Bible in one pinioned fist, and Hardie a handkerchief which he was to drop as the signal for their dispatch. This he did at eleven minutes to three o'clock, and in the moment before the trap was sprung their free hands grasped each other, holding the tight clasp for a minute above the open floor.

When the bodies had hung for half an hour they were cut down and placed on their coffins, their necks resting on blocks and their heads face down above tubs of sawdust. The masked headsman now came on to the scaffold, his axe upon his shoulder, and although many of the crowd were here to see his work, there was a moment of shock, a shudder and angry shouts of *'Murder . . . ! Murder!'* This, and a following silence, unnerved the executioner. He struck three mangling blows before he could sever the head of Hardie, and two for Baird's, lifting each with both hands and crying 'This is the head of a traitor!' He then stumbled away to the Court House, and was heard to say, 'I wish to God I'd not had to do it!'

He was a medical student, and a volunteer for this grisly departure from his studies. Nine days earlier in Glasgow he had beheaded the hanged body of another Radical, James Wilson, whose death was watched by a vast crowd, more than three times the number Baird believed might come to see him die. Wilson was a Strathaven man, a hosier by trade but also a tinsmith and a clocksmith, a trainer of game-dogs and a preacher on Free Thought. An old man when he died, he had been a Reformer since his youth, finally believing that only armed force would secure 'the rights of our forefathers, for liberty is not worth having if it is not worth fighting for'. This simple but ennobling belief had been the spiritual strength of the Radical reform movement for almost three decades. It had frequently found expression in armed protest by the more militant of the artisan classes. Since the end of the French wars in 1815 there had been an increase in social and industrial unrest, wide unemployment and poverty. By 1819 the Radicals were persuaded that only armed protest would move a repressive and unsympathetic Government. The designing leaders of the movement were shadowy, and some perhaps were *agents provocateurs* intent on urging it towards its own destruction. But the emotional strength of the rank and file came largely from the weavers, a literate, thinking, and sometimes staunchly religious section of the under-privileged. It was from them that the Government selected its targets and ultimately its victims. Wilson's fierce conviction that only an armed struggle could now secure liberty and justice was widely and bravely shared. When the fighting came in the spring of 1820, a brief and bloody skirmish along a dyke on the Stirling Plain, the Radical War was already over. A year of squabble and despair, mobbing and moonlit marching, had ended with the imprisonment of the movement's unknown leaders and the provocation of the rest into an unequal conflict with the King's soldiers. Although sixty thousand workers in Glasgow had struck in support of the pikemen who marched to Bonnymuir – on their way to secure guns from the Carron ironworks – there was no possible end to it all, other than flight or death beneath the plunging hooves and swinging sabres of the 10th Hussars.

That long year of unrest had troubled the political loyalties of the Scots almost as deeply as they had been divided by the King's wish to be rid of his wife by a Bill of Divorcement. At times, Scottish society may have found this tragi-comic event – with its salacious revelations and public discomfiture of an unpopular King – less exciting than the omnipresent threat of armed pikemen marching out of the west, but in England the trial of Queen Caroline, and the daily sight of her gross body and painted face on her way to the House of Lords, was of far greater interest than the bloody deaths of three Radicals in North Britain. The English had experienced their own *frisson* of horror two months before the skirmish at Bonnymuir, learning how the Cato Street conspirators had quarrelled over which of them, in their proposed slaughter of the King's Ministers at a dinner party in Grosvenor Square, should have the honour of cutting the throat of Lord Castlereagh. The hanging of Arthur Thistlewood, who had chosen the Duke of Wellington for his victim, was attended by many thousands, and the newspapers' description of it within the unfolding story of the conspiracy, minimized any serious interest in the Scottish Radical War and its brutal ending. But the natural world has a seeming wish to make its own comment on human activity. When the Attorney-General, acting for the King in the trial of the Queen, began his speech for the prosecution there was a violent storm of thunder without Westminster Hall. When he continued the next day, close to the moment when the trap was sprung beneath Baird and Hardie, London was darkened by an eclipse of the sun.

'And that, gentlemen,' said Sheriff MacDonald as the weavers' coffins were taken by cart to the burial-ground of the High Kirk, 'that completes the business.' It did not, of course, for there were attempts that night to frighten or kill witnesses and justices involved in the trial of the Radicals, and later there were armed attacks upon mills and factories. But these were dying eddies in a Radical War that had truly been no war at all, only a restless tide of discontent breaking upon an implacable shore. None the less it had aroused deep fear, and hatred as strong as that once felt for the Jacobins and their British sympathizers a quarter of a century before. Concomitant with such hatred was an inhuman contempt, inspiring vainglorious braggarts like the son of James Boswell to declare that he and his Ayrshire Yeomanry would ride in Radical blood up to their bridle reins.

For this was not a year distinguished by sober calm and reasonable compassion. The field of Waterloo was now a tourist attraction, where Walter Scott and other great men grubbed for souvenirs among the disinterred bones, but the instability and unease the great victory was thought to have ended had now returned. The threat of civil war, it was said, was stronger in Britain than it had been for nearly a century. Even before the discovery of the Cato Street plot it had become Lord Castlereagh's custom to have a bed made for him in the Foreign Office, because he believed his life to be at risk on the streets. It was a year of stubborn strikes by miners and spinners, of rick-burning and window-breaking, of cavalry moving at a gallop from town to town. London was alarmed for three days when a mutiny in the Third Guards left it unprotected, and a fearsome mob flooded through the streets of Westminster, shouting their support for the mutineers, for the Queen and for the Duke of York. The last of these, the King's brother, Guardian of the Royal Person and his heir, ordered the Life Guards to disperse the mob, and by his own efforts brought the mutineers to a proper respect for good order and military discipline. This did not injure his popularity with the mob, and it continued to shout his name as the people's choice for King. George IV had yet to be crowned, had yet to be rid of his wife, had yet to break finally with one mistress and affirm his attachment to another. He was hissed at the entrance to

Carlton House, and if he went abroad in the streets – rarely now, even though it was said that men were paid to cheer him when he did – he had to suffer shouts of 'Nero!' and ribald cries of 'Where's your wife, Georgie?'

That raddled, vulgar, brave, debauched and sometimes likable woman had the shrewd wit to see that if she were to be publicly humiliated by the Bill of Divorcement, she should not miss the opportunity it gave her to ridicule her pitiless husband. To the delight of friends who would soon abandon her, and of enemies who would rather applaud her than show sympathy for the King, she used the House of Lords as if it were a stage for farce. When asked if it were not true that she had committed adultery several times, she replied that she had but once only, and that 'with the husband of Mrs Fitzherbert'. The King so pertly described endured this and his scurrilous critics with an arrogant indifference in public, and fits of childish pique in private. His release from the Queen came soon. Her death was painful, its agony increased by the bleeding and castor oil prescribed by her physicians. She did not object to dying, she said in a moment of clarity, there was sadness but no regrets. This was three weeks after her husband's coronation, from which she had been barred by two prize-fighters at the door of Westminster Hall.

The Scottish Radicals had spent little paper or passion in attacks on so vulnerable a monarch as George IV. His weaknesses and transgressions may have seemed irrelevant to their hopes, and there was little reason to arouse loyal hostility without purpose. When the King spoke to a new session of Parliament, within a month of Bonnymuir, he did not mention the Radicals or their cause by name, regretting only that the 'machinations and designs of the disaffected should have led, in some parts of the country, to acts of open violence and insurrection'. The sentiments were of course composed for him by the Tory administration, which he disliked, but they reflected his own harsh attitude toward Radical reform. Since one alarming threat to his life, when he was Regent, he had a natural fear of what another of his brothers had called the 'abominable revolutionary spirit prevalent in England'. But some of the Radicals, sentenced to the penal colony in New South Wales and now lying in the Thamesside hulk *Bellerophon* (which had delivered Napoleon from *his* angry subjects after Waterloo), believed that the King in his kindness had saved them from the fate of Baird and Hardie. A young blacksmith wrote eight verses of doggerel in praise of the Radical cause and the fight at Bonnymuir, all to be sung, as such amateur verse frequently was, to the music of the Jacobite rant *Hey Johnnie Cope!* The last verses were no doubt sincerely expressed, for the original sentence upon these unfortunate men had indeed been death by rope, axe and knife.

> If mercy to us all shall be shown
> From Royal George's kingly crown,
> We will receive't without a frown,
> And sail the seas some mornin'.
>
> Mercy to us has now been shown
> From Royal George's noble crown,
> And we are prepared, without a frown,
> To see South Wales some mornin'.

Although the Commander-in-Chief in Scotland, and some Ministers in London, would still fret at the thought of another insurrection, the Scottish Radical movement, with its three martyrs and nineteen transported saints, had passed beyond the moment when it had the power to inspire men for a suicidal challenge to authority. The nation it had hoped to lead would shortly be changed by an astonishing *coup de théâtre*, and a new image would fill the looking-glass of Scotland's self-esteem.

In this context the presence of Sheriff MacDonald upon that bloody scaffold in Stirling was dramatic irony, his race, rank and pretensions a forerunner of acceptable vanities to come. He was styled Ranald MacDonald of Staffa, a *duine-uasal*, a Gaelic gentleman, a member of the Celtic Society, the Highland Society of Edinburgh, and the Society of True Highlanders, in all of which he was an officer and thus a player in the theatricals which Sir Walter would shortly devise. Born into the family of the MacDonalds of Boisdale, a Hebridean branch of Clanranald, upon his father's death he inherited, among other lands on Mull, the basalt island of Staffa from which he took his territorial title. The annual rental from his island estates had once been substantial, but must now have been falling since it was based upon the manufacture of kelp, a seaweed industry already in decline. Staffa was a model landlord, or so his peers acknowledged, and considered himself a great authority upon the poetry of his race, although this was based upon his uncritical acceptance of the spurious Ossianic verse in which few now believed. Like his melodramatic mainland neighbour, Alasdair Ranaldson MacDonell of Glengarry, he enjoyed play-acting the role of a Highland chief, ferrying visitors to his Ulva home in an eight-oared galley, welcoming them there with a guard of armed tenants, pipe music, and a noisy discharge of muskets and artillery. Such bold swagger could not fail to delight Scott when he visited Mac-Donald in 1810. His kilted host, he thought, was 'a king of all good fellows . . . a fine, high-spirited young chieftain . . . much loved by his people whose prosperity he studies much'. Staffa's attachment to Clan Donald was flexible, however, and he would later add the surname Steuart-Seton to his own when, by a process that defeats a clear understanding of the rules of titular inheritance, he succeeded his father-in-law in the baronetcy of that name.

His presence was not the only manner by which the shadow of Walter Scott, and the historical pageants he was to create, was cast across the scaffold in Stirling. While awaiting their execution, Baird and Hardie had written many letters to their relations, friends and companions in the Radical movement. Some of these were later transcribed in good copperplate and distributed among those sympathetic to or curious about the nature of the Radical cause. Two such copies – one a letter Hardie addressed to his relations, and another listing points of scriptural debate between himself and the ministers who visited him in the condemned cell – are to be found in the papers of Walter Scott, suprascribed in his hand, *Curious particulars respecting Baird who suffered for High Treason, 1820*. He meant Andrew Hardie, but that is not important, both men may have become one in his mind. What is of interest is that the copies are to be found in Scott's papers for August 1822, the month of the King's visit to Scotland, and among letters relating to his involvement in that event. Their startling juxtaposition may be happenstance only – and the result of careless filing – but considering Scott's obvious interest in the papers, their survival in this chronological order is ironic. His opinion of the Radical Movement, and his schoolboy enthusiasms during the suppression of the insurrection, are the least pleasing aspects of his nature, but they were influential and had much to do with his vision of what a visit from the King could mean to Scotland, and what he should do to make it a success.

The Radical War was a time of great excitement when all that Scott cherished seemed under threat, and when he had an opportunity to strike a blow in its defence. That blow was not thought of metaphorically, for he wrote in fierce expectation of his own appearance on a field of battle. Although he had never fired an angry shot or killed an enemy, he imagined himself to be an old campaigner, and could tell his son – who truly was a soldier – that he had little thought until now that he would need his sword *again*. It was the voice of a High Tory, but the term is too pejorative to be fair to him. He was his own Tory, and his political beliefs were largely directed by his great knowledge of his country's history. He believed that the lessons of the past, the example it set to thought and behaviour, were at grave risk from Radicals and democrats, and he longed for some cathartic experience which would awaken Scotland to a glorious realization of its traditions and its triumphs. This, he thought, would halt the destruction of what remained of the country's nationality, 'the lowering and grinding down all those peculiarities which distinguished us as Scotsmen'. It could be said that his writings had already done much to re-establish and re-inforce Scottish nationalism, but these were for sedentary amusement and did not excite the *action* he thought necessary. When such action presented itself to him, he was profoundly moved and inspired. In 1818 he had been instrumental in the discovery of the lost Honours of Scotland, the residual regalia of a monarchy which had left Scotland for ever two centuries before. Although modest in content – a crown that was perhaps worn by Bruce, a silver mace, the sword of James IV and the sceptre of his son – their golden emergence from dust and crumbling linen in Edinburgh Castle did indeed give Scotland a vision of the past, that glowing, romantic world into which Walter Scott was breathing so much life. On the March evening the old treasure chest was opened, a great crowd waited outside the Castle, applauding loudly when the moment of discovery was announced by the raising of the royal standard – a touch of theatre for which Scott alone could have been responsible.

The past is the key to most of Scott's enthusiasms, to his sabre-rattling during the Radical War, and to the sadness of his last years. He continued to believe that its re-creation could redress the errors of the present and give strength for the future, if only men would remember and remain loyal to it. The fabric of this argument was so delicate that it was constantly at risk from the tearing wind of political change. In the last year of his life, when Parliament and public were debating the first Reform Bill, Scott would travel in pain and sorrow to Jedburgh Court House, and there speak boldly against the Bill, and against a hissing, shouting audience. He answered the catcalls with defiance, as if he were Bonnie Dundee before the Lords of Convention. *'I regard your gabble no more than geese upon the green!'* Their rejection hurt him more than he would admit, but he kept the bitterness of his contempt to his Journal.

> These unwashed artificers are from henceforth to select our legislators. What can be expected of them except such a thick-headed plebian as will be 'a hare-brained Hotspur guided by a whim'.

They were now plebeian workers, but eleven years earlier they had been his Borderers, bold moss-troopers to be loyally gathered under his colonelcy and led against the Radicals of the West or against the colliers and the keel-men of Northumbria, should those ancient enemies of Scotland ever cross the Border to assist the weavers of Strathaven.

When the activities of the Radicals became too strong to be defused by the ridicule of paid newspapers, there was a great recruiting of volunteer regiments of Foot and Horse throughout the Lowlands and Borders, all eager to march wherever glory led. In appealing for three hundred volunteer Horse from the parishes of Galashiels and Melrose, from tenant farms along the Gala Water and the Tweed, Scott was moved by the wonderful feeling that he was not only writing stirring history, he was now living it. There were indeed trumpets sounding below the Eildon Hills, messengers arriving by dark of night, metalled hooves and bridle-chains startling the rooks about Dryburgh Abbey. His piper John Bruce – or, as Scott called him, 'the renowned John of Skye, Piper in Ordinary to the Laird of Abbotsford' – marched at the head of the Galashiels weavers who came to the Tweed with their banners, ready to swear allegiance to the King and their detestation of Radicals. They shouted the words to Scott across the flood-water, like Wallace and Bruce across the Carron, he said. He wished that the boy Duke of Buccleuch, the Scott he called his chief, were old enough to lead his volunteers, to ride out like Dundee at the head of the blue bonnets, the bonnie blue bonnets.

There was always a fear, of course, that the lower class of people would take the wrong turn and declare for the Radicals, if they were not 'humoured and countenanced'. Aware of this, Scott wrote passionately to his neighbours, and to his cousin and steward William Laidlaw, urging them to .

> . . . appeal at this crisis to the good sense and loyalty of the lower orders . . . All you have to do is to sound the men, and mark down those who seem zealous. They will perhaps have to fight with the pitmen and colliers of Northumbria for defence of their firesides, for these literal *blackguards* are got beyond the management of their own people.

He urged the usefulness of amateur soldiers such as his upon Lord Melville, the greatest of the lawyers in the powerful Dundas family, and Scotland's resolute manager in Lord Liverpool's administration. There was no point, he said, in answering the 'ridiculous pretensions' of the Radicals, for so long as the poor believed that they could take the property of the rich by an armed rising, mere arguments were useless. The enlistment of the commonalty in the volunteer corps must therefore forcibly affect the morale of the people.

> It would confirm the loyal of the lower orders by showing confidence in them and it would intimidate the disaffected by showing plainly they cannot rely on even the neutrality of the Scottish peasantry.

Convinced that the country people about him were 'zealously loyal and attached to the Lairds', he offered to send the Gala marksmen anywhere in Scotland they might be needed, or in England north of the Humber, and was encouraged by his own emotions to think that all the new volunteer regiments should be so used. Melville, the cynic and realist, reminded him that however loyal his 'shepherds and hill peasantry' might be, the artisans and other lower-class persons enlisted elsewhere were of a different description. He advised Scott to offer his three hundred as an attached legion to a Yeomanry Corps, a wounding suggestion which Scott nonetheless obeyed, without success. He was now delighted to be able to tell his friends in England that 'the Highland chiefs have offered to raise their clans and march them to any point in Scotland where their services shall be required'. This startling announcement may have been based upon nothing more substantial than his own suggestion to that end, made to the members of the Celtic Society and received by them with loyal but empty promises. The power of the chiefs to raise their clans as regiments of the Crown had been exhausted long before the end of the bloody French wars. The glens from which they had once drawn their rent-roll of swordsmen were becoming pastures for sheep, and there were fewer roof-trees to burn that reluctant fathers might be forced to surrender a son for military service.

Scott's recruiting was reported regularly to his son Walter, a languid, handsome *sabreur* now serving with the 18th Dragoons in Cork and perhaps mildly astonished by his father's fever of warrior zeal. Lest the young man think that his own soldiering was being forgotten, Scott occasionally reassured him. 'Times look still darking about us, and I fear we shall want some of you gentlemen in blue or red or whatever the colour of your jackets may be.' He would have liked to have his son with him at Abbotsford, as a galloper, his aide, or even Quartermaster Commissary, and he wrote without success to Melville asking for the boy's leave of absence. When all the regular battalions in Edinburgh were sent to Glasgow, leaving the Midlothian Yeomanry to garrison the Castle, Cornet Scott's derisive comment may have dampened his father's wish for his military assistance. The young dragoon said he would like to see Edinburgh garrisoned by the yeoman volunteers, 'all the lawyers turning out as soldiers'. His father was, of course, a lawyer, and in his youth had been a cornet of volunteer horse.

Far away from the reality of the Radical War as it was being conducted by professionals – wearisome street patrols and the dispersal of crowds, aching night rides and brutal intimidation by sabre and musket-butt – Scott was able to indulge his unpleasant taste for Sunday soldiering. Inexperienced in the sudden shock of conflict, except through the scratching of his pen, his tireless involvement in the organization of an irregular force encouraged him to think of himself as a military innovator. 'I have always had a strong notion,' he told the antiquarian Robert Surtees, 'that the science of warfare may be much more easily taught than is generally supposed, and the rules for training men to what is really useful might be much simplified.' The partial truth of what he said can perhaps excuse his arrogance, and overlook the fact that he sometimes seemed to be more concerned with the appearance of soldiers than with their proper employment. He had decided upon a uniform for his corps in which grey was to be the dominant colour – grey coat and trousers, a plaid of Galashiels grey, black belts and pouches. The bonnet was to be blue, of course, with a trailing feather, 'or, to save even that expense, a sprig of holly'. He did not see his men marching in sleet and mud, forming line and firing volleys at advancing pikemen. He had not met the old familiars of a soldier's life – dirt, despair and death – but he did know what joy it would be to go a-soldiering. 'We will have shooting at the mark, and prizes, and fun, and a little whisky, and daily pay when on duty or drill.' He suffered also from the blinding disease of patriots far from the field of war, an ignorant contempt for the enemy. Four months before the Radicals marched to Bonnymuir, he thought the danger of conflict was decreasing, and told his son . . .

> The Radical scoundrels had forgot there were any men in the country but their own rascally adherents, but have been woefully chop-fallen since the rising took place. . . . I am sure the dogs will not fight and I am sorry for it. One day's good kemping [fighting] would cure them most radically of their radical malady & if I had anything to say in the matter they should remember the day for half a century to come.

At the beginning of 1820 he decided that his little corps should be modified to form a body of dismounted yeomanry, with 'lads of the higher class such as small farmers etc. . . . as serjeants corporals & lanceprisades'. The employment of this last word, an archaic military term unused since the seventeenth century, is a window to his romantic mind. He was delighted when his friend and distant cousin, Hugh Scott of Harden, offered to raise a company of Ettrick men, and the farmers about Abbotsford promised to send forty of their stout sons. All this in addition to an assurance that he could 'pick at pleasure' from the town lads of Melrose. The promise of so many young and healthful men made him conscious of his own physical disability, the long-ago diseased right leg and its lasting limp, but he told Melville that he would reserve for himself the distinction of being the *only* inefficient member of the corps. No man was being enlisted who was above the age of 35. Furthermore – and here the window opens to the sound of a hunter's horn above Liddesdale – no man would be taken 'who is not fit to run down a buck'. Despite the hours of caring spent upon his volunteers, he was still doing his 'day's darg' at his great desk, composing articles for an anti-Jacobin journal he was proposing and, most appropriately, writing the final chapters of *Ivanhoe*.

Before the book was finished the Radical War had ended in a charge of professional horsemen at Bonnymuir and a rough dragonnade by the 13th Foot in Strathaven and Greenock. There was no call upon the grey plaids and blue bonnets of Scott's little corps, nor ever any real need of them perhaps. But a prompting finger had touched his mind and directed its future attention. He had recognized a threat to all that distinguished Scotland as a nation, and believed it had been checked by a loyalty to the past among people of good will. Once cold, his heart had now warmed toward a King who created him a baronet in this time of unrest, and whose coronation the following year would inspire him by its spectacular magnificence and by the adroit employment of colourful traditions, some ancient and some shamelessly contrived for the occasion. He came back to Abbotsford from the crowning more of a royalist than ever, able to transfer the emotion of his romantic Jacobitism to the man whom he would soon, and most affectionately, call 'our Fat Friend'. He had taken no active side in the dispute between the King and his wretched consort, referring to her supporters as being in a 'high Queen-fever' of which they should be ashamed. But he admired her spirit during her trial in the Lords. She had courage enough, he told his brother, 'to dare the worst, and a most decided desire to be revenged of *him*, which, by the way, can scarce be wondered at'. Her vulgarity also amused him, and he was impressed by her power to win sympathy and support. 'I should not be surprised to see her fat bottom in a pair of buckskins, and at the head of an army, God mend all!'

Aging men, or men weary of aging, look at the past with bitter eyes, regretting it and re-creating it as a sentimental justification for their fear of the present. Scott sometimes thought of the Reformers as a monstrous army, and sometimes as 'a few turbulent spirits' without whom everything in Scotland would be 'perfectly tranquil'. Though he could see much in the new age to delight and impress, and would be an early advocate of gas-lighting, installing it at great expense in Abbotsford, it saddened him to think of what might be obscured by such modern wonders. The meaning of the word *Scot* was being lost, he thought, the history of Scotland untaught, or at best its lessons unlearnt. Throughout Britain the corruption of lying newspapers was creating contempt for authority, particularly the Crown, encouraging pleasure in ridicule rather than joy in respect. He was one of the earliest supporters of the notion that the new King should visit Scotland, the first British monarch to do so since 1650. Sober realists like Lord Melville saw the proposal as a political need, by which the Radical movement might be further weakened and the common people given a solatium of bread and circuses. While the matter was discussed as a possibility only, Scott would take little active interest in it, but once it was determined and his advice sought – indeed, as if he had been waiting for just that moment – he would embrace it warmly, recognizing the opportunity for a splendid pageant wherein ancient Scotland could be reborn. Now the people would be able to see their true King, not the gross debauchee of a political cartoon but, as he would be pleased to report when the visit was over,

> . . . a portly handsome man looking and moving every inch A King, and they expressed the greatest possible indignation at the imposition which had been put on them and their delight with the personal appearance and manners of their Sovereign.

Few of the people would be able to get close enough to their King to form any such opinion, seeing only a fat and distant figure on the deck of the Royal Yacht, on the seat of a fine carriage, briefly astride a spirited horse on Portobello sands, high upon the battlements of Edinburgh Castle with a field-marshal's feathered hat raised above his head, and more intimately in a crimson box at the Theatre Royal, hugely enjoying a dramatic presentation of one of Sir Walter's novels.

Much of the pageant to be devised by Scott would be what his occasionally irreverent son-in-law called 'Sir Walter's Celtification of Scotland'. There was the echo of an old song, an unconscious or deliberate recall of a far-away autumn when the night-fires of the clans were lit on Arthur's Seat, the wynds of the Royal Mile echoed to the wild pibroch of Lochiel's Gathering, and a young Prince in lace and tartan danced through the candle-light at Holyroodhouse. Some of the execrable doggerel Scott wrote for the occasion was based upon the presumption that a Jacobite King was at last enjoying his own again. He clearly wished to believe that the spiritual nature of a Stuart and therefore a Scottish monarchy, purified by exile and the blood of Culloden, had been made manifest in the fat form of the landlord of Brighton Pavilion. Since George IV was by bloodline as much a Stuart as the Young Pretender had been, the suggestion was perhaps not as preposterous as it might appear. Certainly it was not a claim which the King himself would have strenuously resisted.

The moment seemed proper for such felicitous illusions. In the darkness that was finally closing about the exiled house, occasional glimmers of memory seemed to glow more brightly. In the Highlands there were still eyes that had seen the smoke of Belford's guns at Culloden, and living flesh that had plunged through it in a heather charge. On the Braes of Mar, Patrick Grant was still alert in his 109th year, although he spent more time now in his elbow-chair. He had fought with other young men of his name among the Mac-Donalds of Glengarry's regiment at Culloden, and later, it was said, was present when the fugitive Prince left Loch-nan-Uamh for France. If that were true, he was perhaps the last of the Seven Men of Glenmoriston, those agreeable outlaws who sheltered the Prince in their cave for a week, danced and sang for him, and swore to stand firm in his defence though their backs were to God and their faces to the Devil. Another memory was kept warm in a cottage near Dalguise in Strathtay, and this by the widow Margaret Low who said her husband, James Steuart of Tulloch, had carried the royal standard at Culloden. She had seen the Prince when he marched by Dunkeld with the clans, and in her hundredth year she could describe in detail his manner, his dress, and his smile when she gave him a pair of brogues.

The widow of the Bonnie Prince himself also lived, in Florence on a pension of £1600 granted by George III. Louise de Stolberg, Comtesse d'Albany, had not been born when Culloden was fought, but now she was old and tired, tormented by dropsy and bronchitis, by fevers and bitter thirsts, anxious that the right number of Masses – fifty, she thought – should be said for her soul when she was finally released from her agony and her memories. She was alone for much of the time, walking painfully by the river in a summer hat, ribboned dress and shawl, but sometimes she was visited by a curious English tourist, or a tongue-tied young Scot, too embarrassed to ask about her famous husband. Since she had deserted the Prince when she could no longer endure his puking drunkenness, his verbal and physical abuse, her visitors were fortunate that she did not share her memories with them.

Scott had never met the Comtesse d'Albany, but he was fascinated by her continued existence, and was inclined to believe that her paymasters, the Crown and Administration of Britain, must tremble at the thought of it. Henry Fox, who visited Edinburgh early in 1822 and dined with the Scotts, was surprised to hear Sir Walter speaking of her with respect. Fox was an immature young man, a snob and an English snob, as yet without the exonerating grace of wit. He could not see that Lady Scott was asthmatic and perhaps using too much rouge, and so he concluded that she was 'nearly an idiot with great marks of her love for the bottle on her face'. But this, it seemed, was worth tolerating if the occasion allowed him to listen to his host, and to hear him say that Jacobitism – to which Scott professed his own emotional loyalty – still survived 'to a wonderful degree in Scotland, and that it would still be unsafe for Madame d'Albanie to come here, and would make the greatest impression in Edinburgh'. She had, of course, already visited Britain some years before, and had excited a little interest but no alarm. The Prince Regent greeted her warmly and sensibly, making no more of their meeting than a dinner party with Mrs Fitzherbert.

Before the last of the transported Radicals had left the Thames for New South Wales, Scott had finished *Ivanhoe* and was sending complimentary copies to his friends, telling each in his customary phrase that it came 'to kiss your hands'. He had begun *The Fortunes of Nigel*, as always in haste and pain, and aware of his inexorable debts. His mind and heart had been prepared for the pageantry to come, not only by the flurry of his amateur soldiering. His spirit was stirred by what he knew to be a resurgence of loyalty to the character and person of George IV. This was the best physic there could be for treating the disease of Radical and Democratic thought. Returning to Abbotsford from the Coronation, and the long-delayed accolade of his baronetcy, he was astonished by the change of opinion among his neighbours. All about him men were now saying, as he translated their Border idiom to Lord Sidmouth, 'We will fight for the King to the death.' Yet not long since, his Tweedside and Teviotdale friends had been in that high Queen-fever. He told the Home Secretary how strong this had been before their wondrous change of heart.

> I do not know how it was in other places, but I never saw so sudden and violent a delusion possess the minds of men in my life, even those of sensible, steady, well-intentioned fellows, that would fight knee-deep against the Radicals. It's well over, thank God.

The aging and puritanical Lord Sidmouth, who was disliked by the King and cared little for that, was probably unmoved by what Scott had to tell him. He had no interest in a man's emotions, and less concern for his opinions than for the measures necessary to control them – the employment of spies and *agents provocateurs*, the prompt use of cavalry at the threat of disaffection, and a legislature ready to enact such statutes as were necessary to restrict the dangerous licence of the press and the treasonable assembly of seditious combinations. He would shortly surrender his office to his young and ambitious colleague, Robert Peel, and was perhaps relieved that he would not be obliged to act upon the King's decision to visit Scotland. He no doubt shared Lord Melville's opinions, and believed it would be worthwhile only if it further reduced the ferment of Radical ideas among the people and the Whig party, and silenced for ever such inflammatory nonsense as that uttered by James Wilson when he was sentenced to death.

> You may condemn me to immolation on the scaffold, but you cannot degrade me. If I have appeared as a pioneer in the van of freedom's battles, if I have attempted to free my country from political degradation, my conscience tells me that I have done my duty. . . . I appeal to posterity for that justice which has in all ages and in all countries been awarded to those who have suffered martyrdom in the glorious cause of liberty.

*'To the body of the people at large, these
changes when once carried into effect, have been
as acceptable as they have been advantageous.
To the lazy, and to the idle, to the sheep-stealer,
and the whiskey smuggler, they never can, nor
is it desirable that they should be pleasing.'*

– JAMES LOCH, 1820

On the first Thursday of March 1820, in a week when Lord
Sidmouth's spies reported that the Radical Committee was set upon
an armed rising, Sheriff Donald Macleod of Geanies left Dingwall to
enforce writs of eviction upon the Highland people of Culrain. It
was early in the morning and he rode in a well-sprung, well-
upholstered carriage, his old but resolute body warmly wrapped
against the cold breath of the lingering snow. He was accompanied
on foot by forty constables and twenty-five reluctant soldiers. The
latter were the whole of the permanent staff of the Easter Ross
Militia, which the Sheriff himself had raised, and of which he was
the proud colonel. It pleased him sometimes to think of himself as a
military commander, entrusted with the defence of Law and Order
against the prevalent evils of mobbing, rioting, treason and sedition.
His constant strength in this illusion was the memory of his son, a
lieutenant-colonel of the 78th Highlanders who had been killed at
El Hamet on the Nile when Arab horsemen and Albanian infantry
attacked five companies of his battalion. Only eleven Highlanders
were left upon their feet, and when the Arabs rode away they carried
the heads of Patrick Macleod and his young soldiers on the points of
their lances. Some of the dead had been enlisted on the braes of
Culrain.

A large body of mounted gentlemen and their servants also
accompanied the Sheriff this morning. They all held land in the
counties of Ross or Inverness, and the oldest of them had ridden
with Macleod on a similar expedition more than a quarter of a
century before, in *Bliadhna nan Caorach*, the Year of the Sheep. Then

22

the Men of Ross, resisting their lairds' preference for sheep before men, had risen in a peaceful attempt to drive the Great Cheviot across the Beauly Water and out of the county. Macleod had suppressed this 'unaccountable commotion' by two days' hard riding through the glens below Ben Wyvis, arresting twenty of the scoundrels who could not escape his horsemen or the pursuing platoons of the Black Watch. Almost all the prisoners were surnamed Ross, for this was the county of the Rosses, of *Clan Aindrea*, the children of Andrew. Their numbers had been decreasing since the Year of the Sheep as more landowners made their choice between the four-footed clansmen and the race of Andrew, and now Hugh Munro of Novar was to do the same at Culrain.

At seventy-six, Macleod had been Sheriff of the county for forty-eight years and would remain so for another nineteen. It was said in Dingwall that he had asked the Lord Advocate for three pieces of artillery and five hundred foot-soldiers from a marching-regiment to subdue the tumultuous people of Culrain. The request had been dismissed as frivolous, and perhaps with a reminder that such a force must be better employed against the Radicals in Glasgow. The fear of riot and violence, however, the mobbing of persons and property, was real enough among the gentry of Ross. It was believed with some truth that much of the disaffection was created by discharged Highland soldiers, disenchanted veterans of Europe, India, South Africa and America who had come home to find their townships gone, their families dispersed, and their glens under sheep. Their anger had been encouraged by one Thomas Dudgeon of Fearn on the Dornoch Firth. He had enlisted some of the malcontents in his shadowy Sutherland and Transatlantic Friendly Association, each paying a subscription of sixpence, and until he was persuaded to seek another occupation elsewhere for his active mind, he was a galling thorn in the side of society and authority. He told the Highlanders that their extermination had been planned, and he swore to stand by them until his death. He tried to organize southern sympathy for those evicted from Lord Stafford's estates in Sutherland, and then, most outrageously, advocated the issue of Arms to the Populace for the defence of the Crown against such villains as the Cato Street plotters. Since the Populace, in this Highland context, largely stood in the way of Improvement, and deeply resented their removal in favour of sheep, Mr Dudgeon's proposal was naturally regarded as hazardous and suicidal.

He was also suspected, and again with probable truth, of urging the Rosses to resist their removal from Culrain, and of encouraging the people of Sutherland to come to their assistance. Munro of Novar, a rakish young man with a taste for collecting works of art and a purse inadequate for such hunger, had made it known at the beginning of the year that he intended to clear this estate and sell or lease it for sheep-grazing, it being 'well-adapted from its low and sheltered situation for a wintering to a larger farm'. It was a fine property in a green valley along the wide black run of the River Oykel, rich pastures on gentle slopes rising to the south and facing the shire of Sutherland across the water. It was historic ground. Most of the leading Men of Ross in the Year of the Sheep had come from Strath Oykel. The Seaforth Highlanders, the Black Watch and the Ross-shire Buffs had tirelessly recruited here during the French wars, and few fathers had been able to resist their laird's demand for a son or two to soldier under the captaincy of his own. Further back, but not beyond legend, the Great Marquess of Montrose had come here with his sorry army of Orkneymen, fighting his last battle and fleeing to the west for safety, but finding betrayal instead.

An offer for the glen was quickly made and as quickly accepted. On 2 February, Novar's law-agent came to the strath with writs requiring some five to six hundred people, including a hundred who were aged or bed-ridden, 'to flit and remove themselves, bairns, family, servants, sub-tenants, cottars and dependants, cattle, goods and gear, forth and from'. The law-agent and his statutory witnesses got no further than the drystone cottages of Achnagart, the first township in the strath, where they were met by a hostile crowd. Their writs were torn up and thrown upon the snow and they were driven eastward to Invershin.

It was to redress this insufferable affront to authority, and to impose the writs by force, that Macleod came with his little army of gentry, constables and soldiers. A great crowd, no fewer than four hundred, he said, was awaiting him before Achnagart, some barring the road and others crouched behind a stone dyke. There were many women, although the Sheriff believed that most of these were men, wearing their wives' or their daughters' clothes. The noise was intense, the women shouting, young boys blowing whistles and horns. Worse than this, Macleod thought he saw men with guns moving among the white stems of a birch wood. It was also alarming to see more people from Lord Stafford's estates gathering on the Sutherland side in sympathy. They had been summoned by whistles, specially made and sold by Highland gipsies for sounding a warning against the approach of evictors.

Macleod got bravely from his carriage into the cold, the new writs in his hand. When he called upon the people to disperse, the women shouted back, saying that if they must die, they would die here and not in America or on the Cape of Good Hope. 'We don't care for our lives!' The first blow, it was said, was struck by a woman with a stick, following a hideous yell. The swearing constables hit back with their ash-sticks, the gentry leaning from the saddle to beat at the nearest heads with their crops. Gathered about their aged colonel, the militiamen fired one noisy volley of blank cartridges, but one of them, said the *Inverness Courier*, 'a disreputable drummer, and probably in revenge for an injury, used a ball cartridge he had about him'. This hit a woman in the breast, wounding her mortally.

Macleod bravely and angrily held his ground until his loyal militiamen, understandably anxious to put as many miles as possible between themselves and the women of Culrain, took him away in his carriage, followed at a run and a gallop by the constables and the gentry. He refused to go further than the inn at Ardgay by Bonar Bridge, unwilling to return to Dingwall without issuing the writs. He waited for the people of Culrain to storm the little inn, but they did not come. The Minister of Kincardine, Angus MacBean, having protested against the Sheriff's use of force, now sent his catechist to Strath Oykel to chide the people for their madness and their godless resistance to the Law. On March 14 he persuaded seven of the principal tenants to come to the inn and there accept the writs in the name of all. Before that russet autumn they were gone from Culrain, the Laird of Novar concluded the sale, and Major Forbes of Melness put his sheep upon the braes of Strath Oykel.

The Marquess of Stafford had feared that the people of his estates to the north of Culrain might become involved in this brawl, bringing the poison of disaffection on to his ground. His commissioner, James Loch, had no doubt at all that his employer's interests were at risk, and he warned the factors that Dudgeon's agents had been at work, provoking his lordship's people to come down to the Kyle.

> I have just seen a gentleman who was present at the affray in Ross-shire. He states positively that he saw many people with his own eyes on Bonar Bridge and that the blowing of horns assembled a vast number of people who had been assembled for days from all parts of Sutherland and elsewhere.

Since 1813, when he began his work, Loch's Policy of Improvement had brought great changes to Lord Stafford's wide estates in Sutherland. It had been so successful, from a proprietor's point of view, that other landlords in the Highlands had actively pursued it upon their own estates, and the word *Improvement* was now synonymous with paternalistic duty. In human terms, however – whatever the profit to the landlord – it meant the eviction or removal of men, women and children in favour of sheep. It meant the demolition or burning of ancient townships in the mountains, and the merciless destruction of the culture that had once sustained their inhabitants. The people were pressed into unfamiliar labour in new fishing-villages. They were driven to a nomadic life, to the slums of Glasgow and the south. More still sailed for Canada and Australia, harsh, disease-ridden voyages on vessels that were known as coffin-ships. Until now the Sutherland people had made no physical resistance to Mr Loch's Improvements. The bitter removals in Strathnaver and Strath Kildonan were over, and the Marquess and the Marchioness hoped there would be no obstruction now to further improvements in the parishes of Clyne and Rogart, and on the estate of Gruids across the Oykel from Culrain. As Loch strenuously impressed upon the factors, Lady Stafford was 'most anxious indeed that the whole business should go without any disturbance, indeed if it does not you will cause a flame here we shall have much difficulty in allaying'. Particularly irritating to his employers were the petitions they received from their tenants and sub-tenants, asking redress for unjust eviction, for ill-treatment by his lordship's servants, and ingratitude to old soldiers unfairly rewarded. Loch believed that Dudgeon's agents were behind much of this, and he was vexed by the lack of good intelligence. 'Have you any one', he asked his factors, 'you can trust to report to you regularly what the people are about?'

In his seventh decade now, Lord Stafford was an eccentric figure, plagued by ill-health, bilious and rheumatic, a stooped and shuffling man in untidy clothes, his hawk-nose drooping even more over his prim mouth. He was perhaps the richest landowner in Britain, having become so without any talent or effort, inheriting the family fortune in early middle age and then receiving the munificent bequest of his uncle the Duke of Bridgewater's estate. He is remembered as a great art-fancier, spending more in one year upon his collection than the whole rental of his Sutherland property, which had come to him by his marriage. He is also remembered by what is probably the highest statue in the country, thirty feet tall on a pedestal of seventy-six feet, thirteen hundred more above the Dornoch Firth. Much of the cost of this had come from donations by his tenantry, as willingly given, perhaps, as they had once surrendered their sons to Lady Stafford's recruiters.

In her northern country, Elizabeth Gordon the Marchioness of Stafford was known as *Ban mhorair Chataibh*, the Great Lady of Sutherland. She had been Countess of Sutherland in her own right since the age of six, the title secured by costly litigation after the death of her father, the last Earl. Beautiful when young, renowned for her light chestnut hair, her porcelain skin and heart-shaped face, she was still handsome in the fashionable plumpness of matrons of her time. She had a vivacious nature and sometimes imperious manner that fitted the opulence of her several homes, and perhaps believed her best setting to be the turreted castle of Dunrobin on the eastern coast of Sutherland. When she desired, she could charm all, and even in her old age was able to blind Mrs Harriet Beecher Stowe to the fact that the evicted Sutherland peasantry deserved some understanding and sympathy from the author of *Uncle Tom's Cabin*.

The disturbances which she and her husband feared, and which Commissioner Loch had warned the factors to avoid if possible, came a year after Culrain and, predictably, on the estate of Gruids. The land here did not offer the same rich grazing as the Novar estate across the Oykel, but it was still valuable and would be much desired by southern graziers once the people were removed. In April 1821, Sheriff-Substitute Robert Nimmo of Sutherland came to

Gruids with his writs, issued on behalf of Lord Stafford. He and his witnesses were met in a warm saucer of high ground above the River Shin, where a large crowd tore the papers to pieces, stripped Mr Nimmo and his companions of their clothes, and whipped them away. The same violent response was repeated when further writs were taken to the Strathbrora townships in the parish of Clyne – again the rallying notes of whistle and horn upon the braes, the assault with stones and sticks, and half-naked constables running for safety. The resistance here would seem to have been organized or inspired by Gordon Ross, schoolmaster at Ascoilmore, whose family had been roughly evicted when he was away. He was later formally examined with witnesses before Stafford's eldest son, the evidence of all stretching a heavy veil across a clear understanding of what had happened. But the resistance of others to eviction was unequivocal. For the second time only in two decades of Removal and Improvement, Lord Stafford called upon a stronger power than that available from the Sheriff's office.* Companies of the 41st Foot arrived by forced march from Fort George. They were Welsh soldiers, but it was the disarming custom of successive governments to use Celt against Celt, and when their bayonets had dutifully imposed the Rule of Law, and Lord Stafford's will, upon Gruids and Strathbrora the people were gone to Mr Loch's fisheries on the coast, to the mine at Brora or the emigrant ships at Wick. A long lifetime later, a man who had been a child in Strathbrora remembered the clearing of the parish.

> I have seen the atmosphere in Clyne, and for many miles around, filled with the smoke which arose from the burning cottages, from which their inmates had been forcibly ejected, in the straths of Kildonan, Brora, Fleet, et cetera. Other cottages I have seen in the act of being demolished – levelled with the ground; and I have seen the people who occupied them for days without shelter, huddled together at the dykesides and roadsides, and on the beach, awaiting the arrival of ships to carry them across the Atlantic, or wherever they were forced to go.

*The first occasion was in 1813, during the 'Rebellion of the Gunns'. See p. 139.

The Marquess and the Marchioness had been under occasional attack by southern newspapers since the Year of the Burnings, the great clearance of Strathnaver in 1814, and it was fashionable in some malicious sections of society to counterfeit shock at the brutal nature of the evictions, and pretend sympathy for the romanticized victims. The Staffords steadfastly refused to acknowledge in public that they knew of anything harmful in Mr Loch's Policy, or anything reprehensible in the behaviour of the agents delegated to execute it. In private, however, the Marchioness was deeply sensitive to criticism. In 1815, after one of the estate managers, Patrick Sellar, had been tried – and acquitted – on a charge of murder committed during the clearance of Strathnaver, she was angered by an attack upon him and upon Loch, and through them upon her husband, which appeared in the police gazette *Hue and Cry*. Wasting no paper upon intermediaries she wrote to Lord Sidmouth.

> While attacks upon the management of this property were confined to the coarser newspapers, they were treated by Lord Stafford and myself with the contempt they appeared to us to merit, but when I find that such a charge has been published in a paper under the authority of Government, I feel it incumbent on me to have recourse to Your Lordship for your interference and assistance.

The Home Secretary could do no less than respond. He called the editor of the gazette before him, and having discovered that the man had merely copied the account from the last issue of the *Observer*, which in turn had merely printed an account of evidence given at the trial of Patrick Sellar, he did not know what he could do, except tell her ladyship the truth, and that he would do nothing.

> Under the circumstances as thus stated to me by the Editor, who adds that he had no grounds for doubting the accuracy of the article already published; I trust your Ladyship will not consider the result of the inquiry which I have caused to be made an unsatisfactory one.

Before the systematic clearances in Culrain, Clyne and Rogart began, some of the people's angry remembrance of past suffering expressed itself in abusive letters to Dunrobin Castle or Trentham Hall in Staffordshire. They frequently referred to attacks upon the Marquess and Marchioness in the Edinburgh and London news-papers, perhaps knowing how painful these were to both. A few of the pleated slips of yellowing paper were carefully kept among his lordship's correspondence of the time, as if he were confident that posterity would recognize that the charges were disproved by their own absurdity. Thus, *A friend to Humanity* wrote to 'The most abominable George Granville Marquis of Stafford Sutherland butcher' advising him to study the columns of the *Morning Chronicle* wherein he would read 'a true account of your cold-blooded butchery'. Similar letters to the Countess-Marchioness were no more civil.

> It is recommended to a certain Hyena living at Trentham Hall in Staffordshire to read the Gent. Magaseen for Sept 1819 page 221 – and page before. If such a monster has a soul she may reflect and fear – for there is a day coming when she will tremble.

The account in the *Gentleman's Magazine*, one wordy paragraph in an otherwise irrelevant letter, did not mention the Staffords or their estates by name, but the reference was clear.

> [In Scotland] we hear of the tenantry of many parishes being turned out of doors, their houses burnt to the ground, and the district laid waste as far as the eye can reach, or the property of the despots extends, that he may boast of how many thousand acres feed his sheep! Here lonely silence spreads her wings, magnificently it is true, in the grandeur of repose, around his castle; which is like 'the far-famed pyramids of Egypt, pompous amid the desert, the abode of rottenness and death, at once atrophy and a tomb'. Such proprietors possess, not enjoy their estates in the way, no doubt, that is most congenial to their dispositions; for the vulture and the hyena, ravenous wolves, and birds of prey, are fond of seclusion, and generally found in solitude. Here all is terror, all is fear; domestics are eye-servants to such a lord; and their lord, a slave to his passion, carries a torment in his own bosom, from which he cannot fly.

This overblown prose, with its hot air of venomous hatred, was particularly dangerous in a year of murderous plot and actual insurrection, but it may have been curiosity only that persuaded the Marchioness to keep one angry threat to her life. It was signed *Donald Sutherland*, which, in the northern Highlands, was perhaps the equivalent of anonymity.

> You damned Bitch. You are a damned old Cat and deserve to be worried and burnt out for burning out the poor Highlanders. If you dont make a public apology & explanation I will brave you.

It is unlikely that she feared for her life, although the risk to great landlords was always present. In the year of the Stirling executions an attempt was made to assassinate the Duke of Atholl at Dunkeld House, as he sat in an audience room by the porter's lodge where he dealt with the minor affairs of his estate. There he received a native of Strathtay, James Murray, who some said was an avowed Radical. He claimed to have information of a conspiracy which would interest Atholl as Lord Lieutenant of the County, but once admitted to the room he took two bended pistols from his coat pockets. One of them, he said, would blow out the Duke's brains if Murray were not compensated for lands unlawfully taken from him. The other he would then use upon himself. The wretched man had more desperate spirit than skill with the weapons, for the aged Duke was able to take them from him. He was sent to Perth gaol, and ultimately to the penal colony in New South Wales.

The Marchioness gave little thought to the opinions of the mob, of course, or of that greater part of the nation which had no power or influence in public affairs. Among her friends, however, her family's political allies and enemies, and in the Whig party of which Lord Stafford was a now flickering light, it was necessary for the truth to be plain. Thus she circulated a firm rebuttal among her correspondents.

> We have lately been much attacked in the newspapers by a few malicious writers who had long assailed us on every occasion. What is stated is most perfectly unjust and unfounded, as I am convinced from the facts I am acquainted with; and I venture

to trouble you with the enclosed note as a sort of statement of our proceedings. . . . If you meet with discussions on the subject of society, I shall be glad if you will show this statement to any one who may interest him or herself on the subject.

The 'enclosed note' consisted of excerpts from an apologia of the Sutherland Improvements written by their creator, the Staffords' devout and devoted Commissioner, James Loch. He was a fair-haired, broad-shouldered Lowlander, with a small property of his own by Edinburgh and a great pride in a lineage that went back to a Norman incomer called de Lacus, or so it was believed. A skilled advocate, he was called early to the bar at Lincoln's Inn, and was still young when his success at estate management brought him the patronage of the Staffords and lifelong employment as their Commissioner, the powerful manager of their English and Scottish estates. He created the Policy of Improvement which other proprietors would later adopt and adapt. He worked tirelessly and with great spiritual conviction, standing between an angry and bewildered people and his employers, taking without complaint much of the abuse and hatred meant for them. He dedicated himself to the belief that the accumulation of wealth, arising from a wise and proper disposition of its source, with the development of new measures for its investment, could only result in the improvement of the useful lives and moral character of the poor and dependent. Among these he did not include those 'pensioner scoundrels', discharged soldiers who had marched by Corunna and Toulouse to Quatre Bras and Waterloo, and might now be in receipt of a small pittance as Chelsea out-pensioners. 'They are the worst subjects the King has,' he told his principal factor, 'and by far the worst tenants any estate can be cursed with. Admit none of them as tenants if you can help it.'

It was Loch's true belief that 'the emancipation of the lower orders from slavery' was the principal concern of all good Highland proprietors. To men of such patronizing rectitude, a stubborn Gaelic people who stood in the path of well-intentioned improvement could not be reasoned with and should thus be changed by force, if necessary, for their own good. 'In a few years,' Loch wrote in his *Account of the Improvements on the Estate of Sutherland* (from which

Lady Stafford took her excerpts), 'the character of this whole population will be completely changed. . . . The children of those who are removed from the hills will lose all recollection of the habits and customs of their fathers.'

When Walter Scott begged the Marchioness to send a contingent of her people to take part in his pageant for the King's Visit, she and James Loch clearly recognized an opportunity to refute the slanders upon her family, to re-establish it in public esteem, and to demonstrate the loyalty it inspired among the young men of her clan – if a Gordon could rightly claim a tenantry of Gunns, Sutherlands, Bannermanns and Mackays to be her 'clan'. There was also a stronger compulsion, the need to answer a new critic, more influential and respected than the nameless scribblers of the coarser newspapers – a middle-aged gentleman of Strathtay, Colonel David Stewart of Garth, Scott's principal aide and his loyal deputy in the tartan booth at the Royal Fair.

Stewart was a retired officer of gentle compassion and integrity of opinion, a small, weak-sighted man whose serene face and halo of thin white hair would have been better mounted upon the body of a pedagogue or a minister. He was the second of the three sons of Robert, Laird of Garth, and as such was descended from the Wolf of Badenoch, one of the many bastard sons of Robert II. It was a brutal ancestry for so mild-natured a man, and one which as a boy he would not have been able to forget, for on the western marches of the Garth estate, in the narrow black gorge of Keltney Burn, was the ruin of a stone keep built by that lupine ancestor. The immediate past of Stewart's family was, of course, Jacobite, and the Christian name given him was that of a maternal grandfather, one of nineteen officers who died in the suicidal charge of the Atholl Brigade at Culloden.

Commissioned in the 77th Atholl Highlanders at the age of fourteen, Stewart began his actual soldiering five years later, serving in Flanders, the West Indies, Egypt, Italy and Spain, collecting the wounds that seamed his skin and plagued his health in later years. One of his earliest duties, as a young officer of the Black Watch, had been to march with his men under the direction of Sheriff Macleod in the Year of the Sheep. Upon no other occasion, he later wrote, had his feelings been so moved, knowing that his men – who had been largely recruited in the glens of Ross – might now have to use their arms against kinsmen and friends. Throughout his life thereafter, Stewart defended the Highlander, and particularly the Highland soldier, against all slander and criticism, and against their treatment by

> . . . cruel and oppressive systems of landlords who are driving a faithful, moral, chivalrous, brave, independent, loyal race to disaffection to government, hatred to superiors, discreditable and immoral habits . . .

This he wrote to a friend in 1820. It was the language he may have wished to use and might have used in his book had not that same friend and others persuaded him to moderate it. The book, in the custom of the time, was lengthily entitled, *Sketches of the Character, Manners, and Present State of the Highlanders of Scotland, with details of the Highland Regiments.* It would become a seminal work on the Highlands, but it began modestly and in response to a request from the commander of his old corps, the 42nd Highlanders. For a regiment that had been actively and bloodily involved in Britain's wars for three-quarters of a century, the Black Watch was lamentably short of documentary evidence of its service. Its original records had been badly damaged by sea-water in 1771, when a ship taking the battalion to Ireland was driven ashore in a gale. Twenty-three years later, when the 42nd was sent to the Low Countries, the baggage-ship carrying its surviving records was captured by the French at Helvoetsluys. The loss seemed irreparable, there was nothing now but the quickly dying memory of the Watch's history since its embodiment by Aberfeldy bridge eighty years before. In 1817, when the commander of the regiment was instructed to assemble what account he could, he invited Stewart of Garth to supply 'a few notices on the subject'.

Garth began as 'a plain soldier unaccustomed to composition', intending to submit no more than would fill thirty or forty pages of the record book. But as he wrote, the work took hold of him and made itself something more than a regimental diary. Its two volumes, each more than five hundred pages in length, became an account of all the Highland marching and fencible regiments raised in the eighteenth century, together with a history of Highland society and culture. Upon that, itself monumental, he built a spirited and impassioned attack upon the policies of improvement and land use which were at that moment destroying the Highlander's character and way of life, and driving him out of his homeland. Garth wrote with much searching of heart and mind, and in occasional despair. He approached old friends, old officers and soldiers with whom he had served, old men and women who remembered the regiments and the Highlands of sixty years before. He recorded anecdote and legend heard in a wind upon the brae, in the peat-smoke of a cottage, in hunting-lodge and Highland castle. To one friend at least, he also wrote for reassurance and for an understanding of his anger.

The failing eyesight of Sir John MacGregor Murray of Lanrick, the friend so addressed, must have been sorely tried by Garth's spectacular calligraphy. The result of Stewart's own poor sight, it was an Oriental pattern of curves and whorls, heavy strokes for consonants and a light feather touch for vowels. When Murray disentangled their meaning, he was clearly uneasy about Stewart's opinions, his attachment to the interests of the commonalty. He must have reminded Garth of the general fear that the poison of Radical ferment, expressed in the burning of the property of the gentry, could soon reach the Highlands. Garth was never particularly concerned with the Radical War, except in his belief that if the lower orders behaved badly, the explanation might lie in their shameless ill-treatment by their betters. As for torch and flame, he told Murray . . .

> Lady Sutherland led the example of fire-raising . . . When the master burns the tenant's house, despair may make the compliment be returned. If there is no check to the system, the high-spirited, faithfull, affectionate Highlanders will become envious, unprincipled, ferocious Irishmen.

Sir John did not pursue the comparison with the Irish, and it is impossible to know whether Garth would have extended his defence of the Gaelic people to include them, perhaps not. Murray was more concerned with his friend's intemperate words, and was further distressed to discover much the same language in those manuscript pages of the book which Stewart sent to him. In Garth's opinion, Murray was the ideal of a *duine-uasal*, a Highland gentleman, a MacGregor and chief of the name, although there were others ready to dispute that title, bloodlessly in the columns of the Edinburgh *Observer*. All MacGregors were fiercely Jacobite, and Sir John's father had served the Young Pretender as an aide-de-camp. Murray himself had soldiered with the East India Company, together with three of his brothers, and had come home after twenty-five years with a colonelcy, a baronetcy and only tolerable health. For much of his life the use of the name MacGregor had been forbidden by a residual statute of the early seventeenth century, when Crown and Council had endeavoured to 'root out and extirpate' all men of the Griogaraich, and to brand all of its women on the cheek with the scarlet mark of a key. Most gentlemen of this understandably touchy tribe, which traced its descent and therefore its royal blood from Alpin, King of Scots, had taken other names, usually of those great houses which gave them protection and on whose lands they dwelt – Argyll, Montrose and Atholl. This practice, based upon sound common sense, could not escape the imagination of Walter Scott, who gave it a romantic swagger in the mouth of an angry Rob Roy – *'Do not Maister or Campbell me . . . My foot is on my native heath and my name is MacGregor!'* The surname taken by the Lanrick family was that of their overlords, the earls and later dukes of Atholl. When their name was restored to the Griogaraich, and the chiefship to Lanrick, a grateful Sir John raised a regiment of fencible infantry for the grandson of the king his father had fought to unseat, but did not abandon the name Murray. Intentional or not, this was a compliment to his friend John Murray, 4th Duke of Atholl, whose high-spirited daughter Elizabeth was married to Sir John's son.

Garth's retirement from the army, as a brevet-colonel of the 96th in 1815, did not bring him the rest and peace of mind he had earned and perhaps expected. His father was old and incapable, his brother William was simple and inept, and in such hands their estate had come close to irreparable ruin. Garth bravely accepted the burden thus placed upon his shoulders, and wrote of it to Sir John without much complaint.

My father who is not like you, as able for business as when thirty years of age, has for many years given up the whole charge of his affairs to my elder brother who unfortunately has no talent for business, indeed, from natural causes, is totally incapable, and the melancholy failure in my father's mind is too evident from the circumstances that for 14 years he never enquired how matters were managed, or what my brother was doing . . . My brother kept no books, not even rent-roll. He received money from one man, and paid it away to another without frequently even a memorandum, and so incredibly negligent that Bills due my father amount (with interest which has not been called for this last thirteen years) to £4235 10s are allowed to run out, and two of the holders very dishonourably claim prescription and refuse payment. No fortune could long withstand such payment.

In the spring of 1820 Garth came close to quarrelling with his friend. He was astonished to discover that the Duke of Atholl, whom he sentimentally respected as a great lord and chief, was selling a large parcel of his estate to men outwith the Highlands, and thus abandoning its people to eviction and dispersal. Surely, he told Murray, the Duke had greatly changed

> . . . or he would not offer his lands to strangers, desolate his country and drive all his brave Atholl men to cities to become Radicals, or to America to become the most bitter and resolute enemies. My heart and blood was chilled when I read of the whole of Atholl to be laid waste agreeable to the advertisements in the Perth Papers . . . I dreamed for two nights of the misery and perhaps consequent actions to which these outcasts – the moral, the brave, the industrious men of Atholl will be subject to when driven from their ancient homes. The expected excuse of rent is dearly purchased if purchased at such a price as the ruin of so many valuable but unfortunate people.

The Duke would have been irritated and astonished by this exaggeration of an essential property sale, for he looked upon himself as a model landlord who had made an English parkland out of much of

Strathgarry and Strathtay, to the envy of his neighbours and his southern friends. But it had not been done without summary removals such as those now feared by Garth. Coming by Atholl in 1802, James Hogg had spoken to a man who was 'one of nineteen farmers who were removed from the Duke's land to make way for one man'. That the evicted man believed his misfortune to be no fault of the Duke's was customary. The commissioner, the agent and the factor took the force of the successive waves of resentment, leaving the proprietor untouched. Alarmed by Garth's anger, Sir John assured him that Atholl was 'the same, good and worthy man as ever'. He had *never* turned out a tenant, but one or two worthless ones'. Garth was not persuaded. He could not tell his old friend that such an answer was nonsense, but he had a great fund of information, he said, of what had happened and what was happening in all parts of the Highlands, and was thus justified in his forebodings.

> When you have heard that the Duke of Atholl *never* endeavoured to put out a tenant but one or two worthless good for nothing men, you were told so by a person who did not know the circumstances of the case . . . I remember 24 families on the farms of Strathgarry, but it is needless to run over the state of it there, only your informant must have been very ignorant.

He was anxious not to quarrel with his friend, and hoped that they would soon meet again when they could talk about the problems of management as practised by many Highland landlords. They sometimes disagreed, but, he said disarmingly, 'Speaking to a person who agreed with my opinions I could learn nothing.' It may have occurred to Sir John that there were too many matters of this nature upon which they disagreed, and the opinions of one could not be changed by the other. This was clear from Garth's angry response to the news from Culrain. When Murray mildly protested that Hugh Munro of Novar was a 'well composed young man', Garth recognized Murray's loyalty to his own class, and agreed that he too was anxious for the prosperity and honour of many friends among the Highland landlords, but he grieved to see them acting in a way that must eventually bring ruin upon them and upon their innocent tenants.

> Unfortunately, in the management of Highland estates, humanity or pity for the ancient occupiers of the soil is forgot in the display of new theories and plans of Improvement . . . The first object, in general was to extirpate and get rid of them as soon as possible, totally regardless of the misery, poverty and degradation to which the moral, high-spirited peasantry were reduced.

The hypocrisy of some Highland gentlemen embarrassed as well as angered Stewart. Much of his contempt for their pretensions may have grown from his own disenchantment. He had been an early member of the Society of True Highlanders, formed in 1815 by the clownish chief of Glengarry, Alasdair Ranaldson MacDonell. Membership was limited to Highlanders of 'property and birth', and thus did not include the Gaelic people whom some of them were currently replacing with the Great Cheviot. Their aim, apart from the enjoyment of each other's company, was to support 'the Dress, Language, Music, and Characteristics of our Illustrious and Ancient Race in the Highlands and Islands of Scotland'. There were picnics and balls in Lochaber, upon the green plain by Inverlochy where Clan Donald swords had broken the power of the Campbells one hundred and seventy years before. In the warm summer evenings after the joyous celebrations that followed Waterloo, the gentlemen and their ladies danced to the music of Alasdair Ranaldson's pipers, and David Stewart led the mistress of Glen Garry through the torchlight for the first grand promenade. The pleasure of this, born of self-adulation, soon soured. Garth could not stomach Glengarry's egocentric arrogance, his short temper, and his assumption of superior knowledge of the Highlanders and their history. He was no more wrong or right than Garth on some matters, which was itself irritating, but Stewart's final rejection of the Society was due to his bitter discovery of what was happening to Glengarry's clansmen while the man was play-acting his role as their chief. Garth reminded Sir John of this when Murray mildly protested that 'removal of tenants is not extirpation'.

> Is not the clearing away the inhabitants of a whole district, and giving their lands to one or two families thus extirpation?

Glengarry's farms contained 1500 souls, those farms now have 35 persons. Is not this, in more or less similar circumstances, extirpation? and yet Glengarry with an inconsistency only to be equalled by the rest of his character, goes about this country attending public meetings and making speeches *as a true friend to Highlanders*. Who has done more to extirpate the race so far as his power extended?

He knew that his views were not shared by most of his friends and associates, all of a class so badly shaken by the Radical War that the removal of a potentially threatening mountain peasantry was enough to justify the harshest measures of Improvement. Garth believed, in what now must seem to be wasteful simplicity, that the humane treatment of a dependent commonalty, with honest respect between the lower and superior orders, were the only guarantees against anarchy and revolt. He had no violent hatred of the Radicals. Unlike Scott whom he admired and praised – *'His heart is equal to his mind'* – he could not write of war as a romantic experience, and he took no satisfaction in the thought of Scot slaughtering Scot. He knew that the foul killing-trade was not a quadrille performed to delight old men, and he believed that Highland proprietors and chiefs would soon regret

> . . . treating their faithful and affectionate tenants as manufacturers do their labourers – and grieved I am when I hear man of birth, rank and character seek for an apology for their conduct from the traffickers of Glasgow and Manchester, as these claim a right to manage their affairs as best suits themselves, without regarding the misery and poverty they may occasion, and as they dismiss their labourers from their employment without ceremony, so may the landlord sweep away their tenantry. Now when we look to the state of the manufacturing population where these principles are agreed upon, and see the distress, jealousy, danger and horror of the Master Manufacturers with their properties under the protection of the bayonet, and on the other hand see the malicious envy, hatred, disaffection and loss of principle of the labouring manufacturers – are these a people and is this a state of society for imitation by the

honourable, high-minded Highland landlords? and should they not have some regard to humanity and feeling for the despairing and hopeless poverty which follows the forcible ejectment?

If Garth put such passionate language and direct accusation into the first drafts of his book, Sir John's alarmed response when he read the manuscript is understandable. For all that, he clearly did not wish to offend Garth, and his letters throughout the summer of 1820 were cautious but equivocal. In September, Garth delivered the manuscript to the printer in Edinburgh who was then left to decipher its twists and curls and to dust it with the commas, colons and semi-colons that make books of the time an obstacle race for faltering eyes. Stewart was pleased to have to work away from his desk at last, and was now able to spend more time with the violoncello he had carried through all his campaigns. He still suffered from a wound in his right arm, taken at Maida, and playing the instrument must have been as painful as writing. The setting and preparation of the *Sketches* for printing took two years, during much of which he was 'chained to the house', working through daylight 'putting the farms and parks in proper order for letting-out', and spending the candle-lit hours bent over manuscript and proof.

Most of Sir John's letters to him at this time are lost but they had clearly moved from caution to warning as he read more and more of what Garth had written. Stewart protested that all he wrote was founded upon fact, and there he would stand his ground. The future was all too plain for honest men to be silent.

> The system pursued by many Highland landlords is the same as that which has reduced the peasantry of Ireland to their present state. The Highlanders will soon be the same as the Irish unless their superiors relax, and those superiors must have their houses guarded and their rents collected at the point of the bayonet as is the case in many parts of Ireland.

It was that paragraph, perhaps, read in a sunny room in Murray's town-house at Portobello, that persuaded him that his old friend must be restrained from galloping too hard at his enemies. He took what manuscript pages of the *Sketches* he had to gentlemen of his acquaintance, and when they had discussed them they strongly advised Stewart to revise his vigorous attacks upon Highland proprietors, particularly his account of proceedings in Atholl, until Murray 'could make use of them with a view to be of benefit to the tenants'. The reason given for this self-censorship is a recurring argument – that truth, once published, may worsen the injury it reveals.

> It would be advisable to omit the part you meant to introduce relative to Highland proprietors as not being necessary and being a subject that would give offence to many without *any* probability of doing Good, but on the contrary a certainty of exciting discontent where conciliation is most desirable.

How far Garth was persuaded by this appeal it is difficult to say, without knowledge of his original draft manuscript. But it is true that the *Sketches* as published are milder in tone and more restrained in accusation than the letters he wrote to Lanrick, and it must be concluded that he did indeed, in respect for the advice given him, moderate the language of his book. Even so, it was startling in its arguments and its attack, and wrapped as these were in a readable history of the Highland regiments they ensured the initial success of the book. That it made enemies was to be expected, and none more implacable than the Great Lady of Dunrobin Castle and Commissioner James Loch. Garth's references to both by name are oblique, but his disgust for what had been done by their authority is unequivocal. His comment upon the trial and acquittal of the agent Patrick Sellar – for murder during the clearance of Strathnaver – may have convinced Lady Stafford that only the appearance in Edinburgh of a hundred of her loyal Sutherlanders could confound Stewart's slanders.

> The trial ended (as was expected by every person who understood the circumstances) in the acquittal of the acting agent, the verdict of the jury proceeding on the principle that he acted under legal authority. This acquittal, however, did by no means diminish the general feeling of culpability, it only

transferred the offence from the agent to a quarter too high and too distant to be directly affected by public indignation, if, indeed, there be any station so elevated, or so distant, that public indignation, justly excited, will not, sooner or later, reach, so as to touch the feelings, however obtuse, of the transgressor of that law of humanity, written on every upright mind, and deeply engraved on every kind and generous heart.

When George Augustus Frederick reached his fifty-ninth birthday
in August 1821, a month after his coronation, he had been King for
less than two years. During this time he had estranged himself still
further from his Government and become one of the most
unpopular men in Britain. He had grown more obsessed with the
thought of dying, and had attempted to be rid of his wife by one of
the most absurd Bills ever placed before Parliament. The news of her
sudden and painful death, two days before his birthday, was
brought to him at Holyhead where his yacht was waiting to carry
him to Ireland. He was undoubtedly affected by her passing, though
relief was perhaps the dominant feeling. Upon his orders, the yards
of the Royal Squadron were lowered in respect, and all night he
paced the deckboards of his cabin in the *Royal George*. That he could
not sleep is understandable, though what he was thinking is less
easy to gauge. Caroline had not been an agreeable person, and she
had accepted their public dispute with an aggressive vulgarity that
had made her, not him, the favourite of the mob. She departed life
with one last humiliating blow at his self-esteem. On the morning
of his birthday, before the squadron sailed with the tide for Howth,
the King received a copy of his wife's will. The whole of her estate
was left to her adopted son, William Austin. He was said to be the
child of a London docker and his wife. Caroline pretended that he
was the son of a Prussian prince, and gossip was content to believe
that he was in fact the Queen's bastard. He received nothing from
the estate, for she had died with debts greater than her assets.

The King and his companions spent the voyage riotously,
consuming great quantities of wine and whisky, and singing noisy
songs. When he landed in Ireland, wearing a blue coat, black cravat

and armband, he was escorted to Phoenix Park by a yelling crowd which he then invited on to the grass outside the Vice-Regal Lodge, entertaining it with a hearty speech. After a few days spent in private, acknowledged as a mark of respect to his wife, he reappeared again, charming and witty to all. He obediently attended the functions arranged for him, kissed a hundred ladies or more at a Royal Drawing-Room, drank sparingly now and then, and responded to public acclamation, it was said, as if he were a candidate on the hustings. In Ireland he was the popular prince he desired to be. A surviving rebel of the '98 – who would have needed invention if he had not been found – reportedly said that he once had fought against George III but now he would die for his son. This change of loyalties was apparently due to the King's civil enquiry about the old man's health.

When all these duties were done, and he had several times declared that he loved Ireland, that his heart was Irish, the King retired to the country. He was carried northward from Dublin to the valley of the Boyne, where the last British king to visit Ireland had defeated his own father-in-law in battle and driven the Stuart cause into miserable exile. Bleakly exposed on rising ground above the Boyne Water was Slane Castle, the home of the Marquess and Marchioness Conyngham. Here the King was happy and content, as indeed he should have been, for Lady Conyngham was his latest and last mistress.

This liaison was generally treated with hilarity and ridicule. He was no longer the young and handsome prince of the Regency, the days of golden dalliance and midnight gambling, blood horses and noble Corinthians, splendid uniforms and immaculate cravats, fast carriages and tolerable debts. He could no longer take comfort in the fact that whatever the Court, his friends and his Government thought of him, he was at least secure in his people's love. The squalid quarrel with the Queen, unresolved by a crude and sometimes pornographic debate, had occurred at a grave period of Radical unrest, and had stripped him of any honest respect he might have had. Hostile abuse had been scrawled on the walls by Carlton House, *The Queen for ever, the King in the river!* His brother York, popular with the crowd and its choice for the Crown, took that support seriously enough to express his admiration of the King's coronation by declaring, 'By God! I'll have everything the same at mine.' Although, as Madame de Lieven said, it was common knowledge that the police paid men to cheer the King in the streets, his eyes still filled with tears when he heard them, believing or wishing to believe that the shouts of 'Hurrah!' were genuine. An English king, thought de Lieven, should have stronger nerves and be equally indifferent to cheers and boos.

In appearance he was best seen as if upon a stage, elevated and at a distance, where his red-brown wig and rouged cheeks would not be noticed. He no longer used false hair as side-whiskers, but he still prolonged his youthful looks, or so he thought, with oils, creams, unguents and pastes, although less so now than ten years before when his clear grey eyes were not rheumy, his cheeks not sagging, and his legs not yet the dropsical columns they were to become. He lost three pounds from his enormous body during the trial of the Queen, but it soon returned. His abundant flesh was encased in a bastille of whalebone that delighted and inspired the cartoonists, and estimates of his weight at this time vary between sixteen and twenty stones. Because of this fleshly burden he walked slowly, and since all were obliged to wait upon him, his movements had an impressive dignity. At his coronation, wearing rich and swathing robes of immense weight, he acquired a stunning if tasteless magnificence that greatly affected the young ladies present. And if he spoilt the majesty of his appearance by ogling the prettiest faces about him in the Abbey, it did not stop the noble congregation from waving their scarlet and ermine caps and shouting *God bless the King!* The strength and volume of the applause clearly surprised him.

By 1821 he was an aged debauchee, a clownish Prince Hal lifted to the throne too late to be confident of becoming Henry V. He was ready, it is true, to play the King as he saw the role, should the Administration and the public be agreeable, but neither were. His drinking, which had prematurely ruined his youth and his health, was now restrained in the context of its past history, but the Princely Drunkard of the cartoons was the image the public saw – red-faced, round-calfed and round-buttocked in splitting breeches, with a belly like a balloon, one hand holding a spilling glass and the other grasping at the fat thigh or breast of the woman on his knee. His occasional drunkenness, which gave authority to such libels, occurred during times of boredom or despair, and sometimes in the privacy of maudlin love. His courtiers – who did not consider loyalty or discretion essential to the privilege of royal intimacy – gossiped derisively about his behaviour. The selected few who joined him at Phoenix Park or Slane Castle wrote of the amount he drank there, each newly filled glass first touching Lady Conyngham's, her hand held tight in his beneath the table. Castlereagh grumbled that the King 'never spoke to any of his attendants and seemed completely engrossed by his love'. The wife of the Austrian Ambassador, Princess Esterhazy, said the King had no shame before her, constantly kissing Lady Conyngham, and she would have been delighted by the fact that the women of Ireland ignored the Marchioness had she not thereby been burdened with the lady's company when the King was elsewhere. Lord Conyngham, one of the most self-effacing cuckolds in the history of royalty, was diplomatically deaf and blind, telling all who were kind enough to listen that 'The King is a father to us all.'

George IV was an ill man, of course, progressively, incurably, and sometimes bravely ill, and all judgement upon him should perhaps be made in the knowledge of medical treatment in his time. There were some who thought him mad as his father had been mad, although the horrifying torture inflicted upon George III by his physicians could have been sufficient to drive that good man from melancholia to insanity. The King may sometimes have feared inherited madness, remembering the frail, terrified figure of his father, wandering white-haired through the corridors of Windsor Castle in a purple dressing-gown, or playing haunting music on a harmonium. Thoughts of death, however, occupied the King's mind more than madness. When his legs swelled, and a relentless quantity of cherry brandy could not dull their pain, he often thought himself about to die. His doctors, no better than his father's, exhausted him by excessive bleeding, taking sixty ounces from his bloated form at one time, and then calming what remained of his spirit with laudanum, to which he was now addicted. An interested and sharp-eyed observer of his health was pretty Madame de Lievin, the wife of the Tsar's Minister in London. She had also been the mistress of the Austrian Chancellor, Prince Metternich, whom she now served as spy, adviser and plenipotentiary within the King's intimate circle. Since such duties required her to have the King's affection and confidence, she was his frequent companion at Windsor, Ascot and Brighton. When the King's health became important to the plans she and Metternich had for him that summer, she once returned to London from the Pavilion and wrote in rare pessimism to her Prince.

> We left the King very ill. He is tortured by gout and employs the most violent remedies to get rid of it. He looks ghastly; he is plunged in gloom; he talks about nothing but dying. I have never seen him so wretched; he did everything he could to pull himself together but in vain.

There were times when he could hardly walk, and if he did somehow carry himself to the table he could not eat without first drinking a great deal of cherry brandy. The rooms in which he spent most of his time were always overheated, and within this sweating, hot-house atmosphere he would sometimes receive visitors while lying on a couch, dressed in a lilac silk gown, a velvet nightcap on his head, and his bare and swollen feet discreetly draped with pink silk net. 'I got two smacking kisses,' reported Madame de Lieven, having found him thus. 'That is etiquette at official audiences.' The King enjoyed kissing, and his salutations of this kind to women were only marginally more enthusiastic than those his male visitors could receive. It was as if his kiss were more of a plea for affection than a demonstration of it.

His visit to Ireland was followed by another to the Continent where he met Metternich, whom he admired, and who in turn formed a higher estimation of the King's political power than was justified. Both journeys had been too costly to tolerate. Moreover, the Administration was still annoyed, and the Whigs still outraged by the continuing alterations and additions to Brighton Pavilion. It now seemed impossible to talk of the King without money becoming the principal subject of interest. The Duke of Wellington, who watched him closely and judged his behaviour as he might have done an aide-de-camp who appeared with an umbrella on the lines of Torres Vedras, was disgusted by the amount the King had already cost the country. He told his young and platonic friend, Mrs Harriet Arbuthnot, that many difficulties were bound to arise when Parliament came to debate the Coronation expenses. The King, he said, had nine wigs made for the occasion, each costing fifteen guineas, but had worn one only. He had sent 'a person' to Paris, at great expense, to acquire the pattern of Napoleon's imperial robes, that his own might be modelled upon them. The Saint Edward's Crown, made for Charles II's coronation in 1660, was not the King's property at all, but was rented from its mysterious owner 'at a percentage which amounts to £10,000; [and] instead of it being sent back the day after the Coronation, he has kept it ever since in a cabinet which he occasionally opens to feast his eyes upon it'. Without too much heated dispute, Parliament eventually voted £240,000 towards the cost of the Coronation, including £24,000 for the King's robes and £54,000 for the purchase of Saint Edward's Crown.

With such lavish expenditures perpetuating the public image of a profligate prince, Lord Liverpool's administration had little enthusiasm for the suggestion that the King should make a second costly visit to the Continent in 1822, during which he could attend the next Congress of Nations in Vienna. This was to be the meeting unofficially proposed by Prince Metternich and tirelessly advocated by Madame de Lieven, 'the King's journey', as she called it. The invitation to stand among equals with the Emperors of Russia and Austria, a magnificently uniformed triumvirate determining the future of Europe, appealed to the King's vanity, but his Prime Minister and Foreign Minister were naturally alarmed by the thought of their royal peacock (and their own policies) at the mercy of two predatory eagles. The business of foreign affairs was the prerogative of the Administration, not the King. Lord Liverpool and his ministers saw no reason why he should be released into Europe to become a welcome party to Metternich's policy of settling the affairs of Europe in its throne-rooms and not its senates. An alternative diversion seemed desirable, and that could be what Walter Scott would later describe as 'the King's Jaunt'. Since the King's visit to Ireland his ministers had agreed that he should perhaps go on a tour of Scotland in 1823. If this could be advanced a year it would preclude any journey to Vienna, and be of prodigious comfort to the Administration.

But the King had first to agree, and the most powerful influence upon any decisions he now made was Lady Conyngham.

There have been gallant efforts in recent biographies of the King to maintain that the relationship between these sentimental lovers was warmly platonic and no more, and that age, health and obesity made all else impossible. But that is to argue against the survival of lustful enthusiasm, priapic fortitude and physical ingenuity. It also forgets that what made public and private ridicule of their relationship so deliberately cruel was the inelegant image of their coupling. Certainly their contemporaries were in no doubt about Lady Conyngham's role in the King's life, and the passion with which one member of her otherwise complaisant family was ready to fight a duel over her reputation might prove rather than disprove the popular belief.

She was six years younger than the King, the daughter of a rich Yorkshire banker, and for more than a quarter of a century the wife of the Anglo-Irish Marquess Conyngham. Since she was reputed to have taken other lovers before the King, the stunning tolerance of her husband is the only remarkable characteristic in a man who has left but a faint shadow upon history, and that cast by the abundant glow of his wife. At fifty-three she was no longer the buxom, jolly-faced woman painted by Lawrence, and what had once been beautiful in her face was now florid and coarsened. Like the King she was emotional, sentimental and appropriately pious. Although rich, she was greedy to the point of rapacity, with a magpie's fascination for bright objects. She amassed a great store of jewellery in gifts from the King much of which, to her credit, she returned after his death. Her gratitude for this treasure was genuine, and the way she chose to reward him in return made him her besotted slave. Despite this infatuation, or because of it, they quarrelled often, like children, spoiling the winter sunshine of their affection with squalls of bad temper and spite.

Such comic, middle-aged lovers, making no secret of their feelings in public, she simpering as he took snuff from her round white shoulder, delivered themselves to the mercy of the lampoonists. The ridicule was harsher, crueller than that once directed at Lady Hertford, whom the Marchioness had supplanted and who was now regarded as a woman betrayed. They were pictured 'tickling the fat about each other's hips', their kissing lips dripping with the claret they had just taken from the same glass. He was Fat Geordie, and she his Vice-Queen, his 'prime bit of stuff'. Society, too, professed itself outraged, with as much humbug and hypocrisy as the newspapers. Madame de Lieven, younger than the Marchioness and still with some of the beauty that had briefly conquered Metternich, was sickened by disgust at the thought of Elizabeth Conyngham and the King as partners in physical love. This did not prevent her from assiduously cultivating the company of both, if it could serve Prince Metternich, the Tsar and the Emperor. As the King's passion became more demonstrative, she told Metternich that he was now a madman, made so by a foolish woman, a malicious fool who could do him great harm.

> All sensible people regret Lady Hertford, and even though there was nothing worse about his affair than its absurdity, can one imagine anything more absurd than an amorous and inconstant sexagenarian who, at the beginning of his reign, gives up all his time to a love affair? It is pitiable.

Nonetheless, in the cause of the Journey, Madame de Lieven felt obliged to accept the woman socially. Lady Conyngham, she told Metternich, was not the sort of person one usually invited to dinner, but times were changing in many houses. De Lieven was also curious to know how the Marchioness talked, and what she could possibly talk about. The answer to the first, she discovered, was badly, and to the second – against the King's Ministers. That Elizabeth Conyngham complained about the Government was not surprising, for the King could find little good to say of it himself. It may be supposed that they found time to speak of these matters during the calmer moments of the night hours at Carlton House, when the King took her away from a ball to a private room, a page guarding the door and their secrets. Mrs Arbuthnot, watching them retreat to such privacy, thought it outrageous. 'As the King can see Lady Conyngham every day and all day long, I really think he might control his passion and not behave so indecently.'

They cried often in public, holding hands and smiling through their tears – from simple happiness, it would seem, and, for the

King, from the joy to be got in the physical and emotional love of an undemanding woman. Undemanding, that is, with the two exceptions common to most royal mistresses. First was concern and consideration for her family. Her brother William thought her association with the King was an offence to her virtue, but others in the family seem to have accepted it as providential good fortune. It was hoped by Lady Conyngham and her husband that the Marquess would be given the post of Master of the House within the Royal Household – the previous holder, the obliging Lord Hertford, having resigned this and other offices at the time of his wife's eclipse. The appointment was successfully opposed by Lord Liverpool, although it was not in his gift, but in practical terms this scarcely mattered for all the Conynghams used the Royal Stables as if the buildings were their own. The Marquess also failed to acquire the office of Lord Chamberlain of the Royal Household (another surrender by Lord Hertford) and in this matter Lord Liverpool's objections may have been within his powers. Conyngham was finally satisfied with the post of Lord Steward of the Royal Household, an office at least as old as the Lord Chamberlainship. The King's huckstering on behalf of his mistress's husband led to a worsening quarrel between him and Lord Liverpool's administration, including Wellington. At the end of one dispute the Duke faced him as from the ridge at Waterloo and said, 'If you do not like us, why do you not turn us out?' To which there was no reply.

The King sentimentally adored the Conynghams' five children, all adults, lavishing love and presents upon them as if in compensation for the dark and inconsolable loss of his own daughter. With one exception, they took the benefits of this without any introspective doubts about the manner in which they had been secured. The exception was the eldest son, Lord Mount Charles, who invited Castlereagh to a dawn meeting with pistols as a result of what he believed to be offensive Parliamentary references to his mother as 'the King's mistress'. The Foreign Minister coldly rejected the invitation, but the foolish affair can be seen as the first skirmish in an open war between Lady Conyngham and the Castlereaghs.

The second price demanded, or offered for Lady Conyngham's loving submission, was jewellery, valued then at more than £100,000. Dorothea de Lieven, who was no less mercenary in intellectual terms, impaled the Marchioness's greedy desires upon her sharp pen. 'Not an idea in her head, not a word to say for herself, nothing but a hand to accept pearls and diamonds with, and an enormous balcony to wear them on.' The sylph-like de Lieven would naturally consider the King's affection for Lady Conyngham's great breasts incomprehensible, but she also failed to understand that the jewels could mean less to the Marchioness than her lover's desperate need to give them. Nonetheless, the steady accumulation of what Lady Conyngham was obliged to call her family jewels, amused the giggling ladies of the Court. The bright-eyed and vixenish Lady Cowper, one of the gifted flock of Lambs, told her brother that 'The family pearls which she talked of last year have increased greatly, the string is twice as long as it was, and such a diamond belt, three inches wide, with such a sapphire in the centre.'

The story of that sapphire's provenance is rich in historical irony, and if true it is a matter of relief, or regret, that the stone did not make an appearance in Edinburgh later that year. It was sometimes known as the Jacobite or Stuart Sapphire, and was a gift from the Young Pretender's brother in 1807. Senile and slowly dying at Frascati in the Alban foothills, Cardinal Henry of York had been a grateful pensioner of the Royal House that replaced his own, receiving £4000 a year from the Civil List at the wish of George III. The great sapphire, it was believed, was his responsive bequest to the Prince Regent, who later gave it to his daughter Charlotte upon her wedding. When she died in ugly convulsions following the slow delivery of her beautiful and stillborn child, her father asked her husband to return the sapphire, claiming that it could not pass from the possession of the British Royal Family. Prince Leopold at first resisted this attempt at extortion across the body of the woman they both loved, but at last surrendered the gem, salving his pride by saying that it was returned *au Roi comme un hommage*. The final persuasion, said Lady Cowper, was 'the King saying that in particular he must have the stone for his coronation as it was to go in his crown – when lo and behold here it has appeared in Lady Conyngham's waist, *la ceinture de Vénus*'.

If the story of the sapphire's origin is true, it may well have been among the Jacobite relics which the Cardinal also left to the Prince

Regent – a diamond saltire once worn by Charles I and later by the Young Pretender, a ring originally used at the coronation of Scottish kings. Shortly after his accession, George IV contributed to the cost of erecting the Stuart tomb in Saint Peter's, containing the bodies of the Old and Young Pretenders and Cardinal Henry. It was the magnificent creation of Antonio Canova whose work the King had often patronized.

Having no determined notion of how to employ himself as king, only fitfully liking the thought of a Continental visit accompanied by his mistress, the King became more preoccupied with his health, which grew worse or better according to his moods. Sometimes he wept with self-pity upon the gem-encrusted bosom of the Marchioness, sometimes they withdrew apart in angry hostility. When she came to Brighton, Lady Conyngham was often accompanied by her daughter Elizabeth, and the King would walk through the Pavilion with one on each arm, both wearing long strings of glistening pearls. When she boldly ordered the grand salon to be lit by hundreds of candles, he countered some of the resentment this may have caused by taking her arms tenderly, and saying, 'Thank you, thank you, my dear. You always do what is right, you cannot please me so much as by doing everything you please, everything to show you are mistress here.' Such simplicity of emotion helped them to enjoy their bourgeois pleasures, driving together in a pony-chaise through the leaf-dappled sunlight of Windsor Park, or entertaining intimate friends behind the mullioned windows of The Lodge, the mock-gothic cottage designed for the King by John Nash.

By the end of 1821, most of the Court and Lord Liverpool's administration were convinced that Lady Conyngham's influence upon the King was malevolent and destructive. She was thought, perhaps with truth, to have poisoned the King's mind against his amiable but fussy Keeper of the Privy Purse, Major-General Sir Benjamin Bloomfield. This aging soldier was a plodding, pedagogic man whose greatest service to the King, according to Harriet Arbuthnot, was 'buying up caricatures and the newspapers to keep his own and Lady Conyngham's name out of them'. The Marchioness was believed to be urging his replacement by Sir William Knighton, one of the King's physicians-in-ordinary. A round-faced, large-nosed man with mocking eyes, he was known sardonically as the 'man-midwife' or 'the *accoucheur*', a reference to earlier and, some said, darker days when he had a fashionable practice in Hanover Square. He had strong qualities of industry and discretion, but was commonly disliked for his ambition and his unctuous manner toward the King, whom he addressed in a flattering and obsequious style that would not have disgraced the Court of Imperial China. The King's response to this was effusive affection, and he often declared that without Sir William's company he was lost and miserable. An alliance of mutual assistance between the Royal Mistress and the Royal Physician was perhaps inevitable.

At the heart of the popular dislike of the Marchioness was the smouldering hatred of the Castlereaghs. This began, if not with Lord Mount Charles's intemperate challenge, with Lady Conyngham's public declaration of her sympathy for His Majesty's Opposition rather than His Majesty's Ministers. Since Lord Castlereagh was one of the latter, and the Marchioness was presumed to be speaking the King's mind, Lady Castlereagh's loyal response was directed at both. With the hauteur to be expected in the daughter of an earl and the wife of a marquess-to-be when speaking of a banker's daughter, she let it be known that she would never invite the Marchioness to dine or sup because entertaining a King's mistress was unthinkable. This deeply angered the King, as perhaps was intended, and he complained bitterly to Wellington of the way the Marchioness was being treated by his Ministers, declaring that it was all he could expect from such men. He violently abused Lady Castlereagh, the Duke told Mrs Arbuthnot,

> . . . because she took no notice of Lady Conyngham, and said it was a piece of treatment he uniformly met with from his Ministers, that it was enough for any person to be his friend for them to be marked out for all sorts of contempt and insult.

In such an atmosphere of petulant acrimony it was perhaps impossible for Monarch or Ministers to behave with adult common sense. Lord Castlereagh, whose mind was already walking along the black edge of insanity, had a jealous and tigerish regard for his wife's good name. Barred from reasonable access to a King who let it be known that he did not like or trust his ministers, Castlereagh complained to anyone who would listen. He told Harriet Arbuthnot that his wife was incapable of thinking or doing anything unkind. Her refusal to invite Lady Conyngham to supper had not been intended to injure her character, but that

> . . . Lady Conyngham has fancied that, because the King chose to proclaim her as his mistress, all the Ministers' wives and adherents were to pay her court, and that consequently she had not deemed it necessary to seek her out. He said Lady Castlereagh was much too high-minded to pay court to *any* one, much less to a woman whose only notoriety arose from so shameful a cause.

Thus was the beginning of a petty feud that continued for almost two years, during which Castlereagh became convinced that the King's abusive hostility toward his ministers was fomented by Lady Conyngham, and this because their wives would not invite her to their houses. The quarrel was conducted by snub and counter-snub, by gossip and tattle, and the greatest injury was suffered by the King's good nature. The ill-will increased when Castlereagh succeeded his father as the second Marquess of Londonderry. In the hindsight of history, and the little time left to him, it is almost as if another name were needed to protect the achievements of a career of which he at least was proud, and to cloak the grim manner in which he would abandon it.

It would soon become clear to Madame de Lieven that unless there were a reconciliation between Lady Conyngham and the newly-styled Londonderrys, or at least a truce, the likelihood of the Journey being undertaken was small. The King, it was rightly assumed, would not travel to Europe without his mistress. Lord Londonderry, as the accompanying Foreign Minister, could not and would not go without his wife. And neither lady, of course, would at present think of going anywhere in the company of the other.

Madame the Countess de Lieven was close to betraying her angry
impatience, again asking the King if he would go upon the Journey.
Once more she received the same melancholy, self-pitying answer,
'If I live . . . If European politics permit . . .' The year 1822 had
begun badly for everybody at Brighton. With the exception of Lady
Conyngham, and a few close intimates like de Lieven, the King sent
his courtiers back to London. He was tortured by gout and submitted
to the vilest treatment in the hope of relieving his agony. His gloomy
misery increased the waxen pallor beneath the rouge on his cheeks.
He talked of nothing but dying, exhausting the sympathy of his
audience, and he could not see the boredom and contempt in the
eyes of those obliged to listen. Even Lady Conyngham yawned in his
presence. He had also become pathetically suspicious of cabals and
intrigues, desperate to know the thoughts of a hostile world beyond
the glass walls of the Magic Lantern, his private chamber at the
Pavilion. He repeatedly declared that he could not, would not stir a
step without Sir William Knighton's guidance, building his ardent
trust upon the physician's oozing mixture of flattery and rebuke,
and not a little of his respect upon Sir William's attempts at verse
which moved the King to tears and to favourable comparison with
John Milton. Enjoying such royal favour, Knighton did not put it at
risk by provoking Lady Conyngham, making himself her friend,

57

and escorting her to Carlton House in a plain carriage when she wished to avoid the attention of the mob. They also shared a dislike of Benjamin Bloomfield, who offended the Marchioness by his constant complaint that the cost of her jewels must soon empty the Privy Purse. It was now generally believed that Knighton was the King's chief spy, and it was said that not a word was uttered at White's, or any club, that did not ultimately reach the ears of the *accoucheur*. In deep dislike of the man, Liverpool and Londonderry stubbornly opposed his appointment as Keeper of the Privy Purse, once the office was taken from Bloomfield. They also objected to the granting of a peerage to the General, which Bloomfield believed was his due as a parting gift. They were miserably unsuccessful, and the King's will prevailed. The physician received the Purse, and the General not only got his peerage (albeit in Ireland, where he had been buying land) but also a sinecure in Jamaica and the appointment as Minister to Stockholm.

When his mind was not wholly concentrated upon his agonies, the King was still eager to please his mistress. Upon her suggestion, or perhaps at his own prompting, he suggested a marriage between her daughter Elizabeth and Earl Gower, the stiff and proper son of Lord Stafford, and he was ready to make the young man a duke if the union were agreed. It may be assumed that when this startling proposal reached Trentham Hall – the mingling of the blood of a Yorkshire banker (and a King's mistress) with that of eight centuries of Gordons, Granvilles, Gowers, Egertons, Stanleys and Brandons *inter alia* – the Marquess and his lady were at a loss for an inoffensive answer. None was required, however, for when Gower and the girl met they had no interest in each other whatsoever.

The King's short temper in these late winter weeks was to be expected in a man so much a victim of pain and fear. He violently abused his servants for the most trivial errors, even a candle crooked in its sconce provoked him to spluttering fury. He also quarrelled openly with his brother York, two overweight, red-cheeked pouter pigeons facing each other in fury. Rage became a necessary passion, perhaps, a scourge to drive out darker emotions. It had one curious result. His anger with the leaders of the Opposition, upon whom he once smiled, was soon balanced by tolerant approval of the Administration he had once despised.

Despite the chill climate of his uncertain moods, Madame de Lieven bravely continued her advocacy of the Journey. She was one of the few members of the Court whose company was now required at the Pavilion. The King liked her bright, attentive air, her small but pretty face in its frame of dark ringlets, her head coquettishly bent on a white swan-neck. He did not know, or did not care, that she was cold and unsympathetic, ambitious for the power of influence, and contemptuous of his silly mistress. It was enough, perhaps, to see the responsive smile upon that falsely compassionate mouth, and believe that it expressed her loyal admiration. It was often used to hide her frustration. She was angered now to discover that the King and the Marchioness would not speak to each other of the Journey. It was 'a forbidden topic between them', she told Metternich. In order to pique her lover, Lady Conyngham had informed him that she no longer wished to go to Europe, and both had then turned away from the subject in anger. But the Journey could not be ignored, and de Lieven became their intermediary. The King swore to her that he would not budge from England without the Marchioness, and he begged de Lieven to persuade her to accompany him. When approached, Lady Conyngham said that while she would not go to Vienna, she would of course persuade the King to go without her, confident that he would refuse. De Lieven persisted in this childish dispute because, she said, she liked 'challenging silly women', but she knew what the real obstacle was.

> I see no means of bringing about a reconciliation with Lady Londonderry. There is the bitterest prejudice against her, though her husband is regarded with affection . . . [The King] grows more arrogant and despotic every day, the favourite has complained to me; and her son is leaving, because he cannot stand it any longer.

In February the King was obliged to appear in public for the opening of Parliament. Though this was a long and tiring occasion, it was less painful an experience than an ordinary carriage ride from Carlton House or the Pavilion. The red coats and beautiful dark horses of his Household Brigade kept the crowd at a distance where scornful laughter, the jeers and shouts, would be unheard above the noise of beating drums and pumping music. Moreover, he liked to be seen with a crown upon his head, and he had always enjoyed such pageantry – the magnificent uniforms, gilded coaches, harsh primary colours against medieval stone, and the flash of diamonds on white shoulders and breasts. When he stepped heavily from his coach at Westminster he seemed about to collapse under the weight of his robes, his crown slipped forward to his nose, and the drag of his train pulled at his fat neck. He recovered without assistance and entered the Lords' chamber, waiting there for a quarter of an hour before the Commons arrived. At first he was motionless and exhausted upon the throne, his saurian eyes moving coldly over the benches of scarlet and white. Then suddenly he smiled, he saw a charming face and he smiled. This boyish ogling moved on to pretty Lady Cowper, and from her to winsome Lady Morley. He flirted shamelessly, 'his eyelids going hard at it', said Madame de Lieven. The assembled peers and their ladies watched silently, sweating in their robes until the Commons came to end their embarrassment.

There were not many days so happily enjoyed, for soon he was ill again, with dropsy, his physicians said. 'Alas for the Journey!' complained de Lieven, her attention always upon the only important consequence of his agony. Realizing that all possibilities should be considered, not the least the death of the King, she began to cultivate the Duke of York, only to discover that he had old-fashioned views upon all subjects and believed that everything worth doing could only be done by oneself. Since this was not the attitude expected of a constitutional monarch, she suspected that Lord Londonderry, who had once thought that York might make a more tractable king, was now praying for divine intervention to prevent him from outliving George IV.

Londonderry made an unexpected appeal to de Lieven at this time, and one which strengthened her hope for that necessary reconciliation. They met, seemingly by accident, when she was walking and he was riding in the Park. He dismounted, left his horse with a groom, and walked slowly beside her. He told her that he had deliberately chosen this part of the Park to take his ride, knowing that he might meet her. He was eager for news and reassurance, particularly about the Journey of which, he said, he strongly approved. He was firmly convinced that he should accompany the King, holding himself aloof from all discussions if necessary, but ready at the same time to take part when invited. It was an odd conversation for a Foreign Minister to be having with the wife of the Russian ambassador, but he clearly wished both the King and Metternich to know his mind. He was certain, he said, that the Austrian wished him to go to Vienna, and de Lieven, of course, said that *everybody* wished him to go. Unspoken during this pleasant saunter under the plane trees was perhaps the hint that Lady Londonderry, in her proper concern for her husband's career, might now be ready for some reconciliation with Lady Conyngham. If only the favourite would . . .

For the moment the sun shone upon almost everybody. Although still ill and fretful at the beginning of March, the King invited both Liverpool and Londonderry to join him at dinner. He treated both with grace and charm, but neither was comfortable. Lord Liverpool whom many people found comically odd, was so embarrassed by the presence of Lady Conyngham on his right that he could find nothing to say. His discomfort, recorded de Lieven, caused the rest of the guests to 'die laughing'. Apart from this, it was probably an evening of intense boredom, for the King's melancholy pre-occupation with his imminent death now monopolized all conversations. De Lieven stoically endured this when she was alone with him and the Marchioness, her mind concentrated upon achieving some small agreement upon the Journey. She talked about Prince Metternich as often as she could, and once the King took Lady Conyngham's hand and said he would give anything in the world for her to meet the Austrian minister. 'Well,' said de Lieven, 'so she will next summer, I hope.' But the King sighed, and spoke now in German which the Marchioness did not understand. He feared that he might not be able to undertake the Journey. De Lieven was immediately sharp with him, reminding him that he had given his promise and all were expecting him to honour it. He sighed again, and like a sullen child he said, 'If I break my promise, it will be her fault.'

At Ditton Park upon the Thames, a mile from the medieval husk of Windsor Castle which the King and Jeffry Wyatt would shortly change for ever, Lord Montagu observed the King's vacillation with tolerable patience. An urbane, stern and civilized man, he was an example of those Scottish aristocrats who so delighted Walter Scott, and like many of them he satisfied his taste for congenial society by living in England for the greater part of the year. A peer in his own right, he was the brother of the fourth Duke of Buccleuch, and governor of the present Duke, a fifteen-year-old boy who was lodged at Eton College across the green water-meadows to the west of Ditton Park. Montagu was Scott's true and generous friend. This sincere relationship was in no way diminished by their mutual acceptance of their social differences, for if Scott admired Montagu as a responsible Border aristocrat, uncle of the young chief of all Scotts, Montagu in his turn greatly respected the Laird of Abbotsford as an eminent man of letters to whom their country was deeply indebted. They corresponded regularly, shared the same political convictions, delighted in coursing, hunting and the killing of game fish, approved of sensible cross-breeding in landed families and the wise employment of Mr Raeburn for preserving the likenesses of them, discussed all matters of archaeological and historical interest, and were passionately concerned with the preservation of Melrose Abbey. When such matters, and the affairs of the nation, were not filling his time or trying his tolerance in the first weeks of 1822, Montagu was also anxious to know whether or not the King would visit Scotland this year.

Unlike the Great Manager of Scotland, Viscount Melville, Montagu did not think his country needed the purge of the royal presence to rid it of Radical humours. His attitude was, if anything, like that of a modest host who, having been told of a probable visitor, was anxious to be given a date so that the proper arrangements could be made. By the spring he had become sceptical, and did not believe the King would come this year. Since he had been told that one of the objections raised to the visit – and this no doubt by an Englishman – was that there was nowhere in the northern kingdom suitable for the King to stay, he felt obliged to do what he could. It was true that Holyroodhouse, in the lion-headed shadow of Arthur's Seat, was no longer a palace after two centuries without a royal tenant. It had become a draughty apartment house for grace and favour, used as permanent or temporary lodgings by ennobled holders of archaic office, or modest gentry living on sinecures and pensions. In April, Lord Montagu therefore wrote to Robert Peel, offering the King the use – should he come – of his nephew's house at Dalkeith, an impressive but modest Palladian building set in a landscaped park seven miles to the south-east of Edinburgh. It was perhaps the best accommodation available, perhaps the only one offered, for the Earl of Hopetoun by the Forth, Viscount Melville and the Marquess of Lothian in the neighbourhood of Dalkeith, had not suggested Hopetoun House, Melville Castle or Newbattle Abbey as a temporary residence for their King. Peel expressed himself obliged by the offer which, he said, had removed the strongest objection the King had made to the Scottish visit. Dalkeith House was therefore provisionally accepted, but he could not say, of course, whether the King would go to Scotland at all. This was no more than Montagu had expected, and he said so to Scott.

> This is considered as equivalent to *'le Roi j'avisera'*, and from what I hear since, I do not in the least expect he will go. He is bent on going to Vienna, God knows why, but if the Ministers possibly can, they will put a spoke in his wheel.

If the King did not go to Scotland, he added, he himself would bear the disappointment with fortitude, and he turned from what he clearly regarded as a tiresome matter to the pleasure to be got at Easter, when Eton College would discharge his young Buccleuch kinsmen and their friends into the house at Ditton Park.

Of all the hostile Ministers Montagu had in mind, Londonderry was the most irrational and unpredictable. It was upon this gaunt and dark-eyed Anglo-Irishman that Madame de Lieven now concentrated her attention, deciding that she must take the King's mistress to see Lady Londonderry. She did not explain to Metternich how this meeting of mountain and Mahomet was to be arranged – perhaps she knew that the Foreign Secretary and his wife now believed that some resolution of the ridiculous impasse was necessary, even at the expense of an unpleasant hour in Lady Conyngham's company. By this, de Lieven hoped, the King would go to Vienna with the approval of the Administration, the Foreign Secretary would attend him as adviser and British representative, Lady Londonderry would quite properly accompany her husband, and the Marchioness would persuade her petulant lover that all would be for the best if she remained in England. It was a bold try, but successful only in Lady Londonderry's initial agreement to the meeting. Lady Conyngham never intended to honour the arrangement, and welcomed the opportunity to deliver another snub to her enemy. De Lieven was intensely angry.

> I was to take Lady Conyngham to Lady Londonderry's yesterday. I had promised to bring her, and there was great joy at the thought that this wretched quarrel was over, but she gave me the slip and I am furious. She is the most changeable person in the world; and, as her promise to me dated from the previous day, doubtless she was given some advice more charitable than mine. Some people are always sorry to see a squabble finished.

The King was of no assistance, sunk in a wretched trough of boredom, and once more estranged from his mistress, a brief separation which de Lieven thought was due to an unnatural 'attack of prudishness'. The days proceeded remorselessly toward the next manifestation of Lady Conyngham's stunning indifference to diplomatic protocol. Restored once more to emotional and physical bliss, she and the King discussed the entertainment that should be given to the visiting Prince and Princess of Denmark, including the guest list for a state dinner. When the King began this by placing the names of Lord and Lady Londonderry toward the top of his list, the Marchioness declared that if the lady were present, she would herself be absent. The King protested that he could not give a state dinner of this nature without the presence of the Foreign Secretary, and he could not invite the Minister and exclude his wife. Lady Conyngham was obstinate, whereupon the King said that if she would not come, then there would be no dinner. This failed to persuade her, and with great emotion he capitulated, saying the Londonderrys would not be invited. Almost immediately he saw the absurdity of this, and implored the Marchioness to seek the advice of Madame de Lieven. That eager and unscrupulous woman responded with enthusiasm, as always seeing the resolution of the Journey before all else.

She came to tell me what happened, I summoned all my eloquence; I pointed out to her that an official dinner given by the King to a foreign Prince and to the Ambassadors, from which the Minister for Foreign Affairs was excluded, would be in the worst possible taste; that not to invite Lady Londonderry would be to offer her a personal insult to her husband; that the advances she had been making for a year to Lady Conyngham were enough to atone for her past rudeness . . . It was a long battle but I won; and now, thank Heaven, a quarrel of two years' standing is ended, at any rate as far as appearances go. I can think of no more difficult job than getting round a woman's vanity, when one can appeal neither to her reason nor to her decent feelings.

In her satisfaction and delight, de Lieven overreached herself, and foolishly told Londonderry how she had persuaded Lady Conyngham to withdraw her objection to his wife's presence at the dinner. She did not realize that this condescension would be a greater offence to his pride than the favourite's objection, of which he had known nothing until now. He lost his temper with the pretty woman whom he had thought his friend. 'You have shown me my position!' he shouted. 'Our position clearly. Things cannot go on like this. We cannot put up with a Lady Conyngham who is powerful enough to offer us such affronts.' From now on, he said, he would be the King's humble servant, no more. If good relations with his monarch could not last under such conditions, so be it, he would resign.

'I cannot sacrifice my honour and my pride, both are more wounded than I can say. I repeat, things cannot remain as they are. As for the Journey, I wash my hands of it. The King has Liverpool; let him arrange with him. I shall acept his words, and if I continue to serve him, I shall decide according to whether my wife is or is not included in the expedition, what course I have to take.'

Her plans seemingly in ruins, her one great ally in the Administration lost to her, she was further dismayed when Londonderry's half-brother, Lord Stewart, came to see her later that day. He was perplexed and alarmed by his brother's emotional state. The Foreign Minister, he said, was disgusted with the state of his affairs and with his career, and that as a result of 'this woman's quarrel, the cup has overflowed'. Londonderry's unstable mind had clearly stepped into a terrible darkness far beyond the tiresome spat between two vain and ambitious women. Perhaps Stewart suspected this. His brother had enemies, he told de Lieven, 'and he knows it, but he does not know which they are, and thus suspects them all'. Unable to continue his rambling and sometimes incoherent complaint, Lord Stewart broke into tears, begging for an open declaration of hostility from Lady Conyngham, rather than matters to be left as they were.

At Windsor, in the latticed June sunlight that came through the windows of the Lodge, de Lieven worked to sustain the King's enthusiasm for the Journey. He was in a mood of self-indulgent melancholy, at one point indicating the Marchioness with a languid hand. 'Ah, Heavens,' he said, 'if she were what I am!' What he was, or what she was expected to believe he was, puzzled de Lieven. Did he mean that Lady Conyngham ought to be a man? The King then sighed deeply and explained his meaning. 'If she were a widow, as I am a widower, she would not be one for long.' While Lady Conyngham simpered prettily – 'Ah, my dear King, how good you are!' – de Lieven was thinking of Sir William Knighton, the man-midwife's nocturnal visits to the King, and the gossip about his past. A whole chemist's shop flashed through her mind, she told Metternich, leaving him to determine whether or not she thought the King was planning to rid his lady of her husband.

Eventually they spoke of the Journey and her belief that it should also include a visit to Florence, which delighted the King and Marchioness. Neither was sure where Florence was, how far away, and de Lieven had to teach them a little geography. That done, the King said that although he would rather stay in London he could not resist Lady Conyngham's wishes. He promised to tell Liverpool and Londonderry of his firm intention to go to the Congress of Nations, and this assurance, thought de Lieven, was due to her final appeal to his sense of duty and his obligation to serve the cause of freedom from revolutionary terror. 'I made a grand speech, full of the dangers of Jacobinism, and the great moral effect which the presence of the King of England at a congress would produce in Europe.' The King's parting words were of the Journey, repeating his promise to make arrangements with Liverpool and Londonderry when he returned to London, and asking her to keep all secret until then.

As she stepped down from her carriage before her London house, she found Lord Stewart waiting at the door, sent by his brother to discover what the King had decided. She told him that the King had talked of the Journey, and that he was relying upon Londonderry's company in Vienna. Inside the house, Stewart became visibly distressed, complaints and accusations spilling from him as he again spoke of his half-brother's fear of rivalry and of conspiracy among his colleagues. His particular suspicion was that Wellington wished to usurp the duties of Londonderry's office and to go to the Congress himself. His justification for this belief was the curious argument that the Duke was the friend and confidant of Lady Conyngham. Madame de Lieven did her best to calm Lord Stewart before he left, and she told Metternich that she was astonished by 'the illusory terrors that have been conjured up'. Neither she nor Lord Stewart appear to have asked each other whether the Foreign Secretary were not insane.

Whatever Lord Liverpool thought of the King's firm decision to attend the Congress, his reaction is best explained by a small announcement in the *Edinburgh Advertiser* for June 11, its publication no doubt ensured by Lord Melville, as ever managing all things Scottish on behalf of the Administration.

> It is generally believed that His Majesty has no intention of visiting the continent during the present year, and in consequence the report is revived that His Majesty intends to visit Scotland in the course of the present summer.

When Madame de Lieven met Londonderry again she was shocked by his appearance. He looked ghastly, she said, he had aged five years in a week and appeared to be a broken man. He now believed that de Lieven was conspiring with Wellington to secure the Duke's appointment to Vienna, and he was ready to resign his office should this happen. Madame de Lieven blamed Lord Stewart for encouraging his half-brother's jealousies and suspicions, and she thought she was ill-rewarded for the many kindnesses she had shown their family, but she was now confident that the Journey was secure beyond change. 'I think I have pulled it off', she told Metternich on June 17. She had persuaded Lady Conyngham that there would be great prestige for the King if he attended the Congress, and it would be wrong to prevent him going. Moreover, there was an urgent need for the British Foreign Secretary to be present also, and that would be difficult without the excuse of the King's Journey. Therefore, any consideration that prevented either from going – she did not say Lady Conyngham's temperamental obstinacy – would be harmful to the King and the country. This and other persuasive nonsense was successful. 'She swallowed everything I said,' de Lieven gaily reported.

That evening Londonderry was granted an audience with the King, and two hours later he dined with de Lieven. She was eager to discover what had been said about the Journey, whether the King had again declared his firm intention of going to Vienna. No longer looking ghastly, Londonderry was 'radiant', she said, but more inclined to tease her than speak plainly. She tried a score of times to persuade him to give her a message she could send to Metternich, and when he finally did so it was ambiguous and dismissive. 'Tell him that I am hoping to see him soon.'

Three days later, in the Conynghams' house, she understood what that meant. She arrived upon invitation to find the Marchioness in histrionic distress, her eyes swollen and her red cheeks glistening with tears. She held out a letter from the King. 'All is over! He writes to me this morning that his plans have been changed, that he is not going to the Continent but to Scotland, and he has just sent for his Ministers to tell them his wishes.' Greatly alarmed, de Lieven urged her, in Heaven's name, to write to the King at once, to tell him to make no irrevocable decisions, but to wait until she had seen him. At that moment, as if upon cue, Lady Conyngham's son arrived. Where is the King? he was asked. The King is with his Ministers, he said.

Upon that curtain-line, de Lieven knew that all was over indeed. Later that day, her husband was officially informed by Londonderry that the King had abandoned the Journey, and that couriers had been dispatched to Edinburgh to give notice to the Lord Provost that his city could shortly expect a visit from the King. De Lieven acknowledged the Government's victory.

Lord Liverpool has pulled so many strings, and frightened the King so much by means of newspaper articles, that he has made him take up again the plan of a Scottish tour. The King is in tears, the favourite is in tears; they are all in despair. All I have said is that, if I were King, nobody should have the right to make me cry. I give as much autocratic advice as I can; but I have to deal with two women – the King and his mistress. You can see what a weathercock he is; the last person to speak to him carries the day.

It was perhaps characteristic of Dorothea de Lieven to use the occasion to lecture the King on the advantages of an autocracy over a constitutional monarchy. It is doubtful whether the argument was sympathetically received. Everybody at Court, she said, the King, the favourite, *everybody*, was now gloomy. No one knew what to do with the summer, and all looked as if they were on the point of taking their own lives in desperate ennui. The King's miserable state of mind was not improved by the arrival of a letter from the Emperor of Austria, cordially inviting him to the Congress of Nations. Not knowing what to do about this – or rather, knowing that Lord Liverpool would advise doing nothing – the King appealed for sympathy to Knighton. Upon his advice nothing was done, and the Austrian ambassador was blamed for everything from a lack of tact in forwarding the letter, to a machiavellian attempt to embarrass the Administration. The King was indeed a weathercock, and it is possible that having grown tired of all efforts to direct him, he had decided upon the one proposal that would give him the least trouble and provoke the least criticism. Even so, he gave no firm assurance, no promise of this date or that, or indeed any date at all. Thus Lord Melville was obliged to write again to the Lord Provost of Edinburgh, and the *Advertiser* was once more pleased to be of service to his lordship.

The wish of his Majesty to visit Scotland, we understand, remains the same, but the plan is for the present suspended (although by no means given up) in consequence of the doubts entertained by his Majesty's medical advisers as to the propriety of his undertaking so long a journey.

Bitterly vexed by the loss of an opportunity to shine in the great courts of Europe with her royal lover, Lady Conyngham withdrew behind a dignified pique, letting it be known that she and her daughter Elizabeth would be spending August at Worthing, or Hastings perhaps, enjoying the sunlight and sea-bathing so beneficial to the delicacy of the girl's health. Accommodating medical advisers were also able to approve the propriety of this undertaking. The favourite's decision contributed to the King's gloom, and in his contrition he could deny her nothing. The waspish Lady Cowper said that while he was not allowed to see as much of his lady as he wished, 'it still rains bracelets and jewels and side-tables'.

In Scotland, said Walter Scott, one Post hurried upon another with contradictory intelligence. Yesterday the King's coming was announced, and today he is not. Such havering was a bad policy, Scott thought, robbing the visit of the grace it should have, and lowering the temperature of the people's expectations. In the Isle of Man, which he owned and where he was thought of as its king, the Duke of Atholl had little interest in the King's affairs, being much moved by the death at Portobello of his friend, Sir John MacGregor Murray. He was making wearisome arrangements for his return to the mainland and to the funeral when he heard of the proposed Royal Visit. The news came from his London agent, a conscientious man who apologized for sending the information, as if he were somehow responsible for this interruption of his Grace's calm and measured life. Atholl's second son, James, a soldier newly created Baron Glenlyon, was in attendance upon the King in London, but the agent thought he might be released from that duty should the Duke require his assistance to prepare Dunkeld House or Blair Castle for a royal visit. Before Atholl could reply to this, and while he was still humouring his wife's captious complaint that neither Blair nor Dunkeld was in a condition to entertain Royalty, the agent wrote again. The King had changed his mind, or perhaps his mistress had changed it for him. Lord Glenlyon (who seemed disinclined to write himself) had told the agent of gossip recently heard at the French Ambassador's ball – the King was not to go to Scotland.

> Where changes are so sudden and so frequent, there is no saying what his Majesty may do. The apprehension on the part of the Marchioness of meeting with an unpleasant

and unwelcome reception in general is reported to have its influence.

A belief that Lady Conyngham might still abandon the sea-water bathing of Sussex, and risk an unpleasant reception in Edinburgh, would occupy the minds and prejudices of the Scots for the next few weeks, principally, it would seem, because there was no precedent in their recent history that could guide them in their behaviour toward a king's mistress. More distressing than this was the King's continued prevarication. Now at the Clarendon Hotel in London, with a company of healthful children anxious to begin their holidays, Lord Montagu waited for an opportunity to leave for Scotland. He was unaffected by Scott's growing enthusiasm for the Jaunt. It was the King's unavoidable duty, no more. He had not been obliged to visit either Ireland or Scotland, but now that he had visited one, he was in honour pledged to the other. In the second week of July, Montagu gently nudged the elbow of Robert Peel. He was shortly to leave for Scotland, he said, and wished to know if his Majesty had any commands as to his residence at Dalkeith House. He thought this might produce a positive answer, perhaps even a date. Meanwhile, he told Scott, he would take his joyous band of children and their dependants to Scotland, distribute them among other members of the family, and go on to Dalkeith House himself, King or no King. This seemed to be the impatient, if not irascible attitude of most of Scotland's nobility, being close enough to royalty and royal gossip not to believe any nonsense about medical advisers and the danger of long journeys.

Robert Peel was in poor health and in no fit state for the journey he would be obliged to take with the King. Nor had he any great wish to visit Scotland, fond though he was of the country, or at least that part of it where game was most plentiful and people most scarce. But he recognized the need for a firm decision, and on 22 July he asked for it.

> Dear Lord Liverpool
> Has the King made up his mind with respect
> to Scotland?
>
> Ever Yours
> R. Peel

I have not been able to see him, being unwell,
but I desired Lord Melville to be certain to
see him.

>   Yours
>   R.

The answer was yes, although no date was given. Peel told Montagu
that the King intended to proceed to Scotland as soon as possible
after the prorogation of Parliament, and that he wished Peel to
express his thanks for the offer of Dalkeith House. This was enough
for Montagu to order the building to be evacuated by the family, its
plate and china stored, its stables emptied and scoured, the gravel
raked, the gardens trimmed. The young Duke, with his brother Lord
John, the Ladies Anne and Isabella and sundry others, accompanied
Lord and Lady Montagu in a grand carriage procession to Barrie's
Hotel in Edinburgh. Most of the house-servants remained where
they were to accept the authority of whatever staff the King might
bring – butler, grooms to the chamber, doormen, postillions and
coachmen. Stabled near Barrie's, or remaining at Dalkeith House,
were three carriage horses, six riding horses, and three ponies,
although it was known that the King's horses would come by sea as
soon as possible. Dispersed somewhere between the house and the
hotel were nine family servants, one armorial bearer and a New-
foundland dog. The maintenance of the Buccleuch household was
more modest than ostentatious.

Still unconvinced that the King would come, Walter Scott was
inclined to dismiss the subject with a characteristic but now obscure
literary reference. 'The King's affair seems to be the old and oft
quoted line of Sternhold and Hopkins – The Lord *will* come, and he
will not.' Yet there were now firm indications that he was indeed
coming. At the beginning of July, Captain the Honourable Sir
Charles Paget transferred his pennant to the King's yacht *Royal
George* at Portsmouth, with orders to make her ready by 25 July
when she would take the King aboard at Greenwich. Before the
beautiful vessel slipped her moorings on the 17th, and was warped
out of the harbour, her crew had been daily employed in the rigging,
enduring nasty, fretful weather that put none of them in the mood
for a choppy North Sea voyage to the Firth of Forth. The orders to all

the ships of the Royal Squadron were followed by others for the packing of plate, porcelain and clothes, the dispatch of horses and carriages, servants and secretariat, hairdressers, tailors, shoemakers, grooms, coachmen, an army and a commissariat that were to travel northward by sea and road during the next three weeks. On 26 July a conscientious and officious member of the Lord Chamberlain's Office, Thomas Mash, arrived in Edinburgh from London, to originate and direct 'various arrangements'. These, he said, were to follow the pattern of the Irish visit, and of customs observed in England. No one, as yet, told him that he was not in Ireland and not in England, but in Scotland, a kingdom with its own customs and its own ancient traditions (even if Sir Walter had yet to devise some of them).

There was also the matter of the King's wardrobe, or to be exact one part of it, and that the most influential at this time and perhaps for ever since. It is customary to believe that it was Scott who first inspired the King – then Prince Regent – with a warm interest in his Scottish ancestry, in Scottish history, and in the Highlands and the Highlanders. As inheritor of the kingdom of Scotland, and thus its mountain Chief of Chiefs, he learnt that he could rightly and properly swathe himself in what Sir Walter and other endearing romantics called The Garb of Old Gaul – a belted plaid and tartan hose, a velvet jacket and a bonnet pierced by eagle feathers, a basket-hilted broadsword and noble dirk, a *sgian dubh* and two claw-butted steel pistols. This barbaric picture of himself as a royal *duine-uasal* is thought to have been planted in the Prince's mind by Scott on an April evening in 1815, when Napoleon was loose once more in France and London was aflame with a rekindled military ardour soon to be drowned in the blood of Waterloo. They met at a 'snug little dinner', so described by the Prince to honour the 'author of *Waverley*', a title to which Scott pretended he had no right. It was a gathering of great men under the shimmering crystals and candle glow of Carlton House, a roistering and joyous occasion during which, it could be said, Scott persuaded the Regent that he was not only a Stuart prince, but also a Jacobite Highlander.

Before the end of July 1822, and in preparation for what would be his sartorial apogee, the King placed an order with George Hunter & Company, outfitters of Tokenhouse Yard, London, and Princes

Street, Edinburgh, instructing them to make him a complete Highland dress. The cost of this extravagantly executed commission would be £1354 18s, and although it was an age when gentlemen expected tradesmen to submit their accounts at intervals of six months only, the King received his within three weeks of his return from Scotland.

The order included 61 yards of satin, 31 of velvet, and 17½ of cashmere, to make both *feile-mhor* and *feile-beag*, the belted plaid and little kilt, all in the flaming scarlet of the Royal Tartan, later known as the Royal Stewart. The cost of this material was £139 11s 6d, but the most expensive item of the dress, at £375, was a badge for the King's Glengarry bonnet. It was wrought from fine chased gold, the Crown of Scotland set with diamonds, pearls, rubies and emeralds, all held in a wreath of golden thistles surrounding a sea-green emerald. The sporran, costing £105, was made of soft white goatskin lined with silk, its golden spring-top ornamented with the Royal Arms and the Scottish thistle in variegated Scottish gems. Hanging from this elaborate purse were nine heavy tassels and cords, all of gold thread. The King's belts, one to girdle his corseted belly, and the other a sword-belt to be worn across his shoulder, were made of black Moroccan leather. Each had a buckle-plate ornamented with the figure of Saint Andrew in chased gold, imposed upon a saltire of garnets, the whole bordered with Scottish gems. There was more . . . There was a powder-horn mounted with gold and gems, to hang from the cross-belt on a golden chain. There was a golden plaid-brooch in the form of a running hart, also set with Scottish gems. For his fine leather brogues there were golden rosettes, each with a vibrating centre of gold filagree, surrounded by gems. And yet more . . . His emerald-hilted dirk, and the table knife sheathed upon it, were of fine steel inlaid with gold, the table fork being made of the best silver. The scabbard was covered with crimson velvet and richly ornamented with the Royal Arms and the figure of Saint Andrew. The cost of this impossible weapon was £262 10s, more than Mr Hunter asked for the broadsword, which was only £157. This was heavy, two-edged, and made of polished steel, the hilt and

Opposite: The first page of the account submitted by George Hunter and Co for the King's Highland dress *Reproduced by gracious permission of Her Majesty the Queen*

Edenburgh Sepr. 23. 1822

His Most Gracious Majesty the King

Bought of George Hunter & Co.

A fine Gold chased Head Ornament for Bonnets
consisting of Royal Scots Crown in Miniature
set with Diamonds, Pearls, Rubies, and
Emeralds, supported on a wreath of Chased gold
Thistles, surrounding a large green Emerald, large size — 75 ..

A fine White Goatskin Highland Purse, with
massive Gold spring top, with Chased Royal
Arm's Thistle &c Ornamented with Varigated
Scots Gems, blue silk gold bullion Tassels — 105 ..
and Tords, lined with silk &c

A black Morocco Belt for broad Sword Mounted
with gold Buckel, slide, and plate, with
figure of St Andrew in chased Gold, Cross of
Garnets, and whole Mounting bordered and — 63 ..
Ornamented with Scotch Gems ..

A broad black Morocco body Belt, with
fine gold Buckel, Ornamented with — 25 ..
Varigated Scotch Gems &c

A black Morocco Pouch Belt with gold Buckel .... 2 . 12 . 6

A large fine Gold broach Pin, in the form of a
Hart, Ornamented with Varigated Scotch Gems — 14 . 14 ..

A Powder horn Richly Mounted in fine Gold
with Varigated scotch Gems and a Massive — 63 . 10 ..
Gold Chain ..

A pair of fine gold Shoe Rosets, with Debuting
Centre made of Filegree gold, Studed all over — 24 . 10 ..
with Varigated Gems ..

Carried Over .. £ 753 . 6 . 6

mounting inlaid with gold, the blade engraved with the Royal Arms. Its scabbard too was covered in rich crimson. To complete the imagined trappings of a warrior Gael, Mr Hunter supplied a brace of Highland pistols, of polished steel inlaid.

The excessive vulgarity of this theatrical costume was a mockery of the simple belted plaid once worn by the Highlander, his shirt of saffron cloth and his plain knitted bonnet. Few if any of the King's Scottish subjects would remark upon that stark difference when he wore the dress at his first levee in Edinburgh, but one man may have seen the absurdity of it, if only with an aesthetic eye. In David Wilkie's painting of the King in Highland clothes, colour and texture are discreetly muted and there are no obtrusive badges or buckles of gold, no jewelled weapons, fine goatskin or inlaid steel. But closer though it is to a truth the tailors and jewellers distorted, the portrait is still a sad lie.

PART TWO

For the Credit of Old Scotland

'There can be no doubt that the reception
he is to meet with will be one
calculated to gratify all those feelings
with which it is natural to suppose
THE FIRST PRINCE and THE FIRST GENTLEMAN
in the world must be filled upon
such an occasion.'

– Sir Walter Scott, *Hints*

> 'It astonishes me to see that the proprietor takes
> any pleasure in the condition of the hornless
> sheep compared with that of men; and I see
> nothing for it now but that the sheep and the
> deer should be sent away, or the people be sent
> away out of the kingdom . . . If the young
> people go, the old people will die; and it is hard
> for them to see the sheep and the deer enjoying
> the price of their fathers' blood.'
> — DONALD MARTIN, crofter, Lewis

When news of the King's coming was known, said Elizabeth Grant,
the whole country went mad and 'everybody strained every point to
get to Edinburgh to receive him'. In late July her father, John Peter
Grant of Rothiemurchus, responded to his family's entreaties and
agreed to take as many as possible far south to the city, with 'lace,
feathers, pearls, the old landau, the old horses, and the old liveries'.
He owed no less to the honour and obligations of his name, for the
ailing Earl of Seafield, Laird of Grant and chief of the clan, was
sending his brother Colonel Francis as his representative, in a
handsome carriage of green, red and gold. Although a staunch Whig
of the Brougham party, Rothiemurchus had been the King's loyal
man during the squabble with the Queen, forbidding his daughters
to read any newspaper reporting her trial. He was a successful
advocate, a handsome and unassuming man, the inheritor of the
house of Doune and several hundred acres below the boat-shaped
hill that gave the building its name. A Speyside laird of solid
ancestry, his blood-lines were linked with the Grant of Grant and
the houses of Freuchie, Glenmoriston and Ballindaloch, as well as
cadet families of Stewart, Cameron and Gordon. He was none the
less a man of the nineteenth century, with an English wife of Saxon
stock, and he had little enthusiasm for the Gaelic play-acting of men
like Glengarry. He was practising law in Edinburgh when much of
the forest of Rothiemurchus came to him upon the death of an
uncle. Until then the estate had yielded little more than £800 a year

and was largely covered by oak, birch and pine, their remote glades surrounding still and silent lochs. The French wars were prohibiting the importation of foreign timber, and Grant quickly seized the opportunity for establishing a sturdy fortune. At a time when Colonel Francis Grant began the first planting of what would be thirty million trees upon his brother's eight thousand acres, Rothiemurchus employed axe and saw so vigorously that he substantially increased his income. This enabled him to maintain a good house upon King Street in the New Town of Edinburgh and pay the expenses of his electioneering in England. That is to say, he had money enough now to buy the votes that gave him a majority. It was the beginning of a career that would eventually take him to India and the Supreme Court of Calcutta.

In 1822 he had a fragile wife, and of their five children four were already young and vigorous adults. Apart from the eldest, Elizabeth, there was a son, William, and two girls, Jane and Mary Frances. The Grant ladies were all beautiful, accomplished, refined and intellectual, or so thought that peripatetic civil engineer, James Mitchell, who came by Rothiemurchus at this time, helping to plan a new road and lamenting the loss of so many trees on Speyside. The letters which Jane and Mary Frances sent home from Edinburgh during the Royal Visit give no indication of great intellectual powers, but have a refreshing naivety and a mocking sense of fun. Since one of the family was obliged to stay at Doune to care for Mrs Grant – who confessed herself too weak to endure the bustle of the journey – the responsibility fell upon Elizabeth. She rationalized her disappointment by saying that she, too, was perhaps not well enough for the tedious journey, not yet recovered from a severe winter cold. All the girls wrote of these days, Elizabeth briefly in her *Memoirs*, and her sisters in a lengthy correspondence which bubbles with excitement. Meant only for their mother, an aunt and their sister, the letters were refolded and kept in a drawer for three or four decades until they were privately published. Elizabeth's clearest memory of Speyside at this time was her father's urgent request for a good supply of Glenlivet to be sent at once to Edinburgh. The King, it seemed, drank nothing else. As the cellarer at Doune, she regretted emptying her pet bin, 'where was whisky long in wood, long in uncorked bottles, mild as milk, and the true contraband *goût* in it'.

But she dutifully sent it to Holyroodhouse, with fifty brace of ptarmigan, and thereafter was sure that the timely gift had secured her father the Indian judgeship.

The happy party left Doune early on the morning of 8 August, rattling down the military road toward Atholl. Before noon, the old landau and its old horses overtook the Inverness coach, dark red and yellow and crowded with noisy passengers, all eager to see Edinburgh and the King. Dalwhinnie was reached at five minutes past one o'clock, and not long after that the landau went over the high pass of Drumochter in splendid sunlight, coming down to Dalnacardoch in Glen Garry before three o'clock. There the horses were watered in five minutes and put upon the road again. Eight miles on, at a steady pace on the good road which Mr Mitchell's father had built for the Duke of Atholl, the Grants arrived at the village of Blair. The girls were exhausted but excited, sad only that the landau had not been 'more stuffed, Papa and Mamma on one side, their *three* girls on the other, William on Hotspur riding alongside'. And Johnny perhaps, the young brother left at home, a great moment of history lost to him.

Jane and Mary Frances waited in a little parlour of the inn at Blair, while Grant and his son arranged for the horses to be fed and rested until six. The girls leant from the window to watch the arrival of a young gentleman in a carriage and pair, alone except for a servant on the dicky. He was a foreigner and carried those customary letters to men of property which guaranteed gentlemen of the same class the certainty of agreeable lodgings instead of the misery of indifferent inns. One such introduction in his portfolio was to Rothiemurchus, and having discovered who Grant was he introduced himself as the Baron de Staël. While they waited for dinner, the young man took Jane Grant for a walk in the gentle rain, holding his ragged, discoloured umbrella above her. He fascinated her with tales of his travels, and of the old Duke of Atholl with whom he had taken breakfast that morning. Scotland, he said, was pretty and graceful, but not as grand as Switzerland where there were larger rocks. Dining with the Grants later, he contributed a bottle of old claret from the store he was carrying with him, and added some new gossip. In London, he said, it was commonly agreed that the King's visit to Scotland was 'owing to a certain great

Lady who wished to have a few days to herself, and so sent him out of the way'. He was not interested in the occasion himself, and thought he would go on another two hundred miles to Dunrobin, having written to Lady Stafford to tell her to expect him. And, of course, he *had* met Sir Walter Scott in Edinburgh, dining with him on Sunday last and finding him 'quite childish' about the pageant he was preparing.

Childish or not, this was not how Scott had planned his summer. Infected by Montagu's dismissive scepticism, and believing the King would not come this year, he had decided to leave his Edinburgh house as soon as possible and return to Abbotsford. Nearing completion, this remarkable building already looked quite distinguished above the white-stone waters of the Tweed, or so he now thought. In September he would go northward to the Great Glen, to the dark pines and blue hills of Glengarry's country. There among Alasdair Ranaldson's people and upon that wild chief's birthday, he would 'pitch the bar and so forth'. Bewildered by the King's prevarication, and convinced that there was something odd in the reports of his ill-health, Scott's feelings for his Fat Friend were a mixture of loyal respect and irritable impatience and he wished to escape from all the dragging responsibilities of a workaday world. He was not well, and however bright and unflagging his mind would soon be, he was in no physical state to embark upon the exhausting weeks that lay ahead. That spring he had felt a frosty breath upon his neck. The death of James Boswell's disparate sons, one in a squalid and unnecessary duel, and the other of illness in London, had caused him grief and pain. He was also distressed by the state of mind, the unexplained depression of spirits in an old and valued friend, William Erskine, the jurist Lord Kinneder. The loss of friends, he told Maria Edgeworth, always brought a particular melancholy, a sadness more difficult to endure than nagging intimations of his own mortality.

If my limbs are stiff, my walks and my rides slower – if I get a little deaf, I comfort myself that, except in a few instances I shall be no great loser by missing one full half of what is spoken; but I feel the loneliness of my age when my friends and companions are taken from me.

Professionally, he had little to distress him. His publisher told him that *The Fortunes of Nigel*, now in print, would be the most popular of all his works. Seven thousand copies had been sold on the first day of publication in London, and some buyers opened the book to read with the first step they took into the street. He had begun work upon *Peveril of the Peak*, with the enthusiasm that initially propelled all his work. He had been asked to visit London again, but would not go. He did not like that city, he said, there was too much to say, and it made him too excited. On matters political, about which he could usually talk amusingly and at length, he now seemed hesitant and solemn, as if the Radical War had left him with dark and trouble-some doubts about his countrymen. Their sullen, revengeful and long-enduring temper, he told Miss Edgeworth, 'make such agita-tions have a much wider and more dreadful effect among them'.

There were also his business affairs. Upon the surface, they could not have appeared more satisfactory, but his mounting debts, hid-den from his friends and associates, had become a hideous night-mare. Thirteen years before, he had founded the printing-house of Ballantyne & Company with the brothers of that name, friends of his schooldays. He supplied half the capital, lent a quarter to one brother and may have done the same for the other. With that in mind, perhaps, he eventually assumed total responsibility for the company's expenditure and debts. By May 1822, the latter had risen to more than £36,000. After payment of some outstanding and un-avoidable bills, three-quarters of the sum was still owing, for which the house and lands of Abbotsford – the green earth and grey stones that protected his dreams – had been offered as security. A poor businessman, and handicapped by his unswerving honesty, he was slowly driven toward disaster. He had used the name of the company to obtain credit, and the money that should have paid its bills was used to settle the pressing demands of the masons and carpenters who worked at Abbotsford. He would in the end surmount and survive this situation, perhaps at the cost of a shortened life, but in the summer of 1822, as he gathered his strength and spirits to become the King's Pageant Master, there can have been little hope of a resolution to his problems.

There was to be no summer on Tweedside, of course, and no September in Lochaber where, he said, the MacDonalds would have greeted him as a kinsman. And that, presumably, despite the Campbell blood he claimed. There was much he wished to do at Abbotsford, not the least to ensure the safe growth of the cedar and oak seedlings which Montagu had sent him from Ditton. He hoped that some of the oak would be later planted by the ruin of Melrose Abbey, that generations of Borderers yet to come could enjoy the solace of their shade. This task would now be set aside or delegated to others. Abandoned, too, must be his personal direction of yet another stage in the introduction of gas-lighting at Abbotsford. He had decided that his fine new mansion would not be ruined by the smoke of wax-candles or whale-oil, nor his domestic staff burdened longer than necessary with 'the great plague of cleaning lamps'. For modest cost of 3s 6d, a gallon of the best train-oil, processed in the garden, would supply 'one hundred feet of gas', fed by pipes to the walls, ceilings and stairways of the house, bursting into dove-tailed flame within metal thistles and fleurs-de-lys, and filling 'every corner of the mansion with such fountains of light as must have puzzled the genius of the *lamp* to provide for the less fortunate Aladdin'.

July passed, and instead of Abbotsford he was still in Edinburgh at 39 Castle Street. It was the second of the homes he had taken in that arching street, a narrow bow-fronted house of three storeys and an attic, forming part of a block in the classical style of the New Town. Its square-paned windows, behind which he could sometimes be seen, faced westward across the street. To his left he could see the dark rise of rain-wet rock, and the noble Castle upon its summit. To his right was the wide sky and the firthward slope of farmland already surrendering to the eager growth of the city. At the rear of the house, behind the dining-room, was the library where he was to do much of his administrative work this summer. Here he would sit, benign but firm in his familiar blue coat and white linen, greeting commoner and peer, clansman and chief, Highlander, Lowlander and visiting Anglo-Saxon, all who came for advice, orders, guidance or just the pleasure of grasping his hand. He worked at a table by the fireplace, below walls hung with weapons and opposite the portrait of one of his heroes, John Graham of Claverhouse, Bonnie Dundee.

Animals were his fawning, slumbering companions – cats and

dogs, including a handspan of Dandie Dinmonts, each named after the contents of a cruet-stand. And sometimes, brought up from Abbotsford, there was his aging deerhound, a gentle monster called Maida. Six feet from nose to tail, its head as high as the back of Scott's chair, it was a gift from Alasdair Ranaldson MacDonell of Glengarry, an historical curiosity that would cast its shadow five decades into the century and halfway about the globe. Maida was a battlefield in Italy where Alasdair Ranaldson's brother, James, had commanded the 78th Highlanders, and where David Stewart of Garth received the first of his many wounds. Obscured by greater triumphs later, the victory caught the imagination of Britain, and inspired speculators to give its name to the London suburb where they were building discreet villas for the mistresses of public men. Glengarry's compliment to his brother, later the defender of Hougoumont during the long hours of Waterloo, was doubled when the hound was given to Scott. Half a century later, Colonel George Armstrong Custer, whose theatrical temperament had much in common with Glengarry's, gave the name Maida to his own great deerhound, in recognition, perhaps, of the admiration which many American romantics had for Scott. The animal accompanied the Colonel upon all his Indian campaigns, but was left behind at Fort Abraham Lincoln when he rode to the Little Big Horn.

Scott walked abroad a good deal upon Tweedside, but in Edinburgh he rarely left Castle Street on foot, his limping gait hampered by unsympathetic flagstones. He drove out as often as he could, his eyes keenly observant, noting the gulls wheeling in from the sea to encircle the Castle, or a wild wind whirling on the uncompleted Mound, lifting the skirts and revealing 'the legs of nymphs who venture abroad'. He sometimes stopped the carriage and dismounted to think alone in the quiet ruin of Holyrood Abbey or the tall shadows of the Grassmarket, each with its rich memories of martyrs and madmen. He kept a good table in Castle Street and was a warm-hearted host, entering a room full of guests like a schoolboy, rubbing his hands in glee, his smile bright with pleasure, and the household pets tumbling about his feet. The house was renowned for the conversations at its table, for the wit and charm of Sir Walter, the dark eyes and sometimes self-effacing nature of Lady Scott. Few guests acknowledged her presence when recalling the visit, and some like Henry Fox did so without civility. In Scott's city home there was little of the bucolic jollity that distinguished gatherings at Abbotsford. Here behind the door of Castle Street he was still a public figure – Sir Walter Scott, The Bard, The Wizard of the North, and The Author of *Waverley*.

From the beginning there was no doubt that he was the only man who could devise and manage the reception Edinburgh should give to the King. He had established this right by the fecundity of his genius and by his inspirational role in the discovery of the Honours of Scotland. It was he who told the Prince Regent, possibly at that Carlton House dinner in 1815, that the Regalia should be found, restored to the Crown, and displayed before the Scottish people. When workmen broke into that ancient chest in Edinburgh Castle, Scott was the first to lean forward and stare at its awesome contents. Andrew Geddes painted the dramatic scene, but only some of the heads in his canvas have survived the decay of time and neglect. Scott's is perhaps the most moving, his cheeks puffed and sickly, his narrowed eyes undershadowed and dark with pain. It may be the portrait of a susceptible man staring at the relics of an ancient royalty, but since it was painted some time later it was perhaps the face of the tired and ailing organizer who worked himself to the edge of a breakdown during the Royal Visit.

The formal appointment of Scott as master of the ceremonies was more oblique than direct. It began with a nervous request for advice from the Lord Provost, William Arbuthnot, who was understandably alarmed by the enormous responsibility that had suddenly fallen upon him. There was no precedent for the occasion, in the history of Edinburgh or the country. There was, as the newspapers fulsomely explained, the visit of Charles I in 1633, but this had not been a happy occasion, for that luckless King had used the visit to impose his will upon the Scottish Church and Parliament beginning with the introduction of a prayer-book and other innovations of Anglican origin. This had led, by seemingly inexorable steps, to the bitterness and blood of civil war throughout his kingdoms. Charles II had also come to Scotland, in 1650 from his exile in Breda, and had been crowned in a hypocritical ceremony at Scone. This too had ended in war, the bloody destruction of a Scottish army in the fields and ditches outside Worcester, and rule by the English

Commonwealth for nine years. There was no joyous tradition to direct the coming occasion, no custom or ritual, unless Sir Walter could think . . .

His response led to a meeting one Wednesday evening with the Lord Provost and others, including William Adam, an old friend. Adam was a member of that family of gifted architects, a lawyer and a politician, Lord Commissioner of the Scottish Jury Court and one of the most influential men in the country. He was a septuagenarian of taste and sharp intelligence. His fine home at Blair Adam in Kinross was the meeting-place of an exclusive club that took its name from the house. It was a select group of eight or nine like-minded men, including Scott of course, who met on a summer week-end once a year to dine and debate, talk and jest, and make self-important visits to places of antiquarian interest. Following that Wednesday evening with the Lord Provost, Adam wrote to Scott, remembering the committee that had been established to discover the Honours of Scotland, and proposing a similar body upon this occasion. He put forward some names of men he thought suitable, including the Provost. When the list was finally drawn, Arbuthnot was included but the others were men whom Scott liked and respected, friends who could perhaps be relied upon to follow his imaginative lead.

The principal choice was David Stewart of Garth. His *Sketches*, published a few weeks earlier, had brought him modest fame and some unpleasing notoriety. He had made himself the ultimate authority on the Highlanders – their history, culture, customs, arms, dress and military achievements. Lockhart called him Scott's 'Toy-Captain', the man who was to organize and muster, drill and discipline the many self-styled clansmen who were drawn into what Lockhart, yet again, called 'this plaided panorama'. The selection of Garth was a sour disappointment to Glengarry. From the age of twenty-one he had sought to make himself the undisputed authority on the history, culture and dress of the Gaelic people, studying the reading and writing of their language, their songs, legends and fading memories. His behaviour during the Royal Visit clearly suggests that he believed he should have been given the duties and responsibilities undertaken by Stewart of Garth, and if he could not challenge his rival to a duel – as he had other men who offended him – he could at least ridicule the old soldier in private conversation and in the public prints.

The remaining two members of the committee were James Skene of Rubislaw and Scott's distant cousin Alexander Keith of Ravelston. Skene was an advocate, and in their young manhood he and Scott had fished together by torchlight on the Tweed, walked the Border hills, and ridden stirrup to stirrup on Gullane sands as cornets of the Edinburgh Volunteer Light Horse. He was altogether the sort of man Scott cherished, a bold sportsman, physically active but with a passion for scholarship, a linguist and an antiquarian, and sometimes a visionary (he once had a day-dream of Scott upon his death-bed). Though markedly a different man, Keith was also very much to Scott's taste, a paragraph from Scotland's history walking the streets of Edinburgh in solemn broadcloth. Keith earls had been Marischals of Scotland for centuries. Two of them, Ravelston's kinsmen, had gone into exile after the rebellions of '15 and '19, serving as mercenaries of renown in France, Spain, Prussia and Russia. Scott had no doubt that Ravelston, whose father had bought what was left of the exiles' estates, was heir to the rank of Knight Marischal of Scotland, and so addressed him before the title was generally acknowledged. One of Scott's first acts, when the Committee for the Visit was formed, was to write to Daniel Terry in London. The actor was in possession of one of Scott's treasured antiques, the sword of the Great Marquess of Montrose, having agreed to restore it and provide it with a suitable scabbard, presumably from a theatrical costumier. Now Scott wanted the relic returned

> ... with the speed of light, as I have promised to let my cousin, the Knight Marshal, have it on this occasion. Pray send it down by mail-coach. I can add no more, for the whole of the work has devolved on my shoulders. If Montrose's sword is not quite finished, send it nevertheless.

It would perhaps have been more accurate to have said that he had *taken* all the work upon his shoulders, and with the exception of Garth there was little the members of his Committee could do but nod their heads. Even Scott's household was drawn into the preparations. His wife Charlotte, and her circle of ladies, were soon making a gift for the King, an elaborately jewelled saltire. The motto to go with this, he told Terry, was *'Righ Albainn gu brath*, that is, Long Life to the King of Scotland.' From the beginning, Scott had clearly decided upon four major events to express the nation's sense of identity, so necessary for its spiritual survival. The centre of them all would be the King – not the man, not Our Fat Friend but Kingship itself, the enduring spirit of Robert Bruce and the great-hearted warrior-king of Flodden, of Mary Queen of Scots and the hapless prince of Culloden field. The first event involved the Honours of Scotland, still housed in the Castle and an attractive curiosity for visitors to the city. Scott proposed that they should be taken in solemn procession to Holyroodhouse, there to await the King. The second was the Royal landing at Leith, followed by a ceremonial procession to Holyrood, a show of great pomp and dignity, honouring traditions discovered and traditions devised. The third event once more involved the Honours, which were now to be returned to the Castle with the King himself, in a slow progress along the Royal Mile. Fourth and finally was Scott's hope for a great Gathering of the Clans under their Loyal Chiefs. This, and other manifestations of the 'plaided panorama', were to be the day-to-day responsibility of Garth. There were no precedents for any of these events, of course, and it is a measure of Scott's skill that each would give the people of Edinburgh the feeling that they were not only seeing their King among them once more, but were honouring him in the manner his predecessors had been greeted.

There were to be other splendid occasions – a Royal Levee and Drawing-Room at Holyroodhouse, the Peers' Ball and the Caledonian Hunt Ball at the Assembly Rooms in George Street, and a grand review of Horse and Foot on the open ground of Portobello, the city's new seaside resort. The last could be left to the Army, with an assurance that the Chiefs and their Clans, all fiercely armed, would be present and similarly reviewed by the King. The Levee and the Drawing-Room came within the responsibility of the Lord Chamberlain's office, but Sir Walter's wise if unsolicited advice upon dress and behaviour for such occasions would shortly be made known, and generally accepted without dispute.

For the management of all events he respected the advice of his theatrical friends – Daniel Terry, with whom he had collaborated on a stage version of *Guy Mannering*, and the young and inventive actor-manager William Murray. Terry's advice came by mail-coach from London, less often and less influentially, perhaps, than John Lockhart believed when he wrote of his father-in-law's activities at this time as 'the Terryfication of Scotland'. Murray, however, was to be found a short walk eastward along Princes Street, in the Theatre Royal by North Bridge. This shabby, low-storeyed building with a bizarre portico was sometimes known as The Shakespeare from the unmistakable figure on its pediment, flanked by the Muses of Tragedy and Comedy. The playhouse had been jointly managed with Henry Siddons, son of the incomparable Sarah, but when he died in 1816 the management was continued by Murray alone. He staged and appeared in several dramatizations of Scott's works, displaying the skill that was to be energetically employed during the Visit, particularly in the design and presentation of the Balls at the Assembly Rooms. His sister Harriet was Siddons' widow, an actress of no great merit, perhaps, but soon in eager demand by the ladies of middle society – including the Misses Grant of Rothiemurchus – for advice on dress and deportment, on walking, curtseying, advancing and retiring in the presence of Royalty, the discreet lift of a cheek for the King's conventional but hearty buss, the tying of ribbons, the exposure of lace, and the subtle use of the fan as a means of conveying thoughts and invitations that should not be spoken.

Murray was an able collaborator but there were deeper reasons for Scott's interest and friendship. He was no strolling player who had stepped from darkness into a moment of footlight fame. He came from a family of Peeblesshire baronets, and his father had been an actor too, renowned in York, Bath and London. What particularly intrigued Scott was perhaps the fact that his friend's grandfather, Sir John Murray of Broughton, had been involved most bitterly with the heather prince and the old lost cause. One of the eager young men of the '45 Rebellion, he was a leading figure in Jacobite conspiracies before the Young Pretender landed in Scotland, and during the campaign he became the Prince's secretary. After Culloden, from which he was absent, his taste for conspiracy – and also his understandable terror perhaps – finally entrapped him in enduring obloquy. Betrayed by a cowherd, and taken by dragoons from his sister's house where he was hiding, he turned King's Evidence against the Jacobites, saying he was sorry for the distress he had caused his country. His life thus saved, he lived in Edinburgh for the rest of his years, a haunted and hated figure. As a child in George Square, Scott may sometimes have seen this furtive old man, a caller after dark, with his face muffled, coming to discuss his legal affairs with the boy's father. Receiving such a client was no more than a professional obligation for Mr Scott, but once when his wife brought tea for Murray he later threw the cup from a window, saying, 'Neither lip of me nor of mine comes after Murray of Broughton's.' Scott told this story to Lockhart. A compassionate man, he may have felt that he owed Broughton's grandson his friendship.

The work of the Committee had scarcely begun when Mr Thomas Mash, Controller of Accounts in the Lord Chamberlain's Office, challenged Scott's authority, reminding him several times of what had been done in Ireland, and what should therefore be done here in Scotland. Scott's response at last was perhaps more crushing than was needed, but he was already under great pressure. Ireland, he told Mr Mash, was not Scotland, not a kingdom but a lordship, and he wished to hear no more about that country, and no more about England. 'When His Majesty comes amongst us, he comes to his ancient kingdom of Scotland, and must be received according to ancient usages. If you persist in bringing in English customs, we turn about, one and all, and leave you. You take the responsibility on yourself.' Appalled by this threat, Mr Mash retreated, soothing his vanity by involving it in the social trivia of precedence and protocol at the Drawing-Room.

Firm though Scott had been in his proud defence of Scotland's 'ancient usages', much had to be invented, or built upon the shifting sand of accepted truth. No revered tradition was more boldly created at this time than the presentation of the Company of Archers as the ancient bodyguard of the Kings of Scotland. The metamorphosis was undoubtedly due to Scott, and it should perhaps be remembered that the next novel he would write, the idea already germinating in his mind, was the story of Quentin Durward, a Scottish archer in the bodyguard of the King of France. Among the Archers themselves under the leadership of the Earl of Hopetoun, there was no objection to the flattering change. The company had been formed in the late seventeenth century, long after the last King of Scotland left Edinburgh for a greater seat in Westminster. It had never been much more than a club for gentlemen, a gathering of like minds and spirits for the pleasure of hunting, shooting and dining. A Royal Charter and a flaring banner granted by Queen Anne in 1704 gave the Company a noble respectability which it soon put at grave risk during the Rebellion of 1715. Two hundred of its members, dressed as antique bowmen, invaded an Edinburgh playhouse and ordered its musicians to play a Jacobite air, *Let the King enjoy his own again*! Such toothless Stuart sympathies lingered on until the slaughter of Culloden, and the bitterness of its aftermath, destroyed all taste for romantic games. The members settled down to enjoy an agreeable sporting society once more, and were happy to have it so until Sir Walter and Lord Hopetoun persuaded them that they could indeed be Royal, Ancient and Bodyguarding. They were now to be suitably dressed for the King's visit, in tight-fitting Lincoln-green slashed with white satin, long feathers flaunting on a flat-topped bonnet, a *couteau de chasse* at the belt, bright yellow bow in hand and a quiver of clothyard arrows slung aback. Truly a medieval guard, a living tradition saved from neglect, ready to become, upon the King's approval, a quasi-military force with a captain-general and captains, lieutenants, ensigns and brigadiers, adjutant surgeon, chaplain and all.

Not everybody approved of what Scott and his committee were proposing. Sir John Sinclair of Ulbster, the great agriculturalist – whose innocent introduction of the Great Cheviot to the Highlands had begun their transformation into a wide sheep-walk – was one who found the pantomime nature of the occasion deeply distasteful. His feelings were not entirely objective, however, for he thought he should have been consulted on much that ought to be done. Furthermore, he hoped that by giving such advice he would have received the peerage he so much desired and was so certain he deserved. Nevertheless, he spoke for many sceptics when he met Scott in Castle Street at the beginning of August, and ridiculed the absurdity of some of the schemes proposed. Scott was not deeply offended by the hawk-nosed old man, though he was impatient. 'The King is coming *suddenly* upon us,' he said, before passing on, 'and thus we shall be saved from premeditated absurdities.'

It was less easy to deflect those who were facing the coming events with subjective emotions. Members of the peerage and landed gentry were remembering their real or imagined rights as archaic office-holders under the Crown, and were jealous of the distinction this might now give them. It is probable that Scott knew little more about such matters than most men, and certainly less than the Lord Lyon King of Arms, but he strove manfully to answer the claimants. Some had to be told what their privileges were, and others to be dissuaded from claiming those to which they had no right. Wherever possible, their pride, ambition or greed was directed away from Castle Street to the Lord Lyon, to the Lord Chamberlain, or Mr Secretary Peel, but there were some to whom he felt obliged to offer help before he was asked.

Writing in response from Slains Castle on a North Sea cliff-top in Buchan, the 18th Earl of Erroll should have known that there was no reason to remind Scott that he was the Hereditary Lord High Constable and the first among the King's subjects in Scotland, with the right to carry the Sword of State before him. He was also, although he did not say so, Lord Steward of the Household in Scotland, and Lord Lieutenant of Aberdeenshire. His relief at Scott's offer of help was evident in the tone of his reply, and it was clear that he did not know where to begin upon his preparations. 'Nothing can be more gratifying to me than to be guided in the duties of my high office by advice and assistance from such a quarter.' He hoped that Scott would nominate and equip the pages who should attend him upon State occasions, and that Skene of Rubislaw would attend him as his esquire. He begged Scott to give an opinion as to the proper dress which should be worn by his train, his squire, his pages and grooms. There was also the matter of his horse furniture, its correct nature and style. Scott answered with the fullest information where it existed upon record, and with imaginative skill where it did not. He offered the Earl a few Highland gentlemen to march by his stirrups as he led the grand processions, all clad in tartan and armed cap-a-pie with broadsword and targe, dirk and pistols. There was no one to ask whether the last Lord High Constable to ride upon such an occasion would have desired, let alone tolerated, a guard of Highland cattle thieves. But the young Earl was only twenty-one, and he told Sir Walter that the Highlanders would 'form a splendid addition to our national ceremonies on the occasion'.

There was a further, personal matter in which he hoped for Scott's help. If Lady Erroll felt strong enough to come to Edinburgh, would Sir Walter be good enough to find her accommodation in Holyroodhouse? Her indisposition may have been genuine, or at this moment a cloak for caution. Elizabeth FitzClarence, who had married the Earl two years before, was the King's niece, the natural daughter of the Duke of Clarence and that fat, coarse, jolly actress Dorothea Jordan. She and the sailor duke had ten such bastard children, the daughters being as comfortably disposed of as possible before their father reluctantly abandoned their mother for a marriage more agreeable to Crown and State.

Because no other man of authority seemed to be in command of the preparations, or because the opportunity of writing to so august a man could not be neglected, Scott received scores of letters containing what the writers knew to be essential advice. Until he prepared the draft of a simple letter that would satisfy all but the more useful, or more pressing correspondents, Scott answered them all individually. Many of the writers were shocked by the thought of a great increase in the number of residents in the city, as well as those who would visit it daily from the country beyond. The thought of uncontrollable, even potentially hostile crowds was indeed the constant concern of the City Corporation. It also disturbed the mind of General Sir Thomas Bradford, the hard Peninsula veteran who was Commander-in-Chief in Scotland and the victor of the Radical War, but his redeployment of his regiments was yet to be made. Scott was not concerned with riot or violence, indeed he seemed to believe that there could be none upon such an occasion, but he strongly wished the spectators to have a close and uninterrupted view of the King when he appeared in public. This meant bringing one within pistol-shot or stone's-throw of the other. Even this did not alarm him, or his correspondents, there was only a fear that the crowd might not *remain stationary*, and upon this matter James Simpson of Northumberland Street wrote at length.

He told Scott that the greatest risk would come when the crowd, having watched the passing procession, then insisted upon following it to its destination. His transcendent and somewhat incomprehensible solution to this was that everybody 'should make a *social compact* by which every individual, being well aware of it, shall feel himself bound to keep, & what is more to *see kept*, that every person

on the street that day, after *chusing* his place shall *keep it*'. Mr Simpson
thought there would be no difficulty, and if those in the rear of the
crowd could not be trusted to keep the compact, or had not been
informed of it, why then

> . . . some means might be devised – by police men or strong
> cross pallisades at every hundred yards or two, *extending from
> the houses to the front lines*, to prevent this *lateral* movement by
> either checking its beginnings, or, like the small trenches on
> road-side fields, making it useless to take the course so soon, &
> so often interrupted.

His invention then falling back upon cynical caution, he suggested
that bills and posters should inform the public of the need to stand
still without pushing. He was not yet done. Had Sir Walter realized
that the noise of many turning wheels in the processions would
drown, or at least mar the music of the accompanying bands? He
suggested a covering of wet sand upon the roads. 'In London this is
adopted, and by that means the music has its fullest effect.' Returning abruptly to his original subject he suggested chalked lines down
the roadsides of the Royal Mile, crossed by others at intervals and
thus forming invisible enclosures within which the various groups
of spectators – trades, professions, guilds, corporations and so forth –
would be obliged to stand in loyal immobility.

There was one final matter Mr Simpson felt compelled to raise,
and one referred to in many letters with similar apologies. For
centuries, visitors to the old town of Edinburgh had complained
that it was a sink of foul smells and noisome human waste,
although it was perhaps no worse than many of the cities from
which they came, excepting London, of course. By 1822 improvement was still slow, but the coming Visit had increased the indignant shame of some of its inhabitants. Mr Simpson and others told
Scott that persons living in the tall lands on the Lawnmarket, High
Street and Canongate should be persuaded to defenestrate their foul
water early in the morning, or take it to the nearest drain so that
overflowing gutters would not ferment in the sun, a continuing
reproach to the city. Everybody, said Mr Simpson, knew of certain
places where the deposit of night soil was a particular disgrace. The

one he cited as an example was that road out of the city the King must take to reach Dalkeith.

> Nicolson Street & in that direction, about ten at night when tubs are going, is a shocking route to Dalkeith. The South Bridge is even worse. Let all this be over in the morning, and let the scavengers see it done.

It was easier for Scott to pass such letters to the City authorities than it was to deal with those demanding his attention only. The Provost of Peebles, determined to send a 'peculiar and appropriate address to the King', wished to know if Scott would accept the honour of writing it. By way of inducement he was told that Peebles had been patronby The Bruce, 'gifted with many good things' by other monarchs and, of course, celebrated in verse by one of the greatest, James the First. Scott may have regarded this as a salutary rebuke to any excess of hubris he might now be showing, and he did his best to answer such letters without offence. An appeal from one James Spence, who desired the appointment of King's Perfumer in Scotland, was agreeably disposed of by its referral to Mr Mash. Self-described as 'an obscure individual', a widow of modest means asked Scott if he would present the King with a small but treasured relic she possessed, a bead of pure amber cut in the form of a brambleberry. It had been found long since in the neighbourhood of Holyroodhouse, 'at the root of a large pear tree which true tradition says was planted by the fair hands of Mary Queen of Scots'. Scott replied to such simple letters with appropriate grace, quickly writing in the library at Castle Street, its windows open to the warm air and the noise of the city. With the ceaseless, increasing demands upon his time there was no quiet hour for the long reports he customarily wrote to his son, but the boy's letters were eagerly awaited and read. The young cavalryman, now in Berlin, was thoroughly enjoying himself, his father's reputation making him an honoured guest at balls and soirees, banquets and drawing-rooms. He told his delighted father that he had attended one of these occasions in full Highland dress, but not without some initial difficulty. His declared intention of doing so had shocked many ladies of the Prussian Court, and they sent him a discreet appeal, urging him to cover his bare thighs with 'those flesh-coloured things that are worn upon the stage'. The indignant cornet appealed to the King of Prussia who damned the women as a parcel of bitches, and told the young officer to wear his kilt as he pleased.

The desire to wear a modest or splendid uniform now possessed Edinburgh, an uncontrollable itch that affected everybody – students, cordiners, butchers, masons, tilers, lorimers, ferrymen, grooms, Lord Lieutenants and Deputy Lieutenants, gatemen and caddies, canal boatmen, advocates and notaries, physicians, surgeons, booksellers and apothecaries, all manner and style of men. Gentlemen who held no office, had no rank or rights of precedence, no membership of a grand company or corporation, also became obsessed with the desire for *a proper and uniform costume* by which they could demonstrate their loyalty and satisfy their vanity. There was also a wish to know *what should be done*, what would be the correct and incorrect behaviour *upon all occasions.* Sir Walter, of course, was expected to supply answers to such questions.

He had early recognized the need to inspire and direct the nation's enthusiasm, and to that end he soon produced two literary works, although the adjective is perhaps over-kind. Unable for the moment to work upon *Peveril*, and no doubt fretting at this, the quick-penny writing he produced was at least some relief from the increasing strain of the Committee's work. His poor health had been exacerbated by his continuing concern for that of his friend Kinneder, and the nervous sickness from which he was undoubtedly suffering now manifested itself in an irritating rash which his physician decided was prickly heat. The first of the two written works which he released at the end of July was a long and hilariously bad poem called *CARLE, NOW THE KING'S COME! being new words to an auld sang.* When printed in pamphlet form and in the press, Scott's name did not appear above it, only the information that it was 'ascribed to a Celebrated Bard'. There was only one man in Scotland who could be so described, and that was of course the similarly anonymous author of *Waverley*. Intended as an inspiring reflection of the popular mood, but often reading like a Scottish gazetteer, the poem consisted of thirty-six verses, of which the first and the chorus give enough of their cloying flavour and rub-a-dub rhythm for the rest to be considerately ignored.

The news has flown frae mouth to mouth,
The North for anes had banged the south;
The de'il a Scotsman's die of drouth
    Carle, now the King's come!
    Carle, now the King's come!
    Carle, now the King's come!
    Thou shalt dance, and I will sing
    Carle, now the King's come!

Anonymity also disguised his authorship of the second work, finished in great haste and published as a shilling booklet of thirty-two pages.

HINTS
addressed to the
INHABITANTS OF EDINBURGH
AND OTHERS
in prospect of
HIS MAJESTY'S VISIT
by an Old Citizen

Its preamble declared that there could be no doubt that the reception the King would receive in Scotland would be 'one calculated to gratify all those feelings with which it is natural to suppose THE FIRST PRINCE and THE FIRST GENTLEMAN in the world must be filled upon such an occasion'. This was not the happiest introduction for some of its critics to read. The *Scotsman*, a newspaper of moderate Radical sympathies (and as such anathema to its contemporaries) observed that if the King were indeed the First Prince and the first et cetera, 'he must in his heart despise all getting up, all trickery, all pageantry, merely for the sake of shew and spectacle'. This was the *Scotsman*'s way of saying that since it was well known that the King did *not* despise such things, he therefore could not be considered the First Prince and the first et cetera. Moreover, in the same vein of paradox, if corporations and associations felt obliged to give entertainments they should pay for them out of their own funds, for the King, as the First Prince et cetera, would not demand a sacrifice of principle by any of his subjects. Coming as close as caution permitted to a reminder of the darkness at Bonnymuir, the obscene executions in Stirling, the *Scotsman* seized upon Scott's simple hope that the Visit would bridge the differences between Tory and Whig. It was a notorious truth, said the reviewer,

> . . . that the writers and advocates of Toryism in this country have abandoned reason, and attacked their enemies with such fury or brutality, as to shew that, by unavoidably producing quarrels of the most deadly nature, *they sought the lives of all who openly differed from them in political opinion*. It is equally notorious that the persons who did this were substantially patronised by our Officers of State. And is a temporary visit of ceremony, or even courtesy, to extinguish in one day all the feelings generated by such a course of proceedings since the era of the Chaldee Manuscript? We say it is impossible; and nothing but the vilest hypocrisy could pretend to such miraculous charity.

The spirited book-reviewer went on to declare that the people of Edinburgh would not fail in any mark of respect to the King, but he should desire no sacrifice of principle from a free people, and no public body should 'address the throne in the language of slaves and parasites'. It is doubtful whether many readers of the *Scotsman* were much affected by such solemn strictures, preferring the gentler exhortations of the Old Citizen. He hoped, indeed he *knew* that their behaviour would be more restrained than that shown last year in Ireland. The loyal devotion of the Irish could not be more perfect than Scotland's, but the Scots were a quiet race, and the King would not like them the less for expressing their loyalty in accordance with their nature. It was as if Scott were afraid that unrestrained emotion, violent outbursts of patriotic fervour, would mar the gravity of the rituals he was directing. He reminded his readers that by their nature and their education they were an orderly people whose feelings rarely outpaced the restraints of sober judgement. Let them remember that the King would come among them as the descendant of a long line of Scottish kings. 'What ever Honour and Genius can confer upon Ancestry, his Scottish Ancestry possesses.' Still more, he thought, the King was the kinsman of many Scots. The daring of the proposition took hold of him. Not only were many of Scotland's highest nobility acknowledged relations of the King, but there was scarcely a gentleman of the old Scottish families who could not 'count kin' with the Royal House of George IV. Once started, the thought now ran away with him. In so small a country as Scotland it could not be doubted that the greater part of its burgesses and small yeomen could all claim such relationship. Let all Scots remember that this was so, and behave toward the King as to a father, and toward each other as if they were 'ae man's bairn'. In short, said Scott, 'We are THE CLAN, and our King is THE CHIEF.' By one persuasive paragraph the great-grandson of German Geordie and the great-nephew of Bloody Cumberland had become a Highland chief.

Once beyond the preamble, to which readers may have given little attention, the *Hints* cantered briskly through a summary of the events that had been planned, and then slowed to a measured walk as it became a vade-mecum on dress and behaviour. The matter of a suitable costume for ordinary citizens was early resolved. The Magistrates of the city, said Scott, expected all gentlemen to appear in a uniform dress when attending the King's public appearances, or indeed on any or all days during the Visit. It consisted of a blue coat, white waistcoat, and white or nankeen trousers. A low-crowned hat of a sober shade was recommended, upon which should be a cockade in the form of Saint Andrew's saltire, white on a field of blue. The expense of such a costume would be inconsiderable. The *Scotsman* thought this suggestion an insufferable offence to taste, and said the King should be allowed to see his subjects as they normally were. But the proposed costume was widely accepted by gentlemen of all degrees, including William Cranstone, Junior, although perhaps not with gravity in his case. History has no record of him but his name and a summary of his personal expenses during the Royal Visit, but from its excellent calligraphy it may be concluded that he was a clerk. From the impertinent use he later made of the summary it may also be correct to assume he was enviably young. His first entry in his account book was thus:

The following articles ordered by Town
Council and which I got

New superfine blue coat & welcome buttons	£6	6s
White jean trousers and Holland vest	3	3
A silver medal and cockade for breast	1	1
Heather at different times	1	

Gentlemen attending functions at which the King would be present, said Scott, should carry two visiting-cards, to be taken by pages or Lords in Waiting. At the Levee they could present themselves in the full dress of a uniform to which they had a right, and if not a soldier or sailor then 'in a full dress suit with sword and bag*, but hair powder is not now held to be indispensable'. Passing from these magpies to the court dress of his Highland eagles, Scott's prose warms as the picture comes into mind.

> Those who wear the Highland dress must, however, be careful to be armed in the proper Highland fashion – steel-wrought pistols, broadsword and dirk. It is understood that Glengarry, Breadalbane, Huntly and several other Chieftains, mean to attend the Levee with their tail on, i.e. with a considerable attendance of their gentlemen followers. And, without doubt, this will add greatly to the variety, gracefulness, and appropriate splendour of the scene.

Scott made his own appeal for restraint and good order upon the streets. Again he referred to the 'acknowledged truth' that the Scots were not hearty and boisterous like the English, or as wild and eccentric as the Irish. They were, of course, firm and bold, and capable of self-discipline. It was important that the King should have 'a full view of all the various classes of his subjects, while at the same moment they will have the most full and gratifying sight of their Prince'. Therefore,

* A wig-bag, for enclosing the hair at the nape of the neck.

... if the crowd become for a moment unsteady or tumultuous, if they once break their front rank, that is the line of the constituted bodies – if ever they begin to shoulder and press, and squeeze, and riot – the whole goodly display will sink at once into dis-organisation and confusion; and even the very object of the unseemly tumult will be lost, for it is clear, that the most blackguard and insolent would engross the spectacle to themselves, while the great body of the community would be thrown into the rear of this rabble, unseeing and unseen.

Scott's advice upon this, and upon the strict rituals, Levees and Drawing-Rooms ('no gentlemen can come to the drawing-room without having been previously presented at a levee') was gratefully received by a largely middle-class Society – successful tradesmen, professional men, bonnet-lairds and junior officers, all hoping to be received by the King, could they find a peer or baronet to present them. Their strongest desire was to be a representative part of the great entertainment, to commit no gaffes, betray no ignorance and dishonour no name, however humble. Among some of those who had but recently stepped into the lower ranks of the Scottish nobility, there was a desperate anxiety to do nothing that would excite the derision of the English courtiers who came with the King. This feeling, this fear, was strongest among the women. The proper object of a Drawing-Room, as Scott explained, was the presentation of ladies to the King, either by other ladies who had been so presented in the past, or by the Lord in Waiting. With some authority unacknowledged – his reading, his imagination, or perhaps Mr Mash before they were estranged – the author of *Waverley* was able to guide the anxious ladies through the ordeal of presentation.

The lady drops her train (about four yards in length) when she enters the circle of the King. It is held up by the Lord in Waiting till she is close to his Majesty. She curtsies. The King raises her up and salutes her on the cheek. She then retires, always facing the Sovereign till she is beyond the circle. A considerable difficulty is presented to the inexperienced by the necessity of retiring (without assistance) backwards. The ladies must exert their skill to move their trains quietly and neatly from behind them as they retire; and those who have never worn such dresses should lose no time in beginning to practise this. Most painful must be the situation of a young female who is so unfortunate as to make a *faux pas* on such an occasion.

At least nine feathers, he said, should be worn in every lady's head-dress. Here he had perhaps been misinformed by an adviser or by his imagination, for some of the Englishwomen who attended the Drawing-Room later were astonished by the nodding waves of feathers, and hid their smiling mockery behind their fans.

The peers of Scotland proposed to entertain the King with a Grand Ball at the Assembly Rooms in George Street. Scott's announcement of this in his *Hints* referred to it as a Highland Ball. He reminded his readers that Mr Hunter was 'preparing a magnificent dress of the royal tartan for His Majesty' to wear, and without conscious ambiguity he said that everyone who had seen the King must now 'be anxious to contemplate his fine person in this noblest of all British costumes'. There was one unalterable condition upon which admission to the Assembly Rooms depended. With the exception of those in uniform, 'no Gentleman is to be allowed to appear in any thing but the ancient Highland costume'.

If a single occasion can be said to have determined the kilt as the national dress of *all* Scotsmen, should they so desire, this Ball may perhaps have been that moment. Many Scots who were not Highland were intent upon going, and would not miss the occasion for want of a bolt of tartan. Men who had never thought of dressing in kilt or trews would now drape themselves in a belted plaid and walk with the Bard of Abbotsford into the Great Mythology of their fierce pride.

> De'l a care – for what I'se never start
> We'll welcome him with Highland heart,
> Whate'er we have, he's hae his part,
>   Carle, now the King's come!

> *'I was born in Strathnaver in a place called Langall, and was nineteen years of age when we were evicted. I remember well the burning of the houses . . . There was no mercy or pity shown to young or old, all had to clear away, and those who could not get their effects removed in time to a safe distance, had it burnt before their eyes.'*
>
> – GRACE MacDONALD, parish of Farr

'The King is coming after all! Arms and men are the best things we have to show him.' Within a week of the establishment of his committee, Scott wrote this stirring summons to the Highland chiefs, to those who would respond with enthusiasm, and those he thought might reach Edinburgh in time. Sending his fiery cross must have been one of the most satisfying moments of his life. No similar call had gone to the clans for almost a century, and there is an evocative echo of that last haunting occasion in his opening words. It was dispatched on Tuesday, 22 July, carried northward on the military road by the mail-coach *Caledonian*, through Perth to Dunkeld and the Braes of Atholl, over Drumochter to Speyside and Strathnairn, reaching Inverness in seventeen hours and Dingwall in twenty. From Dunkeld it was sent westward by foot-post to the shadow of Schiehallion and the march of Rannoch Moor. From Inverness by foot again down the Great Glen to Lochaber, Morvern, and Mull of the Trees. It was also carried in the leathern hand of a caddie through the greystone streets of Edinburgh New Town, where some of the barbaric chiefs had more agreeable and accessible dwellings.

The letter to each was brief, a literary flourish, and with the exception of a word here and there, one was like another. The first was written to John Norman MacLeod, 24th chief of the name, and was taken by gig and horsemen across the roof of the Highlands, from Dingwall to the silver herring-water of Loch Carron. Ferried to Skye, it then went by foot-post to MacLeod's cliff-edge castle at Dunvegan, and arrived four days after its dispatch if the winds were soft and the roads kind.

MacLeod had been Scott's friend since the summer of 1814 when the author toured the Western Isles aboard the Lighthouse Yacht. An unimpressive man, with dark hair oiled to his round head, and a face made more insipid by a thin moustache and a Byronic collar, he was the unsuccessful son of 'The General'. This was the redoubtable 23rd chief whose example – as a soldier, a Whig, a republican sympathizer and a founder member of The Friends of the People – would have been hard to follow, and John Norman did not attempt it. He enjoyed life in Edinburgh, and in England where he found a wife and a satisfactory Parliamentary seat (although he would have preferred to represent the shire of Inverness). He returned to his island estates when their management required him, and further money was needed for the reconstruction of his castle in a gothic style that would have astonished its earlier inhabitants. Scott thought he behaved very much as a Highland chief should, 'without the fanfaronade of the character'. He also described MacLeod as 'a spirited and judicious improver [who] cannot fail to be of service to his people'. Neither ambiguous compliment was wholly deserved. MacLeod had inherited a debt of £41,000 from his father, and steadily increased this by his improvements and by the ill-advised purchase of the Culloden estate, the latter with uneasy reminders of a rebellion against which his great-grandfather had raised his reluctant clan. The 24th chief was a good-natured man, however, anxious to please Scott and undoubtedly susceptible to the great man's urgent appeal. Arms and men were needed for the King . . .

. . . do come and bring half-a-dozen or half-a-score of Clansmen, so as to look like an Island Chief as you are. Highlanders are what he will like most to see, and the masquerade of the Celtic Society will not do, without some of the real stuff, to bear it out. Pray come and do not forget to bring the Bodyguard for the Credit of Old Scotland and your own old house.

The same cheerful call for the real stuff was sent to others upon whom Scott believed he could rely. To Alasdair Ranaldson, of course, in the weapon-hung valhalla of Invergarry House. To Donald Cameron, 22nd chief of Lochiel, whose debts were approaching £35,000, whose wife was estranged, and whose lands, house and tenants had been abandoned to the management of factors. To old Struan Robertson who was about to die, and the ailing Laird of Grant who believed himself in no better health. To The Maclean, recently restored to some of his ancestors' property upon Mull, and to Mrs Stewart Mackenzie, the homely, impoverished woman who was the sole heir to all the great lords of Seaforth. To these and others, to Neil Menzies in his yellow castle by Aberfeldy, the Drummonds upon Tayside and the Appin Stewarts in Lochaber. The names and titles alone, scratched on the covers of the letters in Scott's hurrying hand, must have been enough to spur his imagination to a gallop, carrying it to distant glens where responsive banners would flicker in the light of a hundred torches, kilted men stand fully armed behind their chief, and eagles scream as they soared in loyal salute. The thoughts of those in receipt of his summons were undoubtedly less picturesque, and the feelings of their sub-tenants were not considered at all. Half-a-dozen or half-a-score, they were to be *brought* before the King.

The gathering proposed was also the belated celebration of an injury righted and an honour restored. When the proscription upon the wearing of Highland dress was lifted in 1782 the belted plaid had not been re-adopted by the people in general. Poverty and dispersal, the loss of old skills in the making of cloth and dyes, and the growth of a generation to whom the clothing was unfamiliar, had made such romantic attachment impossible. The Glen Etive bard, Duncan Ban Macintyre, could sing of the joy he felt in throwing away his coarse tweed coat for a belted kilt, but his fellow-countrymen had little desire for the dress of their forefathers now that it had become the fanciful affectation of an unfeeling gentry. Many saw the kilt as the hated uniform of the young Highlandmen whom oppressive land-owners had committed to endless wars. It is true that in the beginning, in the years immediately following Culloden, the wearing of tartan in military service had been one way of keeping hold on a vanishing past, but by the end of the century that old pride was gone, and a homesick soldier like Archibald Stewart, once a hunter in Glen Avon, could compose its bitter valediction.

If I were as I used to be
amongst the hills,
I would not mount guard
as long as I lived,
nor would I stand on parade,
nor for the rest of my life
would I ever put on the red coat.

The Proscription Act had required those suspected of evading it to swear by a solemn oath, as they would answer to God on the Day of Judgement, that they 'would never use tartan, plaid, or any part of Highland garb', and that if they broke this oath they might be accursed in all their undertakings, be separated from their kinsfolk, and die in battle as a fugitive coward. Few were obliged to take the oath, perhaps, but release from the shame of it was cathartic, encouraging Highland gentlemen to join hands and hearts in fraternal pride of race. The late eighteenth and early nineteenth centuries were an age of scientific, historical and literary societies for the examination of this or the promoting of that. In Scotland they were now increased by a proliferation of small associations in honour of the Gael, inspired in no small part by the supposedly ancient but fictional poet Ossian. In its more sedate form this enthusiasm produced the Highland Societies of Edinburgh, Inverness, Aberdeen, London and elsewhere, their governing committees heavily laden with coronet and ermine. They served their stated obligations with diligence, although their interests were understandably those of the proprietors and the improvers. At no point in the next fifty years could it be said that their considerable political and social influence was truly used to prevent the wasteful diaspora of the Gaelic race or the suffocation of its language and culture.

The Highland Society of Edinburgh was formed in 1784, two years after the Proscription Act was repealed, and ten since the absurd laws against the Griogaraich were lifted. The founding members, one hundred and eighty-nine, were all Highland proprietors – chiefs and little chiefs, lairds, knights, baronets and peers. They included thirty Campbell gentlemen of whom one was the Society's first president, John Campbell, 5th Duke of Argyll. Also enrolled were the dukes of Atholl and Gordon, the earls of Moray,

Breadalbane, Gower, Glasgow and Aboyne. The surnames and territorial designations of others might also have been found in the
order-books and muster-rolls of the Jacobite Army, fathers and
kinsmen who had died in the April sleet of Culloden, or fled into the
hills and exile. There were MacDonalds of Clanranald, Boisdale
and Kinlochmoidart, Camerons of Fassifern and Glen Nevis,
Farquharsons of Invercauld and Monaltrie, a MacDonell of Glengarry, Grant of Corriemony, Mackenzie of Seaforth, MacLeod of
Talisker, Menzies of Culdares, and Stewart of Garth. Their president
the Duke had himself fought at Culloden, but for George II, commanding the Campbells who lined the Leanach dyke and enfiladed
the right flank of the Jacobites' desperate charge.

Within three years of its foundation the Society petitioned the
Crown for a Charter incorporating it as *The Highland Society of Scotland
and Edinburgh*. Its object, it said, was to enquire into the present state
of the Highlands and Islands, and of their inhabitants,

> ... and into the means of improvement of that part of the coun-
> try by the establishment of towns, villages and harbours, facili-
> tating the communications through the different parts of the
> Highlands by road and bridges, extending and promoting the
> fisheries, encouraging agriculture, and introducing useful
> manufactures, and by thus uniting the exertions of the proprie-
> tors of land and others, to call the attention of the public to the
> promotion and prosecution of such beneficial purposes.

The petition reflected the sanguine temper of the age, high-minded
and based upon the tacit assumption that as the rich grew richer, so
must the poor become less poor. Where the changes envisaged were
realized, however, they were often accompanied by the elimination
of Highland townships and the dispersal of their people by removal,
eviction, emigration and nomadic destitution. By 1822 many of
those who had lived on the estates of the founders were now
replaced by sheep, and some of the original members or their inheri-
tors were themselves gone from the Highlands, winnowed by debt,
death or misadventure. Within half a century the Highland Society
of Edinburgh was no longer a generative force for Improvement,
which had become the role of diligent employees like James Loch.

It was now an august association for debate, the reading of scholarly papers, the patronage of agricultural and industrial innovations, and the encouragement of the Gaelic people by the granting of prizes for furrows well ploughed, songs composed, pipes played, and reels danced.

A taste for extravagant masquerade distinguished these associations. The Highland Society of Aberdeen declared that its first object was to 'promote the general use of the ancient Highland dress'. There is no evidence that it succeeded, but to set a proper example all members were obliged to attend meetings in Highland clothes of their own clan tartan. Such gatherings were always well supported. After suitable toasts and speeches of self-congratulation, it was then customary to debate one of the Society's secondary objects, such as the rescue of 'valuable remains of Celtic literature', of which there was believed to be a substantial amount. There were also the need for supporting Gaelic schools, and the relief of Highlanders 'at a distance from their homes', and of these there were indeed a great number, some evicted from the lands of Society members. Finally, there was always much to be said about the preservation of 'the martial spirit, language, dress, music and antiquities of the ancient Caledonian'.

The Highland Society of London professed the same objects, albeit more grandly with a royal duke among its governors. Distance gave strength to the members' attachment to their native heath, and the dress they wore was more wondrous than any seen in Scotland. A belief in clan tartans obsessed them as it did the other Societies, and it was enthusiastically encouraged by Stewart of Garth. He joined the London Society in 1815, when he was briefly resident in the city, and shortly afterwards he moved a resolution which, he told MacGregor Murray, 'was highly approved and applauded with great warmth by the Society and particularly by the Royal Duke'. This proposed a register of clan tartans, for which 'the Chiefs of the Clans should be requested to furnish a specimen of their Clan Tartan, properly authenticated and signed and certificated by their signature and Family Arms'. The royal duke who so heartily agreed with this notion was the King's brother Kent, an old martinet now living in Ealing with his French-Canadian mistress, and freely distributing his creditors' money among sundry charities, including the Society for Propagating the Gospel in the Highlands and Islands of Scotland. Garth urged MacGregor Murray to send an example of his tartan to Mr Hunter's establishment in Princes Street, where Stewart would collect it, and others like it, for delivery to London. The Chiefs so addressed may perhaps have wondered which plaid in their clothes-chest, once acquired for colour or sett alone, should now become their acknowledged, certificated and authenticated clan tartan.

For those gentlemen whose rank or means did not qualify them for membership of the Highland Societies there were countless associations of local appeal, devoted to the study and enjoyment of the history, mythology, geography and geology of their area. Others were shamelessly romantic and self-indulgent. Thus Mr Donald Campbell, an Argyllshire gentleman living by Cairndow upon Loch Fyne, wrote to Scott in the spring of 1822 offering to enrol him as a constituent member of the Highland Mountain Club of Lochgoilhead, of which Mr Campbell was President. This society, he said, had been established seven years before 'with a view to adopt the dress, cultivate the language, and perpetuate the manners and refined sentiments of our remote ancestors, inculcated by the sublime immortal Ossian'. In this naive attachment the Mountain Club was pleasantly behind the times. The immortal bard's Gaelic verse had been produced sixty years before by James Macpherson, an impudent Strathspey gentleman, hack and Government agent, in a bold effort to give the Highlands a literature and a mythology equal to that of classical Greece. Once deeply respected by the great minds of Europe, including Goethe and Napoleon, the works of Ossian/Macpherson were now an embarrassment to discerning scholars but they continued to influence the hearts of men like the president of the Lochgoilhead mountaineers. A description of an outing, which he sent to Scott with his invitation, began with an appropriate Fingalian flourish:

> The Club having partaken of some refection at the Inn, march off in grand style to the top of a lofty mountain, preceded by the bagpipes playing national airs, and their officer bearing their flag . . .

The following thousand words were a lively description of land-scape and seascape unfolding with each upward step to an unnamed peak, probably Ben Arthur above Loch Long. The summit was reached at six in the evening, and the memory of the westering sun robbed Mr Campbell of the power to control his prose, scattering the page with ethereal expanses, floating clouds, reclining rays, cliffy rocks and luxuriant verdure. At ten o'clock the Club

> . . . repairs to a commodious tent previously erected in the centre of a wide plain on the summit, covered with thick moss, soft as velvet. After a sumptuous supper served in the true style of Highland hospitality, and a bumper of genuine *uisgebeag*; the *Cuach Uithair* (Yew bowl) and *Sligean Breachan* (scollop shells) are produced; it being well known that it was out of these our remote ancestors drank their favourite beverage. After every toast there is a discharge of musquetry. The conversation, songs, toasts, and sentiments are principally in gaelic. Thus with occasional marches, strathspeys and reels from the bag-pipes, the time passes joyously and insensibly away, until sum-moned at ten in the morning to drink a bumper of whisky.

The mountaineers then marched downhill 'to the reverberating sound of bagpipes and musquetry'. They dined at the Inn, drank more whisky, and slept if possible until the following morning, when all departed with promises to return upon the summer sol-stice of the following year. In his last paragraph, and perhaps as a final inducement, Mr Campbell told Scott that the Duke of Sussex, who was also Earl of Inverness, was the Club's honoured patron. Yet another brother of the King, whom he infuriated, Sussex was a large, asthmatic man of liberal pretensions, a popular figure in clubs where bibulous Whigs sang noisy verses of *Fall, tyrants, fall!* He never climbed a mountain with Mr Campbell's associates, nor would his example have inspired Scott, but his attachment to Scotland had once been warm and intimate. In defiance of the Royal Marriage Act, and in Rome, he had married Augusta Murray, daughter of the Earl of Dunmore. He married her again in Hanover Square, fathered her two children, but finally brought legal action to remove them from her care, and a further action to restrain her from using the Royal Arms and calling herself his duchess.

In the year the Argyllshire gentlemen formed their club, another was inaugurated in Lochaber, flamboyant and more exclusive. The Society of True Highlanders was the brainstorm of Alasdair Ranaldson MacDonell, *Mac-mhic-Alasdair* the 15th chief of Glengarry and unsuccessful claimant to the leadership of all Clan Donald. He was born in 1773 and succeeded to his title when he was fifteen, and also to a Jacobite barony acknowledged by none except those who had a similar empty rank or cherished the memory of the Old Cause. When he came of age he devoted himself to the protection of his estates and the honour of his name, both of which inevitably involved him in a bitter feud with Thomas Telford and the Commissioners of the Caledonian Canal, whom he regarded as impudent invaders of his country. The value of his estate rose during the French wars and his income was increased by the felling of good timber, the dues from the canal-builders, and the leasing of cleared land to incoming sheep-farmers. Eviction and removal were thus inevitable, from the glen of his name and from the beautiful peninsula of Knoydart, the wildest of all the Rough Bounds.

In his early manhood he played at soldiering, proud and perhaps envious of his brother James. He raised his young tenants to form a company in the regiment of Fencibles formed by his kinsman, Sir James Grant of Grant. He jealously protected them from other officers, and did little to restrain them when they led a spectacular mutiny at Linlithgow. When he later raised a fencible regiment of his own they left Grant to follow him – having first petitioned him for an assurance that their families would not be replaced by sheep during their absence. He was a man of spirited temper, insufferable in angry pride, but capable of a winning charm when the world about him was warm to his touch. Scott was not blind to his faults, but forgave them all in wondering admiration of so splendid an arrogance.

> This gentleman is a kind of Quixote in our age, having retained, in their full extent, the whole feelings of clanship and chieftainship, elsewhere so long abandoned. He seems to have lived a century too late, and to exist, in a state of complete law and order, like a Glengarry of old, whose will was law to his sept. Warm-hearted, generous, friendly, he is beloved by those

who know him, and his efforts are unceasing to show kindness to those of his clan who are disposed full to admit his pretension.

Those who were not so disposed got little kindness, of course. Forced from his land by increasing rents, eviction and despair, it was they who suffered most from his thoughtless prodigality. They went by tens, scores, and eventually hundreds to the forests of Upper Canada, an untitled land which they blessed with the Gaelic names they brought from Lochaber. Nor was Glengarry's warm heart so generous to those who unwittingly offended him. When he was twenty-five, and attending a military ball at Fort George on the Moray Firth, he quarrelled with and was then challenged by Lieutenant Norman MacLeod of the Black Watch, a grandson of Flora MacDonald. The incident was no more than a squalid brawl. Believing Glengarry was monopolizing the company of Miss Forbes of Culloden against her wish, MacLeod intervened and took her away. Later in the mess of the garrison, when the two men quarrelled noisily, Glengarry first struck MacLeod on the head with his cane, and then kicked him. MacLeod drew his dirk and, when restrained by friends, he demanded satisfaction. Glengarry's apology, insisted upon by his companions, was hotly rejected, and the two young men met the next morning on the white-stone beach below the ramparts of the fort. There was one exchange of shots only, in which MacLeod was hit. He stood his ground, however, demanding a second fire or an apology. The chastened MacDonell readily apologized, but MacLeod died on the evening of the following Sabbath. Glengarry was tried for murder before the High Court of Justiciary in Inverness, and MacLeod's kinsmen and friends did their best to have him convicted. He was acquitted, however, and the bards of his own country sang of the duel as if it had been a great exploit in battle.

It was not his last appearance in court, he was called again in the years following, charged with assault or brawling, and with damaging the property of the Canal Company. He conducted himself as he believed proper for a Highland chief, with disdainful pride and condescension, whether he was wearing the scarlet coat and black ostrich plumes of his Fencibles, or the belted plaid and eagle feathers of a Lochaber chief. His public appearances were theatrical and arresting, for he rarely travelled without his *tail*, servants with traditional duties to his person – the carrying of his sword and shield, the defence of his exposed flank in battle, the recitation of his noble ancestry, and the transport of his body dryfoot across a stream. He was strong and resourceful, and often went alone into the hills of Glen Quoich where he allowed no one to hunt but himself, wearing bonnet and plaid only, and sleeping in the open with a stone for a pillow. He would stalk a stag for hours before shooting it. If it stood at bay, he advanced to kill it with the butt of his gun or a thrust from his dirk. His fame was wide as the original of Fergus MacIvor in *Waverley*, and great men came to be his guests at Invergarry House, or in his summer home on the tidal shore of Loch Hourn. All were made to feel how great was their host, and how deep his gratitude for their visit. His pipers strutted about the table as they dined, and his blind bard, Allan MacDougall, declaimed the virtues of Glengarry, his ancestors and his guests. They drank his health and each other's below the mounted heads of the animals he had killed, and when they went at last to bed the blue dusk beyond their windows was flushed with the light of torches, carried by boatmen across the loch. One of those who came to this wonderland was the Duke of Tarentum, Napoleon's great marshal, whose name was MacDonald and whose father had taken that bonnie boat and its prince across the sea to Skye.

The notices of the Society's inauguration appeared in the *Inverness Journal* toward the end of June 1815, with the announcement that ninety-six gentlemen had been enrolled as True Highlanders, and that by general acclamation they had elected Alasdair Ranaldson as their *ceann-suidhe*, their sitting-head, their president. The Society's first meeting was held at Inverlochy in the shadow of its ruined castle, on a field where the clan regiments of Montrose had driven the Campbells into Loch Linnhe and reddened the water with their blood. Glengarry and his kinsmen, his piper and his bard, welcomed the members as they arrived by coach at the Gordon Arms, or stepped ashore on the pier below Fort William. In the warm evening there was feasting and dancing at the Gordon Arms or on the grass about the castle. Glengarry's daughter Elizabeth, described in the Society's minutes as *Miss Banntighearna Mhic 'ic Alasdair*, acted as patroness of the ball, surrounded by her young friends from Edinburgh. Allan MacDougall composed songs in honour of each day, as did the newly appointed Bard to the True Highlanders, Archibald MacDonald. David Stewart of Garth, whose enthusiasm for the Society was soon to fade, was an honoured guest at the second annual meeting in 1816, escorting Mrs MacDonell on to the floor at the Gordon Arms for the first dance of the evening.

Glengarry was his own publicist, writing long and windy reports of the Society's meetings, sending them to the *Inverness Journal* and inviting southern newspapers to copy. Thus his account of the ball on the first anniversary of the Society:

> The guests almost to a man were in the full uniform of their regiments or the Garb of Old Gaul, and such a scene of enthusiastic and harmonious enjoyment was not perhaps to be instanced, and quite beyond description; the richer dresses of the ladies were superbly appropriate, and among the Highland costumes some were mounted with the ancient clasps of Siol Chinn in gold or silver, or hereditary buttons bearing the heads of all the Kings and Queens of Scotland. Colonel Stewart of Garth wore large round cairngorm buttons richly set. Others had the globular silver buttons of their ancestry, and the highly-finished pistols, dirks, powder-horns and other paraphernalia of the rich Milesian costume gave an air of magnificence to the whole, far more brilliant than expectation had sanctioned at their first fête.

Lord Breadalbane's piper played reels and country airs until he was finally exhausted at four in the morning, whereupon Donald Stewart from Glen Spean 'danced high-dances and jigs to his own fiddle, keeping time at the same instance with perfect correctness and extreme activity'. In the morning, for those who could come into the sunlight without flinching, there was cudgelling and exercises with broadsword and targe, a dirk-dance and yet more songs. And perhaps Alasdair Ranaldson truly did, as was rumoured outwith the Highlands, demonstrate how his ancestors had once torn a live ox apart, limb by limb in a vainglorious trial of strength.

More restrained in temper and purpose, the Celtic Society of Edinburgh was also a masquerade, as Scott admitted in his summons to the chiefs. He meant the word kindly, for he was a founding member of the Society and its first President. He was also intensely proud of his Highland ancestry, although it was distant and tenuous. His great-grandfather had married a Miss Campbell of Silvercraigs, which gave him a crooked link with the lords of Argyll and the Neil Campbell who fought at Bannockburn. The Society, which was to cause Glengarry so much chagrin, was the inspired idea of William Mackenzie of Gruinard, a half-pay lieutenant of the 72nd Regiment and captain of the Inverness Militia. Said to be one of the most handsome men in the Highlands he was a stately, aging man who did indeed look well in a belted plaid. So well, in fact, that when the King saw him at Holyrood he asked for the old man's portrait to be painted, and sent to him in England as an illustration of how a Highlander should look. The first object of Mackenzie's association was, of course, to promote the wearing of Highland dress, but despite this – and as he protested when Glengarry's blistering contempt became unbearable – it was 'neither intended to be, nor ever represented as a society of Highlanders'.

Although its first committee of management included men who did not claim to be Highland, there were enough Gaels among its members to brag of an ancestry that even Glengarry could not despise. There was MacLeod of Macleod, sundry Campbells and Grants, Stewarts and other evocative names from Lochaber, and such legendary men as Patrick MacDougall from Lorn, eighty years of age and chief of his clan. Petitioning on his behalf, Scott told Lord Melville that MacDougall had been 'in six battles and thirty times under fire', and suggested that he should have the honour of being the first to greet the King on Scottish soil. The membership of the Celts was in part the same as that of the Highland Society, a noble crust of Argyll, Breadalbane, Fife and Erroll, and below them a rich mixture of lairds, chiefs, lawyers, half-pay officers, bankers and respected members of the mercantile class. As was fitting in an association emotionally attached to the past, there were many members – MacGregors, Stewarts, Mackenzies and MacDonalds *inter alia* – with Jacobite ancestors whose suffering for the Old Cause now gave a paradoxical lustre to their descendants' enthusiasm for its successor.

And there was Ranald MacDonald of Staffa, Sheriff of Stirling, a member of the committee of management who had joined the Society a few weeks before he directed the hangman and the headsman at the execution of Baird and Hardie. The approaching visit of the King now excited him with the hope of obtaining the right and title of Armour Bearer and Squire to the Royal Body in Scotland. It was not a hereditary honour granted to his own family, the MacDonalds of Boisdale, but to the Setons of Touch in Stirlingshire. MacDonald had married a Miss Elizabeth Stewart, daughter of the baronet of Allanton and the niece of the last Seton of Touch, an aged spinster of Bath. Being of mind to change his name to Stewart-Seton, the better to press his claim to his father-in-law's baronetcy, MacDonald now petitioned Robert Peel on his wife's behalf, saying that she should be the acknowledged Armour Bearer and that he should perform the role as her deputy in any future ceremony. The King was come and gone before the matter was resolved. Another Seton, emerging from unsuspected shadows, successfully claimed the title of Armour Bearer, but MacDonald would not be entirely disappointed. His father-in-law's baronetcy would pass miraculously to him, and with yet another change in his name, of spelling this time, he would become Sir Ranald MacDonald Steuart Seton, sometimes known as Steuart Seton MacDonald.

Until Stewart of Garth drilled the more youthful members of the Society into four companies, to act as honour-guards during the Royal Visit, their duties had been no more strenuous than regular attendance at the convivial board of their meetings, and no more exciting than listening to the stirring historical tales of Sir Walter Scott. Glengarry, who had been an early member, soon left them in disgust, and later derided them in a letter to the *Edinburgh Observer*.

> I dined one day with them since, and I never saw so much tartan *before* in my life, *with so little Highland material*. The day went off pleasantly, to be sure, but how could it do otherwise to any man, seated on one hand of Sir Walter Scott in the chair, who had another Highland chieftain on his other. Still, not being dazzled by outward shew alone, I take this opportunity of withdrawing my name publicly from this mixed society, for the reasons already assigned. There may be some very good and respectable men amongst them, but their general appearance is assumed and fictitious, and *they have no right to*

burlesque the national character or dress of Highlands, against the continuance of which, so mortifying to the feelings of all real Highlanders, I, for one, formally protest.

His resentment of the Society was somewhat deeper than an objection to the appearance of its members across a dining-table. He believed it had usurped an honour that should have gone to his True Highlanders. In the spring of the year he had informed the latter of what would be expected of them should the King come, and that 'a select and truly respectable committee' of the True Society should be formed to welcome His Majesty on behalf of his Highland subjects. Membership of this committee should 'not descend below Land Proprietors, Men of unquestionable Family, and Officers at and above Captain's Rank'. He had put his own name forward and expected others to do the same, for it was

> ... desirable to have a large portion of our number from the Chiefs of several Clans; and such men of Rank and acknowledged place in Society belonging to us as would add to the general effect both in the Eyes of the King & The Public, *by encreasing the splendour of the Court in Scotland* in a style peculiarly characteristic of Caledonia, and worthy of Her Mountain Race.

It was, of course, necessary for the True Highlanders to distance themselves from the members of the Celtic Society who 'from the strange jumble of which they are composed, rather discredit our *fine National Dress* & detract from the genuine Highland Character which alone it should enfold in its Tartan Folds'. It was the opinion of the True Society – that is, the opinion of its founder Alasdair Ranaldson – that the Committee of Representatives should wait upon the King and present their duty in *full Highland Garb*. For those Chieftains and Men of Unquestionable Family who might not be wholly familiar with the precise nature of this dress, he enclosed an inventory with his letter.

A Belted Plaid and waist Belt
A Tartan Jacket with T[rue] H[ighlander] Buttons and
    Shoulder Buckles
A Scarlet Vest T. Hrs. Cut with T. Hrs. Buttons

A Cocked Bonnet with Clan Badge and Cockade
A Purse and Belt
A Pair of Highland Garters
A Pair (or two) of Hose
A Pair of Highland brogues (with whangs)
A Pair of Clasps to Do. for Court use
A Gun (or Fusee) with a sling
A Broad Sword and Shoulder Belt for Do.
A Target and Slinging Belt
A Brace of Highland Pistols and Belt
A 'Chore Dubh' or Hose Knife called the 'Skian'
A Powder Horn with Chain and Cord
A short Pouch and cross shoulder Belt

A copy of this summons and shopping-list was sent to Sir John MacGregor Murray, the cover being franked at Fort Augustus, Stirling and Callander before it reached Lanrick Castle below the Braes of Doune. From there it was sent to Sir John in London. He was old and sick, and perhaps aware that he might not live long enough to greet the King in Scotland. His reply to Glengarry was to be expected from someone who had as great if not greater conceit in his name than Alasdair Ranaldson. Firstly, in the matter of approaching the Throne as a member of a committee and under the direction of the Laird of Invergarry House . . .

> If I were determined on paying my dutiful homage to our beloved Chief, the King, in a conspicuous manner, you could not suppose that a MacGregor would present himself in borrowed feathers, or under any other banner than his own. You are the last man to approve of his doing so.

Secondly, he would not share Glengarry's contempt for the Celtic Society, or his belief in the Gaelic purity of his True Highlanders. He reminded MacDonell that their friend, the Marquis of Huntly, was president of the Celtic Society, and that he, Sir John Macgregor Murray, was a vice-president of the same. How then could he desert it?

That Society is a heterogenious mixture of Saxon and Gael, but so are two other Societies to which you and I belong, namely, the Highland Society of Scotland, and the Society of True Highlanders, which last, I had conceived, from the name which, with your request, drew me to it, was limited to genuine Gaels, but I found it to be a compound like the other two. I know less of it than either of the others. I have never observed any election of Presidents and Officers, or seen any mention of the application of the funds of that Society, not even of their having devoted any part of them towards publication of the works of the immortal Ossian, or the compilation of the Gaelic Dictionary, a very arduous undertaking which has been several years in hand.

The works of Ossian could perhaps have done without the True Society's help, although they would have been well matched in harness. Neil MacAlpine's *Pronouncing Gaelic Dictionary*, however, was a worthy cause, and a greater need among true Highlanders than a grand ball at the Gordon Arms, or the dismemberment of an ox. Murray suggested that Alasdair Ranaldson's Society should give at least £100 to 'that important object, to the encouragement of which I have found for myself and others, £250'. To this deflating letter he added a postscript, exposing his nettled pride and contempt. He had been asked for a subscription to the Society, and he now reminded Alasdair Ranaldson that he had paid ten guineas upon joining, that sum being sent to MacDonell's personal account with the banking-house of Sir William Forbes & Company. Sir William was Glengarry's father-in-law.

The response of others to MacDonell's summons was probably as lacklustre as Murray's, for no more was heard of the scheme, and when he came to Edinburgh in August it was at the head of his own clansmen only. There was never any likelihood, perhaps, of Scott considering his quixotic friend for an organising role in his schemes. He stood well back from the touchy squabbles of these Highland societies, and he was sentimentally attached to the Celtic Society, which contained more of his old friends than he would have found among the True Highlanders. He went regularly to the meetings of the Celts, wearing the 'costume of the Fraternity', as

Lockhart described it. More often than not he was accompanied by his piper, John Bruce. The Skyeman was a Gael with the right mixture of mysticism and shrewd common sense that Scott admired. He played well, and was generously concerned about Scott's health and happiness. He once spent a whole Sunday collecting 'twelve stones from twelve south-running streams' for the author to sleep upon and be relieved from the crippling agony of gall-stones.

This was how Scott preferred to see his Gaels, stepping into or out of the pages of his novels. Although he could write of his friends in the Celtic Society with gentle mockery, he was pleased to make them the Highland centre-piece of his planning, drilled and dressed by the old colonel from Garth. From its beginning the Society had given him human contact with a rapidly receding past. At the height of the Radical War, when his military passions were so inflamed, he was able to fit these douce and peaceful citizens of Edinburgh into his fanciful dreams. 'I have been presiding over the Celtic Society,' he wrote to his son, *all plaided and plumed in their tartan array*. It would have done Lord Sidmouth's heart good to have seen them drink the King's Health, claymore in hand.' A gathering of middle-aged citizens, getting closer to their ancestors with each bumper they raised, might not have encouraged Lord Sidmouth, or frightened the marching pikemen at Bonnymuir, but they filled Scott's heart with comforting warmth.

> All the members seemed delighted to escape from the thraldom of their English garments, and it is certain that very ordinary sort of folks seemed to catch a spark of the chivalrous barbarism of the race. The Scotch, more like in that respect to the French than to the English, are not struck with the incongruity or even the absurdity which must to a certain degree attend such a scene, but are completely carried along by the feeling which it is calculated to excite.

And it was in that spirit that he addressed himself to the Chiefs, calling them to Edinburgh 'now that the King is coming'.

PART THREE

Heir to the Chevalier

'We are now all Jacobites, thorough-bred
Jacobites, in acknowledging George IV.
This seems to be one of the feelings that
stimulate the people here, at the
present time, to make such exertions.

– *Edinburgh Observer*

There was no great surge of men and emotion, although most of the chiefs summoned by Scott were ready to come if they could, and with their clansmen if the expense of dressing them and arming them could be met. But where was so much tartan to be had, and where were the arms?

Sir Neil Menzies of Menzies, at Castle Menzies in Strathtay, was a deputy-lieutenant of Perthshire and as such his attendance in Edinburgh would be required by the Lord Lieutenant, whether or not he brought fifty young men from Appin of Dull, all clad in the scarlet and white of his tartan. Although his ancestors had held land in the strath for more than five hundred years, and had maintained that hold by a wise disposal of their loyalties during the Crown's political or dynastic disputes, Sir Neil was not cast from a mould that would have inspired a paragraph in *Waverley*. His immediate predecessor as clan chief, and resident of the Jacobean castle below the escarpment of Weem Hill, had come to both in the last century, rich from mercantile success in the West Indies. Land and wealth, and the influential connections he acquired by marrying a daughter of the Duke of Atholl, had meant more to him than moribund notions of clanship. This he had made clear when sixteen thousand men and women of the strath, including the sub-tenants of his tenants, came to burn him out of Castle Menzies if he did not give his written word that their young men would not be drafted into the Militia. He signed what they put before him, on a table set upon the grass outside his door, and thereby saved his property, repudiating the promise when the riot was suppressed. Sir Neil was a less displeasing laird, although more interested in horses than men. His wife was a handsome and energetic woman who, it was said, could ride the sixty-five miles from Weem to Edinburgh in one day. Their mutual pleasure in equitation prevented Menzies from attending the King in Edinburgh, either as a tartaned chief or a uniformed deputy-lieutenant. He was badly kicked by one of his spirited horses. Although his life was saved by a physician whom Lady Menzies brought behind her saddle for ten galloping miles, he was nonetheless forced to tell Scott and his Lord Lieutenant, the Duke of Atholl, that he could not join 'that universal display of duty, loyalty, and attachment which Our Sovereign will receive from all his subjects in the Kingdom'.

Another absentee was one of the most venerated of Highland chiefs, and one with a feeble foot in the past. Born six years before Culloden – where many of his father's clan were killed in the fierce charge of the Atholl Brigade – Alexander Robertson of Struan was now dying in The Barracks, his remote home at the head of Loch Rannoch. Landless for many years, and exiled by the attainder against his father, Struan had spent his youth and early middle-age as a mercenary, fighting in the Scots Brigade of the States General. Because of his mortal illness he could not go to Edinburgh. He had no sons to lead his impoverished clansmen there, and no grieving gentleman of Clan Donnachaidh was asked or had the spirit to do so for him. When he was dead, and carried to his grave by twelve men of his name, he was succeeded by a cousin whose son, Major-General George Robertson, sent a letter to the King. It was endorsed by almost nine hundred members of the Robertson clan and was perhaps the closest they could get to an apology for their absence from Edinburgh. In other times, wrote the General with some ambiguity,

. . . the Clan Donnachaidh have always been forward to make their attachment to their native Princes, should occasion require it. I feel confident that they would be proud to maintain their ancient character when happily they cannot err in the proper object of their attachment and devotion.

There were acceptances from the great houses of the Highlands, from Argyll and Breadalbane, from Sutherland and Gordon, but from the once powerful Mackenzies of Kintail there was a sad admission of decline. The last Earl of Seaforth, chief of the clan, had died at sea in 1781 while taking his mutinous regiment to the Indies. Few of his soldiers returned to the Highlands. 'Only an odd one surviving of the hundred of us,' said their poet-sergeant Christopher Macrae, thinking of men of his own clan, Seaforth's loyal bodyguard and known as Mackenzie's Shirt of Mail. The lands of the childless Earl went to a kinsman whose son restored a shadow of the old title by securing the barony of Seaforth. This too had no inheritor, dying with him in 1815. His daughter proudly accepted her romantic role as 'the chieftainess of the Mackenzies', although the name itself was almost lost in her two marriages. The first was to a naval knight and the second to a grandson of the Earl of Galloway, James Stewart, who magnanimously relegated his surname to second place and took hers as his own. Now Mrs Mary Stewart Mackenzie, an ailing and emotional woman of 39, she lived beyond the Beauly Firth at Brahan, a dark castellated home hung with the smoke-blackened portraits of dead chiefs. Their spiritual presence must have intensified the disappointment in her reply to Scott. 'Poor *Cabber feidh** is very different to what it was,' she told him, 'and sore pressed and hunted and *hemmed* in.' Mindful, perhaps, of the days when the stone keeps of the Mackenzie lairds had studded the Black Isle and the green plain below Brahan, she asked Scott to convey her apologies and explanations to the King, if that were proper and practicable. But for the deplorable weakness in which her last confinement had left her, making it impossible for her to move from chair to chair without assistance, she would have come to Edinburgh and joined others in duty and homage.

---

* *Cabar Feidh* – deer's horn, the antler badge of the Mackenzies.

I assure you there is not a Chief among them all so anxious, perhaps, to pay their duty to their Sovereign and in *proper stile* as I poor shadow of a Cabber am. Had I possessed at this auspicious moment *health and wealth* like some, I would have paid my duty to the King with 'a tail' that would have reached from here to Johnny Groats house.

Although she knew that some would think it silly and romantic, her dearest wish was that her son Keith, not yet five, might 'see the Royal Pageant and remember in his old age George the fourth in Scotland'. She did her best to find lodgings for the boy in Edinburgh, and seems to have been ill-served by her family and friends. Unable or unwilling to take his son with him, James Stewart Mackenzie left for the capital after George IV had arrived, his law-agent being of the opinion that there might be more chance of accommodation once the visitors who had come to see the King's arrival had gone home. Sponsored by the House of Gordon, he was to be presented to the King by its representative at the first Royal Levee. Mrs Mackenzie's mother, Lady Seaforth, had a fine house in Charlotte Square, but need obliged her to let it for the period of the Visit. No cousin or friend appealed to from the sick-bed at Brahan could offer the boy and his nurse a room or a bed, not even a sofa. A crowded space at a window to watch the King go by could bring ten guineas, and lodgings for one, even a small child, were worth much more. Thus, as it was with the younger son of Rothiemurchus, history passed by beyond the reach of the boy's memory. James Stewart was pleased (as was his wife) to be known as 'Seaforth' during his stay in Edinburgh, and everybody regretted that she was not there with the Mackenzies of Kintail, but sympathy was of little comfort to Mary Elizabeth Stewart Mackenzie.

Scott passed her letter to Robert Peel who, in good time, read it aloud to George IV at Dalkeith House. The King was greatly pleased by it and asked the Home Secretary to tell Scott, who would no doubt tell the lady of Brahan, how concerned he was at the 'cause which has prevented the writer from coming to Edinburgh on this happy occasion'.

The MacGregors, who accepted Scott's summons with characteristic enthusiasm, were to be the most agreeable attraction of his pageant, surpassing Alasdair Ranaldson's MacDonells in numbers and bravura. Old Sir John had died in June, and his son had assumed the ancient surname with the inheritance of the baronetcy. Thirty-seven years of age, Lieutenant-Colonel Sir Evan Murray MacGregor, acknowledged 19th Chief of Clan Gregor, was a handsome man, long-nosed and high-cheeked, his face framed in two waves of dark hair from temples to chin. This was perhaps more considerate than affected, for war had brutally scarred his amiable features. Four years before in India, during a brief but fierce assault on the wicket-gate of a Mahratta fort, he had received one sword-cut across his mouth, and another through his nose. A third had almost severed his right arm about the elbow joint, and four more had wounded his left shoulder, his left and right side. No mark of this incredible experience is visible in the portrait painted at this time by George Watson. Indeed, a brave and honest man is almost lost within the monstrous vulgarity of the Highland costume he proudly wore for the King's visit.

Still weak from his wounds, and from seven years' debilitating service in the East, MacGregor's survival probably depended upon the watchful and constant care of his wife Elizabeth, who had shared his life in India, and some of his campaigning, with uncomplaining loyalty. She also approved his wish to return to military life, or preferably to an appointment of value in the Government service. This, he hoped, might be procured for him by his father-in-law, the Duke of Atholl. When he first heard of the Royal Visit, and before he received Sir Walter's summons, he believed the King would make a progress through the country, visiting the homes of the nobility. This was a common assumption, and some of the proprietors had already prepared their houses or their minds for the descent of so many guests, among whom, it was feared, might be the insufferable Marchioness Conyngham. The Duke of Montrose, who thought such a visit no less than his due, had long since instructed John Nash to alter and extend his castle on Loch Lomondside. While regretting the interruption of his shooting season, Atholl accepted the inevitability of a royal party at Blair or Dunkeld, and was perhaps grateful for an ill wind that might make it unnecessary for him to go to Edinburgh. MacGregor believed that if his father-in-law and feudal lord had to entertain the King he would require an honour-guard drawn from the clans upon his ground – Robertsons, Menzies, Stewarts and, of course, MacGregors. Should the King not go to Blair but to Taymouth Castle, once a black keep but now transformed into a gothic wonder, the Colonel was ready to take his clansmen there as supporters of the Earl of Breadalbane, whose Campbell ancestors had alternated between the persecution and the protection of the hapless Griogaraich.

At the end of July, Sir Evan was told that the King's ministers had forbidden him to travel beyond the outskirts of Edinburgh. This snatch of city gossip was passed to MacGregor by his wife, who was enjoying the calm of Portobello after a storm-beaten voyage from the Isle of Man. Sir Evan thought the news incredible, but was at last obliged to believe it. He accepted the invitation of Robert Roy, secretary of the Celtic Society, and was ready to take his people to Edinburgh. A meeting with Scott – who told him that his clansmen could be the first among those guarding the Honours of Scotland and the King's person – persuaded him that Atholl's banner should be seen in the city, escorted by three pipers and surrounded by Highlanders. He urged the Duke to accept the service of the Griogaraich, for if Atholl believed

> ... that all our Tartan ought not to be thrown away, and intend to distinguish yourself from Lowland Lord Lieutenants by going to the Grand House with some of your Highland follow-ers in your train, I have no doubt it will be in my power to add to your suite, from 40 to 60 picked men of my Clan, properly equipped, who all feel with myself, proud and happy to be near your Grace's person, when you wait upon your Sovereign in the palace of his ancestors.

The 'Tartan' that should not be wasted was a figurative reference to men not yet mustered. Like other chiefs so employed at this moment, MacGregor was finding it difficult to obtain the tartan cloth he needed for his picked men. The orders now being placed with such weaving firms as John Callander & Company of Stirling, and the Wilson brothers of Bannockburn, had greatly increased, particularly since Sir Walter's *Hints* had made it clear that no man could be better dressed if he appeared in tartan at least once during the Royal Visit. Callanders, who wove the tartan for the King's costume, were relative newcomers compared with the Wilsons whose father had begun the business almost three-quarters of a century before. James and William Wilson were now the head of a teeming family all dedicated to the looms and the cloth that had brought them a comfortable fortune. During the long French wars they had made the tartan which Highland regiments had worn at Assaye, Corunna, New Orleans, Toulouse and Waterloo. When peace ended that profitable industry, the Wilsons energetically encouraged the wearing of tartan by men and women of all ranks and all classes, be it only a waistcoat or a shawl. They were the first to introduce soft tartans for women, made from the first pick of wool or from Merino. They invented clan tartans and actively promoted them, filling their pattern-books with 'new' or 'latest' setts for a Mackenzie, a Stewart, Gordon, MacGregor, Farquharson, Campbell and many others. The fashionable novelty of these tartans was a greater appeal than any pretended authenticity, any spurious connection with the clans so named. It was clear to both Wilsons, as it was to their competitors in Scotland and England, that the demand for tartan would be long-lasting, not just for this exciting summer but for endless years to come. Before the Royal Squadron was sighted in the Firth of Forth, the brothers had already established the first of the forty new looms they were to introduce that year, and had begun to build the sheds and employ the labour the machines would need. Throughout the Stirling plain, among the Incorporation of Weavers in the city and the Country Weavers in its surrounding villages, there was great change and activity. 'Almost all the persons formerly engaged in the weaving of muslin in this quarter,' said the *Stirling Journal*, 'have commenced the weaving of tartan, in consequence of its affording a better return for their labour.'

By the first week in August, Evan MacGregor had received the certain assurance of one hundred volunteers, from his own estate and from others in Atholl, Breadalbane and Balquhidder. From these he would finally select fifty to make one of the largest clan contingents in Edinburgh, all wearing his scarlet tartan and a sprig of fir in their bonnets. If kept from his command by his duty to the King's person, he had decided to entrust it to his son John, aged twelve, but at all other times he would lead it through the streets himself, in trews and astride a good horse, carrying the broadsword his grandfather had used at Prestonpans seventy-seven years before. This would excite the admiration of the newspapers and bring a flush to the cheeks of impressionable young ladies, and no one would remember that in that savage engagement MacGregor swords had first sliced through the legs of King George's horses and then through the bodies of his falling troopers.

The gathering of the Griogaraich was perhaps a template for all the clan contingents that came to the city, albeit better disciplined under the practised eye of Sir Evan. Recruitment and equipping of the men was managed by lesser gentlemen of his name, officers now in retirement or on beggarly half-pay, all bored by inactivity after so many years of war, and nettled by a growing indifference to their past service. There was an absurd imbalance in the number of officers in the contingent, one to less than three of the common men, but then few of the gentlemen could be turned away without offence. There were four divisions, three of them raised in the ancient heartland of MacGregor country – Balquhidder, Rannoch and Strathtay. The fourth was urban, four young clerks from the stools of Edinburgh banking-houses. Of the fifty officers and men only nine were not surnamed MacGregor, and of those only four were not called Gregor or MacAlpin. The pipers were John McKay and John MacDonald, both enlisted in Edinburgh where they lived by their skill with the instrument, popular at balls and parties, and now ready to be of service to a chief who no longer kept a piper at his house. Their appointment was made before the arrival of a man from Rannoch, sent to Sir Evan by Major Donald MacGregor who was recruiting there, with a recommendation that he was 'descended from the hereditary pipers *Vu-an Sgeulach* (MacGregors) and I have no doubt will give you satisfaction'. And perhaps he would have done, had he been sent in time.

For every man taken, two or three were rejected, and of all the reasons that brought them to the summons, not the least, perhaps, was a payment of £5 for three weeks under Sir Evan's banner. Some of those who were turned away felt aggrieved enough to complain to their chief. Two self-styled 'zealous clansmen', Donald and John MacGregor who lived in the folded hills of Glen Lyon, had set out early for the recruiting post at Fortingall. 'After attending upon the day desired,' they wrote, 'and going fifteen miles to show ourselves,

James Loch, the young Commissioner who brought Improvement to Lord Stafford's Highland estates. 'In a few years,' he said, 'the character of this whole population will be changed.'

'You are a damned old Cat and deserve to be worried and burnt out for burning out the poor Highlanders.' Elizabeth Gordon, Countess of Sutherland, Marchioness of Stafford.

David Stewart of Garth. 'I dreamed for two nights of the misery and consequent actions to which the moral, the brave, the industrious men of Atholl will be subject when driven from their ancient homes.'

John Murray, 4th Duke Atholl, who did not want more Highlanders in Edinburgh. 'I quite agree,' said Lord Melville. ' I think we have fully as many of the Gael, real or fictional, as is prudent or necessary.'

Elizabeth, Marchioness Conyngham, the King's mistress. 'Not an idea in her head, not a word to say for herself, nothing but a hand to accept pearls and diamonds with, and an enormous balcony to wear them on.'

BONNIE WILLIE.

Sir William Curtis. According to Lockhart he 'cast an air of ridicule over the whole of Sir Walter's Celtified pageantry.'

'The King's yacht, *Royal George*, was towed upstream by the steam-vessel *Comet*, and took up her moorings by Greenwich Hospital on July 31.'

Turner's wild and windswept *March of the Highlanders* for the King's procession to the Castle. More fancy than fact, it none the less reflects the romantic vision of Walter Scott's "Celtification".

Scott's anonymous and quick-penny guide to the Royal Visit 'cantered briskly through a summary of the events that had been planned, and then slowed to a measured walk as it became a *vade-mecum* on dress and behaviour.'

HINTS

ADDRESSED TO THE

INHABITANTS OF EDINBURGH,

AND OTHERS,

IN PROSPECT OF

𝕳𝖎𝖘 𝕸𝖆𝖏𝖊𝖘𝖙𝖞'𝖘 𝖁𝖎𝖘𝖎𝖙.

BY AN OLD CITIZEN.

EDINBURGH:
PRINTED FOR BELL AND BRADFUTE,
MANNERS AND MILLER, ARCHIBALD CONSTABLE AND CO.
WILLIAM BLACKWOOD, WAUGH AND INNES,
AND JOHN ROBERTSON.

1822.

Walter Scott in 1823, 'cheeks puffed and sickly, narrowed eyes undershadowed and dark with pain . . . the face of the tired and ailing organiser who had worked himself to the edge of a breakdown.'

Overleaf. Above: When the King came ashore in Leith Harbour 'he stepped on to a crimson carpet strewn with summer flowers. The slope was not difficult, but he moved slowly and with comic dignity.'

Below: The keys of Edinburgh were offered to the King 'in a wide amphitheatre of meeting streets, thick with people from railing to railing, the tops of immobilised carriages like black islands in a sea of faces.'

Mrs. Mary Stewart Mackenzie of Seaforth, acknowledged chieftainess of that name. 'Had I possessed at this auspicious moment health and wealth like some, I would have paid my duty to the King with 'a tail' that would have reached from here to Johnny Groats house.'

Sir Evan MacGregor of MacGregor was one of the most stunning figures in Scott's pageantry. 'I have no doubt,' he said, 'it will be in my power to add from 40 to 60 men of my clan, properly equipped.'

Left: Alasdair Ranaldson MacDonell, 15th Chief of Glengarry. 'As long as I wear the warlike garb of my ancestors, I will not be *herded* by the best many among my enemies!'

Right: Ranald MacDonell, henchman to Glengarry and one of the clansmen the chief brought to Edinburgh, 'tall, raw-boned, swarthy fellows who carried guns of portentous length.'

we felt very much disappointed to find the Parties are made up without our assistance.' They blamed the 'underhand transactors' employed by Major MacGregor (he of the piper), but wounded pride prevented them from saying how they had been ill-used.

The assembling of the Clan Gregor contingent was, in fact, proceeding in haste, spurred by the news that members of the Celtic Society in Edinburgh were already being drilled by Stewart of Garth. He paraded them every week-day morning and evening on the open green of Queen Street, to the west of Abercromby Place, the sound of their distant pipes coming pleasantly to the open windows of Sir Walter's library. As they impressed their Highland image upon the people of the city, attending to their duties as their Secretary had instructed – 'equipped in all points in the Complete Highland Dress and the usual Highland Arms' – a jealous hostility developed among some supporters of the clan contingents. Major Duncan MacGregor of Learnan was living on half-pay in Edinburgh, having spent two-thirds of his thirty-five years and much of his blood in Highland regiments, fighting in Egypt, the Low Countries and Spain. He watched the morning parades of the Celts with a skilled eye and a sour heart, writing of his chagrin to Sir Evan.

> As the manner in which the Spurious Highlanders are to be disposed of during the Sovereigns visit to Dun Edin to the prejudice of those whose claims to distinction have been often inscribed in characters of blood – do not all accord with my view of the dignity due to the clans – I trust you will excuse my not appearing as a clansman on the approaching occasion.

By the first week of August the MacGregor contingent was ready to leave for the city, each division to march separately and all to rendezvous by the Commercial Bank in Edinburgh on or before the tenth of the month, the day upon which the King was presently expected. The gathering had been made at no small expense to Sir Evan's slender purse. The subsistence pay of the little band was more than £160. The cost of its belted plaids – made from flame-red cloth supplied by the Scottish Tartan, Shawl and Silk Warehouse on North Bridge, at three shillings a yard – was over £55. A cockade for a bonnet cost three shillings, the bonnet five, and a grey goatskin sporran of ordinary quality was seven shillings and sixpence. John MacLeod, outfitter of Castle Street not far from Scott's door, supplied most of the weapons purchased or hired by the clans. A broadsword could be bought for forty shillings, a dirk for thirty-two, and a brace of ordinary, claw-butted steel pistols for twenty-two. Sir Evan's total arms bill – for twenty-eight broadswords with scabbards, three dozen dirks, and forty pistols – came to £148. There were forty-seven goatskin sporrans at seven and six each, and forty patent-leather shoulder belts at twelve and six. In addition to these essential costs there was another no less important, a supply of whisky for a loyal toast and a friendly *deoch slainte*. During the last week of the Visit the ten men of the Strathtay division were disposing of a gallon a day at a cost of twelve shillings, a modest consumption by Highland traditions of conviviality.

The sixteen officers were dressed more splendidly, and their plaids and furnishings, purchased from Messrs Romanes & Paterson at the Scottish Tartan Warehouse, cost two or three times as much as those supplied to their men. The brooches on their plaids, the badges on their bonnets, and the buckles on their shoes were of precious metal, and their weapons were not hired but taken from family walls and chests, and proudly displayed as those used by their grandfathers at Prestonpans and Falkirk. Sir Evan himself was a bird of paradise among them, and his appearance in Highland dress would be one of the most stunning moments of the Visit. He wore his red and green tartan as a coat, plaid and kilt. His bonnet was wide and flat-topped, and from its badge sprang three long eagle feathers. His diamond-patterned hose were white and red, and gartered with scarlet bows. He wore silver-buckled brogues and a monstrous white sporran. There were two long pistols and a longer dirk at his belt, and, of course, his grandfather's legendary sword in a scarlet scabbard on his hip. Much of this he already possessed, and what he did not he now bought from George Willis & Company, uniform suppliers to the Duke of York. From the King's jewellers, Marshall & Sons, he bought a gilt crest for his bonnet, a gold buckle and pendice, a powder-horn with a steel chain. He had decided to wear the belted plaid for levees and balls only. For parades and processions, whereat he had decided to ride, he would wear tight trews and fine riding-boots. His horses, a pair rented from the stabler

Samuel Wadsworth, were to cost him £25 for twelve days. His horse furniture had to be purchased, £20 to the saddler Andrew Paton for two saddles and bridles, spare girths, brushes and combs, green and white rosettes. It was the thought of such requirements, and their daunting cost, that may have persuaded some small chiefs to delay their response to Scott's summons, carrying instinctive hesitation to the point of sound common sense.

It can have been of no comfort to Alasdair Ranaldson of Glengarry, when he brought his contingent into Edinburgh, to have it described in the *Weekly Journal* as 'a small but select following'. His earlier hope of leading his True Highlanders *en masse* had come to nothing, but the men he did command received almost as much attention, perhaps because he attempted to deploy them in the van of most events, usually without authority or invitation and to the fury of Stewart of Garth. It was his belief, for example, that as the direct descendant of Somerled, King of the Isles, and Conn of the Hundred Battles, it was his right to be the first man to receive the King in Scotland. The men he brought were described as 'twelve gentlemen of his house', MacDonells of Scotus, Shian, Barrisdale and others. Each of them, upon Glengarry's instructions, brought a body-servant, 'tall, raw-boned, swarthy fellows, who, beside the sword and target, carried guns of portentous length'. Most of them were foresters from Glengarry's own estates, and few spoke anything but Gaelic. This was perplexing for Scott when he decided to swear in all the Highlanders at a quasi-military ceremony on Queen Street green. He asked Glengarry to translate his words, but the proposal was brushed aside. 'Swear them in,' said MacDonell, 'and I'll take my own time to explain it to them. I am security for their loyalty.' The bold, flamboyant appearance of some of these men – the piper Donald MacDonald, the clansmen Duncan Gilles and Duncan MacDonell, and the henchman Ranald MacDonell – attracted the sharp eye and vivid pencil of the military artist, Denis Dighton, and the likenesses he drew are among the best visual records of the Royal Visit.

Almost lost in this green-tartaned assembly of Glengarry's vanity and pride was a man whose face was perhaps better known by the people of Edinburgh than that of his chief – at least at the beginning. Lieutenant-Colonel James MacDonell of the Coldstream Guards was Alasdair Ranaldson's youngest brother, five years his junior. A modest, even self-effacing man, he was perhaps the clear, sharp image of the man Glengarry ached to be. At six feet three inches he was taller than his brother. He was a better swordsman. He was the 'Hero of Waterloo', and sometimes 'the bravest man in the British Army'. He was popular with all, and duelled with none. He was also untouched by Alasdair Ranaldson's Gaelic mania. He preferred service with the Guards to the Highland Regiments he had once commanded, and his public appearances during the Royal Visit must have been among the few occasions when he wore Highland dress.

Scott's appeal to *Ban mhorair Chataibh*, the Great Lady of Sutherland, was perhaps couched in more personal terms, for he had a great regard for Lady Stafford and always expressed it with affectionate charm. Rank, title and privilege – when well-earned and well-served by the holders or their precedessors – always had his respect, for he saw them as part of the sturdy fabric of history, and in the case of the Marchioness-Countess her family's history had often been the story of northern Scotland. There was a further persuasion. Once a renowned beauty, she was still handsome, and the eye that could be entranced by the glimpse of an ankle and calf on the wind-blown Mound also responded to a fine face in a noble setting. Their association began during Scott's journey north-about Scotland. He wrote to her from shipboard, expressing his regret that the Lighthouse Yacht had sailed 'under the cannon of Dunrobin, but our party was too large to be intruders'. In 1815 he sent her a copy of *Lord of the Isles*, some of it largely inspired by what he saw on that voyage, and when she responded effusively he replied with emotional congratulations upon the engagement of her daughter to a son of the Duke of Norfolk. He was intrigued by the fact that the bridegroom's ancestor had commanded the English army at Flodden, the most haunting of all Scotland's lost battles. The thought of ancient enemies being united in a Dunrobin marriage-bed was history made into romance. To commemorate it, he sent Lady Stafford a silver seal which a Border plough had turned from the earth of the battle field.

This was not long after *Bliadhna an Losgaigh*, the Year of the Burnings in Strathnaver. Scott would later react angrily to the inhumanities of the Sutherland clearances, but unlike his friend Garth he did not accuse the Staffords, or indeed anyone by name. It was perhaps easy for him to exonerate Elizabeth Sutherland, to believe that her charm and condescension had been cruelly exploited by her husband's unprincipled employees. The chief of these – Patrick Sellar the burner of Strathnaver – was now the scapegoat for all the accusations made against the Staffords. She had long ago expressed her contempt for the factor, declaring that he was untrustworthy, that his greed and harshness had been responsible for all that she and her husband, and of course Mr Loch, had suffered from the newspapers. Sellar did not complain of this rejection, although in an address to the Lord Advocate shortly after his arrest, his loyalty to his employers had been less than tactful.

> Lord and Lady Stafford were pleased *humanely* to order a new arrangement of this country ... it surely was a most benevolent action to put these barbarous hordes into a position where they could better associate together, apply to industry, educate their children, and advance in civilisation.

Her ladyship's taste for Scottish historical romance, greatly influenced by the written work of her ancestor Sir Robert Gordon, made the thought of taking some of those barbarous hordes to Edinburgh most agreeable. In her time and in her name, three regiments of Sutherland Highlanders, line and fencible, had been raised to fight the Americans, the French, and rebel Irishmen. They had been enlisted by methods that were traditionally despotic. 'Each father,' as one hapless soldier wrote, 'being obliged to send at least one son to please the lord.' If she had any doubts about such methods, they had been allayed by her law-agent who referred her to the authority of Sir Robert. According to the ancient customs of her people, he said, service in war was the principal qualification for the tenure of land under a lord. Beyond re-establishing the Staffords' reputation in the opinion of their peers, if not the commonalty, another reason for her family's presence in Edinburgh was a matter of fierce pride. This was that one of her sons – the second, Lord Francis, since the first, Lord Gower, was abroad and singularly disinclined to return home – should carry the newly-found Sceptre of Scotland before the

King. Although others disputed it, she believed that to be the hereditary right of the Earls of Sutherland.

James Loch left Dunrobin for the south early in July, eager to prepare for the reception of her Ladyship and Lord Francis, and to make ready for the arrival of the Sutherland clansmen. The responsibility for raising these Highlanders had been left to the factor Francis Suther. He was only marginally less unpopular among the people than Sellar had been, and cannot have improved that reputation if he used the same methods of recruitment as of old. Loch was nervously aware of the delicate situation, and his letters at this time seem to sweat with the concern he was feeling, a desire to protect her Ladyship's name, and to discountenance those whose opinion of her and her husband was based upon the writings of Stewart of Garth.

At the end of July, when it was still thought that Lady Stafford would come to the city, Loch was deeply worried lest the arms and the apparel of the Highlanders would not be to her credit. In the great upheaval of Improvement, the wearing of kilt and plaid in Sutherland had long since been dismissed as a barbaric anachronism, as reprehensible as the keeping of livestock in a dwelling-house, the illegal distilling of whisky, and a belief in the Evil Eye. Staying with friends outside Edinburgh, which he did not choose to enter until it was needful, he reassured Lady Stafford that Sir Walter Scott's help would be available to support her claim to the Sceptre. He also suggested that if she came to the city for the Visit she should reside – 'make your Court' was his phrasing – at the Palace of Holyroodhouse. Upon the matter of the fifty clansmen she would be sending, Francis Suther should order them to rendezvous on the north shore of the Forth at Burntisland (to which they were presumably to make their own way from Sutherland, two hundred miles and more to the north). There he would meet them with one of the Staffords' sub-factors, George Gunn, and take them across the firth to their quarters in the city.

George Gunn was a one-time lieutenant of Marines, a man of modest qualities and small esteem among the vestigial population of Assynt, whose destinies he controlled on behalf of the Staffords. He was also the acknowledged, if not generally accepted, chief of Clan Gunn, and as such had an arguable right to play captain over her Ladyship's warriors in Edinburgh. It may have seemed both proper and politic to give him this honour, although it showed a sorry indifference to recent events in Sutherland. Nine years before, the people of his name in Strath Kildonan had revolted against the threat of eviction and had marched upon Golspie intending, it was said, to expel all sheep-farmers, hang the Staffords' agents, and burn Dunrobin Castle. Faced by the bayonets of the Royal Scots Fusiliers, by fieldpieces of the Royal Artillery, and by sixty retainers of Dunrobin mustered as special constables on the ramparts of the Castle, the Gunns had retreated to their homes where they awaited their eventual dispersal.

In London at this time, Lady Stafford wrote of the bitter affair as 'a sort of mutiny in consequence of our new plans having made it necessary to transplant some of the inhabitants'. The mutineers, she said, lived by distilling whisky and were unwilling to change that occupation for a life of industry. George Gunn, not yet employed by the Staffords, had given no recorded sign of sympathy for the distressed people of his clan, and for that they may have been perversely grateful. Some of them did not accept him as their chief, however obsolescent the title and ironic its privileges under the Policy of Improvement which was soon to employ him. The landless chief was believed to be an old man, Robert Gunn of Achneakin, living on a small farm near Kinbrace at the head of Strath Kildonan. At the beginning of 1822, George Gunn had presided over the first meeting of *The Loyal and United Benevolent Society of Clan Gunn*, a charitable organization from which all 'rebels, swearers, thieves and Sabbath-breakers' were excluded, and the failure to wear clan tartan at its meetings was punished with a fine of one shilling. Nobody disputed Gunn's right to lead when the Sutherland contingent was assembled, and it is possible that few truly cared who led them into Edinburgh under the ancient patronymic of the chiefs of Clan Gunn, *MacSheumais Chataich*.

Although a Lowlander with little patience for Highland custom and mythology, James Loch was nonetheless her Ladyship's devoted servant and thus applied himself diligently to the problem of dressing fifty stout men from her glens.

What occurred to me was that it would be cheap and easy to set the tailors (or Women) of Sutherland at work and give a great many of the tallest men new Jackets, Plaids and Trows of Sutherland tartan, and that they should accompany your Ladyship to Court, two and two walking after your Sedan Chair. It would, if your Ladyship will give me leave to say, be worthy of your rank and situation. If Bonnets enough could not be found in the North, I could get a sufficient number from Kilmarnock in 24 hours.

He thought there should be at least four pipers with the Sutherlanders, and if her Ladyship happened to reach Edinburgh before her clansmen came over the Forth, perhaps she could travel out from the city and meet them somewhere on the Queensferry road. No more than £500 would be needed to pay for the whole affair, and he was confident it would be money well spent. His cautious spirit began to stir with the activity about him. The coach companies and the canal-boat operators, he said, were making arrangements to carry three thousand people a day from Glasgow to Edinburgh. Almost apologetically, he told the Marchioness that she could no doubt perceive that he had 'caught a little of the enthusiasm which animates the whole population here'. So much unusual emotion made him momentarily light-headed. If, through unavoidable absence, Lord Francis were unable to carry the Sceptre before the King, why then ... why should it not be carried by her Ladyship's English son-in-law? 'It would be a remarkable thing to see the Earl of Surrey carrying the Scotch Sceptre for the Earl of Sutherland.' And remarkable that Mr Loch thought his fellow-countrymen would wish to see an Englishman, whose ancestor had come within a spear-thrust of the dying King of Scotland at Flodden, carrying that king's sceptre before a monarch whose dynasty had replaced his. The Commissioner was more realistic when he assured Lady Stafford that 'two hundred well-dressed Highlanders of the clan in Edinburgh would do more to shew the lies about us than all the writing that could be committed to paper'.

By 7 August, with the King's expected arrival only a week away, James Loch was quietly desperate. Despite his bold ideas for enlisting the tailors and seamstresses of Sutherland, and the purchase of bonnets in Kilmarnock, the Highlanders coming slowly south to Burntisland were still inadequately clad, with little tartan and few arms among them. Lord Francis had arrived in Edinburgh, and his pretty, flirtatious wife was now breaking the hearts of all the gentlemen who came to their lodgings in Charlotte Square, or joined them for dinner at Oman's Waterloo Hotel. Loch introduced the young man to the New Club and to all the notabilities he knew in the city. His agreeable lordship opened doors and hearts that Loch had been unable to penetrate. He dined with Scott and finally secured the great man's support for his right to carry the Sceptre. Lord Queensberry offered to put him down for the Peers' Ball as the Earl of Sutherland, which Loch knew would greatly please the boy's mother. More than this, a Colonel Alexander Mackay offered his services as Squire to Lord Francis, saying that he did so as representative of Lord Reay, chief of all the Mackays. The shadow was infinitely more pleasing than the substance, for Lord Reay was in London and unwilling to leave it. He was a renowned spendthrift and was condemned by the Gaelic bards of his far country for wasting his life in drinking-houses and brothels. Loch did not refer to this dark side when reporting the Colonel's offer to her Ladyship. He said that with George Gunn and Lord Reay's representative, Lord Francis would have 'two chiefs under him' during the Visit.

The company of Lord Francis finally solved the vexatious problem of tartan and arms for the Sutherland men. He went with Loch to the Castle where the Commander-in-Chief Sir Thomas Bradford, a man not usually distinguished by generosity of spirit, was most civil, offering Lord Francis his help wherever it might be needed. Thus the storekeeper of the garrison was persuaded to supply on loan all the broadswords and belts the Sutherland men might need. By another fortunate chance, William Wilson had been at the Castle that day, making final arrangements for the dispatch of tartan to the Black Watch in Ireland. With Bradford's approval, a messenger was immediately sent to Wilson by the Stirling mail, instructing him to retain the plaids and supply them instead to the Sutherland men. Whatever the waiting Watch may have felt, in some wet garrison town in Ireland, it must have seemed to Loch that Providence had made him the beneficiary of happy coincidence. The pattern accepted by some as the Sutherland sett was known to others as the Government tartan, a sombre check of green and blue first used to clothe the Black Watch when it became a marching-regiment in

1740. Subsequent Highland regiments also used the tartan, usually
with an addition of red, white or yellow threads according to their
colonel's taste. The 93rd Sutherland Highlanders, however, had
kept the dark sett as it originally was, and had thus made it the
'Sutherland tartan'. Other clans had done the same.

In reporting this good fortune to Lady Stafford, Loch told her that
Lord Francis had that same day acquired his own Highland dress.

> To distinguish him from other chiefs who claim the same Tar-
> tan, he is to have a broad silver lace on the collar and sleeves of
> his jacket. We have given the men trows as we believe that to
> be the distinguishing mark of Clan Chataibh. I wish your
> Ladyship had seen Lord Francis in his blue velvet bonnet and
> Eagles feather. Lord Errol carried the Sword. They will make a
> handsome couple.

So Lord Francis might carry the Sceptre, and Mr Loch now had the
grace of an hour or so to 'run off and see if I can get a full dress suit'.
He had another item of important news to tell his patroness, and
one that showed that the tarnish upon the Staffords' name was
already being erased. 'I was *presented* to Glengarry today at his desire
– which will wipe out many *sins* against the Gaels.' Old Garth might
have seen that as a gathering of birds of a feather.

Before the week ended Loch was told that Lord Stafford was ill
and therefore the Marchioness would not come to Edinburgh. She
wrote to the Lord Chief Commissioner, William Adam, telling him
that Loch would explain her absence, and she enclosed a letter to the
King, expressing her regret. The Marquess had suffered a stroke and
at this point could scarcely move. Loch gave the Lord
Commmissioner what information he could, and repeated Lady
Stafford's hope that her son would carry the Sceptre as was his right,
supported by fifty men 'of his clan'. Loch added that despite the
grave illness of the Marquess the people of his Scottish estates would
gladly celebrate the coming of the King to Scotland. Bonfires would
burn along the mountain littoral of Sutherland, and there would be
feasting and dancing in all the settlements. Returning from his call
upon William Adam, Loch wrote to Dunrobin, saying that since
other gentlemen were sending gifts of game to Dalkeith for the

King's pleasure, the Marquess should perhaps consider a similar offering. 'I believe your lordship could send better red deer venison than any person, and grouse.' He also suggested the dispatch of eagle feathers, for there was a shortage of them in the city and they were in great demand by those Highland gentlemen who considered themselves entitled to wear them in their bonnets.

The Sutherland men came across the Firth of Forth on the evening of Monday, 12 August. They marched through the summer dusk to Edinburgh, where they were met by George Gunn at two o'clock in the morning. Upon the instructions of Loch, who said he was much too busy to write himself, Gunn wrote to Lady Stafford, telling her that her Highlanders were 'now all clothed and comfortably lodged'. Later that week the newspapers acknowledged their arrival in a paragraph that had undoubtedly been inspired by Loch, still jealously guarding his employers' good name.

> They wear the plaid scarf-fashion, and the trews; which though perhaps as ancient a garb, has not quite such a military effect as the belted plaid. The Sutherland men have swords, without any other weapons. It has been disputed whether this great lady's *following* has been diminished by the late improvement on her Highland estate. The following accurate statement will enable the reader to judge. Upon the first intimation, that fifty men were wanted, two hundred volunteered within six hours; and in the course of the next day, a thousand came down to the castle, all eager for the expedition.

Against that splendid claim, which appears to be nowhere substantiated in the Sutherland Papers, must be set the account by a Strathnaver man, the stone-mason Donald MacLeod. He was to become the most relentless and implacable critic of Loch, the Staffords and the Policy of Improvement, suffering eviction and exile as a result. He was in Edinburgh at the time of the King's Visit, and his brief reference to the occasion in his *Gloomy Memories* is perhaps exaggerated, though less than Loch's. He argued that the 'tyranny of one class, and the wrongs and sufferings of the other' on the Sutherland estate had demoralized the people and destroyed their character.

When the clans gathered to honour His Majesty, the Sutherland turn-out was contemptible. Some two or three dozen of squalid-looking, ill-dressed and ill-appointed men were all that Sutherland produced. So inferior indeed was their appearance to the other Highlanders, that those who had the management refused to allow them to walk in the procession, and employed them in some duty out of public view. If their appearance was so bad, so also were their accommodations. They were huddled together in an old empty house, sleeping on straw and fed with the coarsest fare, while the other clans were living in comparative luxury. Lord Francis Leveson Gower, and Mr Loch, who were present, reaped little honour by the exhibition of their Sutherland retainers on that great occasion.

*'My grandfather Ian Ban Mackay lived in
Riphail . . . and he also like the rest of his kith
and kin was doomed. He had served in the
Reay Fencibles and for his good conduct was
made confidential servant to the Colonel of the
Regiment who was himself a Mackay. When
my grandfather was evicted, my mother was
twelve years of age, and she vividly
remembered the incident as long as she lived
. . . When the present was fading from her
memory, she appeared again as a girl of twelve
in Strathnaver continually asking "Whose
house is burning now?", and crying out now
and again, "Save the People!".'*
       – ANNIE MACKAY, parish of Farr

The Grants of Rothiemurchus reached Dunkeld at ten o'clock in the
evening of Thursday, 8 August, fourteen hours after leaving their
home on Speyside. They drank a little tea and went to bed, rising at
seven for more tea before driving on to Perth for breakfast. The girls
were excited and happy, although the brightness of the day, and the
joy of their journey, made the absence of their mother more painful
to bear. The inn at Perth was comfortable, the food wholesome, and
the breakfast-room lively with gossip and laughter. The chamber-
maid told the girls that the road to the south was full of carriages, all
making for the capital. The latest news from Edinburgh was that the
Magistrates had protested against the Highlanders whom Glengarry
had brought into the city, fearing a disturbance now it was believed
that Ranald George MacDonald of Clanranald would come with his
clansmen. The quarrel between these two proud men had been ebb-
ing and flowing for eight years, hot-tempered but bloodless in private correspondence and the press. It had begun with Glengarry's
claim to the chiefship of Clan Ranald and thus of Clan Donald.
Clanranald naturally resisted this, although his life so far had not
been distinguished by selfless concern for his land or his people. A

Regency buck and spendthrift gambler in his youth, he was more at ease in London and Brighton than he was in Arisaig, and since 1813 his debts had been slowly eroding his estates in the Hebrides and on the mainland. In time, he would sell all but the island and castle of Tirrim, receiving £214,211 11s 7d for lands which nineteen generations of his ancestors had held by charter or the sword. Much of the estate was bought by the most ruthless sheep farmer and evictor who came to the Isles. By 1822 the dispute with Glengarry was perhaps no more than a weary jest, but the thought of it excited the Grant girls, and Mary Frances told her mother that 'We shall probably have to describe to you a Highland battle before we leave Edinburgh.'

As the Grants' landau moved southward through the morning sunlight of Friday, the girls were silent and melancholy for a few miles, thinking of their mother again and how she had bravely clapped her hands at their departure, and how their father had been inconsolable for the next two hours. 'But we comforted ourselves,' they wrote that evening to their abandoned sister Elizabeth, 'with putting one another in mind how much better Mamma is looking than she has done of late; and, as for you, we all agree your complexion is much clearer now than it has been since we came north.'

At the Dunkeld inn they had been told that the Duke of Atholl was to leave his great house that morning for Edinburgh, and they may have hoped for a sight of his carriage as they waited by his toll-house to pay for his permission to cross his fine bridge over his stretch of the Tay. This right of portage was already resented, and there would soon be riots against it, but at this time travellers like the Grants may have argued that by building his expensive bridge he had robbed himself of the ferry-dues which, of course, had been his also. This morning he had left for Edinburgh an hour before the Grants, and by evening he had noted in his journal that he had reached the city in 'just 8½ hours going', impressed by the new steam-boat ferry across the Firth of Forth, and the ease with which coaches could be driven on and off the vessels. This was the second visit he had made to Edinburgh within a week, upon the business of the King's Visit, and although he was not frail he was approaching the end of his seventh decade and thus not inclined to haste or excitement.

John Murray, fourth Duke of Atholl, was one of the most power-ful magnates in the Highlands, and the Tory Party's most influential leader north of the Stirling Plain. His favour or displeasure could alter or destroy the careers – civil or military – of most of the gentry of Perthshire. As *Am Moireach Mor* he was the great chief of the Mur-rays, but such a distinction may have meant less to him than it did to an Argyll Campbell or a Seaforth Mackenzie. In thought, spirit and action he was southern and anglicized, dedicated to the improve-ment of his estates and the stability of agriculture and industry. Beyond his obligations as a land-owner, which he observed as con-scientiously as any Sussex noble, he was a passionate sportsman and usually wore hunting-cloth of Atholl grey, whether or not he intended to go on the hill that day. His guests at Dunkeld or Blair Castle came down for breakfast to find that he had ordered their morning for them, one group for stalking, another for grouse, a third for driving through his parkland or riding over its wall of wild hills, and a fourth – usually the ladies – for walking and conversation. In the contrived but beguiling beauty of Strath Garry almost any activ-ity was certain to lighten the heart. 'To render it a masterpiece,' Scott was told by James Hogg, who was never a guest at Blair, 'nature and art have combined their efforts.'

Although Scott did not know Atholl well, he spoke of him affec-tionately, calling him 'Old Ben-a'-Ghlo', a nickname taken from the great escarpment of rock and scree to the north-east of Blair, where Atholl would sometimes drive for rest and thought. Scott the romantic could not fail to have a strong regard for the grandson of Lord George Murray, among the most tragic of Jacobite heroes. He had commanded the Pretender's army for much of the rebellion, and had not Prince Charles assumed that role before Culloden the outcome of the battle might have been different, if indeed Murray would have chosen to fight on ground he did not like. The fact that the Duke's grandfather had died in wasteful exile may have given him a jealous attachment to the land, and a determination not to lose it by political stupidity, self-indulgence or incompetence. This practical view left little room for romantic notions about the Gael, and the principal vision he had of himself was undoubtedly that of a powerful land-owner, Lord Lieutenant of his shire, and the dispas-sionate servant of the best interests of a property-owning class. It was as such that he journeyed diligently if unhappily to Edinburgh, even though he had no doubt that the King had chosen the wrong moment to come to Scotland. The moment, of course, was the beginning of one's shooting.

His duchess shared his views on duty and privilege. She was his second wife, twelve years younger than he, and the daughter of a Scottish baron whose title was four hundred years old. She was a widow when she married Atholl. Her first husband John Mackenzie, Lord MacLeod, had been an old man when they were wed, a Jacobite exile returned from long years of mercenary exile, and dead soon afterward. As the chatelaine of Dunkeld and Blair, the Duchess was conscious of her rank, and of the diminishing perspective of society in relation to it. From the beginning, like others, she had been impatient with the King's failure to make up his mind about the visit. When a letter from Robert Peel, addressed to Atholl in the Isle of Man, told him that it was the King's intention at last to come to Edinburgh, perhaps on 10 August, and that the Home Secretary would be there a week earlier, the Duchess considered the prospect with vapourish irritation. The notice was short, and she remembered that when the King last spoke of the matter to the Duke he had expressed a wish to visit Blair. Mr Peel did not mention this in his letter, which the Duchess no doubt thought was disrespectful negligence, and she expressed her languid displeasure in a long letter to Lady Stafford. The thought of a royal guest on the braes of Atholl was an excuse for genteel despair, and a confession which a rich and titled woman could only make to another similarly blessed. The Duke's houses at Blair and Dunkeld, she said, were old and dirty, the furniture shabby. If the King honoured them by a visit, they would of course do their best, but

> I do not feel so much annoyed in receiving his Majesty, as his suite, as there is no saying who they may consist of. They say *no Ladies* are to accompany his Majesty, but yesterday we heard that Lady Cunningham is to accompany her Lord as far as Dalkeith, on her *way to Ireland*, where it gives out she is going. This is a rumour I cannot believe, however, time will show what is to happen.

Such a letter could not be sent to an old friend without a barb. She envied the Staffords, she said, living so great a distance from Edinburgh, and she presumed they would not think of coming to the city at this time. The Atholls, lack-a-day, were within eight hours' drive and could not escape the obligation. Although she had pleaded with the Duke to spare her the tedium, he thought it proper for her to be in Edinburgh to greet the King. They at last agreed, but hoped that the city would be the furthest north the King would think of going.

> If he should come to us, he must take us as he finds us, for to put Dunkeld and Blair in a fit and proper state to receive his Majesty could not be done in a fortnight or three weeks, as in London, surrounded by everything required.

There was no time to make changes, and no hope of making them if there were, for all the world knew that the Duke of Atholl never did possess ready money, and in these sad agricultural times the land, which is all he ever had to rely upon, was in a poor and uncertain condition. She had received a list of the King's appointments, the levees, balls, assemblies and parades which meant, of course, clothes for each, but she was in mourning for a close kinsman and was separated from a more suitable wardrobe. Apart from this, she could not bear the thought of going to Edinburgh in August.

> To be obliged to think of Court Dress etc etc etc at this time, and in Scotland, I never dreamt of, and being in a long black glove mourning, I left all my finery behind me, and in a way I can't get at, and I am tormented by everybody sending to me to know how they should be dressed.

The Duke's family was scattered across Europe on matters of duty or pleasure, and most seemed unlikely to return to Scotland for the Visit. Lord Glenlyon, his second son, would come from London in attendance upon the King, of course, but his wife would not. 'She is delicate,' said the Duchess, 'I suspect in the family way.' Even this news could be read as an injured protest. It was as if she resented the miraculous speed by which she and her husband had been hurried to these tiresome obligations, only fourteen hours by steam-conveyance from the Isle of Man to Greenock. She longed for October when she would return to the island, and for winter which she proposed to spend in London.

Upon his return from the Isle of Man toward the last week of July, and upon the certain knowledge of the King's coming, Atholl called a meeting of the Perthshire Lieutenancy, and approved the formation of a special committee of eight deputy-lieutenants. This was to proceed to Edinburgh as soon as possible and there arrange accommodation for himself and all of the County's Lieutenancy during the visit. It was stressed that the lodgings found for the Duke, his family and household, should be such that would enable him to entertain handsomely at his table during his stay in town.

The Convenor of the committee, which left for Edinburgh soon after the meeting in Perth, was Sir Alexander Muir Mackenzie. He was a middle-aged, worrying man who would enjoy few of the coming events, being distressed by the chronic illness of his daughter, and forever feeling the burdensome weight of a ducal hand upon his shoulder. Like many of the small gentry of Scotland he had been an amateur soldier during the French wars, an officer of Fencibles and of Militia, and was renowned – if that is not too generous a word – for the invention of a cushion, stuffed with hay, upon which soldiers might sit when transported by cart. From the beginning, as early as June, he had been unenthusiastic about the Royal Visit, dutifully reflecting the Duke's disapproval and declaring at the proper moment that the proposal was ill-timed or alarming. When there was no avoiding the occasion he accepted his responsibilities with melancholy dedication. The search for accommodation needed by the Perthshire Lieutenancy, in competition with the deputies of other shires, he left to his committee, concentrating his own efforts on two important objectives – lodgings for His Grace, and a satisfactory ruling upon the uniform which a deputy-lieutenant might or might not wear before his king.

The offices of Lord Lieutenant and Deputy Lieutenant were a recent establishment, and there was no tradition to guide Sir Alexander in the matter of dress. He was deeply disturbed by this and would worry about it incessantly for the next two weeks. When an authoritative decision was made upon the matter it reached him down a stairway of noble steps. The Lord Privy Seal of Scotland

(Lord Melville) told the senior Lord Lieutenant (Lord Lothian) who told the Lord Lieutenant of Perthshire (the Duke of Atholl) who informed Sir Alexander that, in the words of Lord Lothian,

> There is no dress appointed for Deputy Lieutenants, nor could any dress uniform not recognized at Court be made up for them on the present occasion. They must therefore appear at Holyrood House as private Gentlemen in full Court Dress.

If they were, or had been officers of His Majesty's Navy or Army they could wear the uniform of those services. Elsewhere than at Court, they could appear in whatever dress they had designed for themselves. The unhappy Mackenzie persevered, driven on by vanity and by a hope that the privilege of wearing military uniforms did not refer to officers of the King's *regular* forces only. He still possessed the fading regimentals of his majority in the Perthshire Fencible Cavalry, and his colonelcy of the 3rd Perthshire Local Militia, although the first of these corps had been disbanded in 1800, and the other had been in suspended animation since Bonaparte was sent to Saint Helena. If he and others could not wear such uniforms before the King, he told Atholl, 'It will appear that we are ashamed of them.' Nobody told him, perhaps – if he did not already know – that there was no keener eye than the King's in matters of military dress. He recognized no Court uniform he had not previously seen, approved, and sometimes designed, and he would have tolerated no man to come before him in the dress of a long-disbanded regiment or a drafted corps of shadowy substance.

Mackenzie's attempt to find suitable lodgings for the Duke, the Duchess and their household, was sometimes delayed by his efforts to resurrect a brief moment of past military splendour for himself, and by his sad domestic circumstances. He and his family took modest apartments in the city before the date of the King's arrival was finally known, and for some days his time and attention were centred upon his daughter Augusta. Although her complaint appears to have been a severe inflammation of the throat, her surrender to it made it necessary for her to be carried everywhere, up stairs and down. When Mackenzie was at last able to bend his mind to the Duke's business he reported that the situation was not encouraging. There was no want of houses to be let at £40 to £80 for the duration of the Visit, but these were small and quite inadequate. Charlotte Square was a desirable location, containing large houses that would be most suitable, such as that belonging to Mrs Farquharson of Invercauld, or another to Lady Seaforth. Since there might be stiff competition for these, he hoped His Grace would write to Mrs Farquharson, or to Lady Seaforth, but the Duke did not care to do the work he had delegated to a committee, and Sir Alexander plodded on. He discovered a fine house in Abercromby Place, owned by one Davidson who made it his business to let houses, 'and is therefore prepared to put in additional beds'. The Duke should perhaps place himself and his family there, and his household somewhere in Heriot Row to the west. Davidson would let his house for one hundred and thirty guineas, and another could be got in Heriot Row for seventy, including plate and linen. Mackenzie pressed for this choice, sending a plan of the drawing-room in Abercromby Place, and quoting his committee's opinion that 'there appears to be a total impossibility to procure any one house that can accommodate the Duke of Atholl and at the same time admit of the reception of the Gentlemen of the county of Perth as proposed'.

In the end the Duke decided upon Lady Seaforth's house in Charlotte Square, at a charge of one hundred guineas for the duration of the King's Visit. It was large enough for him and for his household, and for the entertainment he desired, even for some of Lady Seaforth's female servants whom she hoped would be left undisturbed in their attic rooms. Although he could not take up the tenancy before the 3rd or 4th of August he came down to see the house and to conduct other business at the end of July. Before he left Dunkeld he received a letter from Mackenzie who said he had seen Sir Walter Scott that forenoon. The great man had 'expressed a wish that some Highland Gentlemen should come in Highland costume and attended with Highland servants, and seems to entertain a hope that your Grace might furnish some attendants in that Garb'. Atholl had no enthusiasm for this, it was enough that he had already instructed John Findlater, his sub-factor at Blair, to assemble a number of young tenants, clothe them in tartan, equip them with arms if possible and prepare them to parade as a guard should the King come to Strath Garry.

His two days in the city were busily occupied. He lodged and dined at Oman's ('pretty good dinner, but very dear'), saw Lady Seaforth's house, talked with the Lord Provost, the Commander-in-Chief and Sir Walter Scott, and found them all at a loss to know the King's precise intentions, or even the exact date of his arrival. He met some of the deputy-lieutenants of the shires at Oman's, and discovered that little had been done about the scaffolding upon which the Lieutenants, the deputies, the Gentry of Scotland, and their ladies, might watch the King's procession to the Castle. At this time, even Sir Walter's committee seemed to have little prepared and less decided. 'From want of knowledge of any plan respecting the King's reception,' Atholl recorded in his journal, 'little could be done, indeed nothing!' He attended yet another committee meeting and discussed the laying of a foundation stone for a national monument, to be built on Calton Hill in commemoration of the thousands of Scotsmen who had died in the long French wars. On Friday, 2 August, he returned thankfully to Dunkeld, breaking his journey for an hour in Perth where he examined some chimney-pieces, shelves, and a table, all made of marble from his own quarry in Glen Tilt and intended for his house on the Isle of Man.

He spent a rain-whipped week at Dunkeld House, staring through its windows and resenting the weather that prevented him from going further abroad than the length of his gardens. During this time he learnt, as did others of his station in Scotland, that the King would sail from Greenwich on Saturday, 10 August, and would arrive in the Firth of Forth four days later. When the skies lifted on Friday, Atholl left for Edinburgh again, making the journey, as he was pleased to note, once more in eight and a half hours. The Duchess was to follow him later, but his son Glenlyon – one of the King's drinking companions – had already come up from London, and with his wife, pregnant or not. Atholl had a brief meeting with Sir Walter at Oman's Hotel, and was told much about the Celtic Society and the proposed gathering of Highlanders, all of which he thought was fanciful and foolish.

In England that Friday morning, Lord Londonderry called at Carlton House and asked to see the King. He was not expected, and it was a bizarre meeting to which subsequent events would give an overtone of horror. For some time the gossip among the Foreign Secretary's staff in London, and between the servants at his country house in North Cray had been concerned with his low spirits, the lack of his customary affability toward them, and his increasing habit of wandering alone, 'moping' they called it. They also said that he had frequently declared his life to be at risk, but he had thought this for several years now, and sometimes with good reason. When his wife brought him from Kent that Friday morning he left her in their carriage at the doors of Carlton House, and walked aimlessly along Pall Mall for an hour before he went into the palace. He entered the King's study without introduction and seized the startled monarch by the arm, crying, 'Have you heard the news, the terrible news! I'm a fugitive from justice. I'm accused of the same crime as the Bishop of Clogher. I've ordered my saddle-horses. I'm going to fly to Portsmouth, and from there to the end of the earth!' That is how Madame de Lieven recorded his words, having heard them from Lady Conyngham.

The reference to the Bishop was shocking if true, and alarming evidence of an unhinged mind if false. The prelate was Percy Jocelyn, the middle-aged son of the Earl of Roden, one-time Lord Chancellor of Ireland. Within a year of his appointment to the see, Jocelyn was deposed, accused of buggery in a Westminster public-house with Private John Moverley of the Grenadier Guards. A suitable punishment for this offence – considering its social, political, military and ecclesiastical aspects – was still occupying the minds of Lord Liverpool and Mr Peel. The incident had also excited great public interest, and hearing his Foreign Minister refer to it in so personal a context deeply disturbed the King. He took Londonderry's hands and implored him to steady himself, but this stimulated the frantic man to greater confessions. 'He accused himself of every crime,' said Madame de Lieven. 'He threatened the King, and then kissed his hands and wept; for half an hour he alternated between madness and repentance.' Mrs Arbuthnot, who presumably had her account from Wellington, said there were moments during this extraordinary meeting when Londonderry became rational in thought and speech, discussing public business and his mission to Vienna.

Removed from the King's presence, he was conducted or carried outside the palace to his waiting wife. She took him a short distance only, to their town house in St James's Square, from the window of which she called to the Duke of Wellington, at that moment riding by. Sitting on a sofa before his friend, his face shining with tears, Londonderry gabbled about the case against Jocelyn, and of his own fears that his saddle-horses had been made ready for him to flee the country. A stranger had told him so in the street. 'Depend upon it,' said the Duke, 'this is all an illusion. Your stomach is out of order.' But later, as the Minister became more distressed, Wellington bluntly warned him that he could not be in his right mind. Upon this, Londonderry collapsed, covering his face with a handkerchief and weeping bitterly. When the Duke left he called upon Londonderry's physician and dispatched him to St James's Square. By copious bleeding, the distraught man was at last reduced to harmless insensibility, and carried down the Dartford Road to the peace of North Cray. 'Poor Human Nature!' the Duke wrote to Mrs Arbuthnot. 'How little we are, after all.'

Temporarily shaken by his encounter, the King immediately sent for Lord Liverpool, and when the First Minister arrived he said, 'Either I am mad, or Lord Londonderry is mad.' The choice was implicit, but they did nothing to help the man who was thus judged insane, and who must shortly leave for Vienna as Britain's representative at the Congress of Nations. Liverpool may have known more about the crazed man's condition than he was ready to tell the King at this moment. Lady Londonderry, he later said, had been aware of the true state of her husband's mind for some time, and as a precaution she had ordered his servants to remove all razors, knives and pistols from his reach. She was so eager for him to go to Vienna, and so anxious to accompany him, that she kept him away from the public and his friends, even from his physician, while at the same time telling Liverpool that he was well, and that nothing would prevent him from leaving for the Continent on 15 August. But all this Liverpool confided to Madame de Lieven after the matter had reached its grisly conclusion, and it was in his interest, perhaps, to obscure the tragic inaction of the King and the Administration.

On Saturday, refreshed by a sleep that does not seem to have been disturbed by the remembrance of Londonderry's anguished face, the King left Carlton House for his voyage to Scotland. For some days a squadron of ships – men-of-war, yachts, tenders and steam-boats – had been assembling in the Thames, and most of them were now anchored off the Nore. The King's yacht, *Royal George*, was towed upstream by the steam-vessel *Comet* and took up her moorings by Greenwich Hospital on July 31. There in the long, waiting days that followed, her crew were employed in painting ship, drying sails, and taking aboard great quantities of stores. In one morning, from four o'clock till twelve, a city barge brought her 1120 lbs of bread, 54 pieces of pork, 150 lbs of cheese, 75 lbs of butter, 100 lbs of sugar, two bushels of salt and five of peas, 21 gallons of rum, 31½ of brandy, and seven tons of water. Food for the King's own table came aboard later, and was not recorded in the ship's logs.

The Royal Yacht was a beautiful vessel of 330 tons, low-hulled, three-masted and rigged like a frigate. She had been built at Deptford less than five years before, a noble tribute to the last great days of sail. That was how Turner would later see her, perhaps, her sails furled and her masts white, her sharp lines softened by the gathering mists of the Forth, as if the past were closing about her before she could come of age. Her voyage to Ireland the previous year had proved her qualities, and if the gales on her return had reduced the King to sickened immobility she had challenged them bravely and without damage. While her naval escorts plunged bow and sprit into deep waves, the *Royal George*, it was said, scarcely shipped water. It was also claimed that she could outsail any vessel in the King's Navy, a boast which may have made the crew of the steam-vessel *Comet* smirk with superior conceit.

Her interior was modestly palatial. From a larboard gangway, a winding mahogany staircase led below to the middle-deck. Aft of this was the King's dining-room, low in head-room but 23 feet athwart ship and 17 fore and aft. A passage from this reached a large state cabin with arching stern-windows. His bed-chamber was on the starboard side of the passage, and on the larboard was a smaller berth for the most senior member of his suite. The deck-boards of these apartments were snow-white, the panelled walls dark and highly-polished, and the heavy glass of the windows was framed in gilded wood. The Commodore of the Royal Squadron, Sir Charles Paget, could expect to dine with the King. The captain of the yacht, William Mingay, would sit at the King's table at least once during the voyage, dining alone in his cabin at other times. His officers would eat amidships with lesser members of the King's suite, served from a large, steam-powered kitchen in the fore-quarters. Below the dining-room, where the seats could be converted into bunks, there were small cabins for the ship's officers, and hammock space for the crew. Except for His Majesty, no one aboard could expect solitude, silence or undisturbed comfort, from the moment the yacht cast off from Greenwich until the time she came to her moorings in Leith Roads.

During the fortnight the *Royal George* spent in the Thames a small armada of little vessels gathered in a half-moon about her – barges, private yachts, tenders and oared boats. Some made secure at the moorings available, but most moved with the tide, passing and repassing the stately ship, cheering her as the morning sun lifted the veils of mist from her golden tiller, the glistening orbicular glass of her compass, and the red and gold of the royal coat-of-arms on her prow. Every evening a Marine band, brought aboard at Gallions Reach, practised on the after-deck until sunset, its stirring music rolling across the water to the watching boats, and to the listening crowds in Greenwich, Deptford and the Isle of Dogs.

The King did not leave Carlton House until the afternoon of Saturday, but since early morning he had been hourly expected along the dusty length of the Kent Road. At eight o'clock the Lord Mayor of London arrived at Greenwich in his state barge, its scarlet rowers sitting erect with uplifted oars as the Ramsgate steam-packet towed them downstream. They were joined by the ornate barges of the Skinners' and Goldsmiths' Companies, and by pleasure-yachts of the East India Company, aflame with flags, bunting and coloured awnings. Before dawn the youngest and fittest of the crowds waiting along the Kent Road had climbed to the highest spots available, the tops of walls, trees, roofs, steeples and, for some, the Obelisk in St George's Fields. Movement along the road had been reduced to a walking-pace by the growing press of vehicles and foot-travellers. The number of plum-coloured stage-coaches to Greenwich had been increased and all were crowded, atop and inside, the women shaking ribbons and the men waving hats and canes. More fare-stages had also been added to the route, so that the setting-down and picking-up could be done more often in a profitable operation known as *short shillings*.

The bells of Greenwich Church rang their first change at sunrise and would continue until dusk. Rowed over to the Ramsgate steamer for his breakfast, the Lord Mayor had almost eight hours to kill before the King would come. His fine barge, and those of the City Companies, became another attraction on the muddy river. They were soon surrounded by pleasure-boats, many of which, said a journalist filling time and space with words, were 'manned by fashionably attired females, adding their embellishing presence to the spectacle'. The King was delayed, it was said, and no report of him came from the telescopes that searched the Kent Road, or looked up the long stretch of Limehouse Reach. As the noise increased, and tempers became shorter, a company of Royal Marines marched resolutely through the mob to the Grand Square of the Hospital, mounting sentries and forming lines to hold back the crowd from the water's edge. Except for the High Road, down which it was hoped the King would be able to pass to the river, the streets of Greenwich were soon choked with carriages, landaus, chaises, gigs, traps and carts, all pressing toward the square and the river. Most of their occupants would see nothing, nor be able to step down with safety into the human tide that was flowing against the railings of the Hospital. The noisy frenzy of voices was borne upon a carrier-wave of clanging bells and brassy music. There was no pause now in the pumping sound of Scottish dances and military marches played by bands on both sides of the Thames, one picking up when another fell wearily silent. Across the river in the Isle of Dogs, the large crowd which assembled before nightfall on Friday was rapidly increased by the arrival of more sightseers from the city, and from the villages and towns of Essex. Most of them, thought the journalists in their privileged position by the Water Gate of the Hospital, were intoxicated by drink or high spirits, recklessly pressing forward across the mud and into the Thames until the water was above their knees. It was a relief to turn from the sight of this distant mob – so like a menacing army held back by the moat of the river – to the more agreeable scene inside the grounds of the Hospital.

Round the entrance to the Governor's house we observed a number of beautiful females, who waited with great patience for many hours for the gratification of beholding the Sovereign. We noticed many Scotch ladies who exhibited the tartan and appeared to be in high spirits.

Boredom and the flow of the tide now encouraged the growing flotilla of small boats to come closer to the *Royal George*. This, and the increasingly riotous behaviour of the crowd, which threatened to over-run the shore before the Water Gate, began to alarm the Governor. He was greatly relieved when a force of Bow Street Officers came down the river, stalwart blue-coated and red-vested men under the direction of William Broderip, Magistrate at the Thames Police Court. Armed with an authority quickly granted him by the Lord Mayor, Broderip persuaded the City Companies to re-align their barges in a manner that would keep the water clear about the yacht. This worked well until the *Royal George* swung on an uneasy tide, and Broderip needed all the help he could get from the Harbour-Master's boatmen. Even so, he reported,

> There was, during a short time, considerable confusion, for the crews of many boats took this opportunity of forcing themselves into the area between the yacht and the shore, and it required the greatest exertion to clear it. This was, at last, effected, principally by towing out of the area the more contumacious of the intruders.

Ashore, however, the contumacious and defiantly belligerent were less easy to move, for some had been waiting since Thursday when the King's embarkation was first expected. Mounted patrols and foot-men from Bow Street were thinly stretched along the Kent Road, using their elbows and fists, and sometimes their staves to restrain the crowds and to open a central highway along which the King's carriage might safely move. The streets of Greenwich were at last surrendered to the crowd, the scarlet and blue lines of soldiers and seamen falling slowly back to the grounds of Wren's grey Hospital. In the centre of the Square, drawn up in disciplined lines, were eight hundred orphan boys, the sons and grandsons of Nelson's seamen. There were also two hundred girls, 'daughters of wounded and departed heroes'. They were all neat and clean, giving general satisfaction, and it was observed that the girls 'were in a most healthy and apparently happy condition'. But their bright happiness was drooping, their voices faltering as they sang. It was well past noon, and the King would not come until the turn of the tide.

The crowd waiting outside Carlton House, in Pall Mall and St

James's Park, was probably more impatient than the sweating mob at Greenwich, and there was no diversion to be had except coarse mockery of the gentry who had come to watch from the privacy of their carriages. Soon after two o'clock there was a roar of approval when the Spring Gardens gate was at last opened and a line of open carriages came out of Carlton House Yard at a fast trot. They carried His Majesty's luggage only, rocking terraces of shining leather and polished wood. Less than forty-five minutes later the gate was again opened to a fine clatter of hooves and the grinding of iron wheels upon stone. The royal procession was led by two horsemen of the 15th Light Dragoons in dark-blue jackets and sky-blue trousers, each man with a red and white plume, twenty-three inches long, flowing from his bell-shaped shako. They were followed by two outriders and the royal carriage, then more outriders and a detachment of eight dragoons and an officer. The postillions on the carriage were a credit to the King's impeccable taste – coats of pastel yellow trimmed with gold, white beaver hats at a rakish tilt, and whips hung with coloured ribbons. To the rear of this dashing cavalcade was a barouche in which sat Masters Lucas, Holmes and Whiting, His Majesty's young pages, arrogantly bored and languidly indifferent to the occasion. As his carriage came out of the Yard, the King leant forward to the cheers, smiling and nodding in response, before sinking back to the cushions between Lord Francis Conyngham and Sir William Knighton. His costume this day had been chosen with care, complimenting those whom he was shortly to entrust with his life. He wore a plain blue coat, its braiding giving it an intended resemblance to an admiral's uniform. His immaculate stock was black in naval style, and modestly frilled. His belly swelled against a plain white vest, and his gross and painful legs were clothed in white breeches and white silken hose. He was said to look well, which he was not, but rouge and powder loyally maintained the illusion.

The procession passed into St. James's Park, and thence through the Horse Guards arch to Whitehall, Westminster Bridge and the Kent Road across the water. The King leant forward more often now, perhaps surprised by the warmth of his reception – the dense crowds on roads lined with carriages, the broad pendants hanging from taverns, asking God to be his saviour, and the many groups of children, waving in welcome. 'Their appearance was very pleasing,' said a reporter, 'and His Majesty appeared gratified with the artless expression of attachment evinced by his juvenile subjects.'

The Marquess Conyngham, as Lord Steward of the Royal Household, had been waiting in the Grand Avenue of the Hospital for an hour before one of the leading dragoons arrived at a gallop and reined up before him. The King was entering Greenwich. The royal standard slid up its staff above the hospital, the Marine Band began the National Anthem, and a growing cheer came over the roofs from the High Road. But it was another twenty minutes before the four silk-skinned bays brought the green carriage through the crowd to the North Gate of the avenue. The King was greatly moved, bowing and waving to the Hospital above him, to windows filled by women in colourful dresses, to white handkerchiefs and white arms fluttering in greeting. The cacophonic noise increased. Band after band played the Anthem in joyous disharmony, regimental drums began the roll of a royal salute, followed by the rattle and slap of presented muskets.

> When the bands struck up, the acclamations of the people accompanied, and soon drowned the more feeble voice of the instruments. Hundreds of those who were present, particularly such as were close to the north gate, joined in the chorus, and, however, discordant their voices, must have rendered this beautiful piece of national music more grateful to the ears of his Majesty, than if it had been executed by the most finished performers, whether vocal or instrumental.

Whether deafened by the noise, or overcome with emotion, the King seemed to be in a smiling trance. When his carriage reached the shore, the driver of the barouche behind pulled up so sharply that its fore-horses went down, pitching the groom on his face and bloodying his nose. The King saw nothing of this, or ignored it as he alighted. Although the playing of the anthem had now ceased, it was still sung, and the drums still beat a double salute. The King moved toward a waiting barge with the slow and measured steps that gave his overblown figure a paradoxical grace. The crowds on either side pressed toward him, bending the line of militiamen like a scarlet rope. Thrust forward and overthrown, a woman fell upon her knees before the King. He presumably took her reluctant position for obeisance, for he smiled at her pleasantly without slackening his pace. Supported now by a hand on Conyngham's arm, he moved to the barge where Sir Charles Paget was waiting. There he turned, and greatly touched he shouted at the yelling crowd, 'God bless you all!' The woman was still on her knees, unable to rise perhaps, but it was already being said that she was 'some romantic character whose mind, overpowered by the scene around her, could not restrain itself'.

For a few minutes the King paused at the top of the Water Gate stairs, a dark figure in the centre of the scarlet and gold gentlemen assembled for his departure. He lifted his hat again, holding it high that it might be seen above the heads of those above him, and then he went down to the barge. He boarded the *Royal George* at twenty minutes past three, and as he went up her gangway he was again cheered by all who could see him. The white deck of the yacht glowed with uniforms – scarlet, green and blue, glistening bullion, bright steel and the fluttering of white plumes on black cocked hats. Among such sartorial self-indulgence he was the most impressively dressed. His plain blue coat was perhaps a conscious Napoleonic gesture by a monarch who could have appeared as an admiral, a field-marshal, a general of cavalry or foot according to his wish, or to the way he turned at his wardrobe. Awaiting him on the quarter-deck was a very old and very frail man in the blue, gold and white of an Admiral of the Fleet. His head was uncovered, and his hat swept in a curve across his knees as he slowly bowed. John Jervis, Earl of St. Vincent, had joined the Navy as an able seaman fourteen years before the King was born, and was commanding his own ship before Nelson began his naval career. A hard disciplinarian, a great flogger of men, and a dogged sea-fighter, Old Jarvey had risen by one 'smash-'em-up' victory after another. He had resolutely broken the back and spirit of the Nore Mutiny in 1797, and had later been appointed First Lord that he might crush a dockyard strike. 'Manly resistance to mutineers,' he believed, 'is the most meritorious of all military services.' Now brought carefully from a retirement of sixteen years, he spoke his carefully rehearsed and scarcely heard words and was then taken gently ashore. There he was saluted by a detachment of Marines. He nodded an acknowledgement and shouted as loudly as he could, 'Three cheers for the King!' They were given, and as much for him, perhaps, since time mellows the reputation of those who survive.

The Commodore's broad pennant had been lowered from the mainmast of the yacht as soon as the King's barge came alongside, and the royal standard was broken in its place. A flutter of signals in the starboard shrouds asked the telegraph ashore to notify the Admiralty that the King was aboard his yacht and was about to sail. She went downstream at twenty minutes past four, delayed by a difficulty in casting off and in making fast a hawser from her bows to the stern of the *Comet*. She went downriver under tow but with full sail set, her canvas white against the black smoke of the steam-vessel ahead. From the moment she moved she was followed by the waiting boats, more than eighty of them with the Lord Mayor's barge in the lead, towed by the Ramsgate steam-packet. The smaller vessels bumped and bounced in the wake of the larger craft, sometimes colliding and sometimes veering out of control, their frightened passengers crying out in exulting terror. Once the yacht was in midstream, the King went below, quickly re-appearing in the true uniform of an admiral. A fine cocked hat was perched upon his red wig, and frequently lifted above it as he turned to face one shore and then the other, responding to the cheers and the music, the drums and the saluting guns like a delighted child.

By the time the *Royal George* entered Gallions Reach she had left the sailing flotilla well behind, but the King did not go below. The steam-vessels, and the City barges pulled by some of them, were still in pursuit. There were also great crowds waiting to cheer him on both banks. Flags hung from every steeple and the westering sun was bright on the brass of more, yet more military bands. By Blackwall, the boatswain piped to man the yards, and as the seamen sped up the ratlines to their stations they were saluted ashore by puff-balls of cannon-fire and musketry. Eastward toward Dartford and Greenhithe, the sailing-vessels began to turn about one by one, each with a valedictory cheer or a chorus of the National Anthem, and soon only the steamers would remain, riding astern on cream bow-waves, their dark smoke clouding the sun beyond them. As if in acknowledgement of the passing day, the King went below again, returning in a plain blue surtout and a travelling cap. The wind now freshened and towing was discontinued, although the *Comet* and the *James Watt* followed close astern. When the *Royal George* set her studding-sails, the last sailing-vessel gave up the chase. There were crowds still on both banks, and cannon firing bravely from Tilbury Fort. Across the narrows at Gravesend the Mayor and Corporation watched in despair, their address of Welcome and God-speed unrolled and unread as the royal yacht slipped by, heeling slightly under the press of a good south-westerly.

The King remained on deck until dark, his hat still in his hand, ready to be lifted in responsive salute. Upon his suggestion, his suite went thankfully below – six lords, five knights and sundry gentlemen. He did not join them until late, for this was perhaps one of the most remarkable experiences of his life. It held its sweet savour until the last hour of daylight. As each following barge and steamer turned about to go upstream, he heard the cheering of its crew and passengers, the sound of voices singing the Anthem. The Lord Mayor's barge was the last to leave, his worship having dined well aboard the towing packet. Before it left it made one wide circuit of the royal yacht, on the deck of which stood the isolated figure of the King, repeatedly bowing and kissing his hand. At such moments as this the years of hatred, derision, scurrilous ridicule and maudlin self-pity must have seemed a nightmare only. Nor was the wonder of the King's day ended when the *Royal George* at last dropped anchor off the Nore. Awaiting him in the thickening darkness were the other ships of the Royal Squadron – his second yacht *Royal Sovereign*, the frigate *Phaeton*, the sloops *Forte* and *Egeria*, the tenders *Calliope* and *Cameleon*, and the Admiralty yacht *Prince Regent*. They greeted the *Royal George* and its tearful passenger with honour, by manning the yards and by cheering, by saluting guns and soaring rockets. From his stern-windows, as he went at last to bed, the King could see the illuminations burning in the rigging and along the yards of every ship within view – blue, soft and ghostly.

The squadron weighed at four on Sunday morning. It sailed east by north, the *Royal George* leading under tow from the *James Watt*. A cable's length or more behind, the *Comet* took up the *Royal Sovereign*. By six o'clock that evening both yachts, and their black dragon-fly steamers, were far ahead of the rest of the squadron, not one ship of which could now be seen by the maintop look-outs.

'The adoption of the new system by which the mountain districts are converted into sheep pastures, even if it should unfortunately occasion emigration of some individuals, is, upon the whole, advantageous to the nation at large.'

– JAMES LOCH, 1820

Before he had taken breakfast on Saturday, August 10, the Duke of Atholl was driven from Charlotte Square to Castle Hill. There he inspected the scaffolding which was to support the deputy-lieutenants of the shires and their ladies when the King made his grand procession from Holyroodhouse to the Castle. At noon the Duke was to attend a meeting of his own Lieutenancy, and wished to be familiar with this wonderful but somehow terrifying structure in which he had no great faith. Returning to the Square, he ate alone. The Duchess had not yet arrived from Dunkeld, but Glenlyon and his wife came during the morning and made themselves 'busy with a variety of things'. As if to escape them, Atholl went to Holyroodhouse. He hoped to see the Earl of Breadalbane who had sent him a worrying note, saying that fifty Campbells from the Earl's lands in Strathtay were already on the march to Edinburgh. The Earl was not in, and somewhat out of temper now the Duke drove on to 39, Castle Street. Scott's house was full, his library door under siege by a noisy crowd, mostly Highlandmen or city gentlemen so disguising themselves, wrapped in swirls of tartan and girt about with barbaric weapons. Sir Walter was excited and emotional, telling Atholl that Glengarry's clansmen and the MacGregors had been sworn in as a guard for the Regalia of Scotland. More tartan was coming to the city, Drummonds under Lady Gwydir as well as Breadalbane's Campbells, and he hoped the men from the Braes of Atholl would soon join them. The Duke made no promises, and seemed pleased that he had no time before Post Hour to write to his factor at Dunkeld, asking whether a hundred of his tenants could be sent up as Sir Walter desired. That night he recorded his distaste for this

165

foolish fancy, and his alarm at the thought of so many Highlanders 'under no military discipline and who might quarrel with others or among themselves, brought together in such a harum scarum way'. He resolved to speak of this on the morrow to Sir Thomas Bradford. If the Commander-in-Chief shared his concern, he would then write to Lord Melville and to Mr Peel.

The Secretary of State for the Home Department was already in Edinburgh and staying in the seclusion of Melville's timbered estate to the south of the city. Robert Peel had come north with his wife Julia, whose delivery of their son three months before (the second of what would be six children in nine years) had left her fashionably weak. Both the Peels would rather have been elsewhere, perhaps in the pleasant surroundings of Lulworth Castle which Peel had recently rented for its privacy, its clean air and good rough shooting. Their journey to Scotland, leisurely and by carriage, had taken them six days, including a pause in his father's home at Tamworth. The red-haired Minister was unenthusiastic about his obligatory attendance in Edinburgh, but since his predecessor had gone to Ireland with the King there was no escaping the duty. He was in no mood for celebrations, however, and would take little formal part in them. His health was not good. His eyesight was troublesome, and for some time he had been forced to relieve his distress by closing his eyes for a few moments, a habit which many who did not know him took to be evidence of supercilious contempt. The duties of his office, and their relentless accumulation of documents, pursued him to Edinburgh and he now wore a green eye-shade when he worked. His great solace was the company of his wife, her encouraging presence across the room, a pale and oval face within a frame of chestnut hair. He was besotted. 'If I could love you more,' he once told her, 'the sight of others and their odious ways would make me do so.'

Despite his lack of enthusiasm for the Visit, he liked Scotland, provided he saw more of the country than its people, and was not obliged to spend much time in populated places. He had first come in 1809, at the age of twenty-one, with his name on the books of Lincoln's Inn, and a Tory seat purchased for him by his father. The writings of Johnson, Boswell, Pennant and others had filled him with a desire to see North Britain, and in particular he had a 'burning anxiety' to visit the Highlands. He travelled alone, sometimes on foot and sometimes in the saddle, deeply impressed by the magnificent grandeur of Strathspey and the dignified hospitality of the small lairds with whom he occasionally lodged. He returned ten years later, now a blooded and ambitious Parliamentarian with his feet well set upon the political ladder. He came as one of a group, again to Speyside, staying for six weeks during which he fished, shot and stalked, bringing his own cook that he and his companions might best enjoy what they had killed on the hill or on the river. He was in the old land of the Macphersons, renting the castle of their chief at Cluny, and like many susceptible Englishmen of his time he was impressed by 'the simplicity and unaffected kindness among the people'. It was an opinion seemingly without interest in their past, or concern for their future. When he came to Strathspey for a third time, a year before his marriage, he was no longer a solitary wanderer or one of a band of youthful sportsmen. He was the esteemed house-guest of the Marquis of Huntly. The August heat was intense that year, unrelieved by wind or rain, but this did not prevent Lord Huntly's friends from killing seven hundred grouse in seven days.

If he had a lingering nostalgia for those careless vacations, Peel could afford no time or thought for sport during this August of 1822. He was in Edinburgh as an officer of state, and was determined not to be distracted by the festivities. He was never at rest among strangers or casual acquaintances, and his custom of looking into the distance, beyond the shoulders of those who spoke to him, confirmed his reputation for distant contempt. Yet his politeness was genuine, and only his hesitant nature made it appear cold. When he was to be seen abroad in Edinburgh it was always in the background of events, a pale figure with tired eyes, his hair aflame above his black clothes and white linen. He witnessed some of the public events from among the crowd, once with Scott, with whom he developed a mutually respectful friendship. For the rest of the time he considered himself best employed in fruitful conversation with eminent and influential Scotsmen, giving particular attention to what he believed to be the necessary reform of their country's justiciary.

Concern with less weighty Scottish affairs had begun before he left England. From late June he was asked many times by the persistent Lord Provost of Glasgow, John Alston, whether its citizens could expect the King to visit them and enjoy 'the loyalty and affectionate respect which he will meet with from all *classes* of his subjects'. Alston was also anxious to know whether a portrait of the King by Sir Thomas Lawrence, specially ordered by His Majesty for the Glasgow Town Hall, was now finished, and indeed 'in a state of forwardness'. He did not refer to those thousands of subjects from Glasgow and its neighbourhood who had recently been in revolt against His Majesty's Government, or to those long-imprisoned weavers, the last of whom was now dispatched to New South Wales. Nor was the Home Secretary reminded of a letter he had received from Alston earlier this year, the report of a disgraceful riot in his city. The Lord Provost had asked for more foot-soldiers to bring the disaffected to punishment, 'and also be instrumental in checking the lower ranks in future, who seem by the lenity shewn them to have become more bold and ferocious'.

It needed patience and several letters from Peel or his permanent under-secretary, Henry Hobhouse, before the Lord Provost realized that the King did not intend to visit Glasgow, or indeed any of those cities whose senior magistrates were as importunate if not as persevering as John Alston. There had also been letters of regret to be written to the mayors and gentry of such English coastal towns as Lowestoft, Yarmouth and Scarborough whose loyal inhabitants were certain of the King's wish to meet them. Sir Edmund Lacon, a Norfolk squire, offered His Majesty temporary bed and board 'should adverse winds oblige the Royal Fleet to anchor in Yarmouth Roads', and the Earl of Darlington, a sturdy Whig, inveterate fox-hunter and patron of the turf, hoped for 'the high honour that would be conferr'd upon me, if His Majesty would make use of my Castle if he either goes or returns by land from Scotland'. To these and all such correspondents, Peel sent a courteous acknowledgement or suprascribed their letters with a brief indication of the replies his staff should send. *His Majesty regrets . . . gratitude . . . respects . . . your anxious desire . . . not consistent with . . . most probable that arrangements will not permit . . . etc . . . etc . . . etc . . .*

As soon as the King's Visit became a certainty, or as certain as royal vacillation would admit, the resolute Sheriff of Edinburgh, Adam Duff, asked for Peel's assistance in a matter of public concern.

There had been references in the Edinburgh press, culled from English newspapers, to the alarming fact that several 'light-fingered gentlemen of London' were making ready to leave for Scotland and for the profit to be made there during the King's Visit. Duff reminded Peel that this invasion could not be met by the relatively unsophisticated police force of Edinburgh.

> As from the smartness of their dress and appearance these London pickpockets may not excite the suspicion of our Edinburgh officers of police it is necessary that two or three Bow Street Officers who know by sight the principal London pickpockets should be in Edinburgh for the purpose of pointing them out to the Officers of the Edinburgh Police.

The request was not unreasonable. The peripatetic nature of London's thieves had made it necessary for Bow Street Officers to go to Dublin with the King, and Peel now passed this request to Hobhouse for expeditious action. In the ill-matched struggle against what were known as the criminal classes, petty larceny was as common as the itch, and Duff's request was probably dismissed from Peel's mind as soon as it was approved. Of more serious concern was the continuing under-current of social unrest in Britain. Active conspiracy and revolt by the Radicals now seemed unlikely, but the cause of their disaffection remained, and for every man of discontent who was hanged or transported there were others as yet unknown. This year, as in the previous year under Lord Sidmouth's secretaryship, the Home Department had received many disturbing reports of the secret manufacture of dirks, pikes and swords, often in Liverpool where one Thomas Powell was taken up and quickly transported for 'putting handles to weapons of this description'. It was not believed that such arms were being prepared for an English revolt, but for use by the bitter poor and the oppressed Gaelic population of Ireland, where England's running sore was as festering as ever. A vessel sailing to that unhappy land was wrecked near Lundy, and was found to be carrying a cask of iron instruments, each shaped like a scythe and cut into three parts, 'well adapted to be fixed at the top of a pole and used as weapons of offence'.

Although Scotland's Radicals were still numbed, if not cowed by the draconian suppression of their bungled insurrection, there was always reason to believe that the vile Democrat was still a threat to the serenity of England. Since he took office in January, Peel's secretariat had received a steady stream of letters from local authorities, agents and informers, reporting disturbance, riot, barn-burning, assault and conspiracy throughout the shires. To contain this murmuring unrest, if not to eradicate it, there had been a responsive deployment of troops. Light dragoons and yeomanry cantered along the by-lanes and highways from Dorset to Norfolk, and Warwickshire to Northumberland, where the sight of their scarlet, green or blue jackets, the flowing horse-hair on their helmets, was a comfort to those who felt themselves or their property at risk. The new and increasingly prosperous managing-society of post-Waterloo England had yet to acquire the self-confidence of the landed aristocracy upon which it still depended but would slowly replace. It was outwardly complacent and self-satisfied, inwardly thrusting and self-conscious. It was conditionally compassionate, inspired by the verse of Scott, the heroics of Hougoumont, and the power of steam, and sometimes, perhaps, it was aware that all this might be only a hard crust above a latent volcano. In the heat beneath, the masters of that burgeoning Industrial Age fought a relentless war with its hostile victims. As the wages of a Staffordshire collier were reduced by stoppages to six shillings a week, the miners' refusal to work led to bloody affrays between them and the hired forces of the Coal Master. When the dark-of-night protests by the pitmen became a threat to property, the troopers came with carbines booted and sabres on their hips. In the absence of an adequate police force – and in the frank acknowledgement that whatever their quarrel, or with whom, the dissident people were in revolt against Government and Crown – the deployment of soldiers was the only reflex. Thus a regiment of dragoons could be promptly ordered into Frome when its clothworkers lifted their banners and declared their families to be starving.

After reports of this kind it was perhaps a relief for Peel to be in Scotland again. From the tall windows of Melville Castle, looking across the grass to young stands of oak and beech, it would appear that this northern kingdom – where sixty thousand men had recently been in revolt – was now orderly and peaceful. Apart from isolated reports of rural arson (for which Garth ironically blamed the example set by Lady Stafford) there had been no serious incident of unrest during the summer of 1822, and any risk to the success of the King's visit might be no greater than the predatory activities of light-fingered Englishmen from London.

The four experienced officers who left for Scotland by steam-packet, four days before the King's departure, were the most famous members of the Bow Street force. All were men of middle-age and raffish reputation – John Townsend, John Sayer, John Vickery and Daniel Bishop. Townsend, the senior, was no longer employed on the horse or foot patrols of London and its suburbs. He and his crony Sayer had special assignments which they acquired for themselves with an old soldier's cunning. They had regular duties of a formal kind at the Bank of England, the Opera House and the Courts of Justice, for which they were paid in addition to their regular wage of twenty-five shillings a week. Townsend received a further £200 a year for attendance upon the King when required. He was the longest-serving member of the force, London's favourite Runner, a big man in a flaxen wig, light blue coat and red vest, propelling himself forward in long strides by a thrust of his stout stick. So popular was he, so welcome a presence, that invitation cards to society balls sometimes had a pencilled line of reassurance added, *Mr Townsend will be present*. All those to whom he had been of service during the year, muscular or discreet, could expect the knock of his stick upon their door at Christmas.

Townsend's royal favour had begun when he protected the King from an attack by the deranged woman Margaret Nicholson. The monarch admired the officer, as he did other rough and unaffected men, and Townsend shamelessly exploited their relationship. Upon the offer of a glass, or in confident expectation of a coin, he would tell of their meeting, of how his hard white hat had been a gift from the King, and of the many 'freaks', the escapades they had shared.

> Many's the time I've taken him by the skirt of the coat and said to him 'I'd advise your Royal Highness if you have got any money, to leave it with me for safety.' And then he would pull out a purse with 50 or 60 guineas in it and say 'Well, Townsend, you must allow me something to spend, you

know.'; and upon that I used to hand him over about five guineas, keeping the rest and his watch in my own pocket, where few people would have thought of looking for them.

Two of Townsend's companions in Edinburgh were thief-takers in the mould of Jonathan Wild, collaborators as well as persecutors of the inhabitants of Alsatia. All four accepted their welcome as no more than their due, giving Adam Duff and James Logan, the city's police commander, the benefit of their experience. This would have included a finger pointed in the direction of a familiar English face, and a warning that the Scots could expect some of London's most adroit Knuckles and Sneaks, several experts in Touching the Rattler, Milling a Kin and Starring the Glaze, as well as sundry operators of the Hoist.* The Edinburgh press welcomed the Runners more as a curiosity than friends in need, which would not have offended them, and once their arrival had been reported, little attention was paid them. Only John Townsend remained in public view, smiling by the door of an ante-room during the Levee at Holyroodhouse, or in the entrance hall of the Assembly Rooms in George Street, touching his forehead with the knob of his stick as gentlemen of his acquaintance passed up the grand staircase to the Peers' Ball. The old man was perhaps too astute not to realize that the Bow Street Runners had reached the end of their time, that the familiar blue coats and red breasts, belted pistols and hangers, stout arms and malleable principles, would soon be swept away by young Mr Secretary Peel.

Despite testy complaints by Atholl and others that there *appeared to be no plan whatsoever*, the city stirred itself quickly now and moved toward the most lavish and self-indulgent manifestation in its history. The framework of events was a programme hurriedly prepared by Scott's committee in consultation with the civil and military powers. This he presented in his *Hints* as 'a few plain suggestions as to the probable course of things . . . and the part which citizens of all orders may be called upon to take'.

* *Knuckles*, pickpockets; *Sneaks*, burglars; *Touching the Rattler*, stealing luggage from a coach; *Milling a Kin*, house-breaking; *Starring the Glaze*, cutting through a shop-window; the *Hoist*, shop-lifting.

The King would disembark upon the Shore in Leith, to general acclamation and to the lingering chagrin, no doubt, of its neighbour Newhaven, which had unsuccessfully argued the superior advantages of its Chain Pier. Scott had insisted that Leith was the ancient sea-port of Edinburgh and the spot where Scottish monarchs were accustomed to land. He cited, in verse, the precedent of Mary Queen of Scots, although she had landed in a thick haar, almost unwelcomed, and without the 'thousand, thousand shouts' of joy that the verse claimed. The entry to Edinburgh would be by Leith Walk which, in Scott's opinion, was a nobler avenue than any in Europe, even the approach to Waterloo Bridge in London. The procession would halt for the presentation of keys at the entrance to Picardy Place and then proceed by way of Saint Andrew Square and Princes Street to the foot of Calton Hill, entering the grounds of Holyroodhouse from Abbey Hill. After more addresses of welcome the King would go on to Dalkeith, resting there for a day before holding his first Court at Holyrood. In the following days, how many no one could yet say, the King would return the Honours of Scotland to the Castle guarded by Sir Evan MacGregor and the Griogaraich, attend a civic banquet in Parliament House ('every old Scotch dish . . . sheep's head, haggis, hodge-podge etc'), dance at a ball in the Assembly Rooms, parade his cavalry on Portobello Sands, and hold a Levee for gentlemen and a Drawing-Room for ladies. In Sir Walter's opinion, the ladies were Scotland's pride, and should flower most wonderfully when the King went to his Castle. Upon the balcony of the Royal Exchange, he said, over the High Street from the Cross where Lord Provost Arbuthnot and the Magistracy were to be assembled, 'another platform is to be raised, which is to contain what may be regarded as the representative of Scottish beauty, in the persons of several hundreds of the finest women in Scotland'. Aspirants to this exclusive gathering would be admitted by ticket only, obtainable from the Lord Provost.

The Clergy were to have their stand also, before the High Kirk of Saint Giles. At this moment, before the King's arrival, few can have been anticipating this with unqualified satisfaction. The King had yet to say that he would attend the church during his visit, and the only information available – most galling to Presbyterian precept and pride – was that he had no taste for public praying.

With Sir Walter's *Hints* of what was to come, Edinburgh set about its preparations with vigour, and in a mixed mood of vulgar ostentation, sweet simplicity, fulsome homage and unashamed greed. It was sustained in all its activities by an unchallenged faith in Scotland's superior qualities, a belief eloquently expressed by the *Evening Courant*.

> Our gracious King throws himself, as it were, into the arms of his people. He has no guards, but their love; no security but their sound sense and manly respect. Scotland and Scotchmen are altogether a new subject for his observation. We have not the hearty, though boisterous bearing of John Bull, nor any portion of the wild eccentricity of Ireland's loyalty; but we have our own firm, bold, and manly character; and displaying this, as it is our duty and should be our pride to display it, we feel confident that the King will regard us as neither the lowest in his love, nor the last in his esteem.

Although the King was not to reside at Holyroodhouse, as many Scots had wished, it was necessary to make the building as acceptable a royal palace as it once was, if only to be a grand audience chamber for the King's occasional use. The cost of the repairs and refurbishment which became essential, as submitted later to the Lord Chief Baron of the Exchequer, was £4859 and one penny. The work specified was not only executed in the palace, but also in its gardens and on its approach roads. Also included in the cost were improvements to the hall and chambers of Parliament House. The whole was supervised by the Surveyor-General, Lieutenant-Colonel Benjamin Stephenson, with the assistance of Robert Reid, the King's architect, and a worrisome, tireless man invariably but aptly described as 'Mr Trotter, His Majesty's Upholsterer in Scotland'. He was perhaps the most active of the three, for almost two-thirds of the cost of the improvements were expended upon repairs and replacements to the deplorable upholstery of the palace. A fourth man was also involved, more by his own intrusion, perhaps, than by invitation – Mr Mash from the Lord Chamberlain's Office, who probably found the Colonel's wing an agreeable refuge from Sir Walter's candid disapproval.

Stephenson was an aging engineer officer who until now had found his official duties no great strain upon his time or his abilities, but he proved himself to be a man of aptitude and application. In the few weeks allowed him, he worked a miraculous transformation upon the rotting, rat-infested mansion below the northern spur of Salisbury Craigs. Neglected for decades, chilled by bitter draughts and peopled by ghosts, it had become a grace-and-favour apartment house wherein its rooms were part of the payment for noble sinecures, or the lodgings of conscientious office-holders in straitened circumstances, such as the Inspector-General of Barracks in Scotland, Major William Nairne and his lady.

Reporting the changes that were so rapidly appearing in the empty house of Scotland's kings, the *Caledonian Mercury* remembered how there had once been desolate halls, damp air, dust-drenched ornaments and the mouldering remains of unusable furniture. Now, under the direction of Mr Trotter, all was different, as if the sun were seeping through the ancient grey stone to set the walls aflame. The great picture-gallery, where the Court was to assemble before moving to the presence-chamber, was hastily painted in a colour that says much about Mr Trotter's taste, but any hue would have been an improvement upon the layers of grease and candle-soot that it replaced. The colour chosen for the walls and ceiling was a sombre brown – or *fawn* according to those who felt charitable toward Mr Trotter. Where suitable, the walls were sometimes hung with fine scarlet velvet, and the moulding of each public room was extensively re-gilded. Mr Trotter's intention, it was said, was to create a sepia ambience that would emphasize the rich candle-glow of the evening, and reproduce its warm incandescence in daylight.

The industrious execution of the work required the enlistment of a battalion or more of carpenters, glaziers, paviors and painters, tilers, slaters, masons and bricklayers, gardeners, ditchers and iron-smiths. They swarmed over the old building in noisy assaults, repairing floor-boards and panels, relaying stairways and pavements, building platforms, restoring the flags and walls of stables and harness-rooms, for all of which they used a prodigious number of hand-barrows and pick-shafts, rakes, forks, hammers, chisels, gouges, nails and brushes. Plumbers repaired the weeping drain-pipes and sagging gutters, replaced encrusted ball-cocks and rusted chains. New leading was required in almost all the windows, and each stretch of roof needed a dozen or more new slates from Ballachulish. All was done at a cost of £252 8s 5½d in wages to workmen and labourers.

In the cutting of a new road from Abbey Hill to the park of the house, a few small industries and mean houses were removed without argument, but some small compensation. Thus 'George Simpson & Others' were given £60 for the loss of their workshops at the Watergate. Each expense was carefully noted by Stephenson's clerk in fine copper-plate. John Miller received £7 16s 3d for supplying refreshments to the labourers. Fresh timber came from Thomas Hutchison's yards in Leith at a cost of £146 5s 3d. The plumbers who repaired the guttering were paid £4 16s, and James Duff, whose twenty stout horses dragged new cannon to the gates of the palace, was given £15 for their hire. Margaret Craig, who quartered the dragoons standing guard over the palace during the work, received three guineas for their bed and stabling, and Archibald Campbell was paid £5, his precise services unnamed but well-deserved, no doubt for his august presence as the King's Beadle.

There was no recorded compensation for Major William Murray Nairne and his lady. Their summary dismissal from their home on the first floor of Holyroodhouse was made upon a Royal Warrant of 15 July, sent by Robert Peel to the Duke of Hamilton, Keeper of the Palace. Nairne was in his middle-sixties, his wife was 56, and both were members of families broken by past attachment to the exiled Stuarts. The Major's military duties were not onerous and, since they were matched by a beggarly emolument, the Nairnes had been grateful for the quarters that came with the office. Or were so, that is, until the Earl of Breadalbane, who claimed the rooms as part of his apartments, was now required to surrender them for the King's use. The Major and his wife had lived in Holyroodhouse since 1816, when the Earl's chambers were vacated by the Comte d'Artois and his quarrelsome mistress. This fat and melancholy émigré had come from France in 1796, a refugee from the republicans and from his creditors. The latter, when brief moments of international peace allowed them, pursued him to Britain but discovered that residence in Holyroodhouse gave him sanctuary. He enjoyed this until the final defeat of Napoleon restored France to his family. He returned thence, pursued this time by his Scottish creditors who may have discovered that his royal blood gave him sanctuary there also.*

Major Nairne could have accepted the need for his eviction as an ultimate blessing. In the remembered euphoria of the Visit, and upon the earnest advocacy of Scott, the King later lifted the remaining attainders upon Scotland's Jacobite families. A beneficiary of this, the Major was restored to the past honours of his name as the 5th Baron Nairne. His ancestors had been out for the Stuarts in 1715 and 1745, and one had been killed at Culloden, but he had tirelessly served the family they had wished to unseat. He was no longer a young man when his steady but undistinguished military career was rewarded with a post in the Inspectorate of Barracks. In that same year he married his second cousin, Caroline Oliphant of Gask, a spirited and talented woman who – as Lady Nairne – was to become one of the best-known names in Jacobite hagiolatry. A sweet songstress of the lost cause, her romantic loyalty lingers still in every schoolroom voice that pipes the chorus of *Charlie is my darling!*

With her husband, she shared an ancestry among the Murrays of Atholl, but those of her own name were even more fervent in their Jacobitism than Major Nairne's, driven into unrepentant exile and imbuing their children and grandchildren with their own doomed attachment to the Stuarts. At the age of nineteen, her father had ridden into Edinburgh with the first news of the Young Pretender's victory at Prestonpans. In the wrack of Culloden he had shared an emotional farewell with Prince Charles before fleeing to Sweden with his father. His sad collection of sacred relics – the Prince's bonnet, spurs, cockade and crucifix, a lock of his sandy hair – were all carefully preserved and passed to his romantic daughter. From their inspiration, from her own sad longing, and from scraps of traditional verse, she created her Jacobite songs, so beguiling that many take them for the true voices of men and women long dead before she was born.

Old Struan Robertson, whose death prevented his clansmen from answering Scott's call, was Caroline Nairne's uncle, and she is said to have composed her first Jacobite ballads to please him. A year and

---

* He became King of France as Charles X in 1824, but was forced to abdicate six years later. He then came once more to Britain and to familiar lodgings in Holyroodhouse.

more before the Royal Visit, she and other ladies of Edinburgh decided to gather a collection of national airs, and to compose suitable words for them where necessary, discarding the sometimes rough and bawdy language of the originals. Thus the bold strumpet beckoning to the young Prince from an Edinburgh window, and enjoying his robust response, became an innocent lass singing of her darling. When this proposal was put to Robert Purdie, publisher of the *Scottish Minstrel*, he accepted it with enthusiasm, issuing the first part of the collection in 1821. Much of the new work, the writing of suitable words, was done by Caroline Nairne, but she kept her authorship a secret from all but a few close friends, even from Purdie at the beginning. It did not become public knowledge until after her death. Certainly the Major was not informed of his wife's unusual activity. 'I have not told even Nairne,' she said to a friend, 'lest he blab.' She signed her verses *B.B.* and sometimes with the ugly pseudonym *Mrs Bogan of Bogan*, a curious choice for it is an old Scots word for a boil. She often hid her normal hand by writing backwards, and liked to confuse Purdie – who cannot have been deluded for long – by visiting him in the disguise of an old woman. Her anonymity was preserved until her death.

Walter Scott was also unaware that she was the author of the popular work now appearing in successive octavo volumes of the *Scottish Minstrel*. In the close society of Edinburgh, where her family's Jacobite history was well-known, it is odd that he did not cultivate her company. It is not strange, however, that she did not respond to the sycophantic display he devised for the King's pleasure. The lost past was alive to her, the dead Prince's bonnet still warm, and a lock of his red hair deserved more reverence than the fat Hanoverian now being honoured in the palace of the Stuarts. Her name does not appear in the list of ladies presented to the King at his Drawing-Room, at the Peers' Ball or the Caledonian Hunt Ball in the Assembly Rooms, although her husband, as his duty obliged him, was presented at the King's Levee by his kinsman Atholl. It cannot be proved that Caroline Nairne refused to acknowledge or celebrate the King's visit, but it may be that her lifelong loyalty to the memory of the Stuarts hardened into bitter anger when she read the warrant of 15 July, rescinding the order that had given her a home in the palace where her Prince had once danced.

> We do hereby revoke the said order and we require and command you to take care that Major William Nairne and Mrs Nairne quit the said apartments forthwith.
>
> GEORGE R.

The work of restoration outwith the palace was thorough. A jumble of old buildings and collapsing walls on the north and south sides of the building was torn down, and a new porch and staircase erected. Another road was hastily cut from the palace to the Watering Stone, shortening the approach to the Dalkeith road and thus lessening the fatigue of travel the King might suffer. A thousand cart-loads of broken rock and Kensington gravel were needed to make this highway, and also to cover a square in front of the palace where there had been an untended patch of grass and wild flowers. They were now replaced by an iron lamp-post from which a fragile yellow blossom of gas-light would shortly bloom.

The exterior of Holyroodhouse and the streets about were to be illuminated throughout the night during the King's Visit. To produce this miracle, gas-lighting was installed at a cost of £368 14s 2d, less than Mr Hunter would ask for the paler brilliance of a diamond badge to ornament the King's bonnet. Ditches were dug and pipes laid. Lamp-irons, lamp-posts, pedestals and chains came in clanging loads from the foundry of the Shotts Iron Company in Lanarkshire. Still in its wondrous infancy, gas-lighting was to be given an opportunity to capture the imagination and excite the envy of all in the city. The Edinburgh Gas Company seized this chance with enthusiasm, indulging its pride in a great quantity of wrought iron of Renaissance design, and in gilded lanterns for the gates of the palace, large enough and rich enough to be compared with those that decorated the stern-castle of a king's man-of-war. In a final flourish of magnificence, and at a cost of ten shillings each, three hundred lamps were placed along the seven miles from Holyrood to the gates of Dalkeith House, that a sleepy king might go to bed through a corridor of fan-shaped, yellow-petalled jets of blue flame.

Parliament House upon the High Street, set back in proper deference behind the dominating bulk of the High Kirk, had been a debating-chamber in name only since 1707, when the last parliament of Scotland had bitterly argued and irrevocably voted its own extinction. Long accustomed to mundane uses, its great hall was now to accommodate the King and two hundred and fifty guests at a banquet which, the Lord Provost and Magistrates hoped, would honour the monarch and affirm the ancient dignity of their royal burgh. The Surveyor-General and his associates had the briefest of time to prepare the stone-flagged hall for this transient resurrection of its past glory, and Mr Trotter, his painters, carpenters and hangers, were as actively employed as they had been at Holyroodhouse. The Royal Arms and the City Arms, in fresh paint and gilded leaf, were placed at the southern and northern ends of the hall. Thirteen chandeliers were hung between the great hammer-beams of its splendid roof, the three placed centrally being of superb size and shimmering brilliance. Decades of grease and grime were scoured from the great window, cleansing its long shafts of moving light. Below this window the King was to sit at an elliptical table with thirty privileged guests, and here Mr Trotter excelled himself, raising a fine canopy of crimson velvet above the royal chair. The arrangement of the other tables in the hall followed the design of the Coronation Banquet in London, a felicitous notion that can only have come from Scott. In the vaulted chambers below the hall – once prison-cells where suffering Covenanters had cried out for God's damnation upon their torturers – workmen scrubbed the walls, relaid the floors, installed the oil-lamps, spits, oven, boilers, carving-tables, racks, hooks and coal bunkers of the great kitchen needed for this one occasion only.

At seven o'clock in the evening of July 27, the steam-packet *James Watt* had briefly docked by the New Quay in Leith Harbour. There it was rapidly cleared of its cargo, before it steamed south to join the Royal Squadron then assembling in the Thames. Three of the King's carriages were unloaded from the ship that evening, including his principal travelling coach, and also a squad of Artillerymen who manhandled the vehicles across the Harbour Bridge to the barracks in the old citadel. This was the first clear indication to the generality of Edinburgh that the King would indeed be coming, and the news of it increased the steady flow of visitors to the city. Some came by foot, by horse, cart, stage-coach or private carriage, but the greatest number arrived by boat on the Union Canal. This ingenious waterway had been completed only a few months before, joining the Forth and Clyde and thus the two fiercely competitive cities of the

Lowlands. Unlike the reluctant Duke of Atholl, who delayed his arrival until it was clear he could not avoid it altogether, many of the nobility had begun to arrive at the end of July – the Buccleuch family to Barrie's Hotel in Princes Street, the Earls of Erroll, Fife and Morton to the Royal, and others where they could if they had not rented houses. To the irritation of most, there were no rooms available at Oman's, for although the dining-rooms of the Waterloo Hotel were open to the public, its apartments had been reserved for members of the King's suite – English and Scots who were coming with him from London. Now that the hapless Nairnes were gone, Breadalbane could leave his chambers at Holyrood to whatever use the King might make of them, and was perhaps not sorry. He was jealous of his rights and privileges, as was natural in a man whose recorded ancestry began five and a half centuries before, but he was aging and ailing, past ambition gone, and he can have had no wish to risk his health in the discomforts of the palace. He took a house in Saint Andrew Square where his fifty Campbells from Strathtay, when they came, could be seen by all as they strutted before its fine doorway.

Since almost all of the Scottish peers now coming into the city were Freemasons they were entitled or obliged to attend the meetings of the Committee on the National Monument. Having been given no promise that the King would attend the laying of the foundation stone, the members determined to make it an event nonetheless, announcing with pride that ten thousand Masons would attend the ceremony. Indeed, all citizens who had contributed £25 or more to this ill-starred recognition of the nation's nameless dead were invited to join a grand procession to the summit of Calton Hill, along a path which was 'extremely easy and practicable, the ascent not exceeding one foot in eighteen'.

It soon became clear that the King was not so much visiting Scotland as its principal city only. Until the week of his embarkation it had been widely assumed that he would make a leisurely progress which, if all the assumptions were correct, would have needed a season and more to complete. One of the wilder claims had been that he wished to visit the Hebrides in the *Royal George*, with occasional landings of his choice, notably the island of Staffa. Reporting this, the *Scotsman* asked if His Majesty would be required to pay the five or ten shillings which Sheriff Ranald MacDonald demanded from all visitors before he allowed them to slide and clamber among the basalt columns of his uninhabited isle. Once it was realized that the people must come to see the King, and not wait to be visited by him, Edinburgh happily embraced the profitable opportunities this presented. There was scarcely a shop-keeper, tradesman, craftsman, house-owner, inn, hotel, company or corporation whose energies were not directed toward the last penny to be got from the occasion. Nor was there an apparent end to the number of tailors and costumiers, hatters, milliners and jewellers eager to supply dresses, silks, shawls, hosiery, stays, cravats, tartans 'of all clans', ostrich feathers, lace ruffles and tiaras, knee-buckles and shoe-buckles of steel and silver, malacca canes, beaver hats and silk hats 'warranted to resist all moist or rain'. There were suppliers of uniforms to officers of the regular army, the yeomanry, militia and volunteers, and of course the well-buttoned blue coat and nankeen trousers so warmly recommended by Sir Walter and the Lord Provost. Enterprising though the tailoring trade was, it was surprised by the demand for new clothing and was soon forced to appeal for labourers skilled at cutting and sewing. Within a week, three hundred unemployed tailors who had been registered at the House of Call were put to work.

The acquisitive instincts of the city's tradesmen were sharpened by the early invasion of competitors from London. In the advertisements, sometimes placed in the Edinburgh press before their arrival, the English incomers did not disguise their belief that Scottish society was unable to clothe and conduct itself in the proper stylish manner. A costumier, 'Mr Williams of Saint James's Street, London' arrived before the end of July and like many who soon followed him, declared himself ready to supervise the making of dresses and court costumes for those gentlemen and ladies who might not be familiar with the latest modes and fashions. Nobody resented this condescension, for London was the fulcrum upon which the self-respect of the Scottish middle-class could be lifted, and tradesmen had long since learnt how to employ it. William Steven of North Bridge announced that he could supply every article of men's costumes for the Royal Visit, 'made and finished in a very experienced style by an expert tradesman from London'. Having acquired an

English bankrupt's stock of cheap silks, in every shade and colour, James Mackay of South Bridge advertised his 'good fortune in securing them through his agent in London', and advised those ladies who had hitherto honoured him with their custom to make an early call upon him, before rapid demand increased the unprecedented low prices. Mr John Scaife, of J. & A. P. Scaife, tailors of Bond Street, established temporary quarters in Princes Street opposite the Mound where he installed workmen from London. 'By this arrangement,' he said, 'the Nobility and Gentry will have the option of their orders being executed either in London or Edinburgh.' For those whose vanity out-stretched their purse, the House of Solomon & Company of Charing Cross sent its representative to Edinburgh with a supply of court dresses, steel swords, lace ruffles, and 'every article necessary for the King's Levee and Drawing-room, all to be available upon hire to such Gentlemen as may be unprovided.'

All commodities were hallowed by association with the southern capital. Thus Mr Barclay of Barclay & Sons announced that he had come from the Fleet Market in London where his family had conducted their business for a hundred years. He warned the people of Edinburgh that they were at grave risk from an unpleasant and troublesome disorder attendant upon human contact in celebratory crowds. The Itch, he said, could be effectually cured by one hour's application of *Barclays Original Ointment*, a plentiful supply of which would be found at selected vendors of medicines in the city. All sufferers should know, he said, that The Itch could afflict even the most respectable families, which may have been a surprise to those who thought it was common among Highlanders only. Less alarming was Mr Rowland who came from Hatton Garden with a supply of his Macassar Oil, recommending it as regularly used by the King's brother, the Duke of Sussex, and by the Tsar and Tsarina of Russia, as well as the Emperor of China. Available from all perfumers in Edinburgh, it was 'the best and cheapest article for nourishing the hair, preventing it falling off or turning grey, preserving it to the last period of life, and promoting a luxurious growth upon the baldest place'. It could also be used efficaciously during accouchements. One of the tradesmen from whom the Edinburgh alopeciac could acquire Mr Rowland's oil was Signor Gianetti, Perfumer and Patent Peruke-Maker of George Street. For the duration of the King's Visit, and for the accommodation of the Nobility and Gentry, he had increased his staff by assistants from London, 'all of whom have been in the habit of dressing Ladies for Court'.

For those who had the stomach for it, and wished to welcome the King to Scotland before he set foot upon it, the Leith, Hamburg and Rotterdam Shipping Company was the first to offer that exciting experience. Its fast sailing-cutter, the *Elbe*, six guns, under the command of Captain J. B. Forrest RN was now in Leith Harbour and in good time would make sail and put to sea again.

> ... for the purpose of joining the Royal Squadron off the mouth of the Frith. Should time and circumstance permit, it is proposed to give an opportunity to passengers of seeing the beautiful scenery on both sides of the Frith of Forth. Intending passengers should make early application for tickets, price One Guinea and a Half, at the Company's Office, West Dock. Provisions and refreshments to be had on board.

The streets of Edinburgh, Old Town and New Town, were never at rest now, from sunrise until well past its setting. Visitors and residents walked abroad as on holiday, wondering at the skeletal stands on Castle Hill, admiring the gunners at drill in the park of Holyroodhouse, the haughty Highlandmen about the door of 39, Castle Street, and the Celtic Society displaying its tartan on the green by Abercromby Place. At dusk, some climbed eight hundred feet to the top of Arthur's Seat. If they did not have a servant to relieve them of the burden, they carried the wood which Sir Walter had asked them to gather for the great bonfire that was to be lit upon the summit. When they paused to find their elusive breath, they were perhaps grateful for the purchase that morning of *Bathgate's Brunswick Corn Plasters*, 'for the Nobility and Gentry visiting Edinburgh, and prepared from a recipe belonging to her late Majesty'. Through the yellow smoke below, a haze becoming golden with the passing sun, they could see a string of fireflies along the Dalkeith road, where the workmen of the Edinburgh Gas Company were briefly testing their magical lamps.

Every day, it seemed, the newspapers reminded their readers of the direct link between His Majesty and a millennium of Scotland's kings. He was, said the *Courant*, 'lineally descended from our renowned Bruce, and has frequently spoken of this connection, which he seemed to be proud of; and well he may!' In the same heady mood of self-esteem, they were told that they lived in 'the second city in the British Empire, and consequently the second city in the world'. There were some, however, who endeavoured to keep a sense of proportion. The University of Edinburgh, having dutifully voted An Address to His Majesty, was aware of the unease felt by many of its distinguished academics, their disapproval of so much attention being given to the vainglory of costume and uniform, and their subjective concern, perhaps, for their own good appearance among so colourful a gathering. They were assured that court dress, in which all were expected to approach the Throne, was not expensive. Moreover, since members of Oxford and Cambridge Universities attended Court in their ordinary academicals, so might those of Edinburgh. Upon this vexing question of what to wear on the day the King was met, an extraordinary meeting of the Commission of the General Assembly of the Church of Scotland warned its ministers (many of whom were still awaiting word that His Majesty would worship with them) that 'there is a certain costume necessary for admission into the presence of royalty, every clergyman should if possible, bring with him a gown, which cannot be dispensed with'.

The port of Leith was now busy with traffic from the Thames. On the first Saturday of August the steam-packet *City of Edinburgh* arrived with one hundred great cases containing the King's plate and the King's great throne, all of which was brought ashore with care and loaded upon waiting carts. The throne was taken to Holyroodhouse under military escort and followed by a cheering crowd, and the cases of plate, resting upon cushions of straw, were taken to Dalkeith House. And finally, late in the day, crates of live poultry were lifted from the hold of the steamer and sent to Dalkeith also. The excitement such events caused was an indication of the city's emotional mood. There was a great sense of elation, a lightness of heart which John Grant of Rothiemurchus called 'a very entertaining and ludicrous state of bustle and expectation of the sedate and sober citizens of the Scottish Metropolis'. As if it were a household expecting the visit of a stylish and censorious relative of substantial station and means, the city also became hypersensitive about its traditional faults. For some, like James Simpson who had already complained to Scott, the first of these ancient evils was now a cause for outraged shame. The Old Town of Edinburgh was still a place of foul habits and fouler smells. Watching the Surveyor-General's working-men labouring in the policies of Holyroodhouse, and presumably receiving no satisfaction from them or from their immediate superiors, a self-styled *Caledonia* asked the editor of his newspaper whether the King would take a romantic stroll along the foot of Salisbury Craigs, and if he did should he not be warned that at the beginning of such a walk, close to the palace, he would discover

> ... the perfumes of a dung-trap, the proprietor of which is even now busily employed in spreading out its filthy contents, no doubt for the laudable purpose of putting his fellow citizens to shame with the compound 'Sweets of Auld Reekie'. What must strangers think when encountering this nest of nastiness in the refined city, 'the Athens of modern times'?

Little was done about this. The custom of collecting and selling night-soil close to Holyroodhouse was long-established, and there had been small complaint about it until now, except from appalled strangers. Inspector James Logan, in response or in reflex, reminded householders of their responsibilities under the Police Act of providing water-pipes, drains and channels leading to the common sewers. The King was at no risk from the foulness that so offended *Caledonia*, for he would not put a foot outside the palace except to step into his carriage.

The demand for lodgings – houses, a hotel suite, apartments, flats, single rooms, even a bed in a shared chamber – became more desperate as more visitors arrived. Yet as the need increased, so did the offered supply, and no longer was it important for the lodgings to be upon or close to the route of any procession the King might make. In the advertisements of the owners, all that was offered was perfection. *In consequence of His Majesty's Visit . . . to let, genteely furnished . . . a commodious well-furnished house . . . an upper flat at No. 42 . . . elegant accommodation for a few weeks . . . a dining-room, two bed-rooms, a kitchen, two cellars and a water-closet . . . A Good Family House . . . a Parlour and two Bed-Rooms . . . opposite the library and County Hall, four windows commanding a view of the High Street . . . a sitting-room, two bed-rooms, a place for a servant . . . a genteel lodging . . . use of plate, china, bed and table linen, also of a very superior Grand Piano-Forte . . . the use of a Library will be allowed, and a servant will give attention . . .*

The price of the lodgings offered was rarely mentioned in the advertisements, but was the subject of hard bargaining and frequent complaint. As Sir Alexander Mackenzie apologetically explained to Atholl, the rent of a town house suitable for a man of His Grace's station was absurdly high, and he may have thought that Atholl had acquired Lady Seaforth's house very cheaply at £100 for the duration of his stay. A house upon Frederick Street – beyond sight of any procession, but within earshot of Glengarry's piper playing before Sir Walter's door – could be rented at thirty guineas for two weeks, with the attendance of a servant if required. But lodgings on Leith Walk, in Picardy Place, Saint Andrew Square, or any street down which the King might ride, could be twice that sum, and all had been quickly taken upon the first strong rumours of the Visit. As the incomers increased during the second week of August, it became apparent that many of the houses so generously offered and rapidly taken could not happily accommodate all who wished to crowd into them. John Johnston, a woollen draper on North Bridge, offered one solution.

> At this period, when owing to the Royal visit of our Sovereign to this City, Beds cannot be obtained, nor even room fit to contain the common, bulky frame bed, the Public will find an excellent and convenient substitute in the HAMMOCK, manufactured by machinery by Robert M'Call of Glasgow, and just arrived here from the manufacturer.

During the daylight hours, and for much of the evening, there was the relentless and unrelaxing noise of iron upon stone, the clatter of hooves and the grinding of wheels. For every family of established position arriving in the city, there were two, three, and sometimes four horses to be stabled, a carriage to be housed, a coachman to be lodged. The Grants from Rothiemurchus came with two horses drawing their landau, and a saddle-horse ridden by William, a modest number compared with the requirements of larger households such as those of Atholl, Breadalbane or Erroll. In a crowded and fiercely competitive city, concern for their horseflesh took second place in the minds of most visitors, and they were glad of any stabling that could be obtained. The advertisements for this were as beguiling, and as dishonest no doubt, as those for lodgings. *Excellent stabling . . . a large coach-house and experienced ostler . . . two stables, high-roofed, containing eight stalls . . . at the White Hart, excellent stabling . . . fit for any Nobleman or Gentleman's carriage . . .* And for those who had come by stage or canal-boat, and now needed a hack or carriage horses . . . *a brown gelding, six years old . . . in Drummond Street for weekly hire, a horse thoroughly broke to carry a lady . . . a pair of handsome high-bred barouche horses, full sixteen hands . . . a young man has got four excellent bays fit for any Nobleman . . .*

Once lodged and stabled, the visitors had then to decide where and when to see the king, if they had not been wise enough to make this arrangement before coming to the city. The most desired spot was the waterside where the King would land. A place upon The Shore, the crescent-shaped street that embraced Leith Harbour, was the desire of all but the good fortune of a few only. The row of old houses that backed the street before it became a stone pier reaching out into the firth, were largely reserved for deserving notabilities of the town and city. The roadside was to be lined with soldiers, seamen, Archers, Celts, clansmen, magistrates of Leith and officials of its companies and corporations. The scaffolding dangerously balanced on the steep roofs of The Shore, and of the harbour buildings across the water, were the best the visitors could hope for, if indeed any space were now available there. Most looked elsewhere, for a window, a doorstep, a roof-top, a small space upon a stand somewhere along the route from Leith Harbour to the palace of Holyroodhouse. Those who were disappointed, too late or too exhausted, tried for a place upon the Royal Mile where they might see the King on his way to the Castle later in the Visit.

From Leith Walk to Holyroodhouse, by the Royal Mile to the Castle, almost any door, any window, any stretch of coping against an acrid chimney could be turned to profit if the site were advertised with grace. But windows accommodated too few and stands were soon built outside the house from the pavement to the first or second floor, and higher still upon the slates of the roof, providing space for ten or twenty times the number who might watch from a window. The magistrates did what they could to control the building of these fearsome erections, their slender poles held together by fists of rope, and their alarming defects hidden by patriotic bunting, but apart from a few that collapsed during or within hours of their erection, there would be one serious calamity only. The public's hunger for seats upon a stand overcame any doubt about its ability to support the weight of so much movement and emotion. Here and there a householder did consider the risks taken by his competitors, and smugly assured the public that the seats he offered were perfectly safe 'under the superintendence of two professional men, viz. an architect and a builder appointed by the Baillies'. In confident defiance of the laws of gravity, therefore, and of Edinburgh's unpredictable weather, the stands were advertised with public-spirited enthusiasm.

Offering a most interesting view of His Majesty ... a most commanding view of His Majesty ... A grand platform at the foot of Leith Walk, tickets by application to Mr M'Lean, stationer ... a safe and comfortable stand just now erecting in Constitution Street adjoining Dr Colquhoun's Chapel ... the whole procession will be viewed without interruption ... allowed to be equal if not superior to most of the places in the city ...

The early August days were warm and gentle, with no more rain than an overnight shower to lay the dust and wash the streets free of their more noxious smells. Anticipation of the King's coming was whetted by smaller pleasures. In all the attention William Murray was giving to the staging of Scott's dramatic spectacles, and most particularly to his own preparations for the Peers' Ball, he was still able to re-decorate the Theatre Royal for the King's expected attendance, regilding its plaster, making a new entrance to the Royal Box from the office, and draping the box itself in fine crimson. To entertain Edinburgh until it came to see the play he was rehearsing for the King, the company re-staged his dramatization of Scott's *Heart of Midlothian*, 'with the Original Scenery, Machinery, Dresses and Decorations'. His sister, Mrs Harriet Siddons, played Jeanie Deans, a relief perhaps from her daily efforts to teach Court manners and deportment to coltish young ladies from the country. At the conclusion of every performance Mr Mackay, who played the Laird of Dumbiedikes, lifted his fine tenor voice and sang all verses and chorus 'of the popular National Ballad, *CARLE NOW THE KING'S COME!*'

It was a season and it was the weather for walking abroad in the evening, the gentlemen dressed as far as their purse or their disposition allowed in the national costume devised by Scott. A gentle climb to the top of Calton Hill, less arduous than an ascent of Arthur's Seat, was now a favoured outing before dusk, and an opportunity to see the carts and tools, the assembled stones of the great monument. There was also the Nelson Tower, a bizarre column of commemoration rising from a rock-bound shrubbery. The rooms in its broad base had originally been planned as a home for disabled seamen, but were now used for the sale of refreshments, and the view from their windows, according to the proprietor, was 'considered to be equal to any in the world, the Bay of Naples not excepted'. Also unmatched was his establishment, 'its apartments, neatly fitted up where Breakfasts, Confections, Soup, Jellies, Ices, Pastry, Fruits, Tea, Coffee and Mineral Waters may also be had, no Liquors of any kind sold'. The association with Lord Nelson, and perhaps with his distressed seamen, was maintained by the display of a letter in the Admiral's own hand. For a shilling, visitors could climb a winding stairway to the castellated top of the tower, and a view of the city and firth that was breathtaking indeed.

The oddest visitors to the tower this August were a small family from Lapland – Jens, a herdsman, his wife Marine and their child. With a portable hut, and a few reindeer, they had been brought to Britain by William Bullock who had hopes of domesticating and farming the animal. This had proved impracticable and the family had become a raree-show. Harriet Arbuthnot, who went to see them in London, thought them most grotesque, 'excessively ugly, dark-complexioned, and no taller than children of 12 years old in this country'. As interest in them faded, they came to Edinburgh where they were said to be happier, preferring its climate to London, but it was difficult to know what they thought. When the building in which they appeared was needed for more profitable use during the King's Visit, news that they were thus obliged to leave the city revived public interest and brought the offer of another showroom near the Theatre Royal. There they were now, wearing skins and furs and sitting before their hut with a few tools and instruments. Their reindeer were sometimes said to be of greater interest, although it was agreed that the animals were not as pleasing to the eye as a fine Highland stag. To maintain public interest in the curiosity of their presence, the Laplanders were one day taken to the top of Calton Hill. They patiently submitted to the public's close scrutiny, until Jens led his three reindeer up the winding steps to the gallery of the tower. He remained there for an hour, alone, and in longing for his homeland perhaps.

Edinburgh was now rich with uniforms, not only Scott's bluecoats and the tartan of Garth's Highlanders, but the scarlet of footsoldiers, the blue and green of volunteer cavalry. They were present upon the orders of Sir Thomas Bradford, to be quartered in barracks or billets beyond the suburbs, and employed when needed as guards, escorts and sentinels, mercenary spear-carriers in Sir Walter's pageant. In Bradford's opinion, they were also an essential precaution against disorder. An Englishman from the north country, he was regarded by many as the man who had saved Scotland from Radical Terror, and was no doubt pleased to think so himself. He had served in the Peninsula under Wellington, and also in France, and had fought the Irish in the Rebellion of '98. He had been Commander-in-Chief in Scotland for three years, and if he lacked the drawing-room graces so essential to a general officer in peacetime, he had proved himself to be able, reliable and ruthless in face of civil unrest.

In his suppression of the weavers' revolt, Bradford had made frequent use of Volunteer Yeomanry from the Lowlands and the Borders, young men with whom John Lockhart had ridden to the great approval of his father-in-law. If they lacked the discipline and experience of regular soldiers, it was Bradford's opinion that they could make up the omission with their fierce hatred of the Radicals. Now they wished their services during the insurrection to be rewarded with a summons to guard the King and ride before him in all the absurd splendour of their fanciful uniforms. Most eager among them were the Glasgow Light Horse, and of them the most pressing was a young captain, James Oswald of Shieldhall, whose belief it was that 'almost all the lower classes were contaminated and ready to enter into any plan of rebellion'.* With the permission of his

* His estate was eventually absorbed by the expanding city of Glasgow, and became the site of the workshops and factories of the Scottish Wholesale Co-operative Society.

colonel, he offered his troop to Bradford, without pay and with a promise to serve the King in any way His Majesty desired. Bradford sent this and similar requests to Robert Peel, with his own wish to know whether the King would indeed inspect his Yeomanry forces in Scotland. The Secretary passed the letters to Hobhouse with his endorsement, *The King will see the Yeomanry*, and Captain Oswald was told that his troop would join detachments of the Royal Midlothian Cavalry, the Stirling Yeomanry, the Fife Yeomanry, and other mounted regiments of young amateurs. Each passed through Edinburgh during the first days of August, trotting along the streets to the music of their trumpets, metal-bright and leather-polished, their commanders' swords dipping in response to the cheers.

More reliable in the mundane trade of soldiering were the four regular regiments, Horse and Foot, which Bradford quartered about the city. The first was Scotland's only cavalry regiment, the 2nd Dragoons, Scots Greys, each a tall man in scarlet, made taller by his high fur helmet and more fearsome by the downward jut of its visor. Since their spectacular charge at Waterloo they were sometimes spoken of as 'The Immortals', a hard-won title, if not paradoxical, for they had lost more than half of their strength in killed and wounded during that action.

Although fortuitous, no doubt, there was an irony in the selection of the three English marching-regiments – the 13th, the 66th and the 77th. Seven companies of the 66th came from Sunderland to Edinburgh, marching up the Dalkeith road to the storm of its leading drums. Not long before, it had disembarked from Saint Helena where it had been the gaoler of the exiled Emperor of France. Its officers had politely endured Napoleon's courtesy and condescension, and its men had suffered rats and mosquitoes, dysentery and typhus until their duty was relieved by the death of their prisoner. Napoleon's surrender and request for protection after Waterloo, written before he went aboard the *Bellerophon*, had been addressed to 'the most powerful, the most constant, the most generous of my enemies', the man whom the 66th had now come to guard in Edinburgh.

When the Duke of Atholl first saw the double numerals on the black shakoes of the 77th his memory may have stirred uneasily. The regiment was formed in 1787, and was given a number made available by the disbandment of its previous holder. This had been the 77th Highland Regiment, raised in the Duke's name when he was a young man, and recruited largely from his and his neighbours' estates in Perthshire. Enlisted upon an assurance that they would be required to serve no longer than the war against the American colonists, the Highlanders mutinied when an attempt was made to send them to India after that conflict ended. They held the town of Portsmouth under arms for a week until Parliament compelled the Secretary at War to give them their due discharge. They were marched northward to Berwick and there disbanded, condemned as 'insolent cowards' by their officers, but singing their own defiant rant of protest.

The red jackets and yellow facings of the 13th had been familiar to Lowland Scots since 1818, but its association with the country was older still. As Pulteney's Regiment of Foot in 1746, a veteran Flanders battalion, it was moved from the reserve to the right flank of Cumberland's army at Culloden, and there its sustained platoon-fire helped to halt, break and then repel the charge of Clan Donald. During the Radical War it was employed in the brutal policing that followed Bonnymuir and thus, it was said, became the most-hated of all English regiments in Scotland. It guarded the Courts where the weavers were tried, and it surrounded the scaffold upon which Andrew Hardie and John Baird were hanged and beheaded. Sir Thomas Bradford thought well of its service during the insurrection, and its presence now in Edinburgh may perhaps be seen in the context of that opinion.

> *'On Sunday I went to the Kirk, and as the poor*
> *box was much exhausted during the winter, I*
> *put into it a Bank of England £5 note, with*
> *your Lordship's name on the envelope . . . It*
> *was quite necessary, and may be contemned or*
> *not, as is done in Sutherland, as your Lordship*
> *pleases, in the mean time they consider it as*
> *coming directly from your own pocket. A few*
> *old wives had got a little meal, this I have put*
> *in her Ladyship's name, which likewise*
> *prevents it being made a precedent.*
>
> – JAMES LOCH to Lord Stafford, 1829

Sir Humphrey Davy, natural philosopher and experimental scientist, had no wish to stay in Edinburgh for the King's Visit. His tour of Scotland, particularly Inverness and Ross, had been arranged earlier in the year and he was disinclined to change his plans now. Before he left Oman's Hotel on 26 July, intending to enjoy a day's fishing on the Tay while travelling north, he wrote to the Duke of Atholl. When he passed through Perthshire, he said, he would call upon his Grace and accept a long-standing invitation to visit Dunkel House, unless the Atholls had left for Edinburgh. Indeed, they would of course be gone, 'all arrangements must of necessity be in connection with the Royal Visit'. Meanwhile, until they did meet, his Grace was informed that their friend Dr John MacCulloch, the distinguished geologist, needing but a change of air to be rid of the lingering remains of ague, would soon resume those activities so important to Science and their country. Sir Humphrey's reasons for his Highland journey, beyond killing a salmon on the Tay or the Ness, were to cultivate the company of such men, and to enjoy a long talk with the Duke upon scientific matters of mutual interest.

I have been examining the Hyaena's den at Kirkdale in Yorkshire, where amongst the bones of various extinct species on which those Monsters fed are some of the Great Elk. I recognised the same bones in examining the magnificent specimen presented by Your Grace to the Museum here.

Other distinguished men were arriving in Edinburgh for the event, rather then fleeing from it. Joseph Mallord William Turner came a few days after Davy had gone north on the Highland Coach, among the first of the score or so artists who would record the Visit in their own style, according to their own taste, or to the wish of rich patrons. In his tall hat, his old-fashioned coat with a red handkerchief flying from its swallow-tail pocket, Turner's presence was unremarked by the press. He did not seek the company of other artists and preferred a contemplative view from the periphery of events – sitting in a bobbing boat as it was rowed from ship to ship in Leith Roads, or leaning against a column in Saint Giles as he worked upon his sketch-book. He covered a hundred pages with fragments of visual thought – again and again the profile of Salisbury Craigs or Castle Hill, a curve of hunched shoulders in a crowd, the listless drape of a banner, the graceful lines of the Royal Yacht, a Highland bonnet, the pattern of stonework, and an evocative view of the Canongate from the Half Moon Battery of the Castle. Sometimes he wrote a brief colour-guide on the page to hold the memory. *White masts . . . blue cloth . . . green oar . . . scarlet platform . . . gold on blue ground . . . black . . . 6 ports . . . smoke coloured . . .*

He was a dark, private man, short in speech and seemingly indifferent to friendship at times. His association with Scott, with whom he collaborated on a collection of poems, became no closer than each desired, and their professional opinions sometimes clashed. In the waiting days before the King came to Edinburgh he was rarely seen by those few who would have recognized him. On one occasion, however, he was observed outside Oman's, one of a group on the triangular wedge of pavement formed by Leith Street and Regent Bridge. It was perhaps the only time he was in the company of other artists, for all had assembled in the Waterloo Hotel that morning, to meet Scott and his committee and be given the programme of events. After that, Turner avoided committees and all those whom he perhaps suspected of a desire to direct his pencil and brushes. He liked Scotland and the Scots he knew, and during this visit he would make a new friend, James Skene of Rubislaw, a member of Scott's committee and an amateur artist. Left to himself, as he wished, Turner wandered in and out of the city's celebrations. From the wind and the storm, the mist and rain of his imagination he would produce nothing that satisfied his patrons or pleased His Majesty. His painting of the King in Saint Giles would be too human, its atmosphere too bourgeois to please a monarch overcome by the sycophancy of his reception in Scotland. The wild sweep of Turner's brush in his *March of the Highlanders*, whereby a torrent of kilted men surges upon North Bridge, does not picture a true event during the Visit, or even the Highlanders as they were, but how men like Scott wished them to be. And that illusion, perhaps, was what Turner intended to paint.

Other artists who produced illustrations of the Visit included Alexander Naysmyth, William Home Lizars, John Thomson, Alexander Carse and Denis Dighton. The last was the most talented member of a family of military painters, and his imagination was stirred by the Highlanders he saw in the streets. At Alasdair Ranaldson's request, he made vivid pencil portraits of Glengarry and some of his red-shanked foresters, and may well have worked upon the canvas for which they seem to be preliminary sketches. He was English, but most of the attending artists were Scots, some resident in the city. Of recent acquaintance, David Wilkie and William Collins came together from England, one a Scot also, the other an Anglo-Irish-Scot. They travelled with commissions already secured, from Peel, Liverpool and others, to record any event that inspired them, but also those which their patrons desired. Their quasi-official status, and the need to make their way without hindrance through barricades and military lines, required influential accreditation. This they had jointly obtained in a letter of recommendation from Lord Liverpool. He referred to them as 'two of our eminent artists', and asked Lord Chief Commissioner William Adam to

> . . . afford them all the assistance in your power in order that they may see the different ceremonies in the most advantageous manner as I am satisfied there are no Spectators from whose presence the Public and Posterity will derive so much benefit.

Liverpool also told Scott that Wilkie had already made sketches for a great canvas, *John Knox preaching at St. Andrews before the Lords of the*

Congregation. The King had seen these and decided that he would prefer something more humorous. Liverpool had first agreed, but now asked Scott to give Wilkie what help he could with the historical detail. Collins wished to paint the King's landing at Leith, 'after the manner of Cuyp', and in Liverpool's opinion there was no artist more qualified for such work. This may have been true, but Collins' principal reason for coming to Edinburgh at this time was decidedly more personal. He and Wilkie were both in their mid-thirties. The more established of the two, Wilkie was a successful painter in the tradition of his country's best artists. He had known Scott for some years, and although their association was not as active as that with Turner, it was unmarred by the confrontation of conflicting minds. Scott admired and liked him, and had first invited him to Abbotsford with the detailed travelling instructions that characteristically expressed his hospitable pleasure.

> A coach passes three times a week within a mile of my door; it is called the Blucher, and tickets are issued at the Black Bull, Leith Walk; its destination is Melrose and Jedburgh, but my guests stop at the turnpike gate at the end of Melrose bridge, where I will meet you.

Wilkie's professional response to the noisy confusing days he spent with 'the laird' at Abbotsford in 1817 had been a painting of ingenuous charm, a group in which Scott appears as a straddling old rustic surrounded by family and friends. It had been a joking suggestion by one of the friends, but was taken as an excellent notion by Wilkie, a sadly humourless man, with solemn and sometimes death-like features. The coach journey from London to Edinburgh, claustrophobic in an ill-sprung box of wood and leather, must have been a greater strain upon him, for Collins' sense of humour expressed itself in schoolboy puns. They travelled with another Scots painter, Andrew Geddes, who put Collins in such high spirits that he had emptied Geddes' snuff-box before they reached Berwick. At least this pleased Wilkie, for he abhorred both snuff and tobacco. Collins' admiration for his new friend was affectionate and strong. He told his family that Wilkie had been able to draw before he could write, and that when he was a child in his father's manse he would borrow a scoured stool and sketch upon it with a carpenter's pencil. At intervals during that rocking unending journey they were sometimes serious, discussing what they would most prefer to be their subjects in Edinburgh. Apart from the King's landing, Collins had no firm intention, but Wilkie was passionately determined to make the King the centre of 'a fine historical piece', perhaps at the entrance to Holyroodhouse, or in the High Kirk of Saint Giles.

On the first morning of their arrival they plunged eagerly into the heady atmosphere of the city. They delivered their letter of introduction to the Lord Chief Commissioner who took them to see Mr Trotter's preparations at Holyroodhouse. There they met Adam Ferguson, the old Peninsula warrior for whom Scott had secured the new post of Keeper of the Regalia. He told them that The Laird expected to see them soon at Castle Street. 'Collins has got a new coat,' Wilkie wrote to his sister that night, 'which he has been sporting to-day; but I tell him to wait until my sky-blue comes to hand, and I shall then be a match for him.'

What William Collins desired most from Edinburgh was his marriage to Andrew Geddes' sister, Harriet. Their leisurely love affair had all the characteristics of a fashionable novel. They had known each other for eight years and had long ago accepted the fact that marriage was impossible without the approval of their parents, most particularly Mrs Collins. By invoking the terms of a tiresome if transitory Marriage Act, she was withholding her permission until her son's income from his profession was substantial enough for the marriage she thought most proper. Believing that she would accept a *fait accompli*, and growing increasingly impatient, Collins had now decided to take advantage of Scotland's laws, or any law relevant to the situation, and at last be wed. Once arrived in Edinburgh, he sent Harriet instructions on how she should come to the city, and with whom as her chaperone. He and his friends were lodged with Samuel Joseph the sculptor (at that moment working on a fine bust of the King, without a sitting). Mrs Joseph was willing to give Harriet a room in the house that 'we might spend a short time in Scotland, and return to London, cemented by that tie which, please God, may brighten our present prospects'. The marriage, when it finally took place in the English Episcopal Church on York Place, was conducted by the Reverend Dr Allan, 'author of the celebrated work on Taste'.

Another love-sick man also came to Edinburgh, but to find release from his thraldom rather than make its chains secure. The Honourable Edward Fox, aged twenty, was the third son of the third Lord Holland. He was an intelligent, cultured snob, infatuated by what he believed to be his clear perception of the weaknesses of others. He was not a credit to the influence of the Whig circle over which his mother presided at Holland House, and at this early stage of his life may well have thought himself superior to it. He was a delicate young man with an affliction of the hip, which may explain something of his intellectual impatience. He had been educated by a tutor and a bishop and thus his mind, while individual and incisive, had few windows to the realities of the world, such as the correct explanation of Lady Scott's red cheeks and shortness of breath. Round-faced, with a domed forehead and calm, waiting eyes, his entrée to any house was secured by the nature of his birth. He came to Edinburgh upon his father's bidding, a parental hope that he would thus rid himself of his infatuation for yet another Harriet, the daughter of George Canning. Young Fox's miserable state of mind was largely due to the knowledge that she could shortly depart with her family for India, of which her father had been nominated Governor-General.

Fox left London on the evening of Thursday 8 August, travelling with the Earl of Ancram, the first son of the Marquis of Lothian. They were young and impatient, certain of their ability to endure strain and exhaustion, and thus they journeyed the long distance without stopping, except for the regular but brief halts for a change of post-horses. Ancram was an agreeable and good-natured man, but although Fox believed him well-informed he seems to have spent much of the journey talking about the girl he loved and hoped to marry, Elizabeth Grey. He praised her incessantly, she was the best rider, the best dancer, and so on . . . When their coach reached Durham, Ancram insisted they should drive on and change horses at the Lambton Arms in Chester-le-Street, because the ostler at Durham had once been rude to Miss Grey. Reflecting that changing horses at a house allied by name to the Whig interest was perhaps 'out of the Tory line', Fox later noted the incident in his journal with an ambiguous comment, *This looks well!'*. By noon on Friday, sixteen hours after leaving London, they arrived at Newbattle Abbey, the

Lothian home. Fox was once more favourably disposed toward his tendentious companion, even envious. 'I hope sincerely he will marry Elizabeth Grey.'

With the inbred confidence that only the best could befall him, Fox had made no arrangements for his lodgings in Edinburgh. It was enough that one met people who knew one's people. He drove into the city with Ancram on Saturday morning, and quickly decided that it was in a state of wild confusion. He called upon Lord Lauderdale who, of course, offered the young man lodgings in his town house. Fox occupied the rooms for two days, during which he visited Francis Jeffrey, once a youthful duellist, now an eminent judge, co-founder and editor of the *Edinburgh Review*. Fox was amused to hear that the old man was alarmed lest the King should offer to knight him during the Visit, but Mrs Jeffrey seemed half-distracted by the notion. On Monday he accompanied Lauderdale to Holyroodhouse where he was introduced to Lady Breadalbane. He thought her a sensible woman 'with a true *Scotch* understanding', as indeed he might, for she offered him a lodging in those palace rooms for which Breadalbane had no use. The Earl was not present for Mr Fox's critical scrutiny. He was away out upon his affairs, no doubt inspecting the swathes of green tartan which his agent had bought in Glasgow, and which should now make his Campbells the best-dressed Highlanders in the city.

Castle Street was also host to an unexpected guest, although he had a long-standing invitation to visit Abbotsford. George Crabbe, the Suffolk poet, had made the acquaintance of Scott a decade before, but until this year their friendship had been conducted by correspondence only. He was a simple, self-taught man, cast from a mould more common in Scotland than it was in England. He was now approaching seventy and in his long and varied life he had been a warehouseman and the servant to a doctor, had studied botany and practised surgery, was rector of several parishes, a pamphleteer and a journalist, but above all this, or at least most constantly, he was a poet. At the beginning of July 1822 he wrote to Scott saying he had a strong desire to see Edinburgh and wished to know when and where they might meet. Scott's reply was an effusive welcome. The 'Royal motions', he said, were still uncertain. If the King did come he would have have to be in Edinburgh for a day or two. He assumed Crabbe would prefer to avoid that time and place of tumult, 'though if your health permitted it would be a curious sight to see'. Crabbe was advised to take the steam-boat from the Thames to Leith, a journey quickly over in sixty hours, and as pleasant as sitting in an easy chair. He could then take the Blucher from Leith Walk, another seven hours to travel the thirty-five miles from Edinburgh to Galashiels, where the Abbotsford carriage would await him. Scott worried at the thought of an old man, seemingly so fragile, travelling alone, and told him that he could stay at Abbotsford for as long as he liked.

Crabbe gave due thought to Scott's instructions and then decided he would come by the Great Carlisle Coach. When he reached the Edinburgh stage-house he sent his man Hollis to Castle Street to announce his arrival, coming there himself at dusk. Scott was fully occupied with preparations for what he now called 'The King's Jaunt', but he welcomed his aged visitor with great courtesy and honour. Crabbe had told Scott that he had heard much about the Royal motions, but did not think they should cause him to alter his plans. 'I can shrink into myself, and snail-like keep to my own private Apartments till all the Form and Circumstance be past.' Instead of this, he was comfortably installed in one of the best rooms in Castle Street, close to the tumultuous events taking place within and without the house. He watched them all with childlike incredulity. He was happy and well, he wrote to his son. Sir Walter, who was busier than any man in England at this moment, was doing all he could to make Crabbe comfortable.

> Not only that, for here are friends. . . . Here is Mr Mackenzie – with surprise I heard it – the author of *The Man of Feeling* and indeed he is so called. Here is Mr Jeffrey to whom I always count myself obliged. Here is Mr Lockhart, Sir Walter's son-in-law, and his pleasant wife. Here is Mr Murry with whom I dined today, and lastly, not lastly for there are many more, but here is Mr Blackwood, the Editor of the Magazine which goes under his name.

All was bustle and a continual stream of visitors, the wildest of whom was 'the Highland Chieftain and his officers and followers', undoubtedly Alasdair Ranaldson in a bold swing of tartan and a clatter of weapons. Lady Scott, kindness itself to her husband's many callers, was the leading member of the Sisters of the Silver Cross, ladies of Edinburgh so called from the gift they were preparing for the King, in the hope that Sir Walter would present it on their behalf. There were evenings of wine and music that puzzled the old poet's head, each more enjoyable than before, the music becoming wilder and the grand city more wonderful beyond the candle-glow of Castle Street. Crabbe assured his son – as indeed he had promised Mr Blackwood, who would perhaps publish them – that he would employ some of his time on the composition of a few verses in honour of the King's Visit. Not only because of the occasion, but because 'I should like to earn a little money during this excursion.'

Few strangers called upon Scott without an unexpected surprise. The French author, Amédée Pichot, was astonished when the door of Castle Street was opened by a footman in blue and yellow livery, a powdered wig upon his head. When he saw Scott at his writing-table in the library, his majestic head and charming smile, Pichot could scarcely believe that this gentleman was the bourgeois whom he had met in the street the day before, a man in country clothes with sweat upon his face. He might have been more perplexed had he known that the footman was Scott's coachman, Peter Mathieson, so dressed for the brief time of the Visit only, that he might give style to the family's old sociable when he drove the Scotts about the city.

The landau bringing the Grants of Rothiemurchus reached Inverkeithing above North Queensferry before dusk on Friday 9 August. The road before and behind them was crowded with carriages, waiting their turn for crossing the firth. The girls were in a happy but melancholy mood. An hour since at Kinross, John Grant had indulged their romantic fancies by taking them to Loch Leven. Two men in a small boat rowed them out to the little island and the ruined castle where Mary Queen of Scots had been imprisoned, and from which she had escaped with the help of the young and besotted Willie Douglas. Jane Grant had not realized how small, how wretched it would be. 'How could men be so barbarous as to confine a woman in such a miserable little building?' When the Grants dined at the hotel in Kinross they met three young Englishmen on their way north to shoot, and not a bit excited by the King's Visit. William Grant knew one of them, and they greeted each other languidly. The girls thought them bizarre, 'three fair, fine young figures wrapped up in fantastick clothes of tartan velvet, with curious things on their heads by way of hats'.

The Grants were taken across the Forth at seven o'clock that evening, 'horses, carriage and all, very quickly and so easily as really to make this once ticklish passage no trouble at all'. The steam-boat had been at work all day, sometimes with passengers 'loaded as thick as they could stand'. Because it was late, and there were no horses yet for a change, the Grants spent the night in Hall's Inn on the south shore. There was time for the girls to write to Elizabeth, for fitful sleep and an early breakfast. Then a bowling drive in a long line of carriages, all moving in steady haste toward Edinburgh, its distant roofs and the dark prow of its rock coming closer with every turn of the road.

Lodged in King Street, there was much for them to do before the week's end and the expected arrival of the King, not the least a call upon Mrs Siddons in Picardy Place. She lived in a theatrical style that brought the Grant girls close to swooning, 'a beautiful drawing-room on the ground floor, beautifully furnished – muslin draperies excluding half the light; sofa tables covered with flowers and nick-nacks; the grand piano-forte, the guitar . . .'. Here Mrs Siddons worked when not upon her brother's stage, creating her little hats (two of which hung as pretty examples at the entrance to the house), making or re-making some of the gowns to be worn at the Drawing-Room or the Peers' Ball. Here she taught curtseying, retiring, and all the graces necessary for a lady presented to her King. To the delight of the Grants, and as if she were making a grand entrance at the Theatre Royal, she demonstrated the perfect curtsey, and the wide sweep of a gown upon turning. The Grants were to watch the King's arrival from an upstairs window at Picardy Place, and having been told that it was etiquette for young ladies to wear a cap upon such an occasion, they went to the dressmaker, Miss Jolly, where they purchased two, and some ostrich feathers to be dipped in a special pearl colour. Miss Jolly was also making their satin ball gowns which, but for one small fault, were most satisfactory. Hats, gowns, feathers, the expense to Papa was frightening. The box containing more clothes from Doune arrived that night on the Highland Coach, everything packed beautifully and nothing crushed. Mr Grant and William went to the theatre with Mrs Siddons, and later walked home through the cool streets at leisure, with the actress between them and holding their arms. All was excitement, too much excitement. The girls, who had stayed at their lodgings to curl their hair, finally succumbed to the strain. Mary Frances contracted a pain in her chest, and Jane was violently sick.

That night John Grant wrote to his wife. All was well, and it had been immensely gratifying to show off his son and daughters to Edinburgh. The city was in an entertaining and ludicrous state, of course, with the 'whimsical affectation of a sort of highland costume, with about as much propriety in the conception and execution as if it had taken place in Paris or Brussels'. Everybody – and by that he meant men of rank and quality – everybody was sending presents of game for His Majesty's table. Possessing the highest mountains in the King's dominions, Grant thought he should offer ptarmigan. He asked his wife to send two gillies up the glen to kill as many as they could, and one of the men could stay upon the hill in case more were needed. He ended the short letter with a postscript, including a reassurance. 'Mrs Siddons has undertaken to *drill* the girls and they are to dress at her house. She has fixed on a good hairdresser.' The rich forest of Rothiemurchus was making all things possible.

The wood and combustibles taken to Arthur's Seat for the bonfire now made a prodigious mound. The lower slopes of Calton Hill were pricked by the white bell-tents of the artillerymen who had placed twelve guns upon its summit. Six more cannon, with their varnished limbers, were set upon Salisbury Craigs above the Powder House, symbolically trained across the city to the Lowland plain. The illumination of Edinburgh, planned for the evening of the King's arrival, promised to be spectacular. Every window facing a street was to be lit, if only by one of *Bathgate's Special Moulded Candles*. Every corporation, society and association, every trader, every family of rank or self-esteem was preparing a display of burning crowns, thistles, saltires and unrecognizable flowers, heraldic animals, the representation of great events from the nation's history, or stirring incidents from the well-known works of the Author of

Waverley. New variegated lamps were promised, of exceptional brilliance, throwing all manner of hues and colours from behind delicate transparencies. These manifestations were not confined to residents of the city alone. The Magistracy of Glasgow, having stomached its disappointment with the King's refusal to visit the city, was to thrust itself upon Edinburgh's complacency in a blaze of light. The Magistrates had already reserved lodgings for themselves in Queen Street, with stabling and quarters for eighteen horses, the Lord Provost's great coach, his coachmen, footmen, and postillions, all in a special livery. Above the Magistrates' lodgings, or elsewhere if more effective, they proposed to erect 'illuminated transparencies emblematical of Commerce and Manufacture'. And, of course, the city's defiant exhortation was to be spelt out in coloured lights, LET GLASGOW FLOURISH!

A great many of Glasgow's citizens were following their Magistrates eastward. It was said that the number was scarcely credible. Money could no longer buy or hire a carriage in the western city, even stage-coaches were now privately engaged. Extra boats had been put into service upon the Canal, yet they too could not carry all who wished to travel, and coal-punts were being rapidly cleaned and prepared for use as passenger barges. In two days only, two and a half thousand people were carried by water from Port Dundas on the Clyde to Grangemouth on the Forth. Those who could not obtain a place upon boat or barge walked along the tow-path for thirty-five miles, and then another twenty into Edinburgh. Such patriotic fervour, when reported by an admiring press, maintained the high temperature of enthusiasm. It was heartening, for example, to read of the determination of eight weavers from Dalry, in the valley of the Carnock and, most felicitously, the land of Sir Walter's Lochinvar. Uncorrupted by the Radical sentiments of their brotherweavers, they set out for Edinburgh at the beginning of August, ready to walk seventy miles or more to Edinburgh. Pausing at a change-house in Glasgow, they kept its landlord awake all night and spent only four shillings in drink. They had brought their own boiled ham, boiled eggs, cheese and bannocks, enough to feed them for ten days, they said.

At this time the *Edinburgh Observer* reported that the city would shortly be invaded by 'a host of gentlemen who are able to make what is weak powerful, and great things small'. This was perhaps the earliest expression of what would in time become the traditional mockery of London newspapers by the press outside the capital. Almost all the great English journals sent representatives to Edinburgh, where they were shepherded, harried and confused by Sir Patrick Walker. As White Rod, and deeply sensitive of his rights and duties which no one but himself could properly define, he was allowed to exercise a brief authority over the issue of tickets admitting journalists to privileged positions at great events. In return, they treated him with little respect, or so he thought. Competitive journalism was still in its infancy, if yet to be born, and the English correspondents in Edinburgh set aside all hostility for the more agreeable practice of combining their information and sending almost identical dispatches. Approval or disapproval of the King, and the King's reception, was left to their editors in London.

The *Edinburgh Observer* was the emotional trumpet of Scotland's loyalty, and deeply contemptuous of the Radical scepticism of the *Scotsman*. With commendable enterprise it announced that it would increase the number of its editions during the Royal Visit, to keep the public informed as early as possible and, although its resources would not prove equal to that ambition, its panting literary style never flagged. Within hours of the arrival of the King it would publish its declaration of faith, and thereby, of course, the faith of all true Scots. Upon the death of the last male heir to the Stuart cause (albeit fifteen years before), the Jacobite party had become completely triumphant. By this apparent paradox the *Observer* was saying that the House of Hanover had inherited the sacred mantle of the House of Stuart. The bitterness of old disputes could be forgotten in a remarkable transfiguration.

> We are now all Jacobites, thorough-bred Jacobites, in acknowledging George IV. This seems to be one of the feelings that stimulate the people here, at the present time, to make such exertions. Our King is the heir of the Chevalier, in whose service the Scotch suffered so much, shone so much, and he will find many a Flora MacDonald amongst the 'Sisters of the Silver Cross', and many a faithful Highlander attending his Throne with the forester's bugle and bow.

Although the Jacobite King was not yet present, all the King's horses and most of the King's men were come. The first animals to arrive were his carriage-horses, twelve splendid bays that were disembarked at Dunbar. When Mr Billing, senior coachman of the Royal Stables, was satisfied that none was any the worse from the voyage, he took the trotting string of mettlesome beasts into the city, and was cheered all the way to Smith's Stables in Thistle Street. That same evening, the King's riding-horses – two bays, two greys and four hackneys – were brought ashore and taken down to Dalkeith House. Here the King's food was slowly filling kitchens, larders and ice-house. The poultry which had come from London with the King's plate – no bird weighing less than seven pounds – had been delivered to Mr Spike the Royal Poulterer, much to his relief, no doubt, for upon his arrival in the city he had been told that the King would eat nothing that was not the product of his northern realm. The source of this imaginative report was Mr Florance, Purveyor to the King, who had established an extensive dairy at Dalkeith within a few days of his arrival from London. Only the best butter and cream, he announced, would be kept for the King's pleasure. The rest, and the buttermilk, would be distributed among the poor.

Of the King himself, there could be no news now that would reach the city earlier than his arrival. Good weather, it was said, as well as the churning efforts of his side-wheelers, should bring him rapidly to his loyal Scots. On Sunday 12 August, and again on Monday, eager crowds gathered on Calton Hill, waiting for that truly *British* sight, a naval squadron under full sail, heeling to a spanking wind. Although he knew the King could not arrive before Tuesday, Atholl also went up the hill, standing in the lee of the tower with a glass to his eye, watching the blue water beyond Gullane Point. There was much to fret his patience – the bickering of his deputy-lieutenants still worried about their uniforms, the probability that the King would not attend the laying of the foundation stone for the National Monument, and the realization that although it was the Twelfth, he was not upon the braes of Atholl with his guns. Much more irritating was the thought of so much tartan, so many Highlanders in the city.

Not all those clans summoned by Scott had come to Edinburgh. Some chiefs had regretfully declined, some still hesitated, and others would soon be stopped by the events which Atholl's displeasure set in motion. Those who had come, however, had been welcomed by the newspapers in a prose that might have stumbled (rather than tripped) from the pages of *Waverley*. Only five clans would be represented in the city, although there was so much tartan on the backs and about the thighs of unattached gentlemen that the number seemed greater. There would be fifty Sutherland Men with swords only, but dressed in trews of tartan, thanks to Mr Wilson and the Black Watch. The Breadalbane men were expected that weekend, fifty youths from the Earl's estates on Tayside, and their first duty upon crossing the firth would be to belt themselves in the plaids he had sent from the city. Thus kilted in what was taken to be the tartan of Breadalbane Campbells, with a yellow plume in their bonnets and a boar's-head crest on their arms, they were to march into Edinburgh on Monday morning. The Griogaraich had already gathered at the door of the Commercial Bank in Edinburgh, before dispersing to their quarters. An enthusiastic crowd had been delighted by the stunning scarlet of their plaids, the dark fronds of fir in their bonnets, and, of course, the scarred and heroic features of their chief. The *Weekly Journal* was solemnly moved. 'We saw with particular interest this clan, whose sufferings and proscriptions are so well known, come forth so gallantly to attend the Crown of Scotland.'

Glengarry's following, it was said, was 'small and select', but his panache and arrogance made it what he wished to be, a manifestation of all the virtues, habits and customs of True Highlanders. His brother, Colonel James, dutifully played his part in this muster, bravely enduring again and again the story of his defence of Hougoumont where, 'assisted only by a sergeant of the guards, he slew or drove back six French grenadiers who had forced their way into the court-yard'. As for the tall clansmen in Glengarry's tail – his piper Donald MacDonald, his henchman Ranald MacDonell, the Foresters Archibald MacDonell, Duncan MacDonell and others – they all looked 'as if they had done nothing all their lives but lived by hunting and slept in the woods'.

Lastly there was a contingent of Drummonds from Strathearn and Tayside, led by a noblewoman with a Welsh title. Their Jacobite chiefs and gentry had suffered much from their major involvement in plot and rebellion since they first went into exile with the last Stuart king. The bloody seal of this steady loyalty was finally impressed upon their history by the wounding of a Drummond duke and the death of a Drummond viscount at Culloden. In this context it seems probably that Sarah Clementina was given her second name in memory of Bonnie Charlie's Polish mother. Sarah was the only child of James Drummond, 11th Earl of Perth, the title having come to his father when the last claimant was attainted for his rebellious activities. The 11th Earl was acknowledged Chief of the Drummonds in 1785, and now that he was dead his daughter had assumed that leadership, though whether a woman could or should be a *chief* might have provoked warm debate among members of the Celtic Society. The intrusion of a Welsh barony upon this complexity requires patience in understanding. In 1807, Sarah Clementina married the son of the Baroness Willoughby de Eresby, daughter of an English duke and a peeress in her own right. Her late husband had been Lord Gwydir of Gwydir in Caernarvon, and that title was now held by her son. Thus it was that Sarah Clementina led her Drummonds as Lady Gwydir. Although many had been assembled, there were arms and clothing for thirty only, but these were warmly praised by the *Weekly Journal* and other newspapers who reprinted that paper's report. 'They wear sword and targe, have a holly bough in their cap, the ancient badge of their tribe, and are as smart mountaineers as the eye would wish to look on.'

The rest of the Highland Gathering, and by far the largest number, was formed by members of the Strathfillan Society and the Celtic Society. The first was an association of Perthshire gentlemen living along Lochearnside and in the valley of the River Fillan between Crianlarich and Tyndrum. Their leaders were Stewart of Ardvorlich on Loch Earn, and James Graham of Airth. The latter, an officer of the Celtic Society also, was a noisy perfervid Jacobite whose grandfather had been a trooper in the thin ranks of the Young Pretender's cavalry at Culloden, and had himself ridden against the Radicals with the Kilsyth Yeomanry. According to the *Journal*, the Strathfillan gentlemen had formed their association for the enjoyment of sport and games, but also it was to be a benefit society. Their appearance was less impressive than other groups, and they wore various tartans, but in general they were 'well-busked and armed'.

The gentlemen of the Celtic Society outnumbered all others and were more advanced in age, but Garth's patience and perseverance had turned them into a moderately disciplined body. The Duke of Argyll had accepted the nominal command of the Society for the duration of the Visit, and had agreed to ride before it in processions. His deputy, as Captain-commandant of this sedentary body of urban mountaineers, was General Graham Stirling who thankfully left the organization and administration to the senior captain, Stewart of Garth. Stirling was a Peninsula veteran, greatly fond of parades and inspections which he held as frequently as possible. The most important of these took place in the park of Holyroodhouse on 10 August, when the Society was presented with a pair of colours in a theatrical imitation of a solemn military ceremony. The principal standard of silk, bright in many hues and embroidered with the words *Albainn me graidh*, Scotland my love, was to have been presented by a lady of distinguished rank, but none could be found, or none who thought herself equal to the occasion. The honour thus fell upon the Society's most illustrious member, Sir Walter, and Garth was asked to present the second colour. In the centre of a hollow square, formed by eighty kilted members of the Society, the first banner was taken by the man to whom they owed their corporate existence, William Mackenzie of Gruinard. Scott touched the old soldier's heart by saying that he was placing the colour in the hands of true Highlanders, and he knew that it would be honoured and prized by them. This oblique and dismissive reference to Glengarry's Society of True Highlanders cannot have pleased the MacDonell who was present as a spectator, and may explain his theatrical behaviour later. If Garth spoke at all when he handed the second colour to an ensign, his words were not recorded. In general, said a reporter, the members of the Society were

> . . . fully and even superbly dressed and arrayed in belted plaid, and each in his own clan tartan, which distinction gives a rich and half barbaric effect to their appearance. Their grenadiers carry partizans and targets, and are headed by Captain Mackenzie of Gruinard, whose stately and at the same time handsome and active figure, realises the *idea* of a complete Highland soldier. Here and there a white knee betrays the Southron or

Lowlander, in most the limb is as dark as that of *Ghlune dhu* (black knee) himself.

Every day, representatives of these contentious Highland groups stood outside 39 Castle Street, while their chiefs or captains conferred with Scott upon some point of duty, dress, or scalded pride. Scott worked his charm upon them all. His impatience was kindly hidden as he sent them away upon some unnecessary duty, to march through the streets behind their pipers and create that daily entertainment which John Lockhart would soon call 'this plaided panorama'.

So many clans had not come to the summons, however. There had been no Camerons from Lochaber and no MacDonalds or MacLeods from the Isles, no Macphersons, Rosses or Munros, Robertsons or Macleans, although individual gentlemen with such names were most particular in making their presence known. The Gordons were to have come from the north-east under the Cock of the North, their octogenarian Duke whose wife had once helped to raise a marching-regiment and a fencible regiment of Gordons by offering a guinea and a kiss to every recruit. Born three years before Culloden, the Duke had been intent on coming to Edinburgh. His horses, carriage, and servants were already stabled and lodged in the city. But he was ill, some thought dying, although he would live for another five remarkable years. Had he come, said the *Observer*, he would have been accompanied by 'his faithful highlanders, hundreds of whom would have travelled from their mountains.'

For Scott, the continuing absence of the Atholl men must have been particularly disappointing. Not only was Perthshire the heart of the Jacobite Highlands, it had also been a great nursery of soldiers. No story of Culloden could be told without reference to the savage charge of the Atholl Brigade, led by the Duke's grand-father, and shouting *'Run, ye dogs!'* as it struck the left flank of Cumberland's line. Pressed men and unwilling men though many were, they had advanced and died with great courage in the last battle of the Stuart cause. It was the memory of this, in the increasingly euphoric mood of resurgent Jacobitism, that encouraged Scott and many others to believe that the presence of Atholl's clansmen was essential to make the occasion complete.

In Dunkeld and Blair there had been spirited activity among the Duke's servants, if some confusion about his intentions. There was also hurt pride when it was learnt that their neighbours, the Breadalbane men, were away south before their own orders had come. There had been no further instructions given since Atholl's agreement that some sort of honour-guard might be assembled to greet the King, should he visit Strathgarry and Strathtay. It was perhaps assumed that this would now be sent to Edinburgh, although the Duke had not said as much. The duty of raising, clothing, arming and drilling such a force had fallen upon John Findlater, a sub-factor of the Atholl estates who lived at Blair Uachdar in Glen Tilt, a mile from the old castle. He was not a young man, a quarter of a century before he had been Adjutant and Paymaster of the Local Militia, with some probable service in a marching-regiment before that. Nostalgic memories of those days, combined with a zealous attachment to all things Highland, persuaded him to accept the appointment with great enthusiasm.

Atholl had not long departed for Edinburgh when Findlater reported to Frederick Graham, the senior factor who was in the city with the Duke. He had recruited one hundred and ten men, he said, all tenants or sons of his Grace's tenants, and none was under five feet nine inches. He was drilling them regularly, teaching them to march, wheel, and go through their facings with astonishing skill. He was assisted by other members of the Duke's staff at Blair and Dunkeld, all of whom he appointed lieutenants or ensigns in his little regiment. But most of his keen young men had yet to receive their blue coats, their tartan plaids for belting into kilts, their waistbelts, pistols, dirks, swords and sporrans. Each would also need a sprig of juniper for his bonnet, that the ancient badge of Clan Murray might be carried before all the clans. There was no one in Atholl who could supply these needs, no weapons at all to be found in the Highlands, as there had been once, in the old days . . .

Without precise instructions, clear and inspiring orders to march southward by way of Perth and Bridge of Allan, Findlater continued with his drilling, encouraging the young men to borrow blue coats from their neighbours, to be patient until the tartan and the bonnets and the juniper arrived. One of his ensigns, John Duff, who was something of a tailor and had raised a few men about Dunkeld, thought he could have plaiding and bonnets ready in time. 'I have an anxious wish,' Duff told Graham, 'that the Athole lads shall not be outstripped by any who may have the honour of appearing in the presence of his Majesty.' But his Dunkeld men had no arms, and he hoped Graham might be able to buy or rent some dirks and swords in Edinburgh.There should also be a black silk neck-cloth for each man. Some of the lieutenants had gone to Perth to buy these, and it was hoped that they would also find belts, sporrans and dirks. The Royal Squadron was already at anchor in Leith Road when Findlater proudly sent Graham a muster-roll of his command, 'young, stout and fine-looking fellows'. Few were named Murray, but all had good names from the braes – Stewart, Robertson, MacGregor, Blair and Gow – and in Findlater's opinion they were far superior to any man raised in Breadalbane.

> I do feel more than I am at liberty to express for the cause of these fellows being for the present called upon [They] would please the Noble Duchess and you all with their Grand appearance in the Blue Coat and Atholl tartans, and to see fellows in three days doing more than I have seen performed in as many weeks at Drill shows their attachment to their Chief can do more than all the Drills in the Service could have accomplished.

His punctuation was confusing, but his warm enthusiasm was unmistakable. He had received no instructions to put his command upon the march, but he had studied maps, spoken to travellers, and determined upon the quickest route to Edinburgh once the summons came. In the meantime, with only fifteen broadswords available, he continued to drill his hundred men in their use, in case the King should wish to see a display of Highland swordsmanship. He taught them cut, thrust, stroke and charge. It was truly amusing, he told Graham, to see the men waiting their turn to take a sword, and a pity they had no greater opportunity than this. Findlater preferred to think of these days of indecision as *Repose*, the old drill-book word for standing at ease, and although in truth there was little ease among his men he hoped they would soon 'be called upon to appear in uniform somewhere . . .'

They can all face, march and wheel, form four deep and into sections from the line halted or on the march, as well as I could desire. It is a pity they had not to be presented along with those you heard were training in Edinburgh. I should not risk them freely, and I know they would equal them away.

There is a sadness in this report. He has heard, yet cannot accept, that the Atholl men will not go to Edinburgh, that if the King is not to come to Blair there will be no need of them at all. On Sunday 11 August, when the Duke went to see Sir Thomas Bradford, he expressed himself bluntly. He was alarmed by the thought of so much steel and flint and powder on the streets of Edinburgh, and in the hands of so volatile and unpredictable men. Bradford immediately agreed that no more Highlanders should be called into the city. Those already on the march should be sent back, and those who had not yet left their glens should have their orders cancelled. Greatly encouraged by this, Atholl returned to Charlotte Square and wrote at once to Melville and Peel, sending the letters to Melville Castle by the hand of a servant. His advice was briefly put, there should be no more Highlanders in the city. Both Ministers replied before dusk. Peel agreed with the proposal, but his response was oblique in acknowledgement, as if he thought the Duke's Highland pride might be offended by a suggestion he was himself making. Considering the time which must elapse before the Duke's Highlanders could come

> . . . and considering the number already in Edinburgh subject probably to not very severe discipline and exposed to some temptation at a period of general rejoicing, I am inclined to think it might be as well not to summon the men of Atholl.

Should the Duke agree with him, he would not fail to explain to the King the reasons which had induced Atholl to abandon his wish to bring his clan, and Peel himself would take all responsibility for the change. Melville's comment on the Duke's suggestion was more direct, acknowledging its originator and accepting it briefly.

I quite agree with your Grace on both the points adverted to in your letter. I think we have fully as many of the Gael, real or fictional, as is prudent or necessary.

Thus Sir Walter's fiery cross was abruptly extinguished before it had completed its passage through the glens. Even so, those Highlanders who did come seemed to fill the city with tartan, the sound of Gaelic, and the merciless music of their pipes. For some their presence was unbearable and suffocating, but most shared Lockhart's derisive but gentle amusement at Sir Walter's Celtification.

His purpose so swiftly achieved, Atholl sent word along George Street to Breadalbane, advising the Earl to turn his men back before they entered the city. He received a faintly testy answer. 'They are now here,' said *Mac-Chailein-'ic Donnachaidh*. 'I must make the best of them, though they will be very deficient in equipment. It would be impossible for me to send them back, as other Highlanders are to be present.' Plainly and simply put, and saying that no Campbell would happily leave when the Griogaraich and Glengarry's McDonells were allowed to hold their ground.

Atholl turned his attention to other matters in a city 'now filling from all sides'. The King would be here within forty-eight hours. In his relief that this daft affair was at last beginning, he failed to send precise instructions to the literal-minded Mr Findlater. Or it may be that although the sub-factor knew that all his work, the recruiting and drilling, the hours spent upon marching and swordsmanship, were for nothing, his spirit would not allow him to accept the waste. Day after day for the next fortnight he continued to keep his hundred men in formation.

'We shall be going on with the Drilling & Making the Tartan,' he told Graham, 'and holding the men in readiness until further orders.'

At dawn on Monday 12 August a brisk gale blew down the firth,
maintaining its ill-temper for much of the morning. It was the
King's birthday, and many ladies thought him badly used by so
unkind a sea. Seven miles off Flamborough Head, however, the
Royal Yacht was in calmer water, towed by the *James Watt*, with the
Comet in company. At the King's wish, the vessels were brought in
closer to the shore. The cliff above was crowded, men, women and
children looking down to the graceful ship, waving hats and hands
and shawls. On the after-deck of the *Royal George*, a tubby,
foreshortened figure in a blue coat raised its hat in reply. By
Scarborough, the water ahead was filled with small boats, bouncing
and dipping, overladen with more cheering figures. In the bows of
one a man with a long pole, to which was attached a roll of paper,
thrust it upward as the yacht slid by. Deftly snatched by a seaman,
the paper was found to be an address of loyal welcome.

At noon, the other vessels of the Squadron coming up, the King
was smartly cheered by their assembled crews. After he had dined,
his bandsmen were brought over from the *James Watt*, and when
they had played his favourite airs he sent them back to the steam-
ship with a double allowance of rum. He leant over the taffrail as
they went down to their boat, warning them to take care, and later
he sent them a hamper of wine as a further token of his gratitude.
Before nightfall the Squadron reached the skirt of the northern
gales. The tow-rope was cast off and the *Royal George* made what sail
was necessary to use the stiffening wind.

In Edinburgh, the King's birthday had been chosen for the first of Sir Walter's pageants, the carrying of the Regalia of Scotland from the Castle to the palace of Holyroodhouse. There had been some small dispute about this, the English members of the Lord Chamberlain's office arguing that the ceremony should be their concern. But since there was no precedent, no record upon which to base a claim of any sort, the whole matter was finally left to Sir Walter and his committee. He came early to the Earthen Mound where the procession was to assemble before moving on to the Castle. He rode in his own coach, with Peter Mathieson on the box, and he wore Highland dress of the Campbell tartan. Not the kilt, but trews, for he was still suffering from the disfiguring rash that would plague him throughout the Visit. As more coaches arrived, and formed a dark circle on the Mound, the gentlemen stepped down to discuss the day and to reassure Scott that each knew his appointed duty. Pipers of the Celtic Society and the Griogaraich played lustily until the gentlemen got back into their coaches and the procession moved upward toward the Castle, followed by a large crowd.

It was an inspiring occasion and a great relief, it was said, to a public becoming increasingly impatient for the King's arrival. The procession was led by a squadron of the Midlothian Yeomanry, trumpeter and picquets advanced. They were followed by a company of Celts under General Stirling, each man his own dazzling display of tartan, a studded targe on his back and a polished partizan on his shoulder. Behind them rolled five heavy coaches, four drawn by four horses and one by six. Their passengers travelled in the order required by precedence and the solemn ritual devised by Scott. First, the Duke of Hamilton, as the Hereditary Keeper of Holyroodhouse. Then two coaches containing the Marischal's Esquires, followed by Peter Mathieson and his august employer. The coach and six, in which the Regalia was to be placed, carried its appointed bearer the Knight Marischal, Sir Alexander Keith, and old Adam Ferguson into whose keeping the Honours would pass during their stay at the palace. The coaches were flanked by more Yeomanry and more Celts, and more still were to the rear, where Evan MacGregor's clansmen marched in a phalanx of rippling scarlet.

Within a brief moment of its beginning the day's programme was marred by two unexpected and unfortunate events, and before it was ended there would be a third much more ugly. Scott's carriage had scarcely moved when its horses, unused to such attention perhaps, became restive and then unmanageable. He was forced to alight and walk to the rear where the Lord Provost, who was not part of the procession, offered him a seat in his coach. A few yards up the Mound the procession was again halted, by the clattering arrival of an astonishing horseman. Dressed in trews, boots and spurs, a long-feathered bonnet and a flowing plaid, Alasdair Ranaldson had come to ride at the head of the procession. This, he said, was his rightful place. He did not say what right, when and by whom granted, and nobody seemed able to ask him. General Stirling, interrupted in the most solemn parade of his life, was seemingly speechless, and none of the grenadier Celts thought it proper to disrupt the dignity of the occasion (it was later said) by asking Alasdair Ranaldson to dismount and explain, or remove himself and his troublesome horse altogether. Finally Captain Ewan MacDougall, younger of MacDougall, a naval officer of spirit if not caution, stepped to MacDonell's stirrup and by a look, or by words no one else heard, forced Glengarry to ride away. He left in a great temper, and later declared that MacDougall could expect to hear from his seconds. He did not forget the humiliation of this incident. His dislike of the Celtic Society now became an unrelenting hatred of 'that nondescript convention of anything rather than Highlanders'.

The wind-blown procession travelled slowly to the top of the Mound, turning by Bank Street into the Lawnmarket, and thence to Castle Hill, halting at last below the great belly of the Half Moon Bastion. Here at the gate of the castle there was an exchange of challenge and reply, dramatically composed for the occasion by Scott, no doubt.

Officer of the guard (from within)	Who's there?
Herald	The King's Knight Marischal comes to receive the Regalia, which are deposited within your castle, and he demands admission in the name of the King.
Officer (within)	Throw open the gates, and make way for the King's Knight Marischal.

The gate opened, the gentlemen descended from their carriages and toiled upward past Argyle's Battery to the Governor's House. They were gone an hour, during which the waiting crowd greatly increased. The scaffolding which caused Atholl so much concern was still unfinished, but some of the crowd brushed aside the platoon of soldiers who had been placed there to keep them away, and swarmed up the poles and planking for a better view. Workmen and police were still trying to pull them down when the castle gates were again opened, and the scarlet and white band of the 77th came out in a blare of drumming music. The gentlemen followed, pacing solemnly behind the Marischal's Esquires who carried the Honours upon crimson cushions. When all had mounted the carriages, the procession followed the bandsmen down the hill, the escorting troopers sliding upon the stones, and the Highlanders strutting splay-legged to maintain their balance.

As his coach rolled below the high windows of the Lawnmarket, Keith of Ravelston was much moved. Upon impulse, or perhaps a suggestion made by Scott earlier, he took the heavy golden crown from the seat opposite and held it high above his head, smiling at the cheers and the applause. The procession turned down Bank Street to the Mound again, and once beyond the palisade it passed through lines of mounted troopers, and the immobile men of the 77th, the 66th and the 13th. The Esquires now unfurled their great banners, almost hiding Keith's coach behind waves of surging silk, the blue and white folds of Saint Andrew's saltire. The music of two military bands and Clan Gregor's lusty pipers merged with the cheering of the crowd into a throbbing, toneless thunder.

Eastward by Princes Street and Calton Hill, the procession moved slowly to Abbey Hill and the gates of Holyroodhouse, where a guard of honour from the 13th – Culloden no longer a memory – lowered their King's Colour in salute. The Honours of Scotland were taken inside the palace to the room prepared for them, and twelve gentlemen of the Celtic Society mounted their silent guard about the walls. The door was locked upon them, to remain unopened until the guard was changed the next morning, and thus it was to be, upon Sir Walter's inspired suggestion, until the Regalia was returned to the Castle.

Before the procession had left Castle Hill, and while passing the unfinished scaffolding, the monstrous erection began to slip eastward into collapse. Although men and horses may have faltered at the noise of tormented wood and terrified humans, the procession continued without stopping. Before it was gone into the throat of the Lawnmarket, men were climbing over the wreckage, desperately pulling at poles, ropes and planks to reach those trapped underneath. Most of the injured were young. Two were dead when recovered, and ten were gravely injured with fractured hips and thighs, broken skulls, ribs and arms. The Military Hospital within the Castle, and the Royal Infirmary, admitted most of the injured, but 'many bruises and fractures occurred, of which, as the patients were above the rank in life to which, under such circumstances, a public hospital would be considered eligible, we could receive no authentic information'. And the loyal *Observer* did not miss an opportunity to snipe at the *Scotsman*.

> Had the guards on this occasion presented their bayonets to the crowd, and sternly forbidden all approach, what confusion and disaster would have been avoided; though we doubt not but that the radical newspapers would have written many a *lengthy* and wearisome column on the abomination of military tyranny.

Indeed it was generally thought that the incident should not spoil the excitement and pleasure of the day. Many would no doubt have agreed with Jane Grant. 'You will see by the newspapers how foolish people were, mounting a *half-finished* scaffold,' she wrote to her mother that night. 'This sad accident has thrown a damp over everybody. It will make them more particular about the other stands, and after all it was the poor people's own fault.' The Grant girls had watched the procession from Abbey Hill, but it was perhaps less exciting than the arrival that day of their court dresses, 'trains of pearl white satin, trimmed all round with folds of net and bows of satin, beautifully embroidered in a robe shape up the front'. There were silk stockings, slips of satin, and packets of gloves. All so wonderful that the landau was sent to bring Mrs Siddons at once, that she might share their delight.

In England, shortly before seven o'clock that Monday morning,

Lord Londonderry cut his throat, a bloody act which each Cato Street conspirator had claimed to be his right. After that mad audience with the King, the Marquess had been kept to his bed at North Cray and tenderly nursed by his wife. Bled copiously on Friday night he slept deeply, and in the morning his physician, Charles Bankhead, decided that the cupping and some cooling medicines had greatly relieved his condition. It was agreed that he should not leave his bed, however, and a dinner party planned for that evening was cancelled without explanation. On Sunday his mind wandered again, and wildly. He was once more tormented by the thought of the Bishop of Clogher and his unnatural crime. His raving, his tears and protestations were alarming. Upon orders from Bankhead, his servant again removed all sharp instruments from the bedroom, knives, razors, scissors, and also his pistols. When he seemed rested, and was calm again, he was left alone to sleep.

In the morning he was awake early, telling his servants to bring his physician. When Bankhead arrived the Marquess was standing in the middle of his dressing-room. 'It's of no use,' he said, and collapsed in Bankhead's arms. His carotid artery had been severed by a small pocket-knife. His wife came immediately she was called. She flung herself upon his body, and great force had to be used to pull her from it.

When Liverpool was informed, he immediately dispatched a messenger post-haste to Robert Peel in Edinburgh. The King must be told as soon as possible. In London, for a time, the news of Londonderry's death was kept from all but a few, and they were not yet told how he had died. Lady Conyngham was prostrate with an illness that was more diplomatic than real, since it seemed to explain why she had not gone to Scotland. Before he left, the King had told her of his alarming audience with Londonderry, and now, on Monday, she could no longer keep it to herself. She sent for Madame de Lieven, to tell her that because of his odd behaviour Londonderry might not be able to go to Vienna. Nobody, she said, except the King and Lord Liverpool suspected the true state of the Foreign Minister's mind. At this moment, as if upon cue and in keeping with the dramatic form Madame de Lieven's life seemed to take, Lady Conyngham's elder son burst into the room. Londonderry was dead, he said.

Lady Conyngham clutched her head in her hands and cried 'Good God, he has killed himself.' Her son seized her by the arms, thinking she was going crazy. 'But no, Mother, he had an apoplectic fit.' She repeated: 'He has killed himself. He was mad.'

Driving to Calton Hill that day to inspect the hole that had been dug for the foundation stone of the National Monument, Atholl once again studied the mouth of the firth through his glass. At his lodgings in the city, the young clerk William Cranstone was compelled by disappointment to begin an accounting of his expenses during the King's Visit. He had already noted the cost of the blue coat and white jean trousers recommended by the Town Council. Now he estimated that he had spent approximately seven shillings travelling to Calton Hill and waiting there upon a false report that the King would come that day.

That had been Atholl's hope also. 'No vestige of the King's ships,' he recorded in his journal that night. 'Blew every wind from the west.'

PART FOUR

A Plaided Panorama

'His Majesty must now be satisfied, from
ocular demonstration, that the people
of Scotland – of all classes – are *truly loyal*,
by which we mean, that they are
attached to the laws, and anxious to pay
every rational mark of respect to the
CHIEF MAGISTRATE OF THE STATE.'

– *The Scotsman*

> *'With regard to the old belief that the*
> *commonty* belonged to the people, I have*
> *already explained that it no more belonged to*
> *them than their hats and coats belong to me.*
> *. . . They are not slaves; they are not obliged to*
> *live here; and if they don't like the place they*
> *can go away.'*
>
> – FREDERICK WILLIAM
> TRAILL BURROUGHS,
> Lieutenant-General, Proprietor

At daybreak on Tuesday 13 August the *Royal George* was east-north-east of Holy Island, four leagues from Emmanuel Head. Her attendant steam-boats were a few cable-lengths astern, and the rest of the Squadron was still south of the Farne Islands. Before seven o'clock the yacht shortened sail and was taken in tow by the *James Watt*. An hour later she made sail again and cast off the tow-ropes, but the squally weather was worsening and beating up to a gale. She took the Berwick pilot aboard at nine o'clock and made for the roads in the mouth of the Tweed. There she came to and anchored in nine fathoms, furling all sail. In the afternoon she was joined by the *Comet* and the *Royal Sovereign*.

The hostile gale was logged as the reason for the pause in the voyage, but the King's headache, and a longing for a steady deck beneath his painful legs, may have influenced the decision. Throughout the day and despite a rain-whipped offshore wind, the Royal Yacht was surrounded by small boats, by cheering and by patriotic music, but if the King came on deck in response his appearance was brief and unrecorded. Symbolically, he had halted at the historic gateway to Scotland. Although his eyes were perhaps closed beneath a damp towel, from the gilded windows of his state cabin they could have seen the distant rise of the Cheviots, once straddling a contentious Border. And to the north-west, beyond the

*Commonty, commonté, Scots, land held or used in common.

roofs of Berwick, was the black stud of Halidon Hill where the yew-tree bows and yellow arrows of the English had destroyed a Scottish army for the small cost, it was said, of a dozen of Edward III's archers and two of his men-at-arms. Toward evening, the rain slackened, although the wind blew strongly still. The rest of the Royal Squadron passed the mouth of the Tweed under full sail, saluting the King with the thump of their signal guns and a flutter of talking flags.

The wind increased in force during the night, and Commodore Sir Charles Paget was no longer confident that the yachts should sail in the morning, believing that it might be wiser for the King to continue the voyage in one of the steam-boats. Before making that decision, he went aboard the *Comet* and was taken seaward for a few miles, testing the weather. Upon his return it was agreed, seemingly without consulting the King, that the yachts should continue. They were taken under tow before six o'clock, and by seven they had passed St Abb's Head and were making westward for Dunbar. The wind had dropped and although there were squalls, with the promise of heavier rain later, there were also moments of astonishing sunshine.

Before the ships had left Berwick Roads, large crowds were gathering in Edinburgh, and moving toward Leith and Calton Hill. There were now thought to be sixty thousand visitors already in the city, most of them from the west. According to its own newspapers, Glasgow's streets were deserted, 'sombre and still', except by the post-houses where every coach arriving from Edinburgh was immediately surrounded by a great number of anxious people shouting, 'Is he come . . . is he come?' Seven hundred workmen had left the city in a body on Friday, to walk the towpath of the Canal and be among the first to greet the King when he landed. By the arithmetic of the editorial rooms it was agreed that during his visit the King would be seen, however distantly, by three hundred thousand of his Scottish subjects, one seventh of the country's population.

The first to see him – or the first to believe they had – were those who put out from Dunbar through the white smoke of its saluting guns. As the Royal Yacht shortened sail to drop a dispatch-bag into the pilot's boat, any one of the portly, blue-clad figures on the after-deck could have been His Majesty, but no one was sure. More fortunate were the passengers of the steam-boat *Queen Margaret*, Mr Scott RN commanding. A large number of ladies and gentlemen from North Queensferry had boarded the side-wheeler early on Monday morning, and having made one voyage down the troubled firth to the Bass Rock, had returned in great disappointment. At daybreak on Wednesday they sailed again, and at half-past eleven, off the east point of Aberlady Bay, they sighted the *Royal George*. Her bows dipping and her sails filled, she came out of the mist of rain, magnificent in a brief cloak of sunlight. Port and starboard ahead of her, their towing-ropes made fast, were the steam-boats, each a flurry of black smoke and white water. Four cable-lengths astern and losing way, was the *Royal Sovereign*. Mr Scott brought his vessel about and within fifty yards of the Royal Yacht, steaming in pace with her while his passengers sang all the verses of the National Anthem, although they may have omitted those lines which asked the Almighty to frustrate the knavish tricks of the Scots. On the after-deck of the yacht, and grasping the taffrail for support, the King listened to this spirited welcome with obvious emotion, moving only to bow at the end of every stanza. The *Queen Margaret* then fell astern and the King went below.

Edinburgh knew he was coming long before one o'clock when the agreed signal, a salvo from the guns on Calton Hill, was to cough its smoke into the rain. To the east of the island of Inchkeith the yachts came up with the rest of the Royal Squadron, each ship of which fired a salute and fell into line astern. The cannonade was heard, and its smoke seen, from the Telegraph Tower in Leith, and as soon as the Royal Standard was sighted above the sails of the King's yacht every armed vessel in the firth fired its own thundering welcome. By twenty minutes to two the steam-boats brought the *Royal George* into Leith Roads and to her moorings half-way between the harbour and Inchkeith, two miles out and in two and a half fathoms of water. She was now in the centre of a great assembly of ships, the smartest of which – its yards manned and signals strung – was HMS *Dover*, flagship of Admiral Sir John Beresford's station. There were sail and steam vessels from the Lothian and Fife shores, ferries and fishing-boats, and elegant English yachts owned by the titled and privileged members of the Royal Yacht Club. The most handsome of these, certainly the most expensive, was *Die Jonge Vrow Rebecca Maria*, aboard which was her owner Sir William Curtis, once Lord Mayor of London, sea biscuit chandler and banker, a man of wealth and station, and of a girth almost equal to that of his great friend the King.

Before two o'clock the rain became heavy and persistent, drenching the urgent crowds, the riders, carriages, foot-soldiers and cavalry, all pressing toward Leith in a great fear that the King would come ashore before they arrived. Among this noisy but good-tempered crush was Lord Melville's carriage. He and Robert Peel had come into Edinburgh as soon as they heard the signal guns, collecting Scotland's premier peer, the languid Duke of Hamilton, from his rented lodgings, before pressing on to Leith. The harbour was crammed with small boats all eager to put out into the firth, indifferent to the rain and the sickening swell. Peel cannot have enjoyed the wretched boat journey of twenty minutes before Admiral Beresford's barge took him and his companions alongside the Royal Yacht. News of Londonderry's suicide had not yet reached him, but he was unwell, his eyes were sorely troublesome, and he was in no mood for noisy festivities.

Scott was another passenger in the naval barge. He had come down to The Shore in the sociable, its cover raised against the rain. As a tribute to the Royal Visitor, he was handsomely dressed in the Windsor uniform – a blue coat with red cuffs and collar, and fine white trousers. There were some who would believe that so early an approach to the King was an act of thrusting self-importance, but he came upon the instructions of his committee. That morning they had looked at the weather through the windows of Castle Street and decided that the King should be advised against landing that day. Scott also wished to keep his promise and deliver the gift prepared by 'those loyal Ladies of the Silver Cross'. It was a bonnet badge which Lady Scott, in her French way, called 'a pretty cocarde', a silver and diamond saltire on a field of blue velvet. Sewn upon the cloth were small pearls forming the words *Albhain gu brath* which, Sir Walter would tell his Majesty, meant 'Hail to the King of Scotland'.

Like Robert Peel, who sat beside him in the barge, Scott was in no mood for joy. He too was ill, plagued by that irritating rash.

Fortunately it had not afflicted his face or his hands, but he would not be able to wear a kilt. More painful to bear was the death of an old friend that morning. William Erskine had shared Scott's schooldays and had studied law with him. Highly sensitive, easily alarmed and frightened, and still grieving the loss of his wife, he was thought by some to be an odd intimate for a man of Scott's nature. He had been elevated to the Bench as Lord Kinneder at the beginning of 1822 and shortly afterwards became the subject of a slander that would quickly destroy him. It was said that he was the lover of an apothecary's wife, a rumour that appears to have been started by a business rival of the husband. Men of coarser spirit would have laughed at the absurd story, but its effect on Erskine was disastrous, producing what Scott called 'a fever of his spirits'. Despite frequent bleedings, his health rapidly declined and his will for life receded. Two days before the King came, in an effort to arouse her husband's friend, Lady Scott took him to the play, and later helped him to select Court dresses for his daughters. He was thought to be recovering, but again he weakened, was put to bed and once more cupped. Telling the story later to a friend, Scott said

> On the day of the King's arrival he waked from sleep and took a kind leave of his servants (his family were not allowed to see him) ordered the window to be opened that he might see the sun once more, and was a dead man soon after.

Although the shock of this loss deeply troubled Scott, he was perhaps able to put it into proportion as he waited below the larboard gangway of the Royal Yacht. Great events were about to take place, for many of which he had been the inspiration, and private grief should be hidden at a time of loyal jubilation. The solitary misery of the rain now that Peel and the others had gone aboard, the sickening lurch of the barge, and the agony of itching flesh, were quickly relieved when the King heard that he was alongside. 'What! Sir Walter Scott! The man in Scotland I most wish to see! Let him come up!' And up he was quickly taken. Through the gangway port and aft to the quarter-deck where, under a dripping awning and surrounded by his Ministers and his gentlemen, a smiling King was awaiting the Author of *Waverley*. Scott had prepared a speech to introduce the gift he brought, but he began with a warning and an appeal.

> Impatient, Sire, as your loyal subjects are to see you plant your foot upon their soil, they hope you will consent to postpone your entry until tomorrow. In seeing the force of the weather, I am myself forcibly reminded of a circumstance . . .

Which was, of course, the customary comic anecdote. In the agreeable style that had made him one of the best after-dinner speakers in Scotland, he illustrated and enforced his appeal with the story of an old Highlander of his acquaintance who had once apologized for the inclement weather that marred their first meeting.

> 'This is just awful! Sic a downpour! I'm sure it's no fault of mine. I canna think how it should happen to rain in this way, just as a man of this world should come to see it. It looks most personal!'

His speech ended, Scott presented the ladies' gift, knelt on one knee and kissed a royal and pudgy hand. The King promised to wear the badge in public, and so he did, though not perhaps in his Highland bonnet. For that, Mr Hunter had supplied chased gold, diamonds, pearls, rubies and emeralds. There was wine upon a table, but the King called for cherry brandy in which to drink Sir Walter's health, bowing graciously when Scott returned the compliment. Some of the gentlemen asked for the privilege of keeping their glasses, but Scott – seeing a glorious addition to the historical memorabilia at Abbotsford – asked for the King's glass. It was given, and tucked safely into the tail-pocket of Scott's coat.

At three the King went below to dinner, sitting with Scott on his right hand, and Sir William Curtis on his left. Shortly after this, an officer was sent away to Leith. He climbed the crimson landing-stage to The Shore, and outside the door to Young's Crown Tavern he told the nearest officials of Leith that the King would not disembark that day. The word was shouted through the great crowd, up to windows and to the wet, huddled groups clinging to the roofs, but

there was little will or wish to disperse. Many walked to the end of
The Shore, beyond the look-out tower, staring through the rain at
the distant ships. In Edinburgh, great crowds remained upon Calton
Hill and Arthur's Seat, as if, said a reporter, 'deprived of the power of
motion'. The Magistrates and Council of Leith, who had been told
that the Royal Progress from the harbour to Holyroodhouse would
begin five hours after the King's yacht was moored, were now
numbed by indecision. They sat inside their coaches, or gathered
morosely in the doorway of William Reid's Circulating Library. No
more certain of what he should be doing, the Lord Provost of
Glasgow was marooned in his carriage beyond the offices of the
London, Leith and Edinburgh Shipping Company. Yet the crowd
retained its good humour, eddying thickly along The Shore, its
colourful holiday clothes now wet and bedraggled, threaded with
blue, green, scarlet and tartan where Archers, Dragoons, Infantry
and Highlanders desperately endeavoured to reach their allotted
places.

Toward evening, and despite the relentless rain, there was an
increase in the traffic of small boats from Leith to the Squadron.
They gathered on the stippled sea about the Royal Yacht, cheering
and singing the National Anthem until the King appeared. He came
up to the quarter-deck and posed dramatically beneath its protective
awning, wearing an oilskin cap and a military surtout. Some of the
hovering boats contained ladies and gentlemen with whom he was
acquainted, and to these he bowed with a gracious flourish. When a
barge carrying the Duke of Northumberland and his party drifted
past the yacht's starboard quarter, a bottle of claret was dropped into
it, with the King's compliments. It was drunk immediately, the
master of the boat taking the empty bottle for himself and refusing
to part with it even for a guinea. At last the rain, the moonless
darkness, and inexorable weariness slowly dispersed the crowds.
They went reluctantly homeward, many still convinced that the
King was to land, but they no longer had the strength to greet him.
Their spirits were lifted by a sudden burst of flame upon the summit
of Arthur's Seat where the bonfire had been lit. Rain and the misted
darkness hid the familiar lion's-head profile of the rock, and thus
the fire seemed to hang unsupported in the dark sky. Another
suspended miracle was an illuminated crown of yellow flames,

high above the factory of the Edinburgh Gas Company, mounted upon a now invisible chimney.

Henry Fox had not risked his self-esteem or his linen among the crowd. When news came that the *Royal George* could be sighted from Calton Hill he did not go to any vantage point. He called instead upon the Duke of Hamilton 'who was in a flannel dressing-gown, much agitated about his dress and dignities, having received no specific commands'. His instructions would soon come with the arrival of Melville and Peel, but until then the Duke was particularly concerned with the style of gauntlet he should wear for ceremonial occasions. He discussed this vexing problem with a distinguished antiquary who was also present, 'whether it ought to be so long or not, whether it was to be sewed with gold thread &c, &c, &c.'. Fox left them as soon as he could, his boredom later relieved by dinner with the Breadalbanes and the discovery that their daughter-in-law, Lady Glenorchy, was decidedly pretty. Thus amorously aroused, and his yearning for Harriet Canning temporarily forgotten, he went to the Theatre Royal in the evening and greatly enjoyed Murray's production of *Rob Roy*. However, he could not entirely avoid the great event of the day. *'God save the King'*, he wrote in his journal, 'was sung with rapture.' William Grant was also at the play, and his account of its closing, as reported to his sisters, was more graphic.

> There was a row for 'God save the King', and Mr Murray came forward to learn the cause of the disturbance. 'God save the King' was called for, and a wit from the pit called out 'No song, no supper, Mr Murray', to which Murray replied he was sorry he could not give them supper, but they should certainly have their song.

When the Grants of Rothiemurchus heard the first guns, shortly after noon, 'everybody flew to dress, all was confusion'. The carriage was late in arriving and both girls almost had the day spoilt for them by William, who said their new caps made them look old. At the house in Picardy Place, owned by their father's friend John Gibson, a street window had been removed and a stand built between it and the railings. Gibson had taken an early look at the weather and had sent a servant for some sail-cloth to make an awning, but it did not come, and by the time the Grants arrived the stand was so drenched that it could not be used. Mary Frances was sadly depressed.

> All up Leith Walk, and as far as I could see up and down, stages were erected here and there in the same manner; some half way up the houses even, and all empty from the rain, so that it looked quite melancholy. Ladies in white gowns, gentlemen in white trousers all splashed up to their ears, a crowd, but not immense. The yeomanry with their fine new coats and lace, all soiled, the cockades on the horses in the different carriages drooping, and the new liveries of the servants becoming tarnished with the wet.

When the news came that the King would not land that day, Gibson's housekeeper bitterly complained of the 'pairfect wasterie' of her good meats and jellies. The girls went off to gossip with Mrs Siddons, to admire their new plumes, and the large bunches of white roses which were to go between the flounces of their gowns. Across the city, and alone in his lodgings, William Cranstone had now warmed to his accounting, and he recorded the day's expenditure with care.

> Attendance at Leith this day, when I was
> informed that his Majesty would not land
> till tomorrow, detained 3 hours   £1 10s

George Crabbe had spent the day at Castle Street, much of it out of the way in a comfortable chair, taking a copious amount of snuff and becoming increasingly confused by the bustle in the house. Scott now thought of him affectionately as 'a sly old hound', for he could not be sure when Crabbe was pleased or not, and his guests' pleasure was important to Scott. That Wednesday morning he found the old man in the parlour, where two chiefs were waiting. The Highlanders were speaking Gaelic, and Crabbe was talking to them in French, which 'he thought must be more germain to their comprehension than English'. That is how Scott told the story at the time, but sixteen years later Lockhart burnished it to give an unflattering reflection of the Suffolk poet. The two chiefs became 'half a dozen stalwart Highlanders' with whom Crabbe was 'exchanging elaborate civilities in what was at least meant to be French'. The Celts, said Lockhart, took Crabbe for a foreign abbé or bishop, and tried to explain that they were not the wild savages he seemed to think they were. Crabbe did not deserve this condescending mockery, or the distortion of his natural courtesy. He was already feeling the strain of an occasion that had scarcely begun. He wrote to his son that afternoon, before Scott returned from Leith, admitting that he was almost ashamed to say he would be glad when all was over. He had written some five and forty congratulatory lines for the King, but would not presume to believe that they would be presented to him. 'Or that he will read them, but somebody will . . .'. The tone and spirit of his poem was set by the first of its ten verses.

> Of old when a monarch of England appear'd
>> In Scotland, he came as a foe;
> There was war in the land, and around it were heard
>> Lamentation, and mourning, and woe.

Crabbe was sitting in the parlour with Lady Scott and other guests when Scott came home from Leith. Eager to recount every detail of the day, despite his weariness, he dropped into a chair beside Crabbe, and immediately leapt up with a scream. Lady Scott was unmoved, but thinking he had sat upon her scissors she asked if he were injured. His cry had been an expression of spiritual anguish. The King's glass, which he had carefully protected when he sat at dinner, on the boat's thwarts and in his carriage, had now been crushed in the tail of his Windsor coat.

Atholl did not retire before twelve that night. Listening to the incessant rain on the windows of Charlotte Square, and remembering the mist that had spoiled the day, he wished he had been able to see the King's squadron in fine sunlight, the ships dressed and the yards manned. His time had been miserably wasted. With his family – the Duchess, his daughters and eight grandchildren – he had sat or stood by a first-floor window of the Waterloo Hotel, looking out to the curtains of rain on Princes Street and the Mound. He was relieved when he was told that the King had ordered his dinner and would not be landing that day. By the same informant he heard news which he thought explained the postponement. 'In my opinion,' he recorded in his journal, before closing it for sleep, 'the intelligence of the Marquis of Londonderry's sudden death which had at that present arrived occasioned the change.'

He was wrong, for the King had not yet heard of his Minister's suicide when his landing was delayed until the following day. Returning ashore before the King went to dinner, Robert Peel had found Lord Liverpool's rider awaiting him at Melville Castle with an urgent dispatch. *'I must beg of you to break the dreadful intelligence of which this messenger is the bearer to the King. Poor Londonderry is no more. He died by his own hand at nine o'clock this morning . . .'* The carriage was recalled from the stables. Peel returned at a gallop to Leith, to another miserable boat-journey, and to an audience alone with the King. When he returned once more to Melville Castle, greatly exhausted, he had still to write to Liverpool. The King had been very much affected, he said, but as composed as his lordship would expect. Indeed, he had seemed almost prepared for this most melancholy intelligence, speaking of Londonderry with warm affection and bitterly lamenting his loss. All discussion of the Foreign Minister's successor must be left until the King's return. Liverpool was assured that His Majesty was quite well, and had endured the voyage without major discomfort. 'He was not actually sick, but as it blew hard, suffered a little from headache caused by the motion of the vessel.'

A macabre coincidence could not escape the notice of the newspapers, and of course the *Scotsman*, always a firm protagonist of the late Queen, would make the point most forcefully when the news became public thirty-six hours later.

> If we were not those who defied augury, we should say there was something ominous in Royal Excursions. The brave spirit of her Majesty took its flight last year just before the King landed in Ireland, and the Marquis of Londonderry, the most active of her Majesty's persecutors, the apparently least generous of her survivors, has put a period to his own existence on the birthday of our Royal Visitor, and just before his Majesty landed in Scotland.

The obituary which followed did not spare its subject, and the *Scotsman* spoke as if its proper masthead should be *The Englishman*. No name, it said, had ever sounded so un-English as Castlereagh. No one had done more to lower the name of England. No one had done more ill to England in the course of a century. Despising, 'as the most despicable of cant', the custom of speaking no ill of the dead, the writer said it would be gross hypocrisy for the *Scotsman* to profess regret at Londonderry's death. His name would always be linked with tyranny abroad and slavery at home, with the Insurrection Acts, gagging Bills, and transportation laws. He had been a bad speaker, his features repulsive and his manner cold. He was a man of the world without dignity of intellect, conscious of power but without talent, having all the craftiness of a politician and nothing of the patriot statesman. 'We defy the whole corps of his interested worshippers to name another individual who, from the dawning of civilisation, has spoken so much, and said so little that any one would wish to remember.'

Reading this (if it were not kept from him by his ever-closer confidant, Sir William Knighton) the King may have reflected that he did indeed wish to forget the last words spoken to him by Londonderry. To the morbid shock of the news was added the ugly recollection that he had done little to relieve the wretched man's terror. He was perhaps grateful for the protective isolation of his quarters aboard the *Royal George*, even with the knowledge that in this same cabin he had paced a sleepless night after hearing of the Queen's death. And that his feelings then were perhaps the reverse of those now. How he was able to rationalize his emotions and face what awaited him ashore, there is no way of knowing. No events were cancelled, and he said nothing in public of the Minister's death. There is no evidence that he deliberately curtailed his appearances, although whenever possible he seems to have retired from them earlier than might have been expected. Of the fourteen days he was to spend in Scotland, on display before all or some of those three hundred thousand who came to see him, less than thirty hours were to be spent in public, and of these almost half were within doors. Even that, perhaps, was too much for a man who had been so terribly reminded of his own mortality.

> 'If you were going up the strath now you would
> see on both sides of it the places where the towns
> were, you would see a mile or half a mile
> between every town. There were four or five
> families in each of these towns, and bonnie
> laughs between the towns, and hill pastures for
> miles, as far as they could wish to go. The people
> had plenty of flocks of goats, sheep, horses and
> cattle and they were living happy . . . There
> was not a want of anything with them . . .'
> – ANGUS MACKAY, crofter, Strathy Point

At dawn on Thursday 15 August the bonfire still burned on Arthur's
Seat, a bonnet of flame beneath a chieftain's plume of smoke. Now
the rain had stopped and there were becalmed clouds in a blue sky.
The Grants of Rothiemurchus left King Street for Picardy Place at
ten o'clock, in the certain knowledge that the King would land this
day and that an approving sun would shine upon him and his loyal
subjects. The old landau had been splendidly prepared, the metal of
its harness scoured and the leather well rubbed. The horses had new
cockades and saddlecloths of scarlet, and the coachman and
footman were in full livery. John Gibson's house, on the north side
of Picardy Place, was crammed with more than sixty people, all of
whom had been allotted places upon the stand or at the windows.
Henry Fox was there, although he did not think it necessary to
record who his companions were, or indeed that he had any at all.
Mary Frances and Jane Grant, however, bubbled with information
for their sister Elizabeth. There were several ladies of minor title,
two relatives of the Lord High Commissioner and, most interesting
of all, 'Mr and Mrs Lock, he is the man who wrote the book about
the Sutherland Improvements'. The Grants were quite taken with
the Lochs, 'she a nice lively woman, with their three charming
boys'. Jane took the boys to the top of the house, to a back-bedroom
window where they could see the firth, the ships at anchor, and the
puffs of gunfire signalling that the King was about to come ashore.

A scramble then, as Mr Gibson's guests hurried to their places, 'a good many people but not more than could see comfortably'. Mary Frances sat on the top bench of the stand, close enough to the Lochs to prevent their excited sons from plunging headlong to the paving below. James Loch's thoughts were more concerned with the interests of his noble employers than with his own family, hoping that he would be able to report to her ladyship this evening that the Sutherland men – some following the King's carriage, and others on guard at Holyrood – had been a credit to her and had thus brought an end to foul slander. He also hoped . . . no, believed . . . that her first son, Lord Francis, would be the admiration of all in the procession, and the noblest of men when he carried the Sceptre to the King later that day.

It would be two hours before the King's carriage reached Picardy Place, but Mary Frances was not bored. She was amused by the crowds passing and re-passing, by the coaches and hurrying horsemen. There were friends to greet as they came along the street in search of their seats – William Murray and his beautiful wife, Lord Maitland and his two brothers (both colonels). Mrs H.'s daughter Sally Siddons, and Admiral Fleming's wife, a pretty little Spanish woman. The heavens were bright and clear, the whole scene gay and smiling . . .

> All the stages and platforms were crowded with people; the windows of each tall house full to the very top; the Calton Hill covered with tents and spectators; the streets crowded on each side, and a broad empty space lined with yeomenry left in the middle for the coming procession. Even the roofs of the houses were covered with people standing upright by the chimneys or clinging where they could; the doors and steps of the houses all full; boys seated on top of the lamp-posts and hanging up the posts.

Walter Scott had risen early in Castle Street, going down the rise to Queen Street green where members of the Celtic Club were assembling for their march to Leith. He was dressed in Highland fashion, wearing trews of Campbell tartan, a bonnet upon his head and a plaid sweeping from his left shoulder. He was also 'armed and

238

accoutred', said Lockhart, carrying dirk, broadsword and pistols. Peter Mathieson was on the box of the sociable, awful fine in his flaxen wig and yellow livery, ably controlling the same spirited beasts that had behaved so badly on Monday. For David Stewart of Garth, who was invited to ride into Leith with Scott, it was surely a morning of mixed emotions. Although his patience and skill had turned the urban Celts into a tolerable representation of a military unit, his honest conscience was disturbed by the charlatan nature of much of this Highland display, and he had been particularly wounded by Glengarry's ill-mannered behaviour on the Mound earlier in the week. But he had good reason for some personal satisfaction. The first edition of his *Sketches*, one thousand copies, had been quickly sold. So too had a second edition, and now there was hope for a third. If his publishers were as prompt in payment as readers had been in purchase, some of Stewart's financial difficulties might be resolved. There was also the public's esteem, so evident this morning. The cheers that greeted the sociable on its way to Leith were not for the Author of *Waverley* alone, but for his white-haired companion too, a dignified figure in a swathe of tartan, his bonnet cocked and feathered, his broadsword held upright between his knees, and fine cairngorms on his coat of green velvet. Tucked in a pocket of this coat was a pair of small-lensed spectacles, a desperate need should he be required to read an order, or distinguish a distant but important face.

At nine o'clock the procession that was to escort the King to Holyroodhouse began its disorderly assembly in Queen Street, from the corner of Frederick Street to the beginning of York Place. It would be two hours before the marshals and the officers of each component body felt confident or desperate enough to order the move to Leith. The principal music for the march, as Sir Walter thought proper, was to be provided by the pipes. Since there were eight formations of Highlanders, and each was accompanied by at least two pipers, the resulting assault upon the ears and spirit of the crowd was remarkable, and for some most presumptuous and unpleasant. Ready or not, the assembly was obliged to move at eleven o'clock if it wished to arrive in Leith before the King landed. Reaching the harbour, it halted in St Bernard Street and other narrow lanes leading to The Shore. There, in great confusion, another attempt was made to achieve its Order of March, as published in the newspapers that morning. The harassed marshals were not entirely successful, but came close enough to the original plan to avoid undignified dispute.

The column was flanked at intervals by single files of Archers and Highlanders. The honour of the van had been given to trumpeters and troopers of Edinburgh's holiday soldiers, the Midlothian Yeomanry, among whom was John Lockhart, his mind so locked in his scarlet and blue regimentals that he had few personal memories of the day to record later in his biography of Scott. The advance party of the procession was formed by sixty-five Breadalbane men accompanied by two pipers who, it would seem, could play nothing this day but *The Campbells are coming!* and *God save the King*. Inspecting his clansmen in Queen Street that morning, their aging Earl may have wondered why it had been so difficult to find enough tartan for their belted plaids. Two years before, when the King's widowed son-in-law Prince Leopold had visited Tayside, the twelve hundred tenants whom the Earl summoned to greet him had all assembled within thirty hours, and in full Highland dress.

A squadron of Greys was placed between the Campbells and the next body of Highlanders – Stewart of Garth and his urban Celts, the most splendid and most disparate in dress and accoutrements of all the Highland contingents. They were not so wildly cheered, however, as those who followed, the scarlet clansmen of the Griogaraich. Riding before them on one of the horses he had rented for £25, the tall figure of Sir Evan MacGregor was made even taller by the spray of eagle feathers in his bonnet, and by the arrogant lift of his scarred face. His second-in-command, a few paces to the rear in a belted plaid made to fit his small figure, was MacGregor's son, aged twelve and named John Atholl in affectionate respect for his ducal grandfather.

Old Alexander Keith of Ravelston, now a true Knight Marischal, was escorted by brilliantly clothed equerries and by two young pages, one of whom was Charles Scott, the younger son of his old friend. Then came Sheriffs mounted and Sheriffs' Officers on foot, deputy-lieutenants in coats of green, two pipers blowing, and General Graham Stirling with more gentlemen Highlanders of the Celtic Club. When their dark-panelled coaches could be extricated from the crush of other vehicles, the next in the Order of March were the Barons of Exchequer, the Lord Clerk Register, and the Lords of Justiciary and Session. The Marquis of Lothian, as Lord Lieutenant of the county, was then to follow, but since he was also to greet the King upon The Shore he would not take his place in the procession until the last moment, forcing his horse through the crowds that blocked the narrow lanes. Nor were Glengarry and his clansmen prompt in joining the column. Denied those duties he had claimed to be his by right, Alasdair Ranaldson had secured the privilege of escorting the King's empty carriage from Holyroodhouse. When he had brought it to The Shore, and to welcoming cheers, he waved his bonnet in salute and rode away to St Bernard Street with the tacksmen and gillies of his name.

The mounted gentlemen who were to ride before the royal carriages were flanked by a troop of Greys. The Usher of the White Rod preceded the Lord Lyon King of Arms who was followed by the Lord High Constable. Each of these noble officers was accompanied by attendants and heralds in tabards of scarlet and gold. The first of the royal carriages was to contain four officers of the King's suite, his vice-Chamberlain, Comptroller, Treasurer and Equerry. The open carriage following, drawn by eight fine bays, was for the King, sitting alone but facing the Duke of Dorset and the Marquis of Winchester on the opposite seat. This shining, mobile throne would move within a cloud of colourful escorts – ten Royal Footmen and sixteen Yeomen of the Guard, flanking Archers and Highlanders, a squadron of Greys, and Sir Thomas Bradford with his staff, white cocks'-plumes in their hats. The rear of the procession was composed of more detachments of the clans – Drummonds, Sutherlanders and Strathfillan gentry – two squadrons of Midlothian Yeomanry and two of the Third Dragoon Guards, a grenadier company of the 13th Foot, and finally the band of the Scots Greys.

The oddest figure in the procession was undoubtedly Sir Patrick Walker, whose presence as hereditary Usher of the White Rod was a most satisfying personal triumph. Since the beginning of the year he had been diligently promoting the authority of this office, and had welcomed the Royal Visit as an excellent opportunity to confirm it. In March, to the irritation of both men, he had informed Lord

Melville and Robert Peel that as the officer in charge of the King's household in Scotland he wished to nominate a number of trades-men – a bookseller and a wine merchant among them – to the exclu-sive list of Purveyors to His Majesty. Melville advised Peel to have nothing to do with Walker or his *hereditary* office, 'which, I believe, was purchased by his father'. Melville did not know, and did not think it material to enquire what the duties of the Usher might have been before the Union of the Crowns, two hundred and more years ago, but at this date no one but the Lord Steward, the Lord Chamber-lain, or the Master of Horse could so nominate tradesmen. Thus Sir Patrick received a curt note only from Henry Hobhouse, a refusal of his request and a dismissal of his claim to be an officer of the Royal Household. 'Mr Peel is not apprized of your being justly entitled to assume any such character, & must decline attending to any presen-tation founded upon that assumption.'

Walker was not so quickly snubbed. In late July he wrote briskly to Peel, asking whether the King would hold a Chapter or Installation of the Order of the Thistle while he was in Edinburgh, and if so whether the ceremony would follow ancient precedents of which he, as Usher of the White Rod, had assembled a full list during a year of laborious investigation. Lastly, and indeed bravely, he told Peel that when the Royal Arms were displayed in Edinburgh they should be in their proper Scottish quartering, 'for the independence of Scotland does not tolerate the precedence of England within its own part of the United Kingdom'. Peel did not reply to this letter either, but passed it to Hobhouse with a marginal note, *No Chapter or Installation*. Walker was so informed by the Under-Secretary, and as for the other matter raised in his letter, 'I am further to inform you that H.M. has already given directions to the Lord Chamberlain with regard to his Reception.' The King was not to be instructed upon his armigerous rights by an importunate charlatan.

Whether or not Walter Scott and William Murray were deluded by Walker's pretensions is perhaps irrelevant. An historical novelist and an actor-manager, themselves creating an imaginary world for the occasion, could see the dramatic *need* for an 'Usher of the White Rod', and thus Sir Patrick was assured of a part in their pageant. It was therefore fitting that he should wear the most extravagant of all the sartorial extravagances devised for the players. His Spanish cap of black velvet was looped with gold and pierced by a long, drooping feather. His stunning jacket of crimson and gold was almost obscured by a swathing mantle of white satin, lined with crimson. His lower vestments – so described by reporters as if the word *breeches* would be blasphemous in this context – were crimson also, and tucked into brown boots, calf-high and elaborately adorned with tassels and fringes of gold. The horse he controlled with a bridle of crimson rosettes was as grandly furnished as himself, almost hidden beneath a great shabrack of scarlet cloth, edged with white lace and trimmed with silver thistles. His attendants, riding beside him, wore plain blue surtouts lined with white silk, Spanish caps of velvet, and brown boots.

The Esquires attending the Earl of Erroll, as Lord High Constable, also wore Spanish cloaks, deep purple edged with gold. Their breeches were white and gold, and their gold-looped Spanish caps dripped white plumes to the shoulder. And upon their feet they wore brown boots. His Lordship was a crow among these peacocks. His costume, upon the nature of which he had asked for and taken the advice of Scott, had not arrived in time, or indeed at all this morning. Greatly embarrassed by its absence, and very much out of temper, he wore the uniform of an English regiment of Lancers, in which he served as a lieutenant.

The Lord Lyon King of Arms, who followed Errol in the Order of March, was not the Lord Lyon, nor even a Lord, but George Tait, Esquire, a deputy hidden beneath a magnificent tabard of golden scarlet, a red velvet cap and a cincture of gold. And upon his feet, of course, he wore brown boots with golden tassels. As Knight Marischal, Keith of Ravelston was robed in a scarlet frock coat laced with gold, white waistcoat and breeches, and fine hose of white silk. And brown boots. The crowd of attendants gathered about his mettlesome black horse was an eddying pool of scarlet below which, no doubt, there were also more brown boots.

Short Spanish coats and black Spanish caps, white plumes and brown boots with golden tassels – William Murray was surely responsible for these. The like of them could be seen in a hundred historical melodramas, in the gas-light glow of another impossible wonderland.

It was waiting-time. Those who could, got down from their nervous horses or out of their suffocating carriages, easing cramped legs and aching shoulders. The scarlet and black cloud of Law Lords walked solemnly along The Shore to Mr Reid's Circulating Library by the landing-stage. Once inside, they eased their heavy robes, thankfully relieved themselves, and passed the time in agreeable conversation with the Author of *Waverley*, whom they had invited to join them. Lord Erroll – whose blue lancer jacket and square trencher cap looked distinctly odd among the mock-medieval costumes of the eight esquires, ten grooms and twenty-five halberdiers of his bodyguard – retired quickly to the cooler air of the Exchange Building where the King's niece, his wife, was able to soothe his bruised pride.

Outside such retreats all Leith was noisily alive, its grey walls flaming with bunting, with gay uniforms and flowered muslin, burning tartan and burnished steel. The principal trade societies of the burgh had each been assigned a place along the processional route. Shipwrights, Rope-makers, Corkcutters, Carters, Maltmen, Butchers, Porters and others, their banners raised, every cap with a saltire cockade, and every committee member dressed in a blue coat, white vest and trousers. The Magistracy of Leith, assembled before a line of town-constables, stood near but not improperly close to the landing-stage. A few yards from them, and by the door of Mr Reid's shop, General Bradford and his staff, having recently taken this position, now remained resolutely mounted, facing the harbour and sweating in the increasing heat. Along the half-moon of The Shore there was little space between the houses and the lines of constables, soldiers, Archers and Highlanders, but what there was had been packed with privileged citizens of Leith and Edinburgh since early that morning. Every window of every building behind them was crowded. More people were clustered like autumn starlings on the roofs above, clinging to chimneys, straddling eaves, or seated perilously on flimsy scaffolding. There were many more on the narrow Stone Pier where The Shore curved a protective wall about the entrance to the harbour, and the furthest of these, with the Royal Squadron clearly in view two miles away, shouted the news of its movements to those behind. By the Martello Tower, where The Shore became the pier, there was a tall scaffolding upon which was raised a large standard with the woven words *Welcome! In our hearts you reign Sovereign.* Beneath it on benches were the loyal hearts themselves, described by admiring reporters as 'an assemblage of elegantly dressed females'.

The drawbridge at the entrance to the inner harbour had been half-raised, and each uplifted arm was now occupied by 'the beauty and fashion of Leith', that is to say, the wives and families of the officers and officials who were playing their small parts elsewhere. Within the inner harbour, the naval vessels moored there had been drawn up abreast, their ornate sterncastles crowded with spectators, and their bare yards manned by seamen in bluecloth jackets and trousers of white duck.

Special places had been allotted to the visiting artists, on Custom House Quay across the narrow harbour from the landing-stage. Collins and Geddes were there, with Lizars, Skene and others, but Wilkie had decided to make what he could of the King's arrival at Holyroodhouse. Earlier in the day he and Collins had met their most famous competitor. 'To our surprise,' Wilkie told his sister, 'who should start up on this occasion but J. M. W. Turner, Esq., R.A.P.P.!!! who is now with us, we cannot tell how.'* The great man was following his own solitary road. In the wind and foul weather of yesterday he had put out in a small boat to make sketches for an oil he intended to call *The Mission of Sir Walter Scott*, the author's visit to the Royal Yacht. The entry he made on a single page of his book is no more than a shorthand note of simple strokes – albeit distinguishable as yards, hull and uplifted oars – and a few words to guide his brush. *Smoke colored and the shade breaking off becomes darker in the sky & broken by warmth.* Today he had already begun his work, an outline of roofs across the water, a mass of figures on The Shore, *the Authorities in Blue and White Gowns . . . red flags and Gold.*

The noise was unrelenting. The sound of pipes from St Bernard Street, Quality Street and Water Lane . . . cavalry trumpets and the beating of infantry drums by the Tolbooth Wynd . . . a sustained carrier wave of voices and laughter . . . all suddenly stilled at ten minutes to noon when a single gun was fired from the *Royal George*. It was immediately followed by a thundrous salute from the cannon

---

*Turner became a Professor of Perspective at the Royal Academy in 1807.

of the Fleet, joined by the batteries on Calton Hill and Salisbury Craigs four miles away. As the echoes of this violent ovation drifted across the firth, a great swell of cheering rose from the harbour of Leith and the waiting streets of Edinburgh.

The lanyard of the signal gun had been pulled at the moment His Majesty appeared on the quarter-deck of the yacht, dressed in the uniform of an admiral. He wore a thistle and a sprig of heather in his cocked hat, and the saltire gift of the Ladies of Scotland pinned to his breast. Golden and low-hulled, with the Royal Standard dipping to the water from its staff astern, the King's barge had already been lowered on the starboard side by a two-armed crane that had greatly interested Turner the day before. The King went down into the boat with dignity, taking his place on the red cushions in the stern-sheets where he joined two of his gentlemen, one of them the husband of his mistress. Commodore Sir Charles Paget took the helm from Midshipman Tucker and the barge made for the harbour across a still sea, rowed by sixteen muscular seamen in blue frock-coats and black velvet caps. One by one, and without haste, other craft came up astern, first the barge of Admiral Beresford and then the captain's-boat of every King's ship in the Roads. Behind this orderly armada there was soon a swarm of private boats, clamorous, overladen, and almost hidden by flags and bunting.

Despite the planning of Scott, and the eager ambition of Glengarry, the first man to greet the King upon his landing was not a figure representative of Scotland's noble past, but a Mr Kent who did not wait for the King to set foot upon land. He was given a modest immortality in one newspaper report the next day, though it was lamentably incomplete.

> When he was some distance from the shore, his Majesty was saluted by Mr Kent who was walking upon the water, to whom his Majesty bowed.

As the King's barge approached the head of the Stone Pier, where three young gentlemen were playing the pipes, the Royal Standard was broken on the lighthouse tower. Paget put the boat's helm over and brought it through the harbour entrance at twenty minutes past noon. It was greeted by prolonged cheers and the competitive playing of the National Anthem by several bands. The fluttering of hands, handkerchiefs and flags along The Shore, at every window and upon every roof, was so remarkable that the whole harbour seemed to be trembling violently. The noise increased as the barge came alongside the grey landing-stage, its crew rising from the thwarts to stand with their oars upright. Paget's steadying feet, one on the gunwale and the other on the edge of the stage, kept the boat still, and with the help of the Commodore's arm the King stepped on to a crimson carpet strewn with summer flowers. He was welcomed by Lord Lothian, who knelt to kiss his hand, and was then invited to advance up the platform to The Shore. The slope was not steep, but the King moved slowly, and with comic dignity. He removed and replaced his hat several times in responsive salutes, once pausing in obvious pleasure when the seamen on the yards beyond the bridge barked their three disciplined *Hurrahs!*

Once he was ashore, fifteen minutes were slowly spent upon the ritual greetings of lords and knights, magistrates, sailors and soldiers, dignitaries whose names he could barely hear or would trouble to remember later. He smiled to all, bowed to all, and charmed all until he was directed toward his carriage, his feet heavily crushing the flowers scattered by several young ladies of Leith. Before he reached the landau he saw a familiar face among the Archers, their Ensign-General Thomas Bruce, 7th Earl of Elgin, diplomatist and dealer in Greek sculptures. The King shook his hand warmly, an incident that excited no comment but was of some symbolic interest, an unconscious affirmation of their separate descent from the greatest founding-family of Scotland's royalty. The King then mounted his carriage and was joined by Dorset and Winchester. As if his emotions, so deeply disturbed, needed pause to recover, the landau remained stationary, the King gently raising his hat or his hand, and smiling about him. This idyllic moment was shattered by Glengarry. His plaid flowing behind him, he came down The Shore at a clattering gallop, pulling up beside the King with a sweep of his bonnet and a loud cry, *'Your Majesty is welcome to Scotland!'* This was neither planned nor expected, least of all by Scott who had hoped for something less demonstrative, and that from MacDougall of Lorne. But the King accepted Alasdair Ranaldson's greeting as he had acknowledged Mr Kent who walked upon the water. He bowed graciously as his carriage moved off.

Like a brilliantly-scaled snake, the processional column uncoiled itself from the narrow streets and lanes where it had been impatiently waiting. Its tail, three rattling squadrons of dragoons, was followed by another serpent of carriages, both open and closed, and containing fifty peers of Scotland or their representatives. In its slow, slow progress up the long rise of Leith Walk, the column travelled through bright sunshine and the flowered shade of triumphal arches. When he passed a larger assembly of waving arms and excited faces – particularly on those stands which were occupied by women only – the King seemed able to put aside his air of fatigue. He bowed repeatedly, twirling a fat hand in approval, and smiling at the rippling applause before sinking back into his seat. Now and then he bent forward to talk to Dorset or Winchester, and sometimes he leant over the side of the landau to speak to one of the escorting Archers. It is unlikely that his words could be clearly heard, but once, as he called to Elgin, what he said may have been prompted by the banner that hung from the arch above them. *Descendant of the immortal Bruce, thrice welcome!*

Forty minutes after leaving Leith the procession was halted by an artificial barrier to the city of Edinburgh, a palisaded gate of painted wood and coloured cloth. It stood alone in the wide amphitheatre formed by the meeting of Leith Walk, Picardy Place, King Street and Katharine Street. All roads but Picardy Place, through which the column would proceed, were closed and thick with people from railing to railing, the tops of immobilized carriages like black islands in a sea of faces. Here was Sir Patrick Walker's moment of the day. With Mr Tait, the deputy Lord Lyon, he advanced to the mock gateway and struck three ritual blows upon it with his white rod, at which it was immediately opened. The Lord Provost, Magistrates and Town Council (who had spent the waiting hours most agreeably in the house of Mr Craufuird nearby) came through the gateway to the Royal Carriage, offering the King the keys to their city. With great confidence in the skill of his coachmen and the steadiness of the eight bays, he got to his feet and bowed to the crowd. Still standing, his head uncovered, he listened to William Arbuthnot's stilted welcome, and was sentimentally close to tears when he was told that he was also being offered the hearts and persons of the people of Edinburgh. He lifted the keys and then returned them formally to their red cushions, saying they could be in no better hands than the Lord

Provost and Magistrates of his good city. Arbuthnot and his companions then retired, hurrying to their carriages and joining the procession. The King sat down, gratefully no doubt, and the column moved through the gateway and on to Picardy Place.

Here the roadway narrowed, and on the stand outside Mr Gibson's house it seemed to all that they could lean forward and touch the King's shoulder as he passed. To all, that is, except the short-sighted Mary Frances Grant.

> He was very gracious and each lady declared he gave her a particular bow. I could not see his face, I am so blind; but all my party said he was an ugly old man. I saw him take off his hat very gracefully, and everybody said he looked quite pleased and delighted, but when he got further through the town they complained that he looked fagged, and did not raise his hand quite so high.

The King's particular bow, the lecher's smile to which eroding age now gave a harmless charm, was noticed by others. In Picardy Place, said one newspaper, the King held up his hands in wonder at so many women gathered to applaud him, particularly those outside the house of Mr George Spence, linen-draper. Here 'the ecstasies of a beautiful married lady in one of the high balconies attracted the royal regard, and were acknowledged by a bow and a smile'.

A few places from Mary Frances, James Loch was carefully noting all that should be put in his letter to Lady Stafford that evening. It was a *tout ensemble* he had never seen before and one he could not expect to see again. The 'revived ancient dresses' – by which he meant William Murray's theatrical costumes – were well done, and the King looked amazingly well. But Loch's particular interest, as he knew it would be her ladyship's, was the appearance and reception of the Sutherlanders. No man in Edinburgh, he was sure, looked so well as Lady Stafford's clansmen. The trews they wore made them appear taller and more sturdy than other Highlanders. As well as depriving the Black Watch of their clothing, Loch had also acquired scarlet plaids of the Royal Tartan which, he could assure her ladyship, was worn by Sutherlanders in former days. The principal body of her contingent marched in the rear of the procession under two banners, one bearing Lord Stafford's crest, and the other her ladyship's as Countess of Sutherland. In the van were three Esquires to the Chief, all subjects of her ladyship and gentlemen of birth, a Mackenzie, a Mathieson and a Mackay, wearing the tartan of their name and blue bonnets trimmed with gold lace. Then came Lord Francis Leveson-Gower, her son, 'the Chief and a most handsome one indeed'. Four pipers followed, two and two, and then the men of Sutherland, led by the tireless factor of Assynt, George Gunn. Loch was inspired by the appearance of his employers' feudal tribute to the King. 'I mean to write an account,' he told Lady Stafford that night, 'to be placed at Dunrobin, for the whole has done honour to the Clan and the Chief.'

When the King's carriage turned into Princes Street from Saint Andrew Square, the King saw Calton Hill ahead, its slopes alive with people, and its summit belching flame and smoke from the Artillery's guns. He was more impressed by this than he was by the dark silhouette of the Castle to which Dorset or Winchester directed his attention across the long-drained bed of the Nor' Loch. He waved an admiring hand at the hill. 'How superb!' he said, or was thus reported the next day. Mary Frances Grant said that those who heard him declared his words were 'My God, how fine this is!' As the procession curled about the base of the hill, his emotions were so strong that he could no longer speak, only hold his admiral's hat above his red wig and his smiling, sweating face.

Atholl observed the procession from his rooms at Oman's, having a clear and untroubled view as it approached from Princes Street and moved down Regent Bridge to the left of the hotel. Although the Duke had been asked to ride with other peers in the procession – and indeed was reported as having done so – he had chosen to be here, in comfort with his grandchildren. One was Evan MacGregor, a boy of three who was lifted to the window to see his father and his brother John pass below with the Griogaraich. The children's excitement pleased Atholl, although he was irritated by 'the madness for the Highland garb', and amused by 'the different persons dressed by Sir W. Scott in fantastic attire'. But he could not take a wholly crabbed view of the occasion. It had been a finer sight than he had expected, and it was astonishing to see Calton Hill so densely covered by well-dressed people that there was no room for one more.

At another window overlooking Princes Street the procession was watched by another Grant from Speyside. No relation, except by marriage perhaps, to the family of Rothiemurchus, Mrs Anne Grant had been born a MacVicar on Lochaweside in Argyll. She was now the widow of the minister of Laggan and, as she gloomily put it, 'the mother of a perishing family'. A woman of literary pretensions, she lived upon the small pension her modest success had brought her, and upon her lingering reputation as the author of *Letters from the Mountains*, published twenty years before. She was now sixty-seven, and her childhood in the West Highlands, a marriage of love in a small Speyside manse, had left her with a fierce attachment to the past and to the Gaelic race so vividly described by her 'very particular friend', Stewart of Garth. 'The name of the Scotch as a nation', she wrote at this time to the antiquary George Chalmers, 'would perish were it not for these despised Highlanders,' In her *Letters* she had praised the Men of Ross who had attempted to rid their hills of Cheviot sheep, but her sympathy for oppressed Highlanders did not encompass the misery of others.

> As for the mobs in towns, they are mere ebullitions of ignorance and wantonness in a people who were never so rich before, and to whom wealth and freedom are such novelties, that they know not the true use or bounds of either.

She could scarce afford this visit to Edinburgh, but she wished to see her favourite son play his part in the pageant. He was a newly fledged lawyer, having passed his final examination in June, and at his mother's prompting he had become a member of the Celtic Club. He marched below her window this day with his companions, 'in all the Pomp of War, banners flying, pipes playing, badges in their bonnets'. Before he left to join the assembly in Queen Street, she had helped him into his Highland costume. She described this proudly to Chalmers.

> At the head of all, guarding the Crown and the High Constable, marched the Celtic Society, including that tall and sturdy Celt my Son whom like a Spartan Matron I arrayed for the occasion. But unlike a Spartan warrior he wore the Tartan and

broadsword very reluctantly, having a great dislike to all exhibitions of himself, & fearing perhaps the after raillery of his brethren of the quill, the Lowland Cockneys. However, finding himself in very good company, he was soon reconciled to the garb of his ancestors.

On his winding journey about the base of Calton Hill, the King stopped the landau for a moment to look down at the gold-capped turrets of Holyrood, its grey stones and ruined abbey diminished by the great wave of Salisbury Craigs. Seeing this, and listening to the singing of *God save the King* on the Hill, the King was 'visibly moved', as the newspapers delicately described his weeping at moments of unaffected emotion. Moving on, the carriage turned down Abbey Hill away from the main procession and arrived before the palace at twenty minutes to two. Its appearance through the gates was saluted by a party of Sutherlanders, by files of Archers and the flank companies of the 13th, 66th and 77th. When he alighted, and went through the columned doorway, the crowd on Calton Hill shouted its approval, and the guns on the Craigs above fired one last salute.

Inside the palace, the dim light so tastefully contrived by Mr Trotter glowed on the red and gold uniforms of the Yeomen, the yellow bows of the Archers and the burnished steel of the Lochaber axes held by a company of Celts. The first echelon of Scottish nobility was awaiting the King. The Duke of Hamilton, wearing satisfactory gauntlets, it is to be hoped, bent to kiss his hand, and was followed by others whose names and titles had contributed to the history of this modest building in the three hundred years and more of its existence, sometimes in wisdom, sometimes in brotherly harmony, but often in bloody competition – Roxburghe and Montrose, Morton and Argyll, Moray, Home and Lauderdale, Tweeddale, Hopetoun and Breadalbane.

The King was tired, and undoubtedly anxious to be away to Dalkeith where he could relax with his English cronies, his corset unlaced and his breeches unbuttoned. The long day's duty was almost done. After a few minutes alone with Peel and Melville in brief conference, he went to the Presence Chamber and sat upon his throne for the last of the solemn traditions devised by Sir Walter Scott. When he had composed himself, he was approached by the

Knight Marischal, and by Esquires carrying the Honours of Scotland. Each sacred piece was taken from its velvet cushion by Keith and handed to its traditional bearer, who received it upon one knee. Thus Hamilton took the Crown in his right as premier duke, young Francis Leveson-Gower was given the Sceptre in the name of his mother, and the Earl of Erroll received the Scottish Sword of State in his English lancer's uniform. Once this brief and over-solemn ceremony was finished, there were Addresses to be patiently heard. The longest was written by the Lord Provost on behalf of the Magistracy, and read by Mr Cunningham, the Senior Clerk. At this point, Glengarry made another uninvited appearance, albeit with less noise than before and largely unnoticed. An outraged officer of the Highland Guard later described the incident for the readers of the *Observer* under the pseudonym of *A Celt*.

> What did Mr M'Donell do? Why, he forced himself into the Royal presence, in dirty boots and spurs, on the day of His Majesty's arrival at Holyrood when the Lord Provost and Magistrates of Edinburgh were presenting the address, and where *even HE* had no right to enter.

In that crowded, shadowed and over-warm room it is unlikely that the King was aware of Glengarry's uninvited arrival. Despite his weariness he was required to maintain an air of great interest in Arbuthnot's Address. The only sentence that may have touched him was a reference to 'the personal fatigue and inconvenience' he must have suffered during his voyage. When he had thanked the Magistrates, and promised their city his continued favour and protection, he was obliged to remain on the throne while his hand was kissed by the Lord Provost, the Baillies, the Dean of the Guild and the Treasurer. Following this, and more labial compliments from several Judges, he retired to the Royal Closet, preceded by the Regalia. There, in the last ceremony of the day, the Captain-General of the Archers, the Earl of Hopetoun, presented him with a brace of barbed arrows, lying on a cushion of green velvet. This ceremony had required no invention, for the arrows were a *reddendum*, the tribute demanded in the charter which Queen Anne had given to that old club of harmless Jacobites.

The public day was now over. At half-past three, after a few minutes in privacy, the King was driven to Dalkeith in a closed carriage. Henry Fox watched his departure from a window in Breadalbane's apartments. The young man did not think it worth more than a brief sentence in his journal. His egocentricity was exclusive. He did not, for example, record that Lord Ancram, with whom he had travelled from London and whose guest he had been at Newbattle Abbey, had been prevented from taking any part in the ceremonies by an ugly fall from his horse. The 'horrid affair' of Londonderry's suicide was noted in his journal clearly because he thought it might be of advantage to his languishing love for Harriet Canning. He hoped to God it meant that her father would now become Foreign Minister and not go to India. *'If it does!!! . . .'*

Now that the King was no longer obliged to be on display before his subjects his journey to Dalkeith was completed in twenty-two minutes at a steady trot. Dorset and Winchester travelled in the carriage with him, and General Bradford rode upon its right. Thirty troopers and a sergeant of the Greys led the way, followed at an interval by forty more under a captain and a subaltern. Behind the carriage was another detachment of the same regiment. The cavalcade was perhaps a more breath-catching sight than the long procession from Leith, for there was no pretentious absurdity, only a dark carriage with its hidden occupant, the spin of varnished wheels, the thunder of scarlet riders, and the afternoon sun reflected from a hundred shouldered swords. There was a great crowd from the tollbar of Dalkeith to the wide gates of the House, townsfolk and tenants of the young Duke of Buccleuch, held back from the centre of the road by more horsemen of the Scots Greys and by soldiers of the 77th. They saw little or nothing of their royal visitor. Carriage and cavalry went through the gates without slackening the pace, down the dip of the drive and about the trees to the hidden house. The gilded gates were then closed, and guards mounted upon them. The King dined that afternoon with English and Scots peers of his choice, and with particular friends who had come to share his Visit. The people of Scotland would not see him again for another forty-eight hours.

Two of his companions at dinner were Englishmen whose association with him had aroused public hostility or ribald contempt. Sir

William Knighton, the *accoucheur*, sat beside the King, his disappointment at finding no letter from his wife awaiting him in Scotland greatly soothed by this honour. He was not only 'the best of friends' to His Majesty, doctor, counsellor and secretary, he was at last Keeper of the Purse. Although this had increased public criticism, he had defused its effect upon the King by saying that his alone might be 'the voice of opposition to some of your Majesty's schemes' and he feared this might separate them. Not unnaturally, the King had responded to such honesty with even greater affection, and Knighton knew that the apogee of his career was in sight. He wrote to his wife on the morning after his arrival in Scotland, telling her of his delight at being here again, although he had shed a tear in memory of the days when he studied surgery in Edinburgh. He was shamelessly pleased to be at Dalkeith, so beautiful a house, so romantically situated, all wooded and quite delightful. His bedroom was allegedly and truly haunted, he thought, for there were strange sounds throughout the night, which was as nonsensical, perhaps, as his claim that a million people had greeted the King's arrival.

The second favourite, whose fine yacht lay at anchor near the *Royal George*, was a more agreeable man. Now approaching eighty, Sir William Curtis had begun his working life in his father's business, selling sea-biscuit to the Royal Navy and the East India Company. He was the most able of five brothers, and from their Wapping trade he went on to Greenland fisheries and banking, becoming an alderman and subsequently Lord Mayor of London, a Member of Parliament, President of the Artillery Company and of Christ's Hospital. His politics, he once said, could be expressed in a few words. 'I fear God and honour the King.' The latter reacted to their growing friendship with self-centred gratitude, giving Curtis a portrait of himself by Thomas Lawrence, to which the banker responded with one of himself by the same artist. From Ireland in 1821, the King sent Curtis a Coronation Medal, with an accompanying card, *Take this in remembrance of me*. Despite this blasphemy of the Eucharist, the banker offered the hospitality of Cliff House, his rich home in Ramsgate, and the travelling comfort of *Die Jonge Vrow Rebecca Maria* when the King crossed the Channel in the autumn of the same year. Even in his old age, and almost as overweight as his friend, Curtis was still robust and strong, and this may have increased the admiring but pathetic envy of the royal hypochondriac. William Curtis was an uxurious husband and a devoted father. He was not a vulgarian or the thoughtless oaf which a single sartorial error, and its immortalization by George Cruikshank, were to make him.

Dining in Castle Street that memorable day, Walter Scott celebrated the King's arrival with close friends, some of whom had been performers in his pageant, including Alasdair Ranaldson who came with his overwhelming wife. 'Joyous company!' said George Crabbe, writing to his son. It was a sumptuous dinner, all the male guests but himself in Highland dress, and in the evening there were tales and songs, and ballads written by his host. Scott was the life and soul of the gathering. 'It was a splendid festivity,' said Crabbe, 'and I felt I know not how much younger.' Glengarry's lady had captivated him, telling him that he was surely a bard and a harper. He almost believed her, although, as his son knew, he could not strike a note upon a harp.

For the Grants, the great event of the day had passed too quickly. Once the last dragoon and the last varnished carriage had clattered up Picardy Place, Mr Gibson's guests turned to the refreshments he had provided. 'All eating like famished cormorants,' said Mary Frances, 'not a pin's point of meat was left on the table.' She and her sister were determined that the rest of the day should not be an anticlimax. They called upon friends during the afternoon and were given a promise by old Lady Morton, a stranger until now, that she would provide them with tickets for the Peers' Ball should their Papa be unsuccessful. They took some of Elizabeth's songs to be bound, and of course there was another visit to Miss Jolly, 'to see about our dresses'. They returned home to King Street at the same time as their father, and he stood by their open carriage door, reading aloud the latest letters from Mamma and Elizabeth. In the evening they went to the Theatre Royal. Three little pieces were performed, but Jane said she would have preferred one good play and a farce. The girls were separated from their father, who went into Lady Tweeddale's box with the Gibsons, and the girls were seated a row apart, 'uncomfortable and stupefied'. Remembering how she had been placed next to 'a most stupid vulgar woman', Jane's mood became waspish. The performance of *The Magpie and the Maid* was lamentable. 'Mrs Siddons, dying with a headache, had rouged herself up very high, and was not at all herself, though strangers to her acting thought it could not be better.' The only delight in an evening of disappointment was a handsome young cavalryman of the Greys, 'whose moustachios showed him to be an officer' but also prevented the girls from recognizing an old family friend.

The King remained at Dalkeith House on Friday and was not seen outside its gates, 'resigning himself', alliterated the newspapers, 'to the simple recreations of rural retirements'. These included the formal visits of half a dozen peers of Scotland during the morning and afternoon, and a convivial dinner later with half a dozen more.

The emotional deflation which the people of Edinburgh, and its visitors, felt during that long and empty day was dispelled by the wondrous transformation of the city in the evening. The jaded spirits of the Grant girls had been refreshed by a day in the country, visiting friends and relations. They came back at dusk to the unexpected beauty of a New Town glowing with incandescent fire. Hurrying home, the girls quickly changed into warmer clothes and shawls, discarding their pretty white bonnets for something more suitable. The servants, who might also have wished to sally out, were told to stay indoors and guard against any conflagration, and then all the Grants and their friends left on foot to enjoy the unforgettable experience of The Illuminations. Never, Jane told her mother, never would she forget the delirium of this evening.

> Every street in every corner of the town was literally filled with people of every rank; not merely the footways on each side, but the broad pavement held a moving mass whichever way you went. Most of the houses were simply lighted with candles, some one in every pane; others in figures; these certainly look best on the whole, and make a better show than lamps . . . You never saw a small room so crowded the night of a great Rout, as were all the broad long streets of this magnificent town that evening . . . My head was full of the Arabian Nights. Every spot light as noon-day, each house illuminated with splendour, but all empty and deserted.

Not one drunken man had been seen, or an uncivil word heard in the great crowd. Wearing their best clothes, she told her mother, put the common people upon their politest manners.

The Duke of Atholl was pleased by the city's moderate pulse on Friday, and the leisurely manner in which he was able to spend the day. In the morning, as required, he went to Dalkeith House with his wife, hoping to explain the absence of his clansmen, but was given no opportunity, nor was there occasion to speak of it to Robert Peel. When the formalities were over, he made a slow detour on his return to Edinburgh. First he called at Newbattle Abbey, not so much to see Lord Lothian (who had also been at Dalkeith with the King) but to inspect his lordship's property. The house had grown, century by century, upon the site of a Cistercian abbey, and in its present form it was the product of insane alteration and improvement, a romantic illustration for a Waverley novel. Its history clung to it in appropriate legends. The murdered mistress of a king was buried here, and here James IV had first met his English bride, ten years before her countrymen slaughtered his at Flodden, and him among them. The house did not interest Atholl. He thought it small, although there was one fine chamber which Lothian had prepared for the King's reception should he call. The parkland estate had a greater appeal, particularly its noble trees. Atholl had no measure in his pocket, but could estimate their girth with a practised eye, believing the largest to be twenty feet.

He drove on for two miles and stopped for a similar inspection of Melville Castle, the owner of which was also with the King at Dalkeith. Built less than thirty-five years before to the design of James Playfair, and where there had once been a royal hunting-lodge, it was a gothic building in the extravagant style of the time. Modern and good, thought Atholl. Again the trees were admirable, eighty or ninety in number and mostly young beeches, lining the river approach. None exceeded a century in age, and all were remarkably lean in their stems, growing as finely as any at Dunkeld.

His good humour restored by this outing, Atholl enjoyed the illuminations that evening. At dusk he left the house in Charlotte Square, upon which he had ordered an illuminated saltire to be hung, and walked alone among the people for an hour and a half. 'Everywhere crowded to excess, but in civility and quiet, so that a child of five years old might have travelled everywhere.' When he returned to Charlotte Square he did not go to bed until past one o'clock, sitting alone at a window and watching the lights as they were extinguished one by one.

The *Scotsman* said the illuminations had 'much gorgeousness of effect'. They were a mixture of aesthetic innocence and arrogant vulgarity, personal emotion and commercial advertisement. Upon public buildings, such as the County Hall, the Exchequer and the Royal Exchange, an attempt at tasteful dignity was made with representations of crowns, thistles and saltires, cherubs, obelisks and stars, festoons, drapery and patriotic slogans, all formed by coloured transparencies and lit from behind by the clever use of candles, lamps or gas. The *Caledonian Mercury* erected a complex illustration of the King's arrival, greeted by the City of Edinburgh in female form and surrounded by Highland pipers, all against the background of the Castle. The *Scotsman*, more restrained, hid the façade of its building with the thistle of its masthead, surmounted by a crown. Lord Bannatyne's house in the Canongate displayed the King upon his throne, with two seahorses at his feet, receiving his crown from a kneeling woman. Mr Gianetti, perfumer of George Street, graced his fashionable salon with two large transparencies. The first was an imperial crown and the royal cipher. The second showed the King landing upon The Shore, extending his hand and asking, *'How's a' wi' ye?'* Upon the Princes Street premises of Mr Trotter there was a crown and the royal arms, supported by the rose and thistle, all discreetly lit by lamps. The Lord Provost and Magistracy of Glasgow erected a female figure upon their house in Queen Street. She carried a ship and a flag, representing commerce, and supported the city's arms and its vainglorious motto upon her head. The Provost of Stirling was content with the Lady of the Lake, posed before the castle of his royal burgh. Above the portico and pediment of the Theatre Royal, William Murray hung Scotland's shield of red and gold, a lion rampant within a double tressure flory counter-flory, the whole surrounded by stars, festoons and drapery. But the Crown Hotel surpassed all. A muscular Highlander strode from its transparency, carrying the King in his arms and exclaiming, *'Welcome to the land of your ancestors!'*

The exhortations below the illuminations were often banal, and sometimes naively charming. *Vivat Rex! . . . May the King live for ever*

. . . Welcome to Auld Reekie . . . Hail our King . . . Hail Star of Brunswick . . . Happy may he live . . . Salve Pater Patriae . . . Hurra! . . . 'Tis the better for us, boys! . . . May the Learning, Religion, and Valour of the Sons of Scotia be a prop to thy throne.

The fire upon Arthur's Seat burned again throughout this evening, and, now that there was no mist, the outline of the Craigs could be seen against the extraordinary glow. More dramatic still, there were iron baskets of glowing coal on the battlements of the Castle, and cannon firing from the embrasures. Small groups of sailors, on shore leave from the Royal Squadron and the Fleet, danced hornpipes on the pavements, their amiable drunkenness unnoticed in the general intoxication of joy. At regular intervals, rockets were discharged from the squares and gardens of the New Town, climbing in fiery arcs above the blue-slate roofs. Upon the stroke of ten, the guns on Calton Hill and Salisbury Craigs began a series of thundrous salvoes, joined by the Leith Battery and the ships in the firth. In the echoing pauses between these salutes, scarlet infantry on the summit of Arthur's Seat discharged rippling *feux-de-joie* into the night.

Towards midnight, bands of boys appeared on Princes Street, George Street and Queen Street, carrying flaming torches and ready to escort tired sightseers to their rest. The Grants came home wearily. Jane had been separated from the others almost as soon as they set out, and had twisted her ankle on the rough stones in the middle of George Street, but she could not abandon the excitement. When she did return, both feet aching now, she was still ready to go on to a party with William Grant. Mary Frances had returned earlier, 'pale as a ghost and terribly fagged from the heat', and would not budge again. Jane changed her clothes in five minutes, and when a chair was called for her, she followed her impatient brother. This last pleasure of the day was not a success, however, a *stickit* party in Jane's opinion, for the guests kept leaving to see the end of the illuminations. When she came home she could not sleep, but was not unhappy. 'It seemed to me that I had been walking through some enchanted country under ground.'

William Cranstone was abroad in the streets for more than four hours that evening, and had spent the same time at Leith on Thursday, awaiting the King and following him to Holyrood. His account-

John Campbell, 4th Earl of Breadalbane, who refused to turn his clansmen away from Edinburgh. 'They are now here, I must make the best of them, though they will be very deficient in equipment.'

Mrs. Anne Grant of Laggan, author, proud widow and mother. 'The name of Scotch as a nation would perish were it not for these despised Highlanders . . . As for the mobs in town, they are mere ebullitions of ignorance.'

39 Castle Street, Scott's house in Edinburgh and his headquarters during the Visit. 'John Macleod, outfitter, not far from Scott's door, supplied most of the weapons purchased or hired by the clans.'

John Townsend, Bow Street Runner, the King's favourite and his attendant in Scotland, 'a big man in a flaxen wig, light blue coat and red vest.'

Most of the artists who came to Edinburgh sketched the King's landing in Leith Harbour, but David Wilkie was determined to paint the arrival at Holyroodhouse. This was the result, splendid, romantic, absurdly inaccurate, and highly popular with the subject and his people.

The King goes to kirk. 'Turner had visited St. Giles several times, sketching the interior in detail, and had soon decided on his subject – Monarch and Preacher, raised above the floor and facing each other across a crowded congregation . . . The King did not like the work.'

Turner's painting of the Civic Banquet in Parliament Hall shows the granting of a baronetcy to William Arbuthnot. 'The overwhelmed Lord Provost knelt, grasping a royal hand and kissing it effusively until the King lifted him from the floor.'

William Murray's Theatre Royal in 1822. A great crowd gathered here on the night of the King's visit, fighting to get in to the performance. 'The steam that arose from the mob,' it was said, 'was not unlike a vapour bath.'

A solitary, rain-soaked King, waving his hat on the Half Moon Battery of the castle was the most dramatic event of the Visit. 'Good God!' he said, looking down, 'What a fine sight! I had no conception there was such a scene in the world.'

Overleaf: Calton Hill, with its long prospect of Princes Street, and a fine view of the Castle, was a popular assembly point during the King's Jaunt. Many visitors slept under canvas on its southern brae.

The King's grand arrival for breakfast at Hopetoun House, before embarking for England. 'Mr. Blanchflower's footmen had laid the crimson carpet on the wet stones at the last moment before the advance troopers of the escort came down the drive.'

Romantic myth confounded. Kenneth MacLeay's painting of the Atholl fisherman, Willie Duff, and the photograph from which the artist worked, or in which the Highlander was persuaded to pose in sad imitation of the portrait.

book was not a journal, and thus did not record his feelings, but the value of his loyal presence and his expenses were carefully noted. For attendance at Leith, two pounds. Incidentals and travelling expenses, fifteen shillings. For attending a fireworks display in Charlotte Square that night, detained two hours, one pound. And for his wandering during the Illuminations, two pounds and ten shillings.

Robert Peel had now transferred his lodgings from Melville Castle to the Waterloo Hotel. He worked late on Friday night, letters to London and a report to Lord Liverpool of the events of the past two days. He thought highly of the Visit so far, everything had gone admirably, there had been no accidents, and if there had indeed been less acclamation than might have been expected this was because the Scots 'thought it more respectful not to be too clamorous in the immediate presence of the King'. There was a very strong feeling on the part of all classes that the King should go to the Kirk during his visit. Peel had raised the matter with His Majesty at Dalkeith this day, and understood that now there would be no objection.

> He might either go to the Kirk at Dalkeith, go to the High Kirk at Edinburgh, or have prayers read to him by his Presbyterian Chaplain at Dalkeith House. I think if he is to hear prayers at all he had much better hear them in the manner which is most complimentary to the Country and the Established Religion, and to the Kirk in Edinburgh.

During that evening the *Scotsman* had been clearing its editorial throat for the delivery of a leading article that would express a moderate, radical attitude to the King's arrival. On the whole, it thought the ceremonies and celebrations had been picturesque and well-arranged, but too much had been done to 'give a Highland complexion to the whole . . . as if nothing were Scottish but what is Highland'. This, however, was toward the end of the leader, as it degenerated into programme notes of the occasion. The political voice of the paper spoke clearly in the opening paragraph.

> If there be circumstances in the state of the country which, in a general sense, would make us regret some of the consequences

which must attend this Royal Visit, there are other circumstances which make us glad that it has taken place. His Majesty must now be satisfied, from ocular demonstration, that the people of Scotland – of all classes – are *truly loyal*, by which we mean, that they are attached to the laws, and anxious to pay every rational mark of respect to the CHIEF MAGISTRATE OF THE STATE.

> '*My father, when his own house was set on
> fire, tried to save a few pieces of wood out of the
> burning house, which he carried to the river,
> about half a mile away, and there formed a
> raft of it. His intention was to float the wood
> down the stream and build a kind of hut
> somewhere to shelter his weak family; but the
> burning party came that way, and seeing the
> timber, set fire to it, and soon reduced the whole
> to ashes.*'
>
> – GEORGE MacDONALD, mason, Farr

The King reappeared briefly on Saturday afternoon, for a Levee at
Holyroodhouse. He arrived at one forty-five after a rapid drive of
nineteen minutes from Dalkeith. At two o'clock the gentlemen
attending the Levee were admitted one by one to the Entrée Room in
the south-eastern corner of the palace. At three-fifteen the Levee
was over, and within another hour, largely spent with members of
his Privy Council, the King was back at Dalkeith. During his
seventy-five minutes in the Entrée Room, more than twelve
hundred gentlemen had been introduced, kneeling upon one knee
and lowering their lips above his limply offered hand. Each was
thus given an average of four seconds, a literal moment in which
they could henceforth claim to have met His Majesty King George
IV. David Wilkie was more fortunate than most in receiving a
second or two more. Wearing the court dress he had bought in the
city, his hair well-powdered, he rose from his knee expecting to be
recognized. The King stared at him blankly, until he heard Wilkie's
name called from the presentation card Scott had given the artist.
Then he smiled and said, 'How d'ye do?', upon which Wilkie bowed
and moved away.

Henry Fox was presented by Lauderdale. If his journal is
correct, making his moment with the King seem casual and
lengthy, he must have greatly reduced the time allotted to others.

'*H.M. was gracious and spoke a great deal.*' The rooms of the palace were hot and crowded, and Fox was not impressed by some of those with whom he was forced to associate. 'I never saw more ridiculous figures – grocers, tailors and haberdashers were among them.' As indeed there may have been, among others sometimes as worthy – three dukes, three marquesses, sixteen earls, many viscounts, barons, baronets, knights, chieftains, soldiers, sailors, clergy, lawyers, lord and deputy lieutenants, Members of Parliament, and a great number of rank and file described as *Messieurs* in Sir Patrick Walter's list. This day was particularly trying for the Usher of the White Rod, and he later believed his treatment by the press to be most uncivil. The *Evening Courant* accused him of leaving the palace without distributing a list of those attending the Levee among waiting correspondents of the Monday papers. He told them that such information would be available at his home in Drumsheugh after two o'clock on Sunday. Informing its readers of this, the *Courant* apologized for its delay in publishing the list, and explained where the responsibility should rest.

> Finding it impossible to copy off the list of names in time for our Monday's paper, we wrote to Sir Patrick agreeing to pay the fees required, but on delivering the note, we were told that unless we could assist in copying the names, he (Sir P.) was afraid he could not get clerks to copy them for us. We had no alternative, therefore, but to employ our own clerks, and this we were obliged to do after eighteen hours delay.

Walker's failure to understand that the office he had so jealously secured for himself imposed obligations to the press he despised, was as understandable then as it would become incomprehensible in other officials later. Any member of Scott's committee, however, should have realized the logistic complexity of some of his schemes, principally those involving transport and the resultant congestion of streets. Before ten o'clock, on a morning of smoke-blurred sunlight and a hint of autumnal haar, the first carriages bringing the first arrivals to the Levee came down Abbey Hill to the closed gates of Holyroodhouse and were there halted by a scarlet guard of the 77th. Before noon, the waiting line stretched for almost two miles from the base of Calton Hill to Waterloo Place and the arches of Regent Bridge, down the whole length of Princes Street to St John's Chapel and the Lothian Road. With it was a perambulating crowd, gathered to gawk and peer and sometimes mock the wax-like occupants of the carriages. Not all visitors, however, were willing to join this docile queue. The Duke of Atholl assembled his Perthshire gentlemen at 26 Charlotte Square shortly after eleven. They left at noon, their carriages following the duke's own conveyance, its resolute coachman driving against the flood, and although stopped by occasional confusion the cavalcade reached the palace before one o'clock.

By this time the queue was slowly moving, it having been decided that as many gentlemen as possible should be admitted to the Long Gallery and there await the King, rather than detain him upon his arrival. They alighted on the gravel of the forecourt and formed a shuffling line of blue, scarlet, black and tartan, slowly moving through the doorway of the palace and across its central quadrangle to another door. Here a staircase led to the Long Gallery on the northern side. The quadrangle was already crowded. Footmen in state liveries paced meaningless lengths across the stones with their white rods. Members of the Celtic Society arranged and rearranged the hang of their plaids, or combed their fingers through the scarlet tassels on their Lochaber axes. Archers lined all sides of the piazza and the stairway to the Gallery, where there were more Celts and more Yeomen, immobile against its walls. The tall windows of the Gallery were unopened, and its dark panelling, and the indifferent stare of Scotland's dead kings from half a dozen portraits, seemed to increase the heat and the feeling of suffocation. The chamber was already overfull before the Archers at the head of the stairway were ordered to cross their bows, preventing further entry until some of the Company had passed through to the Entrée Room.

The waiting crowd – in the Gallery, the stairway, the quadrangle, forecourt and line of carriages – was perhaps the greatest assembly of the estates of Scotland since the dissolution of its Parliament, and would have given malicious inspiration to a caricaturist, had one been among the artists present. Turner was absent, through his choice or not, but Wilkie had come early with his host, the sculptor Samuel Joseph. The Keeper of the Regalia, Adam Ferguson, admitted them to an attic where they changed into their court dress and then descended leisurely to the Gallery. John Grant of Rothiemurchus and his son had left their lodgings after a great rush and fuss to get them ready, during which the hairdresser called to curl their hair had proved incompetent, and Grant's brother-in-law had been obliged to heat the tongs and do the work himself. The girls dispatched their father and brother with a great deal of giggling and gentle mockery, and when the house was at last empty they practised their bows and curtseys for the Ladies' Drawing-Room next week. They then left to spend the rest of the day with Mrs Harriet and her daughter Sally Siddons, of whom brother William was becoming quite fond. Rothiemurchus was to be presented to the King by the Duke of Atholl, as a Member of Parliament (albeit for an English constituency) and would then present his son. Once in the Long Gallery they stood with other men of their name, more from familiarity, perhaps, than clannishness – their chief's brother, Colonel Francis, and the Lairds of Red Castle and Glenmoriston.

The most colourful and, to some, the most provoking group waiting in the Gallery was a knot of MacDonells, standing about the tall figure of Glengarry in their dark red and green tartan. They were representatives of what he called 'The House of MacDonell', gentlemen of Barrisdale, Shian and Scotus, his brother Colonel James, and other *duine-uasals* of Clan Donald. Alasdair Ranaldson was aware of his growing unpopularity, or jealous envy as he preferred to call it. Stewart of Garth had no doubt now that this hot-tempered and unthinking man had offended and brought ridicule upon all his Highland countrymen. 'Had it not been for Glengarry,' he would tell Scott later, 'the King's visit would have passed without an angry word or an unpleasant feeling.' Alasdair Ranaldson put the blame for any ill-feeling upon the conspiratorial hostility of the Celtic Society. He held it responsible for a malicious rumour designed to destroy his good name. In order to increase the number of his clansmen in Edinburgh, it was said, he had hired a well-built Englishman from Yorkshire and dressed him in Highland clothes. Glengarry answered this calumny with another no less abusive. In the ranks of the Celtic Society, he said, he had seen 'a mulatto, a Jew, a son to the vender of the Balm of Gilead, and some other foreigners equally preposterous'. He was delighted by any public discomfiture of the Celts. Approaching the staircase to the Long Gallery this morning, he saw the watchful Mr Townsend, of the Bow Street Office, successfully stop the entry of a kilted member of the Society. He remembered their conversation and later reported it to the *Observer*.

> Townsend – 'Sir, Do you call yourself a Highlander?' Answer – 'Yes, certainly! You don't mean to offend me, Sir?' Townsend – 'If I mistake not, Sir, I have seen you some twenty years ago, a singing boy in the choir of —— in England.' This remark put the Celtic gentleman quite out.

The King's arrival was announced by the bray of welcoming trumpets in the forecourt and the crash of a band playing the National Anthem. There was a stir of relief in the Long Gallery where the crush was now uncomfortable. Momentarily eased by the beginning of the Levee, it soon came under pressure again as more gentlemen were thrust into the chamber from the staircase. Sir Patrick Walker had gone to the King in the Entrée Room, but his small staff, in their fanciful costumes, pushed and pleaded for order and a respect for precedence.

Once released from the Gallery, the gentlemen were taken quickly through a set of small rooms on the eastern side of the palace, and then a further two on the south side until they reached the door to the Entrée Room. This was guarded, as were all the doors and rooms through which they had just passed, by Archers in green who uncrossed their yellow bows when each approaching gentleman flourished his presentation card. The Entrée Room was the only public chamber in the palace that could be considered comfortable, and in Atholl's opinion (which would have deeply offended Mr Trotter) it was the only one which 'exhibited any marks of being recently cleaned or adorned'. Known also as the Throne Room, it had once formed part of the official quarters of the Commander-in-Chief in Scotland. One of the most astute general officers to hold that position – and one of the few Scots entrusted with it – was Lord Adam Gordon, who ate his meals and entertained his military guests in the room. He was seated there at supper, twenty-eight years before, when dispatches informed him that three regiments of Highland fencibles in his command were now close to mutiny, and that in a fourth a company of armed MacDonells were defying their officers from the walls of Linlithgow Palace. One of these officers, the only one who appeared indifferent to the outrage, was the mutineers' captain and chief, the young Alasdair Ranaldson MacDonell of Glengarry.

The King stood apart at the eastern end of the room, with a lord-in-waiting, Lord Glenlyon, on his left, and the Earl of Cathcart, Gold Stick, on his right. By the great fireplace were the multi-coloured, glittering gentlemen of his immediate suite – among them Hamilton, Argyll, Erroll and Montrose, Conyngham and Melville, soldiers, sailors, and Mr Secretary Peel. The gentlemen from the Long Gallery entered the room by a door in its south-eastern corner, and were then directed to the right where the King was standing in the thin sunlight and the candelabra's glow.

The first sight of him was undoubtedly a shock to many. He was in full Highland dress, the resplendent scarlet of Mr Hunter's belted plaid, jacket and diced hose, shimmering with bright brooches and jewelled steel, his feathered bonnet cocked as Chief of Chiefs. Colonel Stewart of Garth had put the last touches to this vast magnificence before the Levee began, arranging the fall of the plaid and the hang of the dirk, declaring that the King now looked a 'verra pretty man'. Yet the effect desired was not achieved. The sight of so inglorious a figure, in such wildly excessive splendour, amused and disgusted many at the Levee. The cause of complaint was not the prodigious amount of tartan needed to encircle so great a girth, but the insulting self-mockery of the King's appearance. The civilized distaste felt by Atholl was evident in a single sentence of the entry in his journal that night.

> The King stood in the centre of the E. End of the room, habited in the full costume of a Highlander in the Stewart Tartan with flesh-coloured silk or taffeta where the dress should have been bare.

Hugh Scott of Harden, whom Walter Scott called his friend and chief, was astonished by the apparition, sharing his derision with his wife, who passed it on to their daughter.

His Majesty wore the Royal Tartan Highland dress with buff-coloured trowsers like *flesh* to *imitate* his *Royal knees*, and little bits of Tartan stocking like other Highlanders halfway up his legs.

The newspapers reporting the Levee were more sycophantic, declaring that the King's costume 'displayed his manly and graceful figure to great advantage'. David Wilkie told his sister that the King had looked exceedingly well in kilt and hose, 'with a kind of flesh-coloured pantaloons underneath'. But in the magnificent portrait which he later made of this obese caricature, the King's manly knees are bare. The greatest offence given by that expensive and unfortunate costume was not to aesthetic taste but to Lowland pride, and to the self-esteem of those Highland gentlemen who wished to distance themselves as far as possible from the presumed savagery of their ancestors. One of those waiting in the Long Gallery, irritated by the heat and the press of the crowd, was James Stuart of Dunearn, who had recently been tried for the killing of Boswell's son in a duel. He was not impressed by the occasion or its subject.

The King did not seem to move a muscle and we all asked ourselves when we came away, what had made us take so much trouble. He was dressed in tartan. Sir Walter had ridiculously made us appear a nation of Highlanders, and the bagpipe and the tartan was the order of the day.

The pink pantaloons also blunted the edge of the wittiest observation on the King's costume. When someone complained that the kilt had been too short for modesty, Lady Hamilton-Dalrymple ended the criticism with a comment both genteel and bawdy. 'Since he is to be among us for so short a time, the more we see of him the better.' Although, of course, nothing of that nature had been seen. In his concern for what he believed to be the true and ancient Highland dress, Garth would perhaps have persuaded, or tried to persuade the King against wearing the pantaloons, had there not been a strong argument for retaining them. They would give less offence to taste and tradition than the sight of the King's grossly bloated and sadly disfigured legs. There was also a precedent of sorts which the King may have been conscientiously observing, and one which makes this small incident symbolic of the histrionic character of the whole Visit. Actors appearing in Scottish plays, such as *Macbeth* and Scott's *Rob Roy*, usually wore flesh-coloured tights beneath their kilts. As Cornet Walter Scott wrote to his father from Germany, this theatrical costume had now become a fashion which some Scottish gentlemen abroad were adopting at levees and balls.

The general feeling among those who disliked Sir Walter's Celtification was that the King had made a fool of himself by appearing *too Highland*. This stiffened into indignation, or exploded in ribaldry, when it was known that Sir William Curtis had also worn Highland dress at the Levee. Some said it was an exact copy of the King's costume, but Wilkie told his sister that the old man 'was also in the tartan, but without the kilt, and looked well'. Kilt or trews, much was to be made then and later of the King's anger at his friend's presumption, but he was probably more amused by it. John Lockhart, whose opinion of his father-in-law's theatrical activities sometimes has the sound of pious humbug, said that Curtis had cast 'an air of ridicule and caricature over the whole of Sir Walter's Celtified pageantry'. In truth, which is to say in hindsight, the apparent blasphemy seems to have strengthened the bogus sanctity of Highland dress. The grotesque figure of the King does not provoke ridicule now, for it has been hidden beneath David Wilkie's stunning tribute to the belted plaid. But Sir William's comic gaffe, if such it was, is preserved in Cruikshank's cartoon. It might be said, however, that since Highland dress and the spurious tartans of that time and since have little connection with the ancient costume of the mountains, they may perhaps be worn without foolish dispute by any Highlander, Lowlander, or fat Cockney biscuit-seller.

The crush on the stairway, in the Long Gallery and the communicating rooms, had become intolerable before the Levee was half over, despite a great deal of *hurry-hurry* by Sir Patrick's staff and the Chamberlain's ushers. In the Entrée Room a bored Archer estimated that fifteen gentlemen were being introduced to the King within the space of a minute. The Duke of Atholl, standing among the royal suite, watched with approval as his son Glenlyon took the presentation card from each gentleman and boldly called the name upon it. Coming into the dusk of the chamber, from the blinding daylight of the ante-rooms, some gentlemen had to be physically pointed in the direction of His Majesty, and some did not then recognize him in his strange costume. Others had forgotten what they must do. A country laird, uneasy and old, it was said, was told that he should go before the King, make a lower bow than he would to anyone else, and then go out by the far door. This he did, almost without pausing, until Lord Errol hissed at him. *'Kiss hands . . . kiss hands . . . !'* He did so, retiring backwards and almost upon his knees, throwing kisses from his finger-tips. The King's good humour was said to have been wholly restored by the incident, having presumably been thrown out of sorts by Sir William Curtis.

In an hour, or little more, the Levee was over, and the last of the twelve hundred gentlemen joined the noisy wait for carriages on Abbey Hill and the London Road. The King retired to a meeting of his Privy Council, where Atholl thought he was looking remarkably well. The Levee had been a disappointment to the Duke, all too much of a gallop. He also believed that his Majesty should be lodged in Holyroodhouse, for as it was now 'it makes the King's visit less not more than a visit, his residence being seven miles off, rather than in the Palace of the Scottish Kings, and his appearances cannot be half so frequent'.

Indeed he would not return to the city until past noon on Monday, and even then the public would see little of him. He did not go to Kirk this Sunday, as godly men had hoped and expected, but prayers for his divine protection were delivered in all the churches in Edinburgh, and in all the parishes that had received news of his safe arrival. Although he rode briefly in the park at Dalkeith, the King was seen by few of his staff that day. Most of them enjoyed themselves by sight-seeing, taking carriages to Rosslyn Castle, once the centre of a great forest, rich with deer, but now the anachronistic hub of a great community employed in Mr Wauchope's coal-mine. 'Today, Sunday, is a day of peace,' Knighton wrote to his wife. It was also a day of boredom while 'the dear King' was resting. The doctor already felt a prisoner in the house, with nothing to do at one time but stare from its windows to a dozen hares feeding on the lawn. His bedroom, he had now discovered, was historic as well as haunted. A portrait of General George Monck hung above his bed, and in this very room that wily Parliamentarian had signed the paper that restored Charles II to the throne.

At the Waterloo Hotel, Robert Peel put on his green eye-shade and busied himself with reports to and from London. Lord Liverpool told him that by this same post he was informing the King that the Duke of Wellington should perhaps go to Vienna 'with the instructions our dear departed friend had prepared for himself'. Lady Londonderry, he said, was anxious that the same dear departed man should be buried in Westminster Abbey. Liverpool said this would be wrong, leaving Peel to understand, as everybody would, that a suicide could not be interred thus. He would do something about it, he said, if he did not know enough of her ladyship's character to realize that it would not do to disagree with her upon this subject and at this moment. He knew that their friend's death must have thrown a gloom over Peel and the ceremonies in Edinburgh. The Home Secretary was not so much gloomy as unwell, and ill-disposed to join any festivity. He had turned his thoughts to other projects, to the meetings he proposed with the heads of the respective Courts in Scotland. He fervently hoped he would secure their agreement to alterations in those legal practices in Scotland which were 'totally different from English practice, and rather repugnant to English feelings'. He told Liverpool that if they could persuade him that such practices were for the best, he would give his assurance that they would be maintained, but if not he would urge reform.

Walter Scott was now told by his physician that he could expect no immediate relief from his itching rash, and that if he had not been afflicted by this he would have suffered a bad fever, which was perhaps poor comfort as he considered the painful and unsightly condition of his arms and legs, 'spotted like a leopard's'. His guest, George Crabbe, was astonished by the emptiness of Edinburgh on a Sunday, its streets forsaken. London, he thought, also had a diminution of its population on that day, but in Edinburgh there was *stagnation*, although he did not doubt that its citizens were devout. He walked alone, touched by the civility of the city's poor. 'They certainly exceed ours in politeness, arising, probably, from minds more generally cultivated.' He went to Holyroodhouse, which looked run-down, and its tapestries were a great disappointment. But he was impressed by the little room in James IV's Tower, the Supper Room where Mary was sitting with Rizzio when Darnley, Ruthven and others burst in to murder him. In such a place, with such memories, Crabbe was inclined to be credulous, if with a second-thought of caution. Having examined the stains upon the floor, he told his son, 'I see no reason why you should not believe them made by his blood, if you can.'

The King came into the city at two-thirty on Monday, wearing a field-marshal's uniform, his blue pantaloons edged with gold. Since noon, a troop of the Scots Greys, a company of Archers, with Celts, soldiers, members of the Household and several peers had been waiting before the palace and within the quadrangle. There were also crowds in the streets approaching the palace, and upon the slopes of Calton Hill, but not so great as they had been on Thursday and Saturday. An advance picquet of the Greys arrived at two o'clock, and half an hour later the royal coach and six came into the courtyard.

For almost two hours in the Entrée Room, the King listened bravely to long and repetitive Addresses from the Church of both denominations, from the heads of Scottish universities, from the Highland Society of Scotland and from sundry towns, burghs and counties. The room was once more crowded to suffocation. The Address from the Commission of the General Assembly of the Church of Scotland was presented by one hundred and twenty-six ministers, office-bearers and elders, whose sombre clothes and militant zeal provoked evident surprise in the faces of the King and his suite. Their Address, delivered by the Moderator with his renowned pulpit fervour, was distressingly long, and was answered with courteous but salutary brevity by the King. He had then to hear a much longer Address from the Universities of Scotland. The presenters of this were modest in numbers, no more than two chancellors, two rectors, one principal and twenty-four professors. Having accepted their admiration, affection, loyalty, and gratitude for his gracious presence among them, he answered with the same polite brevity. He then retired to a closet where a deputation from the Episcopalian Church delivered its Address in private, thus giving no offence to its Presbyterian brethren beyond.

When the King returned to the Entrée Room and heard the Address from the Highland Society, his response was the briefest of all that afternoon.

> I thank you for this loyal and dutiful Address. It will always be gratifying to me to hear of the success of a society which had for its object the encouragement of the agriculture and manufactures of Scotland.

The Addresses from the towns, burghs and counties were also expeditiously delivered and answered. With that came the last engagement of the day, a private audience to the great agriculturalist, Sir John Sinclair of Ulbster. He wished to present the King with the final result of his *Statistical Account of Scotland*, a monumental work of great industry and value. There was more to Sinclair's motives than this estimable presentation, however. It was his penultimate attempt to secure a peerage. It would not succeed, nor would his last effort a few days later, the gift to the King of six bottles of Mountain Dew whisky from Caithness.

Henry Fox dined with Scott that afternoon, before going on to play écarté with Lady Gwydir in the evening. A turn at cards, particularly écarté, was becoming a pleasant escape from the tedium of Edinburgh during the Visit. The dinner in Castle Street was not as entertaining as it should have been. Scott was 'evidently out of humour with the King', and Fox put this down to a rumour that his officiousness had offended His Majesty.

That evening a messenger brought Atholl a brief letter from Peel. The Secretary still believed, or was considerately pretending to believe, that the decision to stop the arrival of more Highlanders had not originated with Atholl. He now apologized to the duke for not informing him earlier that on the day of the King's arrival he had told His Majesty that many Highlanders were waiting to greet him in the city. At this the King had said, 'I'll be bound the Atholl men will be there!' Peel had quickly explained that

> . . . they had not the same opportunity of preparation that others had, that still a word would bring them, even if they came in the last days before His Majesty's departure, but that there were so many Highlanders already arrived, and such a want of accommodation for them in this crowded city, that Lord Melville and I had entreated your Grace to stop them.

It was true that a word would still bring them, for John Findlater had not yet been told to disband the little company he had gathered, drilled and partly equipped. This day he wrote again to Frederick Graham, at the Duke's house in Charlotte Square. Although the Breadalbane men were thought to have taken all the broadswords and dirks available in Perthshire, Findlater had been able to obtain twenty swords from sources he did not care to name. There were still only twenty sporrans among his hundred men, and there was a grievous lack of white side-belts, which perhaps Graham could acquire from the Castle in Edinburgh, as well as swords and dirks if possible. The men were ready to march now, and he was willing to put the first divisions on the road to save time. Two pipers had offered their services, and would march as private soldiers until their music was required.

Before he retired that Monday night, or perhaps early in the morning, Atholl at last told Graham to order Findlater to stand his men down and dismiss them to their homes. With characteristic generosity, but with an odd failure to understand the nature of the men so recruited, he said that any who wished to make their own way to Edinburgh, to see the King as sight-seers, could expect some help from him to pay their way.

William Cranstone had not thought the King's visit to Holyroodhouse on Monday required his attendance, but he made a note of the four hours he had spent outside the palace during the Levee, standing in the crowd and watching the dusty line of carriages edging down Abbey Hill to the gates. He considered the value of his time to be two pounds.

> *'My ancestors lived and died at Abercross, in
> the parish of Golspie, until 1819 when my
> father was evicted and his possessions set on fire
> by Patrick Sellar, at the instance of Countess
> Elizabeth Sutherland . . . The Law of Eviction
> is the law that ruinates this country. In nine
> years they will have 15,000 removed from the
> interior of Sutherland, and during the reign of
> Charles no more than 30,000 were removed
> out of the whole of Scotland by Prelacy and
> Popery.'*
>
> – JAMES SUTHERLAND, labourer

Four hundred and fifty-seven ladies attended the King's Drawing-Room on Tuesday 20 August. Custom obliged him to kiss each upon the cheek, but in the brisk gallop of their passage through the Entrée Room it was inevitable that some received no buss at all, and later complained that the experience had been most unsatisfactory. Mary Frances Grant said she scarcely felt his lips brush her cheek. She had been too nervous to curtsey, and could give no precise description of the King. 'I saw only a pair of thick lips, and a grave, respectful face bending toward me. He appeared to me a most immense man, much, much above me.'

Like most of the King's public appearances during the Visit, this occasion was affable but brief, taking him away from the pleasant seclusion of Dalkeith House for less than two hours. To others, the day seemed long and sometimes excessively tedious. The first carriages reached Holyroodhouse at ten in the morning, and the last were still coming down Abbey Hill just before two o'clock when the King's coach and its escort of grey dragoons turned into the palace yard. As usual, His Majesty was said to be in excellent health and spirits, which meant, of course, that from a distance rouge and powder disguised the chronic fatigue of his ailing body. He was dressed somewhat aggressively for so feminine an occasion, in the uniform of a field-marshal with a silk sash and the diamond glitter of an Order upon his scarlet breast. After a private audience with Melville, he went to the Entrée Room where the presentation of the ladies began at two-fifteen. By three-thirty all had passed before him, and at three forty-five his carriage and escort took him away from the palace and down the Dalkeith Road at a spanking trot.

He was undoubtedly glad to be gone. The day was warm, and the air inside the palace was insufferably close. The crowd in the Long Gallery and the ante-rooms was greater than it had been for the Levee, the ladies being accompanied by their presenters, and by their husbands or other men of their families. In the estimate of one of Sir Patrick Walker's staff, the number was no less than 2600. The correspondents of the city's newspapers accepted this figure without cavil, glad no doubt that upon this occasion the self-important Usher of the White Rod had provided a list of names, and that someone else in his office, or attached to it, was able to give descriptions of the gowns worn by most of the ladies presented.

In a flowing sea of silk, satin, velvet, lace and muslin, wave-topped by great ostrich plumes dyed in fashionable colours, the women were as representative of Scotland's dominant land-owning classes as their men had been on Saturday. There were two duchesses, three marchionesses, seven countesses, six viscountesses, ninety ladies, nineteen honourables, and three hundred and thirty *mesdames* and misses. All had no doubt begun the day with the same frenetic preparations. The Grant sisters, who were to be presented by the Countess of Lauderdale, rose shortly after seven o'clock. Before they had finished washing, the hairdresser sent by Signor Gianetti was violently ringing the house-bell. He was not a success, a small and obstinate Frenchman, said Jane, 'who having amused himself for half an hour with making us as great objects as he could, and sticking our plumes right at the back of our heads like those of horses at a funeral, took his departure'. At half past eight, brother William accompanied them to Picardy Place where Mrs Siddons finished their toilet and their robing. 'She dressed us all herself, hair, gown, train, everything. Never were we dressed with so little confusion, so *well*, or so comfortably.' Sally Siddons, who helped her mother, was overcome by the occasion, or by the presence of William Grant, and declared that she and the sisters must love each other for ever.

Grant and his son took the girls to the palace before noon. Rothiemurchus was sentimentally proud of them, and told his wife that they wore their gowns as if they had never worn anything else in their lives. The crush in the Long Gallery was almost too much for them, but fortunately they acquired chairs close to the door that led to the Entrée Room. A Yeoman of the Guard promised to give them early warning of the King's arrival, so they might edge even closer to the door, but the shouting and the crash of music beyond the window made a warning unnecessary. The doors to the ante-rooms were opened, and the multicoloured assembly surged toward them in a flood. It was firmly controlled by the Yeomen and Archers who admitted no more than one party at a time. The consequent delay seemed endless, with nothing to do, said Mary Frances, but 'lean against the railings, looking on those who were going in and those who were coming out'. She had time to admire or ridicule the gowns of other women, particularly the Duchess of Atholl's petticoat of red velvet tartan, richly bordered with gold. The absurdly tall daughters of the Earl of Caithness were accompanied by a gigantic Highlander, six feet seven inches in height, but the effect of this was spoilt by the hideous trains worn by the girls, one of blue satin and the other of pink. Mrs MacLeod of MacLeod was also a disappointment, looking fine *only at a distance*. Her husband, however, was majestic in full Highland dress.

At last they were moving through seven or eight ante-rooms, silk and satin slippers whispering quickly behind the relentless advance of Lady Lauderdale, with John Grant and William striding behind. Jane said her courage increased as they passed through each room, but Mary Frances, desperately clutching her train in her arms, abandoned hers with every step. They were halted at the door to the Entrée Room, where Mary Frances could see nothing clearly, nor hear anything but a confusion of voices. One at last became intelligible, an Archer repeatedly telling her to put down her train, until a Lord-in-Waiting stepped in front of him. 'Sir, do not frighten the lady, it is my business to take her train.' And then there was only a blurred picture of those fat lips bending toward her cheek before she was once again in the Long Gallery. Jane thought the kiss she received was no more than a ceremony, and if it were to be done again it would still be the same. But Mary wished it might be repeated, for then it would be much better. She was proud of her affected sister, telling their mother that Jane had looked *beautiful* in her feathers. 'I heard a gentleman say, looking towards her as we were leaving the gallery after all was over, "That's the prettiest girl I have yet seen".'

All the ladies were beautiful, of course, and the Edinburgh newspapers overwhelmed their feminine readers with lavish descriptions of the dresses worn. It had been an *occasion* for ostrich feathers – white, lilac, pearl and sometimes a deep blue or crimson, nodding and trembling above sculptured hair, tight curls in the classical manner created by Joseph Gianetti or his competitors. The cloth of the gowns and the sweeping trains was magnificent, rich silk, silver and golden lamé, blue satin and French tulle, gold lace and tassels, fine point lace, pink velvet studded with silver stars or thistles, striped gauze and white *gros-de-Naples*, tartan silk for petticoats, heavy satin for toques, turbans and Highland bonnets. There was gold or silver for chains and pendants, studded pearls and diamonds, the darkness of rubies on white lace, cool emeralds on black velvet, clear stones from the Cairngorms brooched on yellow lace.

Scott's gay and happy wife, despite her swollen ankles and shortness of breath, recovered some of her youthful beauty in a gown of gold lamé, ornamented with roses and thistles. The Marchioness of Queensberry, in heavily embroidered white satin, and carrying a long train of lilac silk, wore a towering headdress of black velvet, banded with silver and diamonds and flowing with lilac feathers. Mrs MacLeod of MacLeod had to bend her head to enter the Entrée Room, her enormous Highland bonnet of silver net made taller yet by a spray of ostrich feathers clasped in diamonds and pearls.

The King had placed himself in the centre of the room, rather than behind the door where he stood for the Levee. He bore himself well as the feathers and frills surged about him, smiling and bowing, bending courteously to kiss or to bring his lips close enough to a damply glowing cheek for it to be taken as a kiss. In one brief pause he looked at the door through which came this endless tide of women, asking one of his Scottish aides to point out 'the lady on whose account so many Highlanders went down to Elgin two years ago'. He was not disappointed, or so it was said, when she was at last presented to him – Lady Anne Margaret Grant, a stunning matron in gold-spangled net and grass-green satin, Brussels lace and waterfall of Scottish gems. She and her sister Penuel (silver lamé, Brussels lace and more Scottish stones) were daughters of Good Sir James, the Laird of Grant, and in July this year the King had advanced them, and others of their family, to the honorary titles they would have enjoyed had their father lived long enough to inherit the earldom of Seafield. The incident he recalled now – over-dramatically described as the last occasion upon which a clan had been summoned by the Fiery Cross – had occurred during an election for the Elgin Burghs in 1820, in which the Grants supported the Tory interest. During the brush-fire of hostile passion which sometimes accompanied Highland elections, Lady Anne Margaret and her sisters were besieged in an Elgin house by 'a democratic mob', that is to say by townsfolk supporting the Whig candidate. Word for help was sent to Strathspey, in answer to which (and to the beat of a rallying drum) five or six hundred of the Grants' obedient tenantry gathered under the leadership of a major-general, several field-officers, captains, subalterns and post-commanders of the Royal Navy. They marched into Elgin and drove away the demo-crats without blooding any of their ancient dirks. Brought to their knees before Lady Anne Margaret in her besieged house, the Provost and the Sheriff begged her to protect their burgh from looting, which of course she did, insisting only that the town feed her clansmen before she sent them home to Strathspey.

The story of 'The Raid to Elgin' had amused the King, and when its buxom heroine had been given a hearty kiss and a flirting com-pliment he watched her dignified departure and said, 'Truly, she is an object fit to raise the chivalry of a clan.' On the proscenium of Sir Walter's tartan theatre he was now delivering his lines well, and royal approval could be given to a Highland riot which, in a Low-land or English shire, he would expect to see dispersed by a troop of dragoons.

William Cranstone waited at the gates of Holyroodhouse until the King returned to Dalkeith. The young man had been there for al-most five hours, watching the arrival of so many shining carriages, so much silk, satin, ostrich feathers and precious stones. Despite this ostentatious display of privileged wealth, he could still estimate the value of his own loyal attendance at a modest two pounds and ten shillings. Revived by cold water, towels and spirits of hartshorn, many of the ladies presented at the Drawing-Room went that same evening to see *The Merchant of Venice* at the Theatre Royal. Since most of them spent the time exchanging gossip about the King, as if drama could not match the earlier excitement of the day, the play was ill-received. Mrs Siddons was thought to be beautiful as Portia, but Edmund Kean was given little or no applause for what was said to be an execrable performance as Shylock. The sets were also poorly made and well-worn, and most of the audience left before the farce which customarily ended such an evening.

The King remained at Dalkeith House throughout Wednesday, dining with friends on some of the venison and other game sent to him in great quantities by gentlemen of the country. On his behalf it was announced that he would be graciously pleased to attend a banquet given in his honour by the City of Edinburgh on Saturday. He would also visit the High Kirk for divine service on the Sabbath. These announcements were a great relief to the Lord Provost, the Moderator, and almost everybody who believed that the dignity of the city and the protection of the Presbyterian Church were essential for the spiritual and material wealth of the nation. Already prepared, the civil authorities immediately issued a series of proclamations determining the behaviour of the people on both occasions – where carriages were to assemble on the Mound and the High Street, how they were to set down in front of Parliament Hall or Saint Giles, and where they would retire afterwards. Admission to the High Kirk would be by ticket only, obtainable from the City Cess Office at 204 High Street. This created an immediate scramble, with carriages choking the Royal Mile from the Lawnmarket to Canongate, greatly impeding the passage of advance troops of Yeomanry, now riding through the city in readiness for the Grand Review on Friday.

The King's inaction on Wednesday gave the city some time for social pleasures, comforted by the thought that he was still among them, albeit seven miles away and inaccessible. Henry Fox played écarté at Lady Gwydir's, where the whole company agreed that it was distasteful to see Lady Francis Leveson-Gower enjoying herself so openly. The Marquess of Stafford had suffered a second paralytic stroke at Dunrobin, and Lord Francis Leveson-Gower had hired the *Comet* and steamed north at once to his father's bedside. The command of the Sutherland Men was thus abandoned to George Gunn, and the Sceptre of Scotland to whomsoever had disputed his lordship's right to carry it. His wife had not accompanied him, preferring the joy of Edinburgh to the turreted gloom of Dunrobin, even attending a large party on Castle Hill a few hours after her husband's departure. Fox agreed that Lord Stafford might be on the point of death, but the young man could not be too harsh in judgement upon pretty Lady Francis. 'After all, one cannot expect her to care; and though I think it would be much better taste to stay at home, it does not much signify, for, as Lady Gwydir *justly* and *Scotchly* remarks, all the property is entailed.'

Walter Scott devoted part of this day to George Crabbe, who until now had been left to the care of Lockhart. The three men walked by the foot of Arthur's Seat, climbing a spur of the Craigs to the ruin of St Anthony's Chapel, which Crabbe wished to visit, remembering the use his host had made of it in *Heart of Midlothian*. The kindness of his companions affected the old man and encouraged him to speak of his past. He recalled his youth in London when he ate meat but once a week, on Sundays, and then only at a tradesman's house where 'their leg of mutton, baked in a pan, was the perfection of luxury'.

That afternoon Scott went to Dalkeith upon the invitation of the King. It was one of the few occasions they dined together privately, although time would create a belief that Scott was welcomed to the royal table almost every day of the Visit. The evening was very much to the King's taste, the company of men who knew his moods and manner, and whose nature or intellect he respected, most particularly at this moment the Lords Conyngham, Montagu, Melville, Fife and Lauderdale. The master of Dalkeith, the young Duke of Buccleuch, sat upon the King's right and was treated with contradictory affection, sometimes as if he were a royal ward, and sometimes as a favourite servant. The entertainment was given by Gow's Celebrated Band, led by Gow himself. Not Neil Gow, the legendary violinist and composer from the Braes of Atholl, now long dead, but his son Nathaniel. He was more widely known and more popular outside the Highlands than his father had been, and had often taken his musicians to play at Court in London during the Regency, at one time earning £20,000 a year, it was said, from his performances and the sale of the music he composed. The band played whatever air the King and his guests proposed, young Buccleuch being dispatched from the table to carry the request to Gow. When the boy became weary of this, the King slapped his shoulder cheerfully. 'Come now! You're the youngest man of the company and must make yourself useful.' Returning again to the table from one of these missions, he was offered a solacing glass of spirits, but the King waved it away. 'No, no . . . ! It's too strong for his Grace to drink.'

It was the King's usual custom to leave his guests early, retiring to his closet with one or two close favourites until he went to bed at midnight. Though he ate little at table, and perhaps with gastric pain, he drank too much, and often became melancholy and maudlin. This evening, more drunk with Gow's music than the Glen Livet, he stayed later at the table, leaving it once to cross the room and speak to the band. From his earliest years, he said, he had always been fond of Scottish music, but never had he been so entertained by it as he was this evening. He was further honoured to see the son of Neil Gow again, and hoped he would live long. The response of the musicians was in harmony with the age. 'God Almighty bless Your Majesty!' they said, and after more royal compliments Gow was heard to murmur, 'I'm perfectly content to die now.'

Before he retired, the King ordered some of his Glen Livet to be used in the making of a large jug of Athole Brose, delivered to the band before they left. The whisky content was liberal, the oatmeal and honey used sparingly. Thus the musicians went homeward to the city in literally high spirits, playing loudly – if not altogether harmoniously – the appropriate air *I'll ay ca' by in yon town*.

If the King read the Edinburgh newspapers on Thursday – which is unlikely, for most were a strain upon the eyes, and all that he needed to know of their contents was discreetly communicated by Knighton – he would have been heartened by their comments as the first week of the Visit came to an end. The *Observer*, whose uncritical loyalty was a balance to the sour reserve of the *Scotsman*, assured its readers that the King must now be remembered as GEORGE THE PATRIOTIC. By this Visit he had established the seat of his Empire in the hearts of his people, 'not in the smoke of London where *alone* he has ever been reviled and insulted'. Henceforth, he could 'nobly confide himself to the affection of an unattached and admiring people, a great and generous people'. Such sentiments were meant to touch not only the hearts of these admiring and generous people but also their pockets. At the Waterloo Hotel on Wednesday morning, a general meeting of the Institution for the Encouragement of the Fine Arts in Scotland had resolved to erect an equestrian statue of His Majesty in bronze, for which notable sculptors were expected to tender. A subscription list was opened immediately, it being further decided that no gentleman could contribute more than three guineas, and no lady more than one, but contributions from corporations and associations should be unrestricted.

At dawn on Thursday, when the King was to ride in Grand Procession to the Castle, the quiet of the city was broken by the first grinding arrival of hooves and wheels. Before ten o'clock every street leading to the base of the Rock was filled with carriages, and the crowd along the Royal Mile was already immense. Doubt and indecision added confusion to the congestion, for until dusk on Wednesday there had been no certainty that the Procession would take place. It was finally agreed that whatever the weather – which threatened to be wet and hostile – all should proceed as proposed. The event and its planning were Scott's work alone, and on this occasion he did have some precedent to guide him. There was an historic platform upon which to stage his pageant. The great thoroughfare of the Old Town had been the route of many popular processions, some bright and triumphant, and others vengeful and bloody, as century by century the people and governors of the nation had acted out their contentious history. Certainly there was no honoured tradition of a Scottish king making a ritual journey from his palace at the foot of the Rock to his castle upon its summit. There was, however, the ancient Riding of Parliament, the ceremonial progress of the Estates of Scotland, and it was in the last record of such an event, four years before the Parliament of Scotland voted its own extinction, that Scott found some inspiration and guidance. If there were nothing in the records to say how a German king in a

British field-marshal's uniform was to be received, the evocative ground upon which he was to appear would give invention the impressive stamp of truth.

From the foot of Canongate to Castle Hill, both sides of the Royal Mile were lined with stands, webs of scaffolding, planks and benches decorated with flowers, flags and patriotic exhortations. Between them and the centre of the steep, cobbled way there was room for standing spectators, many of whom arrived long before dawn and were now reluctant to edge more than a pace aside to admit late-comers, or give passage to those who wished to reached more privileged accommodation at the windows of the lands above. The Magistracies of Edinburgh and Leith had stands in the Canongate, for themselves or their dependants. Along the High Street to the High Kirk and through the Lawnmarket to the narrow throat of Castle Hill Street, more stands and roadside space were reserved for every manifestation of the city's professional and commercial life. For candlemakers and barbers, journeyman printers, bookbinders and booksellers, advocates and notaries, surgeons and medical students, butchers, gardeners and porters, chairmasters and carters, colliers and the sailors of Leith, bright-faced schoolchildren, the clergy of Edinburgh, parochial and private teachers, and the Senatus Academicus of the University. A gallery for peeresses and another for merchants, for the Commissioners of Police and the Royal College of Physicians. By mid-morning all was wild colour and relentless noise, despite a yellow and persistent drizzle. The windows of the lands were filled with heads, leaning over waterfalls of bunting. The officers of the trade societies, assembled in their allotted spaces, were uniformly dressed in blue, with white saltires on their breasts and white rods of authority in their hands. The gardeners of the city had worked all night to weave hollyhocks into a great spray of Prince of Wales feathers, but the glass-blowers had excelled all in ingenuity. And in courage. Their rods were made of white glass, and their leader was a brittle Highlander with a glass bonnet, glass coat, glass sword and glass shield.

The stands for the Army and Navy, and for the lieutenancy of twenty-four shires, were erected on both sides of Castle Hill, the wide but sloping approach to the barrier-gate below the great Half Moon Bastion. Since the accident ten days before, the Committee of the Lieutenancy had remained uneasy about the safety of the scaffolding, and the strongest critic had been the Duke of Atholl, unimpressed by so much defiance of the laws of gravity and the persuasions of common sense. At seven o'clock this morning he inspected the Perthshire stand with an architect, and was at last satisfied that it was as secure as it could be. There was still the irritating matter of the seats, however, more being available than there were applicants for them. He was now obliged to return a hundred tickets to the Committee or pay for them himself. He decided that the latter was the honourable course, and went away through the crowds and the increasing drizzle to take his breakfast in Charlotte Square.

All lieutenancy parties were instructed to reach their stands through the garden gate on the north flank of Castle Hill. They were further advised to go no further in their carriages than the top of the Earthen Mound, proceeding thence on foot to the gate. Thus no one arrived dry-shod, and there was a long queue moving slowly upward under a glistening roof of umbrellas. Like many others, the Grants waited at home until the last moment, lest warning guns announced the cancellation of the day. By the time they arrived on Castle Hill the drizzle had turned to rain, and the scarlet draperies and painted awnings above the stands were now more decorative than useful. Sitting in the front of the Inverness Gallery, Mary Frances was glad to escape the worst of the weather, even though her sister could not.

> We sat for a long time; the rain pouring in torrents, and only ceasing now and then for a moment or two to pour down with more violence. At last it penetrated through the seams of the awning, and umbrellas and parasols were lifted up without our caring whether the poor people behind could see over our heads or not. I was most happily placed, just out of the dripping. Jane was in the very midst of it.

Robert Peel left his wife at the Waterloo Hotel and made an uncharacteristic sally into the streets with Sir Walter Scott. He had perhaps grown weary of the continuing work of his office. He also needed relaxation for his bruised spirits, having felt obliged to protest against Sir William Knighton's arrogant intrusion upon the private ground between the Monarch and the Administration. Scott may have known of this irritation, and hoped to disperse it by inviting Peel to 'mingle with the crowd' upon the Royal Mile. Scott was a familiar figure in the streets of the city, and today he made himself more conspicuous by wearing the blue and red coat of the Windsor Uniform. Before they left the hotel to cross North Bridge, Peel told his eager companion that they would never get through the crowd. But they did, by separating themselves from it and walking together in the rain and in the middle of the High Street, where Scott lifted his hat in acknowledgement of the cheers that greeted him. It was a story Peel often told.

> I said to him – 'You are trying a dangerous experiment. You will never get through in privacy.' He said – 'They are entirely absorbed in loyalty.' But I was the better prophet: he was recognized from one end of the street to the other, and never did I see such an instance of national devotion.

William Cranstone, doggedly faithful, stationed himself at the foot of the Royal Mile ('Detained 4 hours £2'). He was there before the Procession began to assemble, its main body coiled in the Abbey precincts and its head advanced up the Canongate. Throughout Wednesday there had been rumours that the King had no enthusiasm for the occasion and was out of humour with Scott for organizing it. He was said to be angry because all had been arranged without consultation, and thus he would not budge from Dalkeith. In the foul weather of Thursday's early hours it was easy to believe such gossip. During the morning the King rode alone in the park of Dalkeith House, not so much for pleasure as from need. Horse and rider were strangers to each other, and one at least must have been uneasy as the other climbed a ladder to mount in comfort. The animal had been purchased that week, for two hundred guineas and from the Riding-Master of the Greys. Since the King intended to ride it on Friday when he reviewed the Yeomanry, the familiarizing exercise this morning was necessary for man and beast. When he had walked, trotted and cantered the great animal beneath the dripping leaves of the park, and perhaps executed a modest caracole to the left and to the right, he returned to the house and was dressed in his field-marshal's uniform for the day.

The first arrivals in Palace Yard, shortly after ten o'clock, were the aging gentlemen of the Company of Archers, briskly marching to the hurrying notes of a bugle as if they were youthful light-infantrymen. Today they were supporting players only. Once more imposing a Highland image upon the nation's pride, Scott and Garth were determined that the Procession should be a triumph for what was now called (not always with affection) 'The Tartan Confederacy'. Less spectacular than they would later appear in Turner's wild and windswept watercolour, the clansmen came down Abbey Hill to the palace an hour or so before noon, their pipes screaming against the cheers from Calton Hill. First the Drummonds, led by the Anglo-Welsh husband of their chieftainess. Then Glengarry's MacDonells and the Sutherland Men, the latter wearing kilts for the first time. Garth's companies of the Celtic Society – captained, among others, by MacDougall of MacDougall, MacLeod of MacLeod, and MacDonald of Staffa – were to flank the march and be honour-guards to the Regalia, Scott having decided that the King could not go in state to his castle without his Crown, Sceptre and Sword. The van of the Procession was given to the Breadalbane Men and the MacGregors, deep green and defiant scarlet marching twelve abreast as the first division of the Marischal's Guard. The rear-guard, also twelve abreast and following the Lord High Constable behind the King's carriage, was composed of Lord Gwydir's Drummonds and more men from Sutherland.

Within this tartan encirclement was the medieval flummery which Scott had devised to support the sparse relics of the Regalia. There were trumpeters and heralds, pursuivants in red and yellow tabards, yeomen and henchmen, macers, esquires, equerries and grooms. These, and the principals they served or escorted, were as splendidly and as gaudily dressed as they had been on the day of the King's arrival. The Knight Marischal, Alexander Keith of Ravelston, was again in the saddle of his black Arab, wearing a mantle of flowing crimson over his white satin doublet and hose. Two henchmen at his stirrups were dressed in rose-coloured satin, white stockings, and white roses on their shoes. Lord Kinnoull, who had held the office of Lord Lyon King at Arms for the past eighteen years and would continue to hold it for another forty-four, had recovered from the indisposition that kept him from the arrival at Leith. He too rode a spirited Arab, and wore a gold crown upon his cap of crimson velvet, a scarlet cloak above a green surcoat edged with gold and scattered with golden thistles. The vain and irresolute Duke of Hamilton, on a black horse led by two kilted officers of the Celtic Society, was dressed as a seventeenth-century cavalier in black satin slashed with white, a rich vandyked collar of lace on his shoulders. He carried the Crown of Scotland, although his right to this honour was being disputed before the Privy Council by an aged kinsman who had already maintained a claim to some of the Duke's titles and estates.

All this colourful magnificence was sadly marred by the grimy drizzle long before the King arrived at Holyroodhouse. He came at two o'clock in a closed carriage, not the open landau expected, and little was to be seen of him, or of his companions Dorset and Glenlyon, but a face at a lowered window, bowing and smiling. The Procession moved up the Royal Mile almost immediately, the royal carriage and another containing five members of the King's suite taking their places behind the Duke of Hamilton. The cheering began as soon as the hooves of an advanced troop of Yeomanry danced upward on the wet cobbles, but from the children on a low scaffolding by the Canongate Church there was no sound of intelligible voices, only a strangled piping, accompanied by an excited flutter of flags. The sign above identified them as asylum children, deaf, dumb and deaf-mutes. They believed the King greeted them with particular warmth, for some had written to him earlier this week. James Bain had said he was sorry the King was visiting Old Reekie for so short a time, but the children's hearts were full of joy to have him here. 'When the King passes to the Canongate near our scaffold, we wish we could cry "God save the King!", but we cannot.'

In reporting the occasion later that week, the *Scotsman* was cautiously impressed by so great a welcome on so miserable a day.

The High Street presented a most brilliant and spirit-stirring spectacle. The windows and the galleries in front of the houses were filled with the assembled beauty and fashion of Scotland. The street, excepting the narrow path in the middle, was one dense mass, diversified by flags, symbols of various kinds, bands of men in coloured clothes, ranged in lines, and small parties of military . . . Not a single person was seen whose exterior indicated squalidity or wretchedness. All were dressed decently, and a very great proportion handsomely. There was not the least symptom of turbulence or disorder, no battling for places, and scarcely anything like confusion.

Before the King's carriage had travelled seven hundred yards the rain became so heavy that his view of the crowds on both sides of the street was obscured by the umbrellas raised above them. The Procession paused for a ceremonial moment at the site of the Netherbow Port, the old gate in the wall that once surrounded the city. Here the King waved his plumed hat from the window, applauding a pleasing addition to his train. Six girls in white sashed with blue, and all beautiful of course, now walked before the clanging hooves of the King's bays, strewing wild flowers on the wet stones. The rain, the *Scotsman* would say in a jest that was already senile, was not heavy at all, indeed it might be called a *Scotch mist*. But it was heavy enough to soak Hamilton's vandyked collar, and the rich velvet cushion upon which he carried the Crown. It glistened on the gold of the Sceptre and of the Sword, and darkened the bright tartans of the clans. Outside the Royal Exchange it dripped through the awning to the scarlet and fur shoulders of the Lord Provost and the Magistrates. The King waved his hat to them as they bowed. He waved to the cheering, red-faced boys from the High School, and to yet another group of girls, with more flowers to be sweetly crushed beneath the wheels of his carriage.

When the leading divisions of the Procession moved to the right and left of Castle Hill Street, the way was clear for Mr Small, the Marchmont Herald, to canter up the slope with his trumpeters. They brayed a salute to the bastion wall, and Mr Small hammered on the Barrier Gate, informing the waiting Lieutenant-Governor beyond that the King was come. Before the officer could give his rehearsed order there was a crash of saluting arms, the first anguished chords of the National Anthem, and a roar of excited voices. The crowd began to cheer, said Mary Grant, before the royal carriage appeared on Castle Hill, and continued to shout as the King was driven slowly past the dripping stands and the drenched lines of tartaned Celts. He alighted at the Ditch, stepping down to a red-carpeted platform where the Lieutenant-Governor and Sir Thomas Bradford were awaiting him with their staffs. Offered the keys of the Castle, he touched them lightly, signifying their acceptance and their return in trust. He then crossed to the drawbridge, passing through the gate to the Inner Barrier. Mary Grant said he 'walked up the winding road to the castle', but she could not have seen him from the Inverness stand. The pathway below the north-eastern wall was then a steeper and more stony ascent than it is now, and the breathless monarch could never have dragged the burden of his body through the Portcullis Gate to the Lang Stairs. A light carriage was waiting at the Inner Barrier, and this took him upwards, surrounded by his trudging officers and the grenadier company of the 66th Foot, all very wet but determinedly cheerful.

From the foot of the Lang Stairs, the King was carried round the western escarpment, through Foog's Gate to the summit of the old citadel, and then on to the Half Moon Bastion, a bellying breastwork of immense thickness. Here he alighted and walked alone to the battlements. Two days before, Joseph Turner had diligently placed himself in this same position, sketching the view of Castle Hill below, the downward stretch of the Old Town and the gleam of bright light on the golden turrets of Holyroodhouse. On so dour a day as this, the King saw little, only the thickening haze of rain, and white faces staring upward beneath waves of black umbrellas. When he removed his cocked hat, holding it high above his head, there was a responsive cheer. He twirled the hat in delighted acknowledgement, bowing and waving for fifteen minutes.

> He turned and looked about on every side, and still they shouted; and as he turned from side to side, speaking and pointing, the loud huzzas seemed to gather strength. Sir Alexander Keith, who was with him on the battlements, told us he lifted and clasped his hands when he came out on top of the castle, and said 'Good God! What a fine sight. I had no conception there was such a scene in the world; and to find it in my own dominions; and the people,' he added, 'are as beautiful and as extraordinary as the scene.'

What he did say, before his words were improved by the Knight Marischal or Mary Frances Grant, was perhaps something of that nature. He was an emotional man, and nowhere in England, among its hating and hateful people, had he been received with such decorous enthusiasm. The sunlight of this good temper conquered the misery of the foul weather. 'Rain?' he said, when his gentlemen begged him to take shelter, 'I feel no rain. Never mind, I must cheer the people.' At last he did step away from the battlements and was hurried to a warm room in the Governor's House, where the windows were draped with gold-fringed scarlet, and the floor newly covered by a crimson Brussels carpet. The King drank one glass of wine only, toasting the damp officers about him. He also thanked the Governor *in absentia*, having heard that Sir Robert Abercromby's absence was due to the afflictions and indispositions that plague old soldiers well past their eightieth year. He then left, carried down to the Barrier Gate and rising cheers. After more twirling waves of his hat, he entered his carriage and was borne away to the Earthen Mound, and thence to Princes Street and Regent Bridge, all at a fast pace, the great horses of the Greys pounding in escort.

As the little procession went by Abbey Hill, a cloud burst above the city, and the people awaiting the King on Calton Hill turned from it and ran for shelter. He leant from the window, cheering them on and laughing like a schoolboy. But the day had exhausted him. He was anxious to return to Dalkeith, and paused briefly at Holyroodhouse. Coming down the great stairway to re-enter his carriage, he stumbled and would have fallen heavily, had he not been saved by the shoulders of the groom preceding him.

On the Royal Mile and Castle Hill the anticlimax that follows all euphoria was made more dismal by the rain and by the scrambling press of the crowd. Passage down the Royal Mile was almost impossible, the whole street was now a bobbing cataract of umbrellas, coloured banners rising and falling above it like flotsam. Pushing through the Garden Gate on Castle Hill the occupants of the county stands found the descent more hazardous than the climb had been. 'We had to walk down a dreadfully dirty way to get to our carriages,' said Mary Frances, 'the ladies with their fine dresses actually complete mud up to their knees, the feathers in their hats drooping, and hanging all different ways down to their waists.'

Henry Fox had viewed the occasion in comfort, from a window overlooking Castle Hill, in a room where he had dined the night before. He thought Hamilton looked well in his cavalier's dress, though whether the crowd was applauding the Duke or the Crown he was carrying, Fox could not be sure. As for the chief performer of the day, 'The King went up to the top of the Castle and bowed, rather absurd, and useless. It was, on the whole, a failure.'

> *'Our places were crowded first when the*
> *neighbouring township of Milasta was cleared.*
> *Six families of that township were thrown in*
> *among us; the rest were hounded away to*
> *Australia and America, and I think I hear the*
> *cry of their children till this day.'*
>
> – NORMAN MORRISON, crofter, Lewis

Henry Fox's journal for Friday 23 August was once again characteristically brief. 'Heaven only knows why,' it began, 'but I passed the day in tearing spirits.' He had lately written to Harriet Canning, declaring his passion, and knew that she would receive the letter this day. Borne upon the heady exhilaration of that knowledge, he went to Portobello Sands to watch the Royal Review of the Yeomanry, travelling with Lady Gwydir who was not only a clever flatterer, he thought, but also a good-natured and long-headed woman. Thus, by evening, the self-esteem of this impossible young man was sufficiently restored for him to record a properly dismissive, if somewhat ambiguous account of the occasion. 'The review was beautiful. The King rode a white horse he bought here. It went off admirably.'

Three thousand volunteer cavalrymen from the Lowlands and the Borders were assembled for the Review, their conceit and their braggart patriotism reinforced by the recent employment of their corps in the Radical War. Young farmers, tradesmen and citizens of the burghs, armed with carbine and sabre, officered by the middle class and commanded by titled men of property, they were theatrically costumed in scarlet, blue and green, each rider's height increased by the tall plume on his shako or the dipping roach of his metalled helmet. Affirming an earlier promise to review these holiday-warriors, the King had also agreed to honour the Highlanders at the same time. On Wednesday morning he sent his elegant friend Lord Lowther to Stewart of Garth, with an assurance that if the clansmen were also drawn up on Portobello Sands, to the right of the Yeomanry line and some distance from it, 'he will look at them in passing and they will afterwards form a guard round his person when he reviews the troops'.

Garth's response was immediate and enthusiastic. He summoned all the Highlanders to a practice drill on Thursday, the Celtic Society, Strathfillan Society and the clans, marching and counter-marching on the sheep-cropped grass of Holyrood Park. He assembled them again at an early hour on Friday, this time in Queen Street, drilling them once more until the unhurried arrival of the Duke of Argyll, magnificent in a green belted plaid and eager to lead this tartan gathering to the Review. By the casting of lots on Thursday the Highlanders had agreed upon their order of precedence, and the result, of course, had not reflected their proud traditions. To James Loch's loyal satisfaction, the van and thus the right of the line, an honoured place in battle, fell to the Sutherland Men. The second place in the column of march was taken by the MacGregors, commanded this day by the young son of their chief. Sir Evan had sent Garth an apology – he was indisposed, exhausted by strain, perhaps, and the lingering discomfort of his wounds. The Tayside Campbells marched behind the Griogaraich, and were led by Lord Glenorchy. The Drummonds, under Lord Gwydir, formed a sparse rearguard and the left of the line.

Such arrangements read as if designed to provoke Glengarry, and he reacted with familiar fury. Although nine of his MacDonell gentlemen came to the assembly, he did not, and he was not seen on Portobello Sands, except by the imaginative eye of the *Observer*, which described him as the only chief present whose ancestor fought *as a chief* in the last Jacobite Rebellion. Those interested enough in his wayward behaviour sought an explanation for his absence in the musty mythology of Glencoe and Culloden, deciding that his obsessive family pride would not permit him to march under the leadership of an Argyll Campbell, or agree that Clan Donald's traditional place on the right of a Highland battle-line could be transferred by vulgar lot to the breeched men of Sutherland. A week later, in a tediously long letter to the *Observer*, he confirmed this opinion. His absence from the Review, he said, together with his brother James and two of their immediate kinsmen, had been due to 'accidental circumstances'. He did not say what they were, but unconsciously exposed them as his letter moved turgidly on to an envenomed attack upon the Celtic Society, warning its hostile members to 'leave my plaid alone'. None of his ancestors, he said, would have been mustered under a Campbell chief, or served anywhere but on the right of the line. Deriding the pretensions of Lord Gwydir and Lord Francis Leveson-Gower, he said that in the past no Drummond or Sutherlander would have 'suffered Englishmen (whatever their rank in South Britain) to assume the place of their ancient chiefs'. Not only David Stewart of Garth, but many present in Queen Street must have been grateful for the absence of this prickly man. But within the archaic framework of the charade they were enacting he was perhaps closer to the truth than they cared to be.

Historical parallels to this day were and are inescapable. No such assembly of armed and kilted men had been seen by the people of Edinburgh for more than three-quarters of a century. Not since that September day when the Jacobite clans marched into the city from the victory at Prestonpans, lighting their bivouac fires in the King's Park and mounting their picquets within cannon-shot of an obdurate Castle. The *Observer*, again, reminded its readers that the site of this brief and bloody triumph – a mining village three miles to the east of Edinburgh – was less then half an hour's walk from the reviewing-ground on Portobello Sands. Unremarked by this newspaper, or any other, was a more recent affray within the memory of many still young. On another day late in summer the colliers of Prestonpans and its neighbour Tranent, rioting against their conscription under the Militia Act, had been dispersed by the hysterical horsemen of an English Yeomanry regiment. Many were killed in a field of standing corn, and their little towns were raped and pillaged.

Twenty-five thousand spectators were expected to watch the King's Review, and the first of them arrived shortly after dawn. The day was warm and sunlit, with no threat of rain, to the relief of the young Yeomanry officers who idled below Calton Hill for gossip and displays of horsemanship before riding on to their regiments at Portobello. They were watched and cheered from the slope above, where those visitors who had failed to find lodgings were now encamped under makeshift tenting and patriotic bunting. So strong was the general wish to see the Review that by eight o'clock that morning it was impossible to hire a post-horse from any stabler, and well before noon there was an unbroken line of carriages, two miles long, moving slowly along the road to Portobello. The landau of the Rothiemurchus Grants joined this queue in excellent time, said Mary Frances, but the crush on the road was heavy and exciting.

> Officers in scarlet coats, their horses neighing and richly caparisoned, pranced along the road; open landaus full of gaily dressed ladies, barouches, barouchettes, curricles, gigs, open chariots, one-horse chaises, carts full of hearty farmers and their rosy-cheeked families, stage coaches loaded outside and in with laughing *countenances*, every sort of equipage the world could furnish, was to be seen this day.

Before Rothiemurchus and his daughters left Queen Street he had dispatched a hasty letter to his wife. First there was joy to report, another ticket for the Peers' Ball had been promised, and thus both girls would now be able to attend. Secondly, most importantly, there was the gift which, in the opinion of his eldest daughter, would later secure him a seat on the Calcutta bench.

> [The King] drinks nothing but *whiskey*, and he is an admirable judge of glen livat. Lord Lauderdale carried out two bottles today as a grand present. Pray send a dozen of our best. William and I believe Eliza knows where to find it. Address it – GLASS, J.P.G. of R., 25, Great King Street. For His Majesty's use.

By noon the great parade had taken its waiting position on the Sands. Nine gaudy regiments of Yeomanry, three thousand mounted men in three ranks, their faces to the sun and their backs to the sea, supported on their right and left flanks by Light Artillerymen and troopers of the First and Second Dragoons. The noise was continuous and deafening, the music of competing bands, brief trumpet-calls, the impatient neighing of horses, clattering metal and thudding hooves as spirited gallopers rode from one regiment to another. Beyond the mile-long line of black shakos and burnished helmets was the water of the firth, the sunlight strong upon a watching crescent of ships – yachts, ferries, lighters, oared boats and a steamer's dark funnel.

By one o'clock the expected crowd of twenty-five thousand was twice that number, and a thousand vehicles were stationed along the ridge of the dunes. Some of the spectators had seats in the high stands erected for the occasion. Some, like Walter Scott who came with the Duke of Montrose, watched from the comfort of carriages, but most were standing fifteen or twenty feet deep on the uneasy slope of sand. This great mass moved forward eagerly when the sound of pipes was heard from the Leith Road, and patrolling dragoons were obliged to press their horses against the crowd to force it away from the line of Yeomanry. There were cheers and shouts, catcalls and hysterical waving as Argyll led the Highlanders in a plunging march across the sands, wheeling the column into the position indicated by the marshals. Here they were unexpectedly joined by Sir Evan MacGregor, pale and obviously ill, but determined to resume the leadership of his clan, which his son surrendered with great gravity. MacGregor was riding the better of the two horses he had rented from Wadsworth the stabler. According to his adjutant it was 'a quite showy grey which was intended for Sir Patrick Walker'. Having failed to take up this option, the Usher of the White Rod was obliged to come by carriage, if indeed he thought the occasion merited his presence.

As the King desired, the Highlanders were *some distance* from the Yeomanry and thus did not challenge the Light Artillery's jealous privilege of holding the right of any British line. Dragoons began immediate patrols to keep the gap clear, but it would prove disastrous for the Highlanders.

Twenty minutes later, the thump of saluting guns and the fluttering rise of the Royal Standard above Portobello Quay announced the King's arrival from Dalkeith. His open carriage, escorted by Greys, took him to the front and centre of the line, to the thunderous playing of the National Anthem, the shimmering flourish of three thousand sabres, and the dip of silken standards to the yellow sand. The King was as delighted as a schoolboy, touching his field-marshal's hat and sometimes lifting it, a smile of pleasure appling his reddened cheeks. Such an occasion as this was the happiest of his public appearances, the centre and the object of loyal cheers, gunfire and stirring music, splendid horses and magnificent uniforms, all the artistic grandeur of war without the tiresome inconveniences of reality. His happiness was so apparent, so much an *honest enjoyment*, that it is easy to believe that sometimes he really did think he had ridden with his Household Cavalry against the French at Waterloo.

When Lord Lothian, the welcoming Lord Lieutenant of the county, had risen from his knees beside the royal carriage, the King stepped down and moved toward the great horse he had purchased from Cornet Edlman of the Greys. Hidden for a moment by his encircling suite, he emerged at last in the saddle, riding toward the right of the Yeomanry line, followed by his escort and military staff. He always looked well on a horse, once the difficult problem of mounting was over, and in the sunlight today, before so great a mass of young cavalrymen, he came as close to perfection as he ever could. Standing in the Grants' landau, Mary Frances was transported by the grand panorama before her.

> The sea was as clear and blue and glittering as possible; the beautiful opposite coast of Fyfe perfectly distinct. The King rode three times up and down the sands, and we saw him perfectly. He bowed and touched his hat repeatedly as he moved slowly along the lines of the regiments drawn up in single file with their backs to the sea, and all presenting arms, and every time the King bowed, the crowd of lookers-on cheered him so heartily.

If the King remembered that he had promised 'to look at them in passing', there was little he could do now to honour his word to the Highlanders. As he moved along the third rank of the Yeomanry, the cavalry picquets were unaccountably withdrawn from the gap on the right flank. A great number of the crowd, with some vehicles, surged into the vacated space, isolating the Highlanders from the main body of the Review. When his inspection of the third rank was completed, the King returned to the front for yet another royal salute. That received, he dismounted and walked toward his carriage. It would be later said, and perhaps kindly believed by the journalist Robert Mudie, that the King 'was observed to mount and dismount from his horse with great ease, agility and neatness'. If that were indeed possible for a painfully disabled man of more than sixteen stones, it was perhaps the most spectacular event of the day.

The Highlanders were numbed. Throughout the inspection of the Yeomanry they had stood patiently at ease, one knee bent and the weight of the body supported upon a weapon-hilt in a pose that made the wearing of a belted plaid both fearsome and graceful. Their leaders, gathered about Argyll, Garth and Stirling, were demanding that one of their number be sent to the King, reminding him of the honour they had been promised. After some debate, Doctor Mackintosh, the worried adjutant of the Celtic Society, was asked to find a Scottish lord among the royal suite who would make the Highlanders' disappointment known to the King. He went at once, pushing through the crowd, and he spoke to Lord Lowther, who spoke to the Earl of Fife, who spoke to the King, who had just realized how many people had come to see him and was now standing by his carriage, staring at them with delighted astonishment. His reply was quickly carried to the isolated clansmen. Of course His Majesty wished to see his brave Highlanders, and would do so if they joined the Grand March Past, taking a position to the rear of the Yeomanry.

The King mounted his carriage and the order for the March was given, cry upon cry of young voices, the rise and fall of extended sabres. Upon the brief lilt of a trumpet-call the regiments closed ranks, formed open columns of half-squadrons and trotted by the royal carriage. As the Highlanders passed, trudging well to the rear of the dusty sand kicked up by the hooves, the King was said to be much affected, touching the tears from his eyes.

Returning to their former positions in line, the Yeomanry regiments now moved toward the King, halting at fifty paces and lowering their standards to the National Anthem. With that, the Review was over. The regiments rode away in quick time to their quarters, and the King was driven to Dalkeith. The smarting pride of the Highlanders may have recovered during their march back to Edinburgh, led by Argyll on foot and by Fife on a splendid horse. They were watched by 'an immense multitude of well-dressed people,' said Robert Mudie, 'who constantly cheered His Grace from Portobello to his house in George Street, where the whole body formed in line, opposite the door, and saluted him accompanied by three hearty cheers from the assembled multitude'.

William Cranstone had spent seven hours on the sands at Portobello, and the value of his time, he thought, was three pounds and ten shillings, with 'incidents and travelling expenses £2 15s'. The Grant girls returned to King Street in chattering excitement, anxious to write an account of the review to their mother before they prepared for the Peers' Ball that evening. Their view from the open landau had been clear and uninterrupted, and the Yeomanry had played their parts exceedingly well. The Scotch Greys, said Mary Frances,were beautiful and their colonel looked like the King of Prussia.

> The breaking up of the whole thing was most beautiful; officers flying up and down the course; carriages and people scattered over the sands promiscuously, and all hurrying off; altogether it was the most splendid scene and far the most worthy of anything I have seen yet.

The King was of much the same mind as he was carried quickly to Dalkeith. He told his travelling companion Dorset, and through that agency the expectant gentlemen of the Edinburgh Press, that 'he was never at a review with which he was more delighted'.

There was little delight that afternoon and evening in the town of Musselburgh, two miles along the shore from the reviewing-ground. Late on Thursday, its Magistrates had been encouraged to believe that the King wished to pass through their town on his way to Portobello. A group of labourers was therefore rapidly summoned and instructed. By working throughout the night and early morning they built a triumphal arch, decorated with flowers and coloured bunting, and at noon the Magistrates gathered beneath it with their white rods of authority. All able-bodied inhabitants of the little burgh were assembled in the high street, confident that the King would of course extend his journey by a detour of three miles to pass through their town. This touching faith was maintained until twenty past one, when it was destroyed by the measured thud of saluting guns to the west, the distant sound of music and cheers from Portobello Sands.

The King's day was not over with his return from the Review. He arrived at Dalkeith House shortly before four o'clock and dined almost immediately. Less than five hours later he was again on the road for Edinburgh to make an appearance at the Peers' Ball in the Assembly Rooms. It was to be the greatest social event of the Visit, for which all other gatherings, parties and balls had been preparation only. For the Misses Grant of Rothiemurchus, and for most of the young women who had been able to acquire an invitation from a titled friend or patron, it was also to be the greatest event of their lives. Even those who had already seen the King, and knew that he was, in sad truth, a *fat and ugly old man*, could still believe in his romantic transfiguration beneath the chandeliers of the Assembly Rooms.

The evening began with a disappointment for the Grants. The extra invitation promised had not come, only apologies. Jane nobly insisted that the one ticket available should be used by her sister, upon an assurance that both of them would go to the Caledonian Hunt Ball next week. Thus Mary Frances went alone, her 'melancholy puckle of hair decorated with feathers' by her self-denying sister, and without a chaperone except a friend, the daughter of the lawyer John Clerk. Instructed to take the open landau as close to the Assembly Rooms as he could, the coachman obediently joined a long queue of carriages below Charlotte Square, half a mile away. From there it moved 'at a foot's pace by regular intervals' along the broad length of George Street.

Tonight the classical façade of the Assembly Rooms was fancifully lit by spirals of gas-lamps, their flower-coloured transparencies wreathed about its arcade, columns and pediment. Built thirty-five years before upon the Augustan model of similar erections in England, it was one of the finest public buildings in the New Town and was intended, in the words of those who managed it, to be 'contributory to the purposes of benevolence as well as public amusement'. It contained two ball-rooms, two supper-rooms with their dependent kitchens, card-rooms, retiring-chambers, and a columned entry-saloon where a splendid staircase lifted its encircling arms to embrace a wide glass dome. The principal ball-room on the first floor was ninety-two feet long, its seven windows overlooking George Street, and its walls hung with mirror-glass and smoke-darkened paintings, all lit by shimmering falls of crystal and orange candle-light. This evening, under the imaginative direction of William Murray and the supporting talents of Mr Trotter, the Upholsterer Royal, it had been transformed into the throne-room of a theatrical palace. The windows were heavily draped in blue velvet richly fringed with gold. Flanked by white and gold candelabra of an antique design, the elaborately gilded throne was set upon a low dais at the eastern end of the room, below an ornate canopy and crown, boldly swathed in crimson velvet. A narrow stage, one step high, was built about the other sides of the room, where guests could wait and watch if they were not dancing. Murray placed gold and scarlet sofas at points along this stage upon which the King, should he condescend to dance and thus become fatigued, might discreetly rest. The second ball-room, on the southern side of the building, was thought to be more appropriate for the young and fashionable taste in lively quadrilles, and although the King was not expected to visit it, it too was heavily dressed with crimson and gold, and provided with restful sofas.

All Murray's theatrical skills were handsomely employed. In the card-room, converted now to a supper-room for the King and his immediate suite, the actor-manager had laid a floor of crimson carpeting and draped a large Venetian window with kilted swathes of the Royal Tartan. The room was scattered with fragile gilt chairs upon which actors alone might have been able to sit without discomfort or danger. A great side-board of mahogany, covered with damask, was laden with gold plate and those cold collations known to please the King's taste. Except for its patient staff, the room would remain empty. Having dined at Dalkeith, and being anxious to sup there later with his friends, the King would express no wish for food or drink.

At Murray's wish, the bay windows of the second ball-room had been removed to give access to a temporary erection of wood in the courtyard beyond. Polygonal in shape, and designed like a tent, its slender pillars supported a ceiling of white and rose-coloured muslin, falling in soft folds from a central chandelier. At the far end, mock curtains were drawn back to show a romantic countryside, the whole being the evocative work of Mr Roberts, scene-painter at the Theatre Royal. This room, too, was not visited by the King, but when he was gone the young and beautiful came to sit, to sup and gossip in its refreshing air, as if happy to escape from the dark crimson and thick velvet of the other rooms.

Murray had created a *sense of occasion* in great haste and, it seems, without neglecting his responsibilities as an actor-manager. Coming to George Street at four o'clock that last afternoon, he was met by a member of the Peers' Committee who angrily complained about some of the decorations. 'Good God, Mr Murray, see what's been done! There's no time to alter it, and it will disgrace us all. What must be done?' Murray was unruffled. 'What must be done, my lord? Why . . . *this!*' And he pulled down the offending drapery. By six he had replaced it with something else to the satisfaction of all. He then walked down George Street to Saint Andrew Square and thence to the Theatre Royal, where he was to appear that evening.

The doors of the Assembly Rooms were opened at eight o'clock. As the guests came in from the hot August evening they walked beneath Murray's most shameless touch of theatre – Scotland's lion shield of scarlet and gold, surrounded by the bold banners of its history and hanging perilously below the candle-lit dome. At first the great crowd before the arcade and along the street was noisily good-humoured, but as more carriages came, and the frustrated coachmen used their whips upon any human obstacle, order became disorder, and disorder threatened chaos. John Townsend and the other Bow Street Officers who had been lounging against the pillars of the arcade, looking for familiar or furtive faces in the crowd, were now pressed back into the building, beyond the entrance to the stairs. Those guests who arrived by sedan were more fortunate than the carriage passengers, for their Highland chairmen used the ends of their long poles to force a passage through the crowd. Shouting wild cries in Gaelic, they ran fiercely forward, retreating from each shock to charge once more. Watching this from beneath the portico, Robert Mudie thought the noise and violence was enough at times 'to shake the democracy from its propriety', which was to say, perhaps, that there were moments when an enthusiastic crowd threatened to become a hostile mob.

It was curious to observe many sylph-like forms, decorated with every ornament that could enhance their charms, encompassed in their chairs by a dusky multitude of people; and their fragile vehicles reeling to and fro amidst the agitation of the enormous mass, which acknowledged every new impulse and heaved into waves that threatened to overwhelm whatever resisted their progress. The situation of those ladies, however, was merely whimsical; for the pressure was altogether involuntary on the part of the populace, who conducted themselves with the greatest possible civility and even delicacy. By the exertions of a small party of dragoons and some police officers, a free approach was at length opened up for the company.

As the landau moved slowly along George Street, Mary Frances occasionally waved to the windows above, each with its sash lifted high, dark figures silhouetted by the lamplight in the room beyond. The sensation of riding in review was so exciting that it overcame the tedium of the journey, and before she was ready the carriage had reached the arcade where it was surrounded by the great horses of the Greys, anxious voices calling upon her to alight. When she and Miss Clerk entered the Rooms, their shawls were taken by 'a well-dressed woman'. At the top of the stairs, one of several languid gentlemen of the Ball Committee accepted their invitation cards and waved them on. As if in a dream, they passed through lines of Beefeaters to a room hung with glazed calico, blue and yellow and looking as fine as silk. There were columns wreathed in flowers, arched doorways through which they saw 'lights and covered tables, glittering with barley sugar temples and iced mountains'. The light and heat from the chandeliers in the great ball-room was remarkably strong, and the crowd was immense. Some of the ladies were magnificently robed, and those men in Court dress were 'all like gentlemen'. In a musicians' gallery, lifted above the floor on fluted pilasters, Nathaniel Gow's band played sentimental Scottish airs.

The King left Dalkeith House at nine o'clock, reaching George Street in forty-five minutes. There were crowds all along the road into the city. Troopers of the 7th Dragoons had been patrolling the route since the afternoon, and a squadron from the same regiment now rode as escort to the closed carriage, forcing their horses against the crowd in George Street. Inside the Assembly Rooms, the King proceeded as rapidly as he could through a welcoming circle of lords and ladies, all rising and falling in a wave of bows and curtseys. At the head of the stairs, which he slowly mounted with a happy smile, he was greeted by another group of peers and taken in to the ballroom. He wore a field-marshal's coat and blue pantaloons, either the uniform he had worn at Portobello Sands that afternoon, or another like it. He was also wearing riding-boots, which many thought was decidedly odd. Mary Frances Grant, who had a mind for pursuing such puzzles, was told that the King had recently been lamed. By what and when was not known, but 'he had been obliged to wear boots for the review in the morning, and his surgeon had advised him not to change'.

The dancing began with a reel, said some, because it was the King's favourite, but Mary Frances believed it was a strathspey, following quickly upon the National Anthem after the King's entrance. Gentlemen who were not in Court dress, having observed Scott's warning that a belted plaid would be obligatory, leapt into the dance with the wild animation usually displayed by those to whom the costume is unfamiliar. Seated upon the throne, the King soon looked hot and weary, but he responded to the infectious music and motion, sometimes applauding, sometimes snapping his fingers in time and nodding approval to Gow's energetic fiddlers. He did not dance, and when he left the dais and walked among the dancers it was to clasp the arm of Atholl, Melville, Argyll or another, drawing him aside for a short and whispered conversation. Later he was visibly moved, and wept a little when William Moray of Abercairney and his lady performed a strathspey. 'He was quite enchanted of Abercairney's dancing,' said Mary Frances, 'and made him dance an immense deal.' Then so quickly, so soon after his arrival it seemed, the King was gone. The *Historical Account* said he left at a quarter past ten o'clock, a misprint perhaps, for Henry Fox and Miss Grant said he stayed for almost two hours. Whatever the exact time, a change of costume for so brief an appearance would indeed have seemed excessive.

When he was gone, the Ball continued with increasing spirit and noise until past one in the morning. Before his departure nothing but country music had been played, but now the dancing became less Highland and more fashionable. While the youngest danced, others stood on or about the stage, some ladies in flowering, gossiping groups. Much of their talk was of the King, what he had said, what had been done before him, and upon whom had fallen his rheumy, ogling stare. The story of the absurd hand-kissing old laird at the Levee was now elaborated to explain the King's lameness and his surgeon's advice. When the laird bowed so extravagantly, it was said, one of his heavy Highland pistols fell from his belt and struck the King's foot. Lady Hamilton-Dalrymple's *bon mot* of seeing so little of the King and thus relishing that much revealed by his kilt, was again retold, to the discomfiture of old Lady Saltoun whose prim disapproval had first inspired the witticism. No one could remember much of what the King had said this evening, except 'Ah, how d'ye do, Lord Chief?' to Commissioner William Adam, and 'Good-night, my dear Duchess!' to Argyll's handsome English wife. There had also been an oblique compliment. Recalling the ladies at his Drawing-Room on Tuesday, he said he had never seen so few diamonds or so little dirt. 'In London,' he said, 'they put on their diamonds to hide their dirt, but it don't do.'

Mary Frances did not dance that night. 'It was not in fact a dancing ball,' she told her mother. 'The whole evening was confusing. Walking from one room to another, one saw a recognizable face for a moment and then lost it, never to see it again.' She wanted to dance when the quadrilles began, particularly when she recognized the back of a Mackenzie gentleman whom the Grants had met at the Northern Meeting, but he did not turn and see her. She rested at last upon the stage, where she could watch, and perhaps rehearse in her mind those biting observations she would later write in her letters home. The Duke of Hamilton, in full Highland dress tonight, was not impressive. He looked like a dancing-master, or an Italian greyhound, and when he trod upon her foot he made 'the most ridiculous bow and grimace, with his hand upon his heart, by way of apology'. The Duke of Atholl, she thought was a great pig, and the Duke of Montrose was ugly. Even the Duke of Argyll, that green-plaided chief who preferred the King's court in London to his home and clansmen on Loch Fyne, was only 'very interesting'. The Duchess of Argyll, however, was splendid, 'and looked lovely in a kind of Highland bonnet, done with gold; a beautiful eagle's feather and a large plume of fine black feathers sweeping her neck and cheek'. Most of the younger ladies looked ridiculous, and one was 'very ungenteel, bouncing about with tartan under one arm and pinned to the other shoulder, and a streamer flying about on either side'.

At one o'clock the guests began to leave. William Cranstone, who had been waiting outside the Rooms, was long gone before this, as soon as the King himself was away. His time and trouble, the young man thought, were worth thirty shillings. Inside the Rooms there was soon confusion and uproar, the saloon and stairs so densely packed that any forward movement was both difficult and painful, and many ladies were manhandled down the stairs regardless of broken feathers and torn clothes. As each carriage drew up outside, said Mary Frances, its coachman cried *'Ready . . . !'*

> 'Coming down,' was screamed from the top of the stairs by those who were coming, and in whose name the carriage had been called; but if they did not run down like lightening and shoot themselves in, the carriage, without half a minute's delay was sent off. I saw three carriages in this way ordered to drive off, though the parties were putting on their shawls on the landing place.

The crowd in George Street had become a mob, ill-tempered, groaning and hissing. When the surge of its hostility threatened to flood into the Rooms, the Highland chairmen struck out with their poles, and the soldiers of the 13th, who were intended to be ceremonial guards only, now charged their bayonets and stamped their feet in advancing menace. Liveried footmen, defending their employers' right of precedence, fought violently amongst themselves, sometimes aiming blows at master as well as man. Caught in this noisy brawl, young Lord Erroll, the King's High Constable and the first of his subjects in Scotland, was struck down by a footman's fist and badly injured. When the last chair and carriage were gone, and the extinguished lamps had turned the noble Assembly Rooms into a grey husk, the happy mob drifted away into the first light of dawn.

It was agreed by all who knew him that the Ball had been a triumph for William Murray. His sister, Harriet Siddons, told the Grants that the Peers should be under eternal obligation to him. In addition to his responsibilities as an actor-manager, which were increased by Mr Kean's appearance at his theatre,

. . . he has been indefatigable about helping the Peers, and has besides been consulted as to all the processions, fitting-up Holyrood House, and of the Parliament house when the Lord Provost entertains the King. In short, nothing has been done or attempted without him, and he has acted every evening.

Serving his fellow-countrymen and Scott's Jacobite King in this conscientious way, Murray may perhaps have hoped to lift his family name from the dark shadow of his turncoat grandfather.

*'Formerly when a person did a clever thing it
was said of him that the black blood had gone
into his bones, meaning he was well-nourished
upon milk and meat once a week at least; and
now we have become so low in condition that
those whom I have seen with ten cows, three or
four cows yielding milk, cannot now keep up
two cows because of the scarcity of land, and
they can never have any meat.'*

– MURDO MACKAY, crofter, Lewis

On Saturday 24 August the *Scotsman* applied its leading article and
most of its front page to the subject of loyalty, keeping in mind the
quotation from the *Letters of Junius* which was daily printed below its
masthead – 'This is not the cause of faction, or of party, or of any
individual, but the common interest of every man in Britain.'

In the context of the King's Jaunt, the common interest of every
North Briton might well have been the manner in which the
Scotsman reconciled its radical sentiments with its grudging
enjoyment of Sir Walter Scott's pageant. There was nothing so
fulsome, it said, or so disgusting as the cant of loyalty, and nothing
so mean or selfish as sycophancy. It should be remembered that the
King's family had been placed upon the throne to preserve the civil
liberties of Britain, and any man who advised a departure from
these constitutional principles was a traitor to his country.
Moreover, it should be remembered that the behaviour of the
Emperors of Europe, in their Holy Alliance, had excited a universal
hatred of monarchy. But an honest Whig could welcome a King
without denying his principles. Providing he did not abandon all
common sense, it was possible for him to enjoy a *rational elation*, and
such a man would have been disgracefully insensible during these
past few days if he had not been carried away by this feeling. Times
were changing, however, knowledge was no longer locked in a
closet, the voice of truth was attended by principles of justice. With

this hollow platitude, the *Scotsman* then raised a chimera which many thought had been strangled by the hangman at Stirling, and should now remain buried beneath the loyal enthusiasm for the King's Visit.

> Monarchy cannot exist long if it perseveres in its present continental course. It is kindling a spirit which must speedily throw Europe into a flame. We wish to prevent this evil abroad; we are still more anxious to prevent any similar evil at home . . . We have exposed, and think it our duty to expose, all those ultra Tories, monarchists, or whatever else they may be called, who, under the cuckoo-song of loyalty, see the improvement of their own fortunes at the expense of their country, who honour the King by dishonouring his services, and who support the laws by bringing them into discredit by their mode of administering them.

Few who read this can have felt obliged to alter any plans they had for welcoming the King when he came to dine in Parliament Hall that evening. But it may well have given encouragement to one 'honest Whig', the tenth Duke of Hamilton, strengthening his determination to tell the euphoric diners how matters now stood for the Crown, the Administration, the People and, of course, the tenth Duke of Hamilton.

In the forenoon of Saturday, the public was entertained by another small but colourful ceremony. The Honours of Scotland, for which Sir Walter's pageant had no further use, were taken from Holyroodhouse and returned to the Crown Room of the Castle. This was the Griogaraich's day, and the last the MacGregors were to spend in the city as a formal body. The modest procession up the Royal Mile was flanked by troopers of the Greys and by axe-carriers of the Celtic Society, but the Regalia Guard was composed of Sir Evan's clansmen only. He rode in the van, once more upon the finest beast from Mr Wadsworth's stables, followed by his temporary pipers and by the MacGregors' now-familiar banner – a green oak crossed by a naked sword with a crown upon its point. The first division of the clan preceded the Marischal's coach, within which sat Alexander Keith and his squires, in their theatrical costumes again and with the Regalia upon their cushioned knees. Behind the carriage came the second division of the Griogaraich, in scarlet tartan like their brothers ahead, belted and braced with sword and dirk, a sprig of fir in every bonnet. When the Marischal and their Chief had placed the Regalia in the Crown Room, the MacGregors marched over the Mound to Queen Street green, where their pipers played a last salute.

They took their own way home to Tayside, to Glen Dochart, Loch Earn and Balquhidder, most of them leaving early on the Sabbath. On Saturday evening they had prepared a civil petition which Hugh MacGregor, a ground-officer on the Cuilt estate below Ben Lawers, took to Sir Evan. Before they left, they wished to inform their chief of a small grievance, an irksome feeling that they had been treated less generously than other Highlanders who had come to honour the King.

> Breadalbane's men have been allowed 7/- a day while travelling to and from Edinburgh, and 5/- a day while there. Their clothes were also provided for them, ready made, including purse, silk stock, and medal; all of which they have been allowed to retain as their own. Sir Evan's men have likewise been allowed each 5/- a day, and had cloth sent them for their dress. They, however, paid for making them, and furnished themselves with other little articles necessary to complete their dress, for which they had made no charge against the chief.

They did not complain of this, they said. They were *perfectly satisfied*, but would be grateful if Sir Evan could place them on some level footing with the Breadalbane men by allowing them to keep their sporrans. Many had come from the same glens as the Earl of Breadalbane's followers. 'It will be a fertile source of boasting to the Campbells,' they said, 'that a mark of distinction was conferred on them by Breadalbane which the Chief of MacGregor denied his men.' Such an argument was unanswerable, and before they said farewell to him on Sunday morning, Sir Evan granted their small request.

At his cottage in Blair Uachdar this weekend, John Findlater at last accepted the harsh truth that the Atholl Men would not be called to Edinburgh, nor would they be required to parade before the King at Dunkeld or upon the forecourt of the Castle. He had previously ignored all warnings to the contrary, and Frederick Graham's tardy dispatch arrived just in time to prevent the first division from marching south to Perth where, Findlater hoped, it would be ready for a rapid advance to Edinburgh when the call came. As to the Duke's offer to those who might wish to come to Edinburgh on their own, Findlater must have pondered long upon a dignified but tactful reply. He succeeded with the skill of one well-schooled in respect toward disrespectful superiors.

> There are none inclined to imbrace the opportunity of His Grace's kind office in coming to Edinburgh upon the allowance of expenses for the occasion, but observed that they wish it to be known that their Voluntary offer was entirely for the Credit of Atholl, in appearing in the tartan and dress in name of his Grace the Duke of Atholl's Men, and by *none* going upon the other pretence, it will appear to their countrymen that such was their sole intention, although at the same time they will be proud in boasting of the kind of honour done them.

In both order and decorum, the civic banquet that Saturday evening greatly exceeded Scott's memory of the King's Coronation Dinner in London. The Baillies of Edinburgh, he said, were Roman senators compared to the English aldermen who 'broke their ranks in procession to charge the turtle and venison'. His own contribution to the occasion in Parliament Hall, beyond broad advice, is best illustrated by one characteristic incident of romantic if doubtful tradition. When the King had dined, he cleansed his fingers in a basin of rose-water brought to him by a young Midlothian laird, William Howison Crauford. This hereditary honour, it was said, had been granted to his maternal ancestor four centuries before. The King of Scotland, isolated from his hunting-party, was attacked by gipsies. He was saved by a passing husbandman who drove off the robbers with his flail and then brought water to wash the royal wounds. True or not, the legend appealed to Scott's love of a dramatic balance between courage, service and reward, and in introducing it this evening he was also able to involve himself in its ritual. His young son Charles, and his nephew Walter, acted as pages to Crauford, one holding a silver ewer and the other a salver and a damask napkin. The King thoroughly enjoyed the ceremony, and played his part with practised gravity.

There were three hundred guests in the great Hall of Parliament House, five more then there were covers set, but extra chairs were hurriedly found before too much self-esteem was wounded. The exclusively masculine company included the greater part of Scotland's nobility, its officers of State, the Navy, Army and Judiciary. And, of course, the King's hosts, the civic power of the City of Edinburgh. Most of the gentlemen wore court dress or the uniform of their service, but as was now to be expected there was also a flamboyant display of belted tartan, eagle feathers and diced hose, and silver-buttoned coats foaming with lace at throat and cuff.

William Murray's creative role in the setting was an impossible dream miraculously realized, a production too great for his modest stage, and lit by a brilliance of light impossible in any theatre. The normally chill Hall, with its bleak memories of pain and betrayal, now glowed with the heat of scarlet cloth and rich gold. Three great lustres hung from the timbered roof, the central and largest at a cost of £1200. Six more, smaller but still impressive, were suspended from the dark hammer-beams on each side. In addition to these glistening fountains of light, and the candelabra along the walls, four more lustres were hung above the King's Table, itself raised upon a crimson dais at the southern end of the Hall. The great Gothic window behind was hidden by scarlet swathes of drapery, and by the blue, gold and blood-red splendour of the Royal Arms. The stiff linen on the King's table was laid with gold and silver dishes, crystal decanters, wine-coolers and water pitchers. With the exception of that placed before the King, all the glassware on this table had been made for the event. Each heavy goblet was cut in the form of a thistle, and the same wild and intractable emblem was etched upon its side. They were the product of John Rankie's Flint-Glass Manufactory of Leith Walk, as he was not slow to inform the public as soon as possible. The goblets from which the King would drink were antique, two centuries old and Sir Walter's gift.

The guests began to assemble in the Signet Library at half past four, and all took their places in the Hall an hour later, directed to their places by stewards with white rods. The waiters, standing patiently against the walls, wore blue coats, white vests and breeches, their particular duties indicated by orange ribbons. The table-waiters wore an orange sash about the waist, wine-waiters a bow on the right arm, and butlers a rosette on the breast. Guests, stewards, waiters and butlers sat or stood in their designated places for an hour, immobilized by a stunning tedium until a distant bray of trumpets announced the King's arrival in Parliament Square.

He did not come immediately to the Hall. He was met at the door of the House by Lord Provost Arbuthnot and several Baillies, all bowing low to his fat but delicately pointed legs as they stepped from the carriage. He was then taken to the Library for more formal introductions. He endured them cheerfully. He loved banquets, not so much for the enjoyment of their food as for their splendour, of which he was always the glorious centre. Once again he was dressed as a scarlet field-marshal, the barrel of his chest glimmering this evening with the pointed and jewelled star of the Garter. Red-cheeked and red-haired, his eyes wet with emotion, he gave the Magistrates all the flattering attention they desired, until Baillie Henderson whispered in the Lord Provost's ear. Dinner was ready to be served, as indeed were the three hundred guests no doubt. Ushered into the Hall, and welcomed by loyal applause, the King walked toward the dais with slow and stately steps, now a short bow, then a lifted hand, sometimes a smile or a brief word to a familiar face.

When he was seated below his scarlet canopy, Arbuthnot to his right and Lord Errol upon his left, Grace was said by the Very Reverend Principal Baird, and dinner began with a clatter of plates and a surge of voices. The meal was long and varied. As the courses arrived from the great kitchens below they were directed to the tables by George Stevenson, master-manager of the Albyn Club. Turtle and grouse soups, stewed carp and venison, roast grouse, lobster and vol-au-vents, pigeon pâté, sole, veal, roasted chickens hot and roasted chickens cold, ornamented ham and cold roasted ham. . . . And, of course, those traditional Scottish dishes promised by Sir Walter Scott – hodge-podge, haggis and sheep's-head.

The King ate little and drank cautiously, some moselle and a little champagne at the beginning, and then claret for the remainder of the evening. In narrow alcoves eight feet above the floor, Nathaniel Gow's musicians and the English band of the 77th Regiment played Scottish airs, and none other, among them *Roy's Wife of Aldivalloch* and *I'll gang nae mair to yon Town*, *Scots wha hae* and *The Campbells are coming, hurra!* Now and then the King beat time upon the table, or waved a hand, moving his body in rhythm. His lacklustre interest in the food was quickened only when dessert was brought, a golden dish of peaches, apricots, raspberries and pineapples, but among all the courses he briefly tasted that evening the water-ices pleased him most, and a simple sweetmeat of dried orange-chips. Toward the end of the dinner he sat back in his chair, suddenly grave and scarcely moving as he listened to the young voices of a choir. When they sang *Non Nobis Domine*, he rose to his feet with the rest of the company, lifting his bass voice in the canon.

Forty-seven toasts were proposed and emotionally drunk, some with acclamations three-times-three. The first was of course the King's health, proposed by Arbuthnot and drunk by the whole company standing. When the Lord Provost raised his glass two rockets were discharged outwith the Hall, a signal immediately answered by artillery salutes from the Castle, Salisbury Craigs, Calton Hill, and the Fleet in Leith Roads. While the guns were still firing, the choir sang the National Anthem. 'A grand symphony of the thunder of the guns,' wrote Mudie, 'that rolled along the vaulted roof, gave an effect to the music of almost preternatural sublimity.' The King answered briefly, but with feeling, his voice gathering strength as he returned the toast to the company. 'Words fail me were I to attempt to describe to you my feeling . . . I consider this one of the proudest days of my life, and you may judge with what truth, with what sincerity, and with what delight I drink all your good healths.

The remaining toasts now proceeded with solemnity, affection, hilarity and occasional braggadocio. Most had their own supporting music, played by Gow's musicians or the band of the 77th, *Highland Laddie* or *The Garb of Old Gaul*, *The Bold Dragoon* and *Kind Robin love me*, *Up and waur them a', Willie* and so on. During the table-thumping that followed one libatory compliment, the King rose again. He hoped the company would all do justice to a toast he wished to make – 'All the chieftains and all the clans of Scotland, and may God bless the Land of Cakes!' The response was thunderous, led by wild, skirling cries from Glengarry and other Highland gentlemen of like voice and enthusiasm. Thus encouraged, the King was not done. Bending to his right, he asked the Lord Provost if he had any objection to becoming a baronet, to which there was only one proper answer. 'Then call a bumper!' shouted the King. 'To the Lord Provost of Edinburgh, Sir William Arbuthnot, Baronet!' The overwhelmed Provost knelt beside him, grasping a royal hand and kissing it effusively until the King lifted him from the floor.

There was no end now to the toasts that followed, not while invention was inspired. To the British Constitution and to the Lord President of the Court of Session, to Distinguished Strangers from England amongst us, to the late Lord Nelson, to the Duke of Wellington (accompanied by the music of *See the Conquering Hero*), and to the Yeomanry of Scotland, real defenders of Government. To Mr Robert Peel, absent through indisposition, to the City of London and Sir William Curtis, to the Memory of Mr Pitt, and to the Author of *Waverley*, to the Chief of Chiefs – the King, to Lady Arbuthnot and the Flowers of Edinburgh, to the King's young landlord the Duke of Buccleuch, and then the King again as Baron Renfrew. To the Health of the Duke of Atholl and the National Monument . . . Atholl was touched by this compliment. He was, he said, a Scotsman born and bred, and loved his country most sincerely. He hoped that all those who respected the brave men who had fought the battles of their King would come to Calton Hill on Tuesday and honour the foundation-stone of their National Monument. He also proposed a toast himself, uncharacteristically sentimental but with hint that His Majesty would also be welcome on the Hill. 'May the Radiant *Sun* of Royalty see what the *Sons* of Scotland are made of!'

Long before the toasts were finished, the King was gone. He left at nine upon a wave of valedictory applause, 'the choir and instrument bands', said Mudie, 'singing and playing at the same time'. The Lord Provost and others solemnly escorted him from the Hall, waiting patiently when he paused for a bow to this side or that, to turn about and bow again. When the royal carriage and its escort had clattered across the square to the High Street, Arbuthnot returned to the now uninhibited company which greeted him with cheers and a noisy rendering of *A man's a man for a' that!* The toasts began again with Alasdair Ranaldson MacDonell of Glengarry, one foot upon his chair and the other upon the table in True Highland style, calling his toast in Gaelic and in English, 'To the health of his Majesty as King of the Isles!' The title was his own invention, but the toast was drunk with enthusiasm.

There was one distasteful moment in the wine-drenched emotion of the late evening, provoking anger, gossip and amusement for some days. There was also an historic irony in the incident, unremarked by any who recorded it, even by Scott who might have recognized the dramatic parallel. Answering a toast to himself, Lord Melville expressed his great admiration for Edinburgh and for all Scots 'from the highest peer to the meanest peasant'. This led him to propose his own toast, not to the meanest peasant but 'To his Grace the Duke of Hamilton and the Peerage of Scotland'. The Duke began his reply with an admission that it was painful for him to speak upon the subject, feeling inadequate to do it justice, but as he proceeded it became clear that he wished no one to take that confession seriously. Much of what he said was about himself, and almost all of it unpleasing to the company, since it was plain he held many of them in contempt. Moreover, he truly did not speak well, or so thought Scott who later sent a brief but mocking account to his friend John Morritt.

> The Duke's speech was delivered like a schoolboy, and lest we should not be aware of his folly, he spoke it twice over in great trepidation, and yet with an air of his usual assumption . . . His Whig friends, whom I scrutinised closely, showed great signs of distressful impatience, and Lauderdale covered his face with his hands. There was no applause but a gentle murmur, which only respect for time and places prevented from being a decided hiss.

Hamilton's political opponents were outraged. Atholl and the Earl of Morton rose at one point as if to protest, but were restrained by others. Morton sat and turned his back upon the speaker, but Atholl remained on his feet, staring at Hamilton in anger. The vain duke of the worrying gloves, the cavalier lace, flowing tartan and

Italian manners, had chosen an odd occasion for a statement of his political faith. Encouraged by that morning's *Scotsman*, perhaps, he appeared now in another fanciful costume, this time the mantle of Mirabeau, Friend of the People. Having thanked Melville for the toast, he said that no one had a warmer reverence for the King than he, and none was more ready to pay homage to the dignity of the Crown.

> But at the same time I may not forget the just and jealous care which I am bound to observe toward the rights and interests of the people under this free constitution. I feel a pride in showing every respect and honour to the person who wears the Crown of these realms, but in doing so I must not forget the respect due to myself. I must repeat that I have duties to maintain for the people which are interwoven with the best rights and securities of the Crown, and which, in fact, form the basis of true power and constitutional glory of the Sovereign.

At the worst this was an expression of petulant vanity, at the best it was a brave effort to lift the scales of euphoria from the eyes of the nation, and remind it of those liberties for which many Scotsmen had recently, if misguidedly, placed their lives at risk. He succeeded in alienating his Whig friends by what appeared to be a crass lack of tact, and all he said was challenged by the angry, silent figure of Atholl. And there was the historic irony. This was not the first time that two men of their rank and name had faced each other across this Hall in such hostility. One hundred and fifteen years before, when the last vote upon the Treaty of Union was being taken by the Parliament of Scotland, the first Duke of Atholl, leader of those who were determined to vote *Against* once more, waited for the fifth Duke of Hamilton to honour his pledge and vote with them. It was confidently believed that his influential voice, as the premier peer of Scotland, would win over the waverers and bring defeat upon the supporters of Union. He was to have spoken the day before, upon Article 22 of the Treaty, but was absent upon a plea of toothache. Now he rose uncertainly, and when he spoke it was not what the Duke of Atholl, and indeed most of the Estates in the Hall, expected to hear. He wished to declare, he said, that in any reconstituted

House of Lords in a Union Parliament at Westminster, he had the right of the first seat and the first vote among all Scottish peers.

There were several toasts to Scott during the evening, either by name or as 'The Author of *Waverley*, whoever he may be'. Responding to one proposed by Lord Erroll – 'Sir Walter Scott, and our thanks to him for the share which he had in bringing us together' – he said he was in need of the power to express himself. As reported by Robert Mudie, his speech was a small gem of such shameless modesty.

> He was even happy that his want of expression arose from the warmth of his feelings, which rendered him incompetent to utter what he would wish at such a time. He could, however, say that he did not deserve this mark of their attention; and if, as *amicus curiae*, (for in no other capacity had he a right to interfere) he had thrown out a few hints, he had only to say that he had an easy task, as he had to communicate with Magistrates, who, whatever was proposed that had taste or propriety to recommend it, were ready to command, and who had to deal with a people who were equally willing to obey. That he had himself any, the slightest, share in the late arrangements, would always be to himself a matter of the deepest pride.
>
> (*Loud applause*)

> *'I have a distinct recollection of seeing a notice
> that was posted upon the door of the parish
> church, intimating that any person who was
> known to have given shelter to, or to have
> harboured any of the evicted people, would, in
> turn, without warning, be summarily ejected
> from his or her house, and be compelled to leave
> the country; and this harsh decree applied
> irrespective of any ties of relationship
> whatsoever.'*
>
> – JAMES MacDONALD, parish of Clyne

'The King goes in state to the High Church to-day,' Jane Grant wrote
to her mother, 'which will do more than any other thing to make
him popular.' His belated decision to worship at Saint Giles was a
relief to those who had doubted his real understanding of Scotland
past and present, to others who had feared a royal snub to their
Presbyterian Church, and to still more who had taken a surfeit of Sir
Walter's rich pageant and would now welcome the cleansing
experience of a Scottish Sabbath with its principal player.

He was driven to Holyroodhouse in a closed carriage, and thence
to the High Kirk, arriving at a quarter past eleven. According to
some, he looked greatly fatigued and ill. He was once more wearing
the uniform of a field-marshal, this day with the green sash, the
jewelled saltire and star of the Order of the Thistle. The High Kirk
had been open since seven o'clock that morning, and all seats were
filled with ticket-holders before nine. The crowd outside
Holyroodhouse, along Canongate and the High Street, was large but
not dense. It was also soberly dressed and quiet, all gentlemen
removing their hats as the royal carriage passed. There was no
cheering, and when a number of schoolboys seemed about to do so
they were stopped by the men who had them in care.

There was no agreeable precedent for an occasion like this. The
last British King who passed this way to Saint Giles had been
accompanied by an English archbishop whose chaplains celebrated

an Anglican service in the church, before a table clearly meant to be an altar, and beneath a tapestry of the Crucifixion. This had been one of the first intransigent steps that would ultimately cost that king his crown and his head. Such incidents in its sometimes bloody history were not happy memories for the Church of Scotland, and its past relations with a Scottish or British monarch had never been mutually inspiring. But in May this year, confident of a Royal Visit, the General Assembly had addressed the King and directed his attention to past assurances – which he may have forgotten – that they could count upon his 'zealous co-operation and support in all our exertions to promote the great cause of Religion'. In an oblique reference to the Radicals they told him that they had

> . . . witnessed with deep concern the wicked and persevering efforts, which, in certain parts of the Kingdom, have recently been made to subvert the religious Faith of Your Majesty's people, especially in the humbler and more numerous classes of Society, by means of publications replete with scepticism and blasphemy. We are sensible that it will require the most active exertions of every friend of religion, of every lover of his Country, and above all of the Ministers of the Gospel, to counteract so great and alarming an evil.

There was undoubtedly a preening arrogance, albeit a recognition of Divine justice in the thought of a British monarch, the pinnacle of Anglican episcopacy, humbly kneeling where his heretical church had once hoped to triumph. The point would be forcibly made in Mudie's *Historical Account*.

> It was a spectacle worthy of the present age, to behold in that sanctuary which was once the *arena* where the adherents of Presbytery and Episcopacy long struggled for dominion, each sect arming itself with the darkest passions of the human heart, where the storm burst out which laid Prelacy low, and led to the establishment of a system which, whatever be its merits, was most consonant to the wishes and feeling of the people, and in this very spot the head of that rival church, once triumphant, now *tolerated* in Scotland, joining in worship with his Presbyterian subjects.

The King was not naive, and must have known that his presence in Saint Giles would be seen in this patronizing light. The thought of such humbug may have encouraged him to resist the early advice given by Peel and others, that he should not consciously offend the established religion of the country. Thus the visit to the High Kirk became a chore, but nonetheless one that he performed well and with affecting humility. He had been hurriedly briefed for the ceremony. He was given a pencil sketch of the interior of the church, drawn from the spot he would occupy, and also a detailed explanation of the manner of Presbyterian worship, written by the Reverend George Husband Baird, Principal of Edinburgh University. He diligently studied both in his carriage that morning, during the journey from Dalkeith.

Baird received him at the door of Saint Giles and led him into the church, behind the Sword of State held erect by Lord Erroll and through a black file of ministers and elders, his uniformed retinue following in a blaze of scarlet and gold. His entry was watched by Turner, Collins and Wilkie, each hoping for some inspirational moment, or for confirmation of one already chosen. Wilkie had decided that the most dramatic would be when the King paused at the door and placed a gift upon the Poor's Plate. This was undoubtedly his intention, for having been informed of the offertory dish by Baird's little tract, he was carrying a sealed packet endorsed *One Hundred Pounds from the King*. To his confusion and Wilkie's chagrin, however, the plate was not there. A church official, believing that a common dish with a pile of vulgar coins would be an offensive sight, had ordered its removal. The King paused for a moment only, then thrust the packet into Baird's hands and moved on.

The congregation rose as he entered. Aware of the faces turned toward him, the rustle of voices dying to silence, he paused again, covered his face with his hat and turned half about, his head bent in brief prayer. This, the press later explained, was 'according to the English Form of Worship'. He was then taken to the gallery, facing the pulpit down the length of the church. He stood there for a moment as his suite discreetly arranged themselves behind him. Here was the scene which Turner had chosen for his painting. He had visited the church several times, sketching the interior in detail, and had soon decided upon his subject – Monarch and Preacher, raised above the floor of the church, and facing each other across a crowded congregation. Turner emphasized the King's pathetic majesty by placing him at a distance, diminished and remote. David Lamont, Moderator of the Church of Scotland, dominates the painting. Where all else is brightly sunlit, he stands aloft in a dark, canopied pulpit, and it is easy to think of the scene as a court of judgement wherein the relentless, ungiving authority of the Presbyterian Church accepts the submission of a profligate prince. The King did not like the work.

Profligacy was indeed the subject of Dr Lamont's discourse. He began the service by giving out the first version of the 100th Psalm, whereupon the King rose, psalm-book in hand, obliging the rest of the congregation to stand with him during the reading. An eloquent prayer from the Moderator was then followed by the singing of four verses of the 23rd Paraphrase. After the recital of the Lord's Prayer, Lamont began his discourse upon Paul's Epistle to the Colossians, chapter three, verses three and four, *For ye are dead, and your life is hid with Christ in God* . . . After two centuries, much of it spent in great suffering and under cruel persecution, the Presbyterian Church had a degenerate Monarch and an idolatrous Episcopacy at its awesome mercy. As if he were conscious of History's encouraging hand upon his shoulder, Lamont spoke directly and cogently, and with great skill for a man in his eighth decade. Without the use of notes, he developed his theme beyond the chosen verses to embrace the whole chapter from the Epistle. That is to say, he spoke of the sins of fornication, concupiscence, anger, wrath and mendacity, and of the obligation upon all husbands to love their wives. It was, thought Robert Mudie, 'altogether a good specimen of Presbyterian preaching'. There is no record of the King's reaction to the discourse or its theme. Perhaps his face showed none, not even when Lamont concluded with an encouraging prayer.

> May the choicest blessings descend on the head of our sovereign King George. Grant him, O God, a long, a happy, and a prosperous reign. May he be adorned with every Christian virtue. May the paternal regard he has shown in visiting this part of his dominions, which has diffused joy throughout the

land, have a lasting influence on the hearts and conduct of the people.

If the King made no public comment on the Moderator's discourse, he was generous in his praise of the singing that day. His taste for music, and his intelligent knowledge of it, could comfort him in moments of tedium and trial, and before he left the church he declared his admiration for the skill with which the musicians and the ordinary people of the congregation were able to keep in tune and time. Reporting this compliment, the press deflated it. The usual choir of the Kirk had been strengthened by several young ladies from respectable families, all renowned for their fine treble voices. In addition to these, a number of professional teachers of vocal music had also been recruited – twelve trebles, eight counter-tenors, eight tenors and seven basses.

The service over, the King bowed gravely to Lamont and walked slowly to the door of the church, preceded by Erroll and the Sword of State. He talked briefly upon unheard matters with Lord Montagu and young Buccleuch, and he had a final word with Baird. All was generally satisfying, he said. Then he was gone, through the same quiet crowds on the Royal Mile and back to Dalkeith.

As the King left the church by one door, a small family party entered by another, bringing a child for baptism. The father, a print-worker, had delayed the ceremony since midsummer, determined to have his son baptized on the same day and in the same church as that attended by the King. He had not thought this important enough to interest his colleagues on the *Observer*, and the newspaper's subsequent comment that it was 'not displeased' to discover its association with the event was perhaps its only understatement during the Royal Visit. The child, of course, was baptized George Augustus Frederick.

The atmosphere in the Old Town that Sabbath morning was grave and sombre, reflecting the boredom which accompanies the more demanding exercises of Christian worship. In the New Town, in Leith and in Portobello, however, those who could do so without risk of ministerial rebuke took boat or barge on to the firth for a tour of the Royal Squadron and the Fleet. The Grants went down to Newhaven at one o'clock with a gaggle of relatives and friends,

including MacLeod of MacLeod and his lady, and as the guests of
Captain Charles Adam of the *Royal Sovereign* they went aboard his
barge for their tour. Before it cast off from the Chain Pier, rain fell
suddenly, and until the clouds were lifted all sat miserably on the
wet thwarts, hunched beneath umbrellas and waterproof cloaks.

By mid-afternoon the Lothian water of the firth was crowded
with pleasure-boats, moving aimlessly about the anchored ships.
Their passengers stared upward to the gilded sterns, to decks
'crowded with officers in full uniform, and well-dressed visitors'.
Adam first took his guests aboard his own vessel, telling them that
although it was the King's old yacht it was more magnificent than
the *Royal George*. His junior officers were waiting at the stair-head,
and escorted the ladies upon a brisk scamper through the after-
quarters and the lower decks. Everything in the state cabins, said
Jane, was beautiful. The lobby leading to the dining-room was so
high that the tallest man could pass erect with his hat on. The large
mahogany dining-table was covered by a wonderful crimson cloth,
the walls hung with damask, and where there were not sideboards
there were rich sofas. The drawing-room was equally magnificent,
panelled with inlaid rose-wood. The sleeping-cabin, which interested all the ladies, was also hung with crimson damask and furnished 'with a good-sized French bed'. Their prurient curiosity
aroused here, they were then rowed across to the *Royal George* and to
a privileged inspection of its sleeping-cabin, so recently occupied by
his august Majesty. But it was something of a disappointment, being
severely plain, and its simple china wash-stand was unimpressive.
The white and gold drawing-room, however, pleased everybody,
and the ladies were delighted by its chintz hangings, piped in the
French fashion, and by the sofas of unbleached holland. Returning
to the *Royal Sovereign* they dined upon cold chicken, ham, veal,
pigeon-pie, grapes and peaches, with claret and barsac to their
pleasure. Jane's short-sightedness provided the company with their
most amusing moment. She said that she had been pleased to see 'a
nice little library' in the King's drawing-room aboard the *Royal
George*, whereupon everybody laughed and declared that there had
been one book only, and that entitled *Les Malheurs du Mariage*.

The Royal Visit was slipping slowly into anticlimax. Its great
events were over, and little would be seen of the King during the

four days remaining before his departure on Thursday 29 August. It was known that he would appear twice only in public, at the Caledonian Hunt Ball on Monday, and at the Theatre Royal on Tuesday, but some still hoped he would also attend the inauguration of the National Monument. Although sightseers were still coming into the city, more had left or were about to leave. The departure of some of the clans, and country gentlemen of the Celtic and Strathfillan Societies, had taken much of their tartan from the streets, but enough of the enthusiasm they had aroused still remained to sustain the euphoria of Walter Scott's Celtification. He was in good spirits, he said, although weak and weary, and his unhappy rash was a persistent affliction. Robert Peel was fretting at his prolonged exile in Scotland, being anxious to return to Westminster where Londonderry's suicide had opened many doors to advancement, not the least his. Meanwhile he served the King conscientiously, and with what Liverpool may have thought to be an over-zealous attachment to trivial detail. Thus Peel told his lordship that he had promised an annuity of £50 to Flora Macdonald's granddaughter, and that the King had agreed without argument. Such was the current Jacobite mood that it seemed only proper that the House of Hanover should honour the memory of a woman who had saved the life of its last active rival.

The King's emotional attachment to his Stuart ancestors also compelled him to make a private visit to Holyroodhouse on Monday afternoon. He came without ostentation and without a dragoon escort, riding in a closed carriage with Lord Graves and the Duke of Dorset. Two coachmen in undress livery sat upon the box, and four servants rode behind. The King had dressed himself with thoughtful modesty, as if he were a well-to-do country gentleman coming to town, in a blue surtout and trousers, black neckcloth and a hard round hat. He had insisted upon no formal reception, and only Thomas Mash awaited him at the door, escorting him quickly to the State Apartments where the Duke of Hamilton, Keeper of the Palace, was attending.

The King had but one wish, and without it he might not have troubled to make this visit. Before he left London he had insisted that in the preparation of Holyroodhouse there should be no disturbance of Queen Mary's Apartments on the second floor of the

327

north-western corner. These consisted of an audience chamber, a bedroom, and a turret cell from which David Rizzio, the Italian secretary of Mary Queen of Scots, had been dragged and murdered by her husband's confederates. The King went directly to these rooms, accompanied by the palace housekeeper who described their history in the same parrot words she used to all visitors. The monotony of her uninspired drone at first amused the King, but he quickly tired of it, turning from her to absorb himself in the atmosphere of the rooms. He spent fifty minutes there, sometimes motionless, sometimes moving slowly, touching the bed in which his ancestress slept, a post from which Rizzio's hands had been torn as he screamed, *'Sauvez ma vie, Madame, sauvez ma vie . . .'* When the housekeeper told the King that the blanket he held was the selfsame used by the Queen, he was astonished that it could be so well preserved.

He did not stay long after he left the Queen's Apartments. He gave the housekeeper ten sovereigns, but took nothing from the palace, no object large or small as was expected of him. He had already accumulated a number of small relics of the Stuarts, although no one had offered him what he desired above all – a dirk worn by the Young Pretender during the Rebellion. There was one gift he could not escape this day. As he approached his carriage he was halted by the Reverend George Tough. This minister of a Berwickshire parish wished to present the King with a copy of his most recent sermon and also a clockwork model of the planetary system, described in Mr Tough's accompanying letter as 'the workmanship of a Scottish clergyman in a remote situation, during his leisure moments, by the help of rude implements'. The King accepted the orrery with tact and grace, passing it to the care of Mr Mash. He then bowed to all the palace servants gathered about him, climbed into the carriage and was driven away. At the gate of Palace Yard a woman ran forward and curtseyed, almost under the horses' hooves. The King took off his hat and bowed in salute.

When the Royal Visit was over, Mr Tough discovered that his gift was still in Holyroodhouse and much neglected. He called upon Mr Mash at the Waterloo Hotel, and when he received no satisfaction he asked for Scott's help. Sir Walter referred him to William Knighton in London, who did not reply. Now much distressed, Mr

Tough again appealed to Scott whose influence was this time successful, and the minister's 'curious and scientific piece of machinery' was given a lasting home in the Royal Library at Windsor.

That Monday evening, after a relaxing dinner with his closest companions, the King was once more tightly laced and enclosed within a gorgeous uniform, this time as a colonel of the First Guards. He was then driven into the city again for the Caledonian Hunt Ball, arriving at the illuminated portico of the Assembly Rooms shortly after half-past nine o'clock.

The occasion was in most respects a repetition of the Peers' Ball, an extravagant expression of self-conscious loyalty by the illustrious members of the Caledonian Hunt, each of whom had contributed £50 toward the expenses, and £43 10s for every ticket they subscribed. It was perhaps made more exclusive by the *English* snobbery of some of its members, and more vulgar by the undignified scramble for the tickets they distributed. Henry Fox did not think the affair important enough to record how he came by his invitation. Of first concern to him that day was the sleepless night he had spent, wondering whether his latest letter to Harriet Canning had been delivered. He recovered well enough in the morning to take a walk with her brother George, climbing Calton Hill to Nelson's Monument. In the afternoon, the young men dined with Lady Francis Leveson-Gower in her room at the Royal Hotel. The spirited and independent flirt, who seemed to live without sleep, had now decided to join her husband in Dunrobin and share his vigil at the bedside of his stricken father. Since none of her family was left in Edinburgh, George Canning offered to escort her on the steam-vessel to Sutherland. Fox thought this was a rash promise, and told his friend so when they went to see *Macbeth* at the Theatre Royal. They watched two acts only of Edmund Kean's performance, and then left for the Hunt Ball. That too was tedious, and Fox gave it the briefest acknowledgement in his journal. 'The counterpart of the Peers' Ball, but not so full.'

The King entered the grand ball-room within a circle of his lords-in-waiting, all dressed in the Windsor uniform, blue coats with red collars and cuffs. His hosts, the Committee of the Hunt, wore their recently designed uniform, a scarlet coat faced with green, white breeches and white silken hose. Beyond them in the crowded ball-room was the now obligatory swing of tartan plaids, the bright gleam of candle-light on silver brooch and buckle. The dancing this evening, to music from Gow's Band, was less formal and restrained, and before the King was gone it became a wild swirl of reels and strathspeys. The red-faced monarch was quickly excited by the music and the movement, standing on the dais to wave his arms and shout his encouragement to the dancers. Once more his wish was being observed, that while he was in Scotland he would have no music that was not 'purely national and characteristic'.

He left the Rooms before eleven-thirty, bowing to all. He looked sadly tired, and he descended the stairs slowly, as if he were consciously pacing out the beat of Gow's valedictory rendering of the National Anthem. When he was gone the dancing became more noisy, strathspeys and reels abandoned for wanton country-dances and the racing delight of galop and quadrille. Jane Grant thoroughly enjoyed herself, and for once was not critical in her report of the evening. In the supper-rooms, she said, there was champagne and fine wine *in oceans*.

> Besides this, there were ices in abundance, in one of the small rooms during the whole evening, and a supper for the King in another. He merely went to look at the tent, but did not take anything. We saw him go away as well as we had seen him come in, and I managed besides to make a tour of the great room, so as to stand behind him for a considerable while, and as he constantly turned round his head, I now know his countenance quite familiarly.

It is probable that the King had become bored with the formal impositions of the Visit, relentless presentations, unfamiliar faces and perplexing names, the tiresome reading of public addresses, the continuing language of cant and sycophancy. No reason was given for his absence when the foundation-stone of the National Monument was laid on Tuesday 27 August, the inauguration of a memorial 'designed upon the model of the celebrated Parthenon, and consecrated to the Deity, in testimony of the nation's gratitude for the signal success of British arms during the late war'. Many people, including Atholl's founding-committee, had presumed that the King would wish to be present, not only in respect but also because the ceremony on Calton Hill was to be a manifestation of the omnipresence and the power of Scottish Freemasonry. This may or may not explain his absence, although he had been admitted to the Order in his youth. He agreed to be a patron of the memorial but no more, remaining in the quiet of Dalkeith House until past two in the afternoon. He then left for Lord Melville's home, to enjoy a cold collation and say farewell to some of those who had shared his private life during the Visit, Walter Scott among them. Some of the guests came to Melville Castle at express speed from the ceremony, but others, like Robert Peel and his wife, used his lordship's invitation as a welcome excuse to avoid one more noisy, crowded occasion of vulgar enthusiasm.

The representatives of every Masonic lodge attending the ceremony formed their companies in Parliament Square before marching to Calton Hill at two o'clock. They were escorted by troopers of the Greys and the 3rd Dragoons, and also by detachments of foot-soldiers. Each military contingent and each lodge was accompanied by its own band, all playing together, said Robert Mudie, and 'independently of every feeling connected with the mysteries of the craft'. But when the procession climbed the hill he was reminded of 'those pious celebrations upon the Holy Mount which are so sublimely described in the sacred writings'.

The foundation-stone awaited them in bright sunlight, poised above its shallow bed and in the middle of a great crowd. More than seven feet square and weighing six tons, it was in fact three stones, strapped together by iron and lead. It was placed in the centre of what was intended to be the south wall of a noble classical building, 228 feet long and 102 wide, and no one here this day would have believed that indifference and a lack of funds would eventually leave so grand an undertaking unfinished. The ceremony proceeded upon a wave of eloquent platitudes, with more reference to the Scriptures than to the young Scotsmen whose bodies had been scattered across the globe from India to the Bay of Mexico, South Africa to the plain of Waterloo. As premier duke and Grand Master, Hamilton spoke at length upon the high qualities of his brother Masons and of the 'pure age of Grecian refinement' which the monument would ultimately reflect. When he was finished, the nearest band played *Hail, Masonry!* After several bottles containing coins and newspapers were buried beneath the stone, it was solemnly lowered. The Duke of Atholl then closed the day with a speech of thanks to all worthy Masons, including a curious but perhaps not inappropriate cross-reference. The ground for the National Monument, he said, had been broken

> . . . on the anniversary of his most gracious Majesty's birth; and the foundation laid by us, the Commissioners, acting in the name and on the behalf of his Majesty, on the anniversary of the day when Christian slavery was abolished, when the captive's bonds were broken, and the prisoners were set free by British valour under the wall of Algiers, thus gloriously terminating the achievements of our gallant countrymen.*

Upon his return from Melville Castle the King rested alone. Shortly after seven o'clock he left for the Theatre Royal to see a performance of Scott's *Rob Roy*, adapted and produced by William Murray. Earlier in the day, when the long procession of Masons passed the theatre on their way to Calton Hill, workmen were still changing the façade of the shabby building. Two of the six cast-iron pillars supporting the pediment were removed and a crimson platform was built in the space thus available, that the King might step from his carriage without descending to the pavement. By dusk, other workmen inside the building had transformed the foyer, covering its stained walls with gold-fringed scarlet drapery, all lit by clusters of gas-lamps, lustres and girandoles of glittering crystal, brilliantly reflected in tall pier-glasses.

It was to be the King's last public appearance, the only one, perhaps, wherein it could be said that he was at ease among his Scottish subjects. There were to be no stifling Court formalities, no absurd pecking at feminine cheeks, no repetitious bowing or clockwork saluting, no prayers or pulpit homilies, only an evening of boisterous enjoyment shared by an amiable old man and so many loyal

---

* The bombardment of Algiers in August 1816 and the destruction of its fortifications by a fleet under the command of Admiral Sir Edward Pellew, as a result of the Dey's refusal to abolish Christian slavery.

friends. The passages, rooms and auditorium of the theatre were lit at seven o'clock, when heavy rain-clouds produced an early dusk. At this time, too, English Yeomen took up their stations in the foyer and upon the stairs, wherever the King might walk and wherever his eye might rest. Thomas Mash arrived with them, believing this evening to be within his authority and not Sir Walter's, fussing at length over details of no consequence, but honestly impressed by Murray's ingenuity. He said so generously, when the two met in the royal box, but to redress the balance of his conceit he moved the royal chair an inch or so to what he said was a more agreeable position. The King's play-bill was placed upon a velvet cushion before the chair. It was a unique production, handsomely printed upon white satin, lined and bordered in crimson velvet and heavily embroidered with golden thread.

The first members of the audience had taken their places outside the pit and gallery doors shortly after one o'clock, and by three there were two hundred at each entrance. Within another hour there were more waiting than the theatre could accommodate, and by the time the doors were opened at seven, every approach to the building, by Princes Street, North Bridge and Leith Street, was choked from railing to railing. Brief showers of rain increased the press of bodies toward the theatre, and in the constant and turbulent movement some collapsed from the heat, and others fought to reach the closed doors. Watching from the windows of the Waterloo Hotel, observers remarked upon the curious behaviour of the crowd. As the pressure on its perimeter increased, it surged like an incoming tide, reached its swell and then receded to surge once more. The steam that arose from the mob, it was said, was not unlike a vapour bath. When the doors to the theatre were finally opened, men and women struggled to keep their positions. Younger or more daring men, too far from the building for hope of entry, now climbed upon the shoulders in front and attempted to run across the press of bodies. Almost all of them failed, falling or dragged down, bruised or broken by stamping feet. Murray sent some of his staff outside to post notices saying the theatre was now full and, when they were ignored, he called upon the dragoons and men of the 13th to drive the mob from the portico.

Once inside, the crowd was noisily good-humoured, but so compressed in pit and gallery, said James Ballantyne's *Weekly Journal*, that it would have been difficult to insert the point of a sabre between any two persons. The boxes were filled at comparative leisure as the carriages of the gentry forced a way through the crowd. Some of them found their boxes filled by enthusiastic claimants from the pit. These interlopers were expelled by force, dragged or thrown back by the box-keeper and his staff, assisted by Colonel John Mair, the one-handed deputy-governor of Fort William. The audience cheered this veteran wildly. They cheered the Lord Provost when he entered his box. They sang songs to soothe their impatience, and they cheered every chief who came in tartan. They madly applauded the arrival of Garth, but Sir Walter Scott, said the *Scotsman* with sour approval, 'was also cheered, though not enthusiastically or very generally'. The noise of the singing and the applause, reported the same newspaper, was not unpleasant, though it sometimes excited a fear that the house might become unruly.

At eight o'clock a dragoon came over North Bridge, plunging his lathered horse into the crowd and shouting *'Make way! The King is coming . . . make way!'* The main doors of the theatre were again opened. The Duke of Montrose, as Lord Chamberlain of the Household (having succeeded the abandoned Lord Hertford in that office), walked to the edge of the platform with William Murray, each carrying a great candlestick and holding its rain-whipped flame above his head. Others followed them from the theatre, all peers of Scotland, and all in evening dress or regimentals except the Duke of Argyll and the Earl of Fife who were wrapped in tartan, the wing-feathers of an eagle in their bonnets. Dramatic in its silencing effect upon the crowd, this scene had been cunningly devised by Murray, and the King made an entrance as if upon cue, stepping slowly from his varnished carriage to the crimson platform. He followed the candle-bearers into the theatre with 'that benignity which never abandons him', according to Robert Mudie, but there was perhaps equal concern for his own infirm legs when he called out to the tottering Lord Chamberlain, *'Don't be in a hurry, do not on my account walk too fast for yourself!'*

There was an uncanny silence in the auditorium when it was known that the King was in the house, a 'momentary pause of death-like stillness', said one journalist, before the roar that greeted the King's appearance in his box. He received the welcome with evident pleasure, bowing, bobbing and smiling, lifting his own waving hand in response to the great flutter of handkerchiefs, hats, bonnets and tartan scarves. He sat at last in his theatrical chair, surrounded by a colourful semicircle of his suite, all standing despite their age and the intolerable heat.

When Murray had gathered the whole cast upon the stage for an emotional singing of the National Anthem, the play at last began. It was neither good nor bad but immensely popular, and Murray was said to have made £3000 from its repeated presentation. It was performed tonight at the King's request, as a compliment to Scotland and to the author of the novel from which it had been drawn. The King's reaction to the play was affable and courteous. He applauded with the audience, laughed boisterously at familiar comic lines, whether or not he understood the language or the allusions. His laugh, said Ballantyne, 'was by no means a stage-box whisper, but hearty and sonorous, such as belongs to the most frank and generous nature'. When he was bored or disappointed, he hid the feeling by taking snuff, 'elegantly and without affectation'. He was perhaps happier during the *entr'actes*, joining the audience in singing such songs as *My love is like a red, red rose*, and beating time more successfully than when he attempted to follow a Gaelic song.

At the close of the play, the house shouted for the Anthem to be sung again. All stood and faced the royal box, singing the chorus with great emotion. An additional verse had been written for the occasion, said the *Scotsman*, but it 'was totally lost upon the audience by being sung in parts, in place of being legibly delivered by one distinct and intelligible voice'.

> Bright beams are soon o'ercast,
> Soon our brief hour is past,
>   Losing our King.
> Honour'd, beloved, and dear,
> Still shall his parting ear
> Our latest accents hear,
>   God save the King.

When the King left his box, with a last lift of his hand, the audience continued to applaud his emptied chair. In the corridor outside, he spoke briefly to William Murray and his sister Harriet, saying how pleased he was to see Mrs Siddons, for she was one of his favourite actresses, as she had been his father's. In his euphoric humour he was perhaps confusing her with her immortal mother-in-law, Sarah. He was in excellent spirits during the drive to Dalkeith House, recalling lines from the play and laughing again at their humour. He had spent three hours in the theatre, the longest of his public appearances, and the most human and relaxed. No other occasion during the Visit had aroused such intimate emotion, and to no other had he responded with such unaffected warmth. Indeed, nothing in Scotland had so pleased the fat, infirm and increasingly melancholy old man as this evening in Mr Murray's theatre, the willing prisoner of Scott's inspired imagination.

Watching the play from his own box, the author's feelings may have been mixed. He had written *Rob Roy* six years before, under growing financial and physical distress. He had at times despaired of finishing it, he said, 'with such a *curmurring* in my guts'. It had marked the end of tolerable health, and the beginning of chronic sickness, depression, and the occasional use of opium to ease his discomfort. Before the writing was done he was anxious to be rid of it, but it became one of his greatest novels. More than *Waverley*, perhaps, it presented a persuasive view of the Highlands and the Highlandman, an image that fitted firmly into his Celtification of Scotland, standing between romantic myth and bitter reality for more than a century. In the context of hindsight, no more appropriate play could have been chosen for the King's Visit.

*'We poor people have been sent to a headland of
the sea where it was not worth while to send
sheep forty years ago, and that was the reason
we were sent there. We were crowded all
together upon it. In my father's days there were
sixteen crofters there. There are forty houses
now. Many of these were sent from other
townships that were cleared – poor people that
could not get away to America. Because there
was no other place for them, they were hurled
upon that headland. When I open my door
there is no place within the range of my sight
except where there are big sheep.'*

– ALEXANDER MacDONALD, Lewis

Archibald John Primrose, the fourth Earl of Rosebery, was in an understandable huff, his pride touched and his dignity offended. It was now known that the King would leave Scotland on the afternoon of Thursday, 29 August, and that he would sail from Port Edgar, this being close to Hopetoun House where he would take breakfast before embarking. His journey there would take him by the gates of Dalmeny Park, Lord Rosebery's home, and Commissioner Adam thought the Earl would naturally wish to compliment the King in passing. He therefore suggested that some of Rosebery's retainers should be stationed at the entrance to his estate. Indeed, the gates could be opened, enabling the King to make a detour from the Queensferry road and travel through his lordship's park.

The Earl's reply, written in haste on Wednesday, pointed out that since he had received no official intimation that the King was to pass by his estate he had some doubt about the propriety of Adam's suggestion. He had heard 'from a private communication by a friend' that the King was visiting Hopetoun, but that did not oblige him to dispose his servants as proposed. 'Had I received in any official manner, notification of His Majesty's wish to see the park in his way to Hopetoun House, there cannot be a doubt of my acceding to have my grooms at the gate to shew the way, and of placing myself near the house to make my bow to the King in passing.' This was a flourish of conceit, no more, for Rosebery did not expect to be at home that day. The informative friend above, the Earl of Hopetoun, had already invited him to the royal breakfast.

Such hauteur and testiness was common during these last days of the Visit. There was also a languor, an emotional exhaustion, unrelieved by the publication of a great deal of indifferent poetry, including the verses George Crabbe had written upon his arrival in Edinburgh.

> Aloud strike the harp, for my bosom is cold,
>   And the sound has a charm on my fears.
> A City new-clothed as a Bride I behold,
>   And her King as her Bridegroom appears.
>
> 'Tis he whom they love, and who loves them again,
>   Who partakes of the joy he imparts,
> Who over three nations shall happily reign,
>   And establish his throne in their hearts.

James Loch and his family had left Edinburgh for Dunrobin at the week-end. What remained of his employers' immediate affairs in the city was now in the hands of their law-agent, William Mackenzie, a worrying and sometimes inept man of whom Lady Stafford had a low opinion. He was unhappily aware of this and therefore fretted even more at the spate of rumours and newspaper speculations that followed the sudden departure of Lord Francis Leveson-Gower. This, it was said, was not because of the young man's wish to be at his father's sick-bed, but because the Sutherland claim to carry the Sceptre had been disproved, and he had accordingly surrendered it to the Earl of Moray. Mackenzie sent a paragraph to four Edinburgh newspapers, refuting this and other vile errors printed by the *Observer*. Writing to Lady Stafford, he blamed them upon Sir Patrick Walker who, he said, 'is sole proprietor of the Observer & is also White Rod and chooses to think he is wiser than the King's Council & does not hesitate to support his opinion by any misstatement of facts'.

The public saw little of the King on the last day before his departure, only his red face, smiling momentarily at the window of the closed carriage that took him to Newbattle Abbey. This was a pleasant drive southward along the River Esk, two rolling miles beneath a vault of yellowing leaves. His host at Newbattle was the Marquess of Lothian, Lord Lieutenant of the county, an aging man now and sentimentally affected by the condescension of his royal guest. He was proud of his ancient home and of its recent improvements in the gothic style, and he was anxious to have the King's approval of its books and its paintings, particularly a portrait of Charles II, the last British monarch to visit Scotland, albeit disastrously. Lothian had gathered a small group of family and friends, including the Peels, and had cautioned his seven younger children, all born to his second wife, on their deportment and manners. Finally, he had engaged the celebrated Mr McGrath to play upon the organ throughout the royal visit.

The King reached the Abbey gates at two-thirty. The pillars supporting them had been specially heightened, and the Royal Standard was broken from one as the carriage and its escort clattered by. The foreman of the masons who had completed the alterations within two days, and had himself renamed the entrance The King's Gate, stood beside it now with his gang, shouting a stentorian *Huzza!* Lothian's estate workers and his tenantry lined the long approach to the house, and in the hillside village of Newbattle, which stood within his lordship's walled bounds, the mounted staff of his own Edinburgh Militia saluted grandly as the King went by. When the carriage halted at the columned entrance to the Abbey, a signal was quickly passed to the drawing-room where Mr McGrath at once struck up the National Anthem. Lothian knelt in the doorway, ready to kiss the King's hand, but carefully watching the slow descent of the first royal foot. He explained why to Scott later.

> I had played him a sort of *trick* on his arrival, having managed matters as that the crimson cloth from the stair case within should reach no further than the very threshold of the House door – by this means he was obliged to place his foot (when alighting from his carriage) on the stone in front of the door. I marked the spot, and the impression of the foot-step is now

(indelibly, I hope) described by a rim of brass round the outside edge of it.

The King stayed for no longer than an hour, during which the redoubtable McGrath played without pause, including Mozart's duet *Ah, perdona* which the King particularly requested. He also admired the house, having an experienced eye for architectural detail, commending the grand staircase and the library. In the dining-room he ate little, staring upward again and again to the ceiling upon which was a magnificent Tudor Rose, commemorating the first meeting here between James IV and his bride Margaret Tudor. He sternly advised Lothian against any alteration or enlargement to the room, for this would surely spoil its effect upon the eye. He spent a playful and caressing moment with his godchild Georgina Augusta, the youngest of Lothian's large family, and before he left for Dalkeith he said he had never seen a more comfortable and enjoyable house.

In the late afternoon, before he prepared for dinner, he gave considerate attention to yet more gifts that had arrived from societies and corporations, from honest individuals and others with a keen eye for profit. At the wish of the cartographer Knox, Commissioner Adam sent a copy of that gentleman's plan of Edinburgh, showing all the completed and proposed changes in the city and its environs. The magistrates of Leith had also sent a map of their own town and harbour, the spot where the King landed upon The Shore being marked by an imperial crown. It was more handsome than Knox's effort, being printed upon satin and enclosed in a box of crimson velvet embroidered with thistles. A lady of Edinburgh, whom Adam described as 'highly accomplished, and of great respectability', sent several panoramic views of the city as seen from the Braid Hills in the south. More than the maps, these so pleased the King that he said they should be brought before him frequently when he was again in London, that he might remember his visit to the city.

There was a flamboyant gift from Matthew Lyon, a hosier from Hawick. Having discovered, he said, 'a method of working travelling cloaks on a stocking-frame', he had made a garment of rippling silk, mazarine blue and lined with scarlet wool, six feet four inches long and thirteen feet six inches wide at the bottom, with a large

cape and a standing collar. His letter describing this mephistophe-
lean cloak was passed to Robert Peel. Lyon hoped that he would be
allowed to present the gift himself, and that he could also make one
of tartan should the King so wish. 'If his Majesty condescended to
take the Scotch cloak about him, it will not only make an *old Lyon*,
but *Lyons* yet unborn, to rejoice.'

The King was intrigued by the hosier's description of the cloak,
although it would surely have appalled his now-abandoned friend
George Brummel. Lyon was told to bring it to Dalkeith on Wednesday, where he was received by a servant whom he mistook for a
lord, and was given a Bank of England note for twenty pounds. He
was further informed that if he called on the following day, he
might be given another order. In conclusion, the King had insisted
that the hosier should drink His Majesty's health. Therefore, would
he take hock or burgundy? His honest response greatly amused the
journalists who listened to his story.

> He, who had never heard of such wines, but thought from that
> circumstance they must be too good for a man of low degree,
> hinted that he would prefer port or sherry. Accordingly, a gob-
> let was filled up to the brim, to the drinking of which Mr Lyon
> modestly demurred, on the score of its enormous size, but
> being told that such was the custom of the place, he drained it
> dry to the health of His Majesty.

The King's last evening in Scotland was passed without ceremony.
He entertained those members of his suite who, having been lodged
at the Waterloo Hotel, had not yet dined with him at Dalkeith
House. Also included were a number of Scots to whom he had
become fondly attached, pre-eminently the Author of *Waverley*.
Aware that the evening was perhaps the simple climax of his personal involvement in the Royal Visit, Walter Scott was moved by
affectionate sadness. Proposing one of many toasts, he hoped that
this would not be the only occasion when Scotland saw its noble
monarch. The tearful King, forgetting the squabbles that had preceded and provoked his jaunt, declared that on the contrary Scotland would see him *frequently*. The wine of the country made the
foolish promise. The King's liking for Glen Livet, liberally supplied

by Rothiemurchus and others, had now developed into a taste for its regrettable use in Athole Brose. He drank two large glasses of this mixture during dinner, and under its potent influence he declared his passionate admiration for the dress, manners and characters of his Highland people.

After dinner, at his request, reels and strathspeys were danced by twelve of Lord Breadalbane's Highlanders, and by twelve more from the lands of the Earl of Fife. During a pause in this wild and noisy entertainment, Scott raised his glass to *The Chief of the Clans . . . the King!* He translated the toast for the benefit of the dancers, none of whom, it was uncharitably assumed, could speak English, although for much of the preceding century the teaching of their own language had been forbidden in their schools. The leader of the Breadalbane men politely repeated the words in Gaelic to the others, and then presented the King with a sprig of heather. 'May God bless you all!' he cried, and ordered whisky to be sent to their quarters. Shortly after this he said good-night and good-bye to his guests, and went away to his bed in happy sorrow.

Orders of the Day, posted for the Scots Greys stationed in Dalkeith, instructed all but the King's Escort to march for Hopetoun House at eight in the morning, the band to proceed to Queensferry at first light, dressed in review order. The music of cavalry trumpets, sounding the close of the evening, could be clearly heard in Dalkeith House.

> *'I have seen in my grandfather's house and my
> father's house, a pile of correspondence
> describing the vicissitudes they underwent. They
> were left exposed on the north coast and they
> had to find their way from Hudson Bay to the
> Red River settlement; and they were exposed to
> the rigours of a lengthened winter, and, to
> crown all, the Indians came in and killed some
> of them, and the rest fled over the winter's
> snow. Only seven or eight managed to settle in
> Canada afterwards.*
> — ANGUS SUTHERLAND, Helmsdale

The weather on Thursday was drear, the wind blowing from the east with rain. 'This is a vile day,' wrote Scott, in a valedictory letter to William Knighton, 'but it is right Scotland should weep when parting with her good King.'

At four o'clock that morning, the *Royal George* slipped her moorings in Leith Roads and made sail up the firth to Port Edgar beyond Queensferry. There she anchored a mile offshore, joining the rest of the Royal Squadron which had come upstream on Wednesday afternoon, eleven vessels including Sir William Curtis's yacht. Shortly after six, the *Comet* and the *James Watt* arrived, making a great deal of white water as the brisk wind turned to squalls. Port Edgar was one of the oldest harbours in Scotland and recently enlarged, its rock-shore cut and blasted to make a fine quay and breakwater. An historic footnote to the King's embarkation from this spot was no doubt noted by Walter Scott. Almost eight centuries before, according to legend, the last Saxon claimant to the English throne, Edgar Atheling, had landed here to seek refuge with his brother-in-law, the last truly Celtic king of Scotland.

Westward for a mile beyond the harbour, a winding shore-road ended at the Society Gate of the great park surrounding Hopetoun House, to which its owner had invited three hundred and eighty-five guests to take breakfast with the King before his departure. The invitation was not to be taken literally, of course, for only thirty of them would sit at table with His Majesty, sharing an excellent *déjeuner à la fourchette*, but all would consider this the most memorable day of their lives.

John Hope, fourth Earl of Hopetoun, had held the title for six years, having succeeded a stepbrother twenty-four years his senior. An amiable and uxorious man, broad in view but fussy in detail, he had been a career soldier of merit, and upon the death of its commander he had successfully completed the embarkation of Sir John Moore's bloody army at Corunna. The house he had inherited, and further enriched with fine paintings, was the work of two of Scotland's greatest architects, William Bruce and William Adam. Grandly disposed on a green rise above the firth, its curving colonnades of elegant beauty reached out from the central block like welcoming arms. The Hope family believed they were French in origin, and they had been of small importance until the rise of a seventeenth-century baronet, sometimes described as 'a lawyer and leadworker'. That is to say, he was a member of the Scottish bar who married a rich heiress and thereby became the possessor of lead and silver mines. He applied himself to their management with such vigour that he brought what his descendants called 'the art of mining' to a state of near perfection.

The fourth Earl had anticipated a visit from the King as early as the end of July, and with military precision he had prepared a detailed and unequivocal list of instructions for his grieve, John Cockburn, and his house-steward, Henry Blanchflower. His principal guests were to be entertained in the house, if not all at the King's table. The remainder, more than fifteen hundred of lower station or less importance, were to be assembled, marshalled and fed within the policies of the great building. More still, if issued with tickets of entry, could be accommodated at designated points above the park and along its approaches, where they might watch the King pass and where he could receive their loyal greetings. In addition to all these, there were of course the yeomanry and dragoons who, with their bands, were to give the day its necessary dash and colour. The front of the old grey house, its curving colonnades enclosing green lawns and gravel drives, provided a noble amphitheatre for a unique occasion, and was to be used with a sense of theatre that

William Murray must have admired. 'It is intended,' his lordship declared,

> . . . to place as many of the well dressed women & children upon the tops of the two colonnades and Pavilion as possible, & the Grieve will either himself or by means of others, direct them to go by the Carpenter's Stairs and the Hay loft to the roof. None but Women & Children are to be admitted to the colonnades, & a person will be kept always at the foot of the stairs to shew them up.

Tables for privileged tenants, for some yeomanry and dragoons, were to be laid below the colonnades. For lower orders there would be bread, meat and beer available at the Farm Offices, or on the green meadow eastward of the stone sphinxes that guarded the main approach to the house. No spirits or liquor of any kind were to be allowed within the grounds, except that distributed from the estate carts, and six hogsheads of ale and porter were to be brought to the Farm Offices as early as possible on the morning, ready for distribution on the Green. The estate foresters were to issue the beer, calling up more hogsheads if needed, but were to 'stop the supply if there is any appearance of drunkenness'. To reduce the risk of disorder, Cockburn was to put reliable men at all entrances to the park, at the Society Gate, the Obelisk, the Blue, the Middle and the Abercorn. If necessary, the Sheriff at Queensferry would supply constables to assist.

When the carriages and horses of the gentry had delivered their owners to the Great Front Door, they were to be driven round to the stables, but Cockburn was warned that his lordship would have no common hacks received. The horses of the West Lothian Yeomanry (of which the Earl was colonel) could be put in the Riding House when not on duty. All other animals were to be directed to the Farm Office. The Head Forester would be held responsible for order and discipline outwith the house, and most particularly the superintendence of the ale-carts. No one should be permitted to come close to the house except those with tickets, and no horseman would be permitted within the embrace of the colonnades. To keep the lawns and the gravel court clear at all times, as many of the grieve's staff as possible were to be employed as marshals. Those stationed at the gates were to prevent the entry of 'all Carts, Hack Chaises, or Gigs belonging to persons who have no tickets of admission, & must direct them to wait outside the Gates'.

Within the house, Henry Blanchflower was advised where to place his best footmen, two of whom should be at the Great Front Door to lay a crimson carpet upon the steps immediately prior to the King's arrival, and to take it up promptly after his departure. Blanchflower was warned that he must be in attendance at the door as much as possible, and that in the dining-room he should stand by the side-tables, where he could best observe all things. The eight waiters at the King's table should have their peculiar duties explained to them, and each should be given a list of the wines and dishes on the side-tables. If the King brought his own servant, all wines and dishes were to be handed to him for laying before His Majesty. Blanchflower was to remember, most particularly, that 'no wash-hand glasses must be put upon the King's table'.

The wine to be decanted for the King was red and white Hermitage. Iced champagne and white burgundy were also to be ready. The order of drinking was set down clearly by the Earl. First, an iced punch made from rum, madeira, champagne, sugar and lemons. Second, old sherry and white burgundy. Finally, red and white champagne, and more Hermitage. There were to be two kinds of soup on the side-tables, with patties, crockies, cutlets plain and cutlets dressed. The principal dish, grouse, was to be eaten from silver, but china was to be used for all others. Coffee would be served after the ginger fondant and cheesecakes. No dish was to be served to any guest until the King had accepted or refused it.

The number of persons to be entertained by the Earl this day, within and outwith his house, was almost two thousand, at a cost of more than one thousand pounds. This included the employment of extra cooks and waiters, the hire of plates and glasses, and payment to the bands of the Greys and the 77th. The cost of 'the collation in the grounds' was a quarter of the total sum. The Royal Visit was indeed a great expense to Hopetoun, beyond this extravagant breakfast. His tailoring account with George Hunter was £400, largely expended upon his splendid uniform as Captain-General of the Company of Archers which he wore this day – coat and trews of the

Government tartan lined with satin, a rich blue bonnet and eagle feather, a silver-buckled belt and a silver-mounted dirk, linen ruffs and tartan hose. There were also bills to more tailors, to her ladyship's dressmaker, to saddlers, butchers and bakers, confectioners and fishmongers, and to the suppliers of hay and corn for the visiting carriage-horses. The shore-road from the Society Gate to Port Edgar was virtually rebuilt at great speed in ten days, by eighty men and boys using sixty teams of horses. Almost half of the total cost of £130 was expended upon the levelling of two small hills.

And there was Mr John Borman who presented the Earl with a bill for painting and papering at Hopetoun House, including 'hanging French paper, making up the landscape designs of the paper with pencil . . . painting part of wall's mock sky . . . dining-room walls washed with gall and water'. His account for £15 6s 9d was paid the following January.

The continuing squalls of rain did not depress the spirits of the large crowd which began to arrive early in the morning. Detachments of the West Lothian Yeomanry and the Greys arrived before nine o'clock. Upon that hour two field-guns from the Royal Artillery battery at Leith came up to the house at a brisk trot, entertaining the crowd with their wheel-spinning drill before moving on to Blackness Castle, there to fire royal salutes when required. The gentlemen of the Company of Archers, in dark tartan sashed with blue, travelled to Port Edgar by the steam-vessel *Tourist*, and thence by carriage to Hopetoun House. At noon, and preceded by a band, Lord Elgin marched them to the Great Front Door where they were welcomed by their Captain-General. He apologized for the weather as a good host should, invited them to take a glass of wine with him, and then dismissed them to their guardian posts along the colonnades. The arrival of the Earl's particular guests increased with the morning, the exclusive few who were to sit at the King's table being quickly conducted to quieter rooms on the first floor. The remaining three hundred and fifty-five were taken to a circle of tents outside, in the park behind the House, where there were tables 'most lavishly furnished with every delicacy and the richest wines'. Also deserving a condescending welcome were those whose interests were favoured by members of the Hope family – local tenantry, townsfolk of merit, boy scholars from the parish school of Abercorn, and girls

from another at Bluegate, the last being under the patronage of the
Countess. They were interesting children, thought Robert Mudie,
'all dressed in their holiday suits, wearing thistle and heath in great
profusion'.

The Greys and the Yeomanry were drawn up in line on the lawn
by the south colonnade, and a hundred mounted tenants in similar
formation on the north lawn, all to endure a long, damp, muscle-
aching wait for the King's arrival. A great multitude, said Mr Mudie,

> . . . from Edinburgh and the surrounding country, many of
> them from a distance of twenty miles, were now assembled
> upon the lawn, bidding defiance to the pelting of the storm.
> Among them were a considerable number of respectable farm-
> ers' wives and their blooming daughters, dressed with great
> taste and elegance. These were admitted upon the roofs of the
> colonnades and wings of the building, which were now com-
> pletely covered. There they stood, some of them for hours,
> exposed to torrents of rain, and completely drenched, but
> seemingly proof against the wildest fury of the elements.

At half past twelve a galloping dragoon came through the rain,
handing a dispatch to Mr Blanchflower at the door of the House.
The King was upon the road.

He had left Dalkeith at eleven-twenty, dressed in the blue and
scarlet of his Windsor Uniform. Before going, he thanked the small
group of Buccleuch's servants who had remained in the House to
attend him, most particularly the housekeeper. He gave her a silver
breakfast service, and others received gold watches which he
insisted should be suitably inscribed. There was no doubt that he
was deeply affected by this parting, bowing to all and saying, 'I shall
never forget the kindness I have received. May God bless you all!' He
travelled with the Duke of Dorset in a plain four-horse carriage,
troopers of the Greys giving him a last escort. He was taken rapidly
through Edinburgh, by Nicolson Street to the North Bridge and
Princes Street. There were cheering crowds along most of the way,
and girls from the Asylum for the Industrious Blind sang the
National Anthem to the noise of passing hooves. The guns of the
Castle began a long salute when the carriage turned into Princes

Street, a measured thunder still heard when it was long gone by the Water of Leith. At Cramond Bridge, two troops of the West Lothian Yeomanry relieved the Greys who were said to be 'well-pleased for the sake of their horses'. The change was made with the minimum of delay, and there was no time for ceremony when Sheriff Duff of Edinburgh, whose carriage had escorted the King this far, surrendered that responsibility to Sheriff Macrae of West Lothian.

The King had decided to pass through Lord Rosebery's estate after all, though he did not stop at the house. Having recovered handsomely from his earlier huff, the Earl assembled two hundred of his tenants to greet the passing monarch, who responded by waving his hand three times. His lordship then got into his own carriage with his wife and drove off to Hopetoun House, leaving his tenants to drink a toast to the King and a toast to the Roseberys at tables generously laden with meat and drink.

The rain lifted as the King came down the narrow shore-road to Society Gate. To his right he could see the Royal Squadron at anchor, broadsides starboard to the shore. With the exception of the *Royal George*, every ship was dressed overall with flags and streamers, and the bark of disciplined cheers so clearly heard across the water greatly affected the sentimental man in the carriage. His arrival at Society Gate, and the rapid approach up the rise, was announced by a bugle. When the challenging notes were heard at the House, the Yeomanry formed along the colonnades, and the Archers lined the great steps to the door.

Mr Blanchflower's footmen had laid the crimson carpet on the wet stones at the last moment before the advance troopers of the royal escort came down the gravel drive. They were quickly followed by the escort and carriage, the noise of wheels and hooves lost in the great blare of the Anthem, played by the competing bands of the 13th and 77th. At the opened windows of the House, upon the roof of the colonnades, on the lawns and the great green beyond the guardian sphinxes, the brightly coloured air trembled with waving shawls, handkerchiefs, hats, umbrellas and plain blue bonnets. Patrols of Sheriff's officers, with fifty special constables, kept the eager mass from breaking over the low wall between the wings of the colonnades, and thus little was seen of the King, except by those close to the House. Most of them saw only his back as he walked up the steps, pausing for a moment until, with the help of Lord Hopetoun, he felt able to enter the House. The Countess was waiting inside the marbled hall, and the King at once released the Earl's arm and offered her his own, walking with her into the dining-room and nodding happily to the slow rise and fall of bow and curtsey. A richly ornamented chair had been placed at the centre of the table, but he refused it, jovially offering it to Lady Hopetoun and taking another beside her.

As the bands played patriotic airs, the crowds outside turned eagerly to the food available. In the Granary there were cold meats and ale for household servants, the coachmen and grooms of visitors. There were more tables and more hogsheads of ale on the green for Lothian's stout farmers, their wives and their blooming daughters. In the happily styled Pleasure Ground, between dark yews and tall elms, there were two booths made from rough-sawn timber and covered with sailcloth from the Naval Yard at Leith. Here four hundred more were able to eat and drink. And then, of course, the rain began again. According to the *Narrative*, written for the Earl's archives, this was of the greatest inconvenience to those guests who had not been admitted to the dining-room.

> The unfavourable state of the weather prevented the Ladies generally from going out of doors – accordingly tables were set out in the Library, Garden Room, and others adjoining, for their accommodation, and at which they partook in succession of some refreshments.

The entertainment in the grounds was curtailed or abandoned, although the gentlemen Archers did their best. Some of them, said Mudie, 'equipped with their bows and quivers, amused themselves by running about under the greenwood, sometimes darting out upon the lawn, and again as suddenly disappearing'. An attempt to bring Locksley and the outlaws of *Ivanhoe* to further life by a display of archery ended almost before it was begun, with wet bow-strings, drooping bonnets, and the soggy weight of soaked tartan. There seemed little else to do but surrender to the power of so much water, and great admiration was expressed for Lord Hopetoun's celebrated fountain, propelling a feathered column fifty feet into the air.

The Earl had hoped that his royal guest, like others, would spend the night in his house, and Henry Blanchflower had prepared apartments on the drawing-room floor, including the Red Silk Damask Bedchamber. But the King gave no indication of staying the night, or even staying long. He ate sparingly, a little turtle soup and three glasses of wine. He talked vigorously and familiarly, for he knew almost everybody there. When one of the Earl's small sons came into the room and stood by his mother's chair, the King asked her how many children she had. Ten sons, she replied, and an infant daughter. To which, and understandably, the King could only say, 'Good God, is it possible?' As if the point therefore needed proving, the girl was brought by her nurse, followed by several of her young brothers. The King kissed the child and teased the boys. He lifted the frock of one, grasped a leg and exclaimed, 'What a stout little fellow!' Such comic-uncle interest encouraged the presentation of yet more children, including nephews and nieces, all of whom enlivened the King's spirits until he was ready to leave.

Before he went he borrowed a sword to knight old Adam Ferguson, Keeper of the Regalia. He borrowed another to give the same accolade to Henry Raeburn, Scotland's greatest portraitist, a tired old man within a year of his death. This was the righting of an old wrong. Scott had urged the overdue honour, and it was therefore fitting that when Raeburn died he was working upon two portraits of the Author of *Waverley*.

The crimson carpet, removed from the steps during the worst of the rain, was now relaid for the King's departure. The Archers, the Greys and the Yeomanry again took up their positions. The women and children waiting upon the roofs of the colonnade, and the great crowd upon the green, once more cheered, waved, and shouted huzza. And again little was seen of the object of so much enthusiasm, only a dark figure coming slowly down the steps, turning for a last touch of hands, a last bow, before entering the carriage. He was thought by some to be excessively melancholy, and others noted that he did not smile again that day.

Followed by the Earl of Hopetoun, riding the best horse in his stables, the King was driven down to Port Edgar. A green carpet had been laid along most of the quay, the rest was covered with small white pebbles. Walking alone with Hopetoun for the last few yards, the King had little to say, except that he had been impressed by the Earl's great house, as indeed he should have been, for it was the noblest of its kind in the whole of the northern kingdom.

The yacht's barge was waiting at the end of the quay, manned by eighteen seamen in blue jackets and black caps, their red and white oars held steadily aloft. The King shook hands solemnly with all about him, and then went down the steps to his seat. As the barge moved out into the uneasy waters of the firth, the guns of the squadron began their long salute, followed by the two guns at Blackness, and two more across the firth at Broomhall. The crowd on shore cheered as a small figure appeared on the after-deck of the *Royal George*. This was the last William Cranstone saw of the King. The young man had been at Port Edgar for seven hours, and considered them worth £3 10*s*, with £4 18*s* for 'travelling expences and incidents'.

Before the Royal Squadron weighed and moved downstream, the rain began again, heavily now. As on the day of its arrival, the King's yacht was surrounded by an attendant shoal of small boats, dropping astern one by one with a last cheer or a final verse of the National Anthem. Among those remaining to the last was a small sailboat, full of gentlemen draped in tartan. They had placed a tall piper in the bows, and because of the movement of the little vessel, or the state of his stomach, three of them crouched beside him, holding him upright. Watching this with grave interest, the King observed that the piper had been 'making too free with the Glenlivet'. They were his last recorded words in Scotland.

Under tow now by the *James Watt*, and leading the Squadron, the royal yacht came by Leith Roads at four o'clock, to the thunder of more guns. At the firing of the first salute from Leith, a spark from the match fell explosively into the powder-keg, killing one of the gun's crew and mangling the rest. For a brief while as the *Royal George* passed through the roads toward Aberlady Bay, it seemed she would be carrying an unwilling passenger on to England. Wilkie and Collins had taken breakfast aboard the vessel that morning, both artists hoping to make sketches of the embarkation. Wilkie went ashore before the King came, but Collins remained, still working when the ship sailed, all thought of Harriet Geddes and marriage driven from his mind by the elation of the moment. When the yacht came by Leith, running fast under tow and a gathering wind, it was only with great difficulty that he was dropped into one of the shore-boats.

By six o'clock the Squadron had passed the northern tip of Inchkeith, the guns of Edinburgh Castle firing a last salute. The Royal Standard flown daily on the Castle and on Salisbury Craigs, the Union flags hoisted elsewhere, were all lowered, and the King was officially gone from Scotland. He remained on deck for a few minutes more, waving his hat to the boats that still followed. Then he went below. Without doubt he was hungry, having eaten little this day. The Earl of Hopetoun had not ignored this possibility, and had sent a cart to Port Edgar that morning, with the gift of two fine bucks, some boxes of pineapples, grapes, melons, apricots and pears.

There were many gifts stored in the hold of the *Royal George*, and in the baggage carried by the steam-vessels, most of which the King would not see again. There were also two hundred and more Loyal Addresses from cities, towns, burghs, societies, associations, corporations, guilds, assemblies, faculties and presbyteries. The King had already listened to enough of these for him to lose all desire to hear the remainder. Among the gifts, great or modest, there was one he may have cherished, and not only because it was presented by Scott. It was a sycamore snuff-box, its lid inlaid with wood from several trees, all of them renowned in history, legend or verse. There was a splinter of yew from Wallace's home at Elderslie, from the oak that protected him from his pursuers, a piece from another yew beloved by Mary Queen of Scots, a particle of the *Victory*'s anchor-stock, and another from the elm that sheltered Wellington at Waterloo. All were enclosed in a border of blackened oak from the Armada galleon sunk in Tobermory Bay. Whether their authenticity could have been proved was perhaps of no consequence.

The homeward voyage took three days. At night, beacons and lamps burned on the cliffs and hills to starboard. During the day there was the white smoke and laggard thunder of saluting guns, the pulsing strains of patriotic music. Flotillas of small boats came out from Whitby, Lowestoft and Yarmouth, sometimes surrounding the *Royal George* at great risk to it and themselves. Although he was now a very exhausted man, the King came on deck as often as he could, wearing his sailor's blue surtout and cap. Standing alone, he smiled and bowed, turned and waved until distance or dusk made it all unnecessary.

Greenwich had been ready for the royal arrival since Saturday afternoon, the King's carriage and others for his suite waiting in the park of the Hospital. Because great crowds were expected, a large force of Bow Street Officers, mounted and on foot, took their positions at seven on Sunday morning, with detachments of the Guards and the Marines. The seamen pensioners of the Hospital, called early once more from their beds, and warmly wrapped against a chill September hour, were left to stand or sit behind the Water Gate of the park. As the morning continued, and until well past noon, the crowds in Greenwich, on the water and on both its banks, steadily increased until they were as large, if not larger than those who had watched the King's departure. The welcoming guns began their salvoes as soon as the royal yachts and their attendant steamers had passed through Gravesend Reach. Aboard the revenue cutter *Fortitude*, as if to balance a similar occurrence at Leith, the premature explosion of a charge shattered one arm and destroyed one eye of the ship's carpenter. The arm was being roughly amputated as the *Royal George* passed by, the sound of cannon drowning the carpenter's cries of agony.

The first intimation in Greenwich that the King was near was a black column of smoke to the north-east. At four o'clock the Lord Mayor's barge, which had gone downstream to meet the Squadron, now reappeared in tow by a steam-vessel. Behind them, belching more smoke, the *James Watt* brought the *Royal George* up the reach from Blackwall to Greenwich. Drums began to beat within the Hospital park, the urgent drag and paradiddle calling the Guards and Marines to parade. At four-thirty the royal yacht's tow was cast off, and she dropped anchor within a cable's length of the position she had taken twenty-two days before. The King came ashore almost immediately, amid gunfire and cheers, and once he was gone the royal yacht was taken upstream to Deptford by the *Comet*.

The tide was on the ebb and the river low. The King was in difficulty stepping from the barge, tiring almost immediately as he began the walk up the slope of the platform to the Water Gate, helped by the ever-ready arm of Commodore Paget. There were a dozen gentlemen awaiting him, and behind them a guard of honour composed of officers both naval and military. He smiled at them all, nodding to a familiar face. 'How are you . . . how are you . . .?' And a particular smile, a warm handclasp for two pretty girls. The greetings, the introductions and the civilities were soon over, the words lost in the sustained noise of cheering, music and gunfire. At last he was helped into his waiting carriage, sinking back on the cushions beside Lord Francis Conyngham, the son of his mistress. Led by a fast-riding escort, his carriage and those following travelled quickly up the Kent Road to Westminster Bridge, not slackening the pace until Carlton House was reached at five-fifteen. The bells of St Martin's, St Margaret's and St James's had begun their welcome as he crossed the bridge, and they continued to ring at intervals throughout the evening.

It had been left to Robert Peel, on the day of the King's departure from Edinburgh, to address the Scottish officers of state and inform them of His Majesty's gratitude. 'He takes leave of Scotland with the most cordial feelings of affection toward her people, and with the deepest anxiety to promote their welfare.' That same evening Lord Melville wrote to the King, begging leave most humbly to add his gratitude to the many proofs of loyalty His Majesty had received during the Visit. Despite the stilted phrasing of his letter, the minister's relief is evident, and his satisfaction that political need had been served beyond all expectation.

> When your Majesty announced your intention to visit Scotland, Lord Melville had no doubt that the people of that country would not be deficient in dutiful respect to your Majesty; but he did not anticipate to its full extent the determined and deep-rooted Monarchical feeling which evidently pervaded the great body of the people.

The Duke of Atholl went thankfully home shortly after mid-day on Friday, 30 August, travelling through showery weather but reaching Dunkeld in less than eight hours. There was more rain on Saturday but he could not remain inside the house. He took a fine pike and some trout from the Loch of Lowes, and then ordered his coachman to take the phaeton along the narrow track below Craig More and Deuchary Hill, where he was happy to see that the stand of larch he had planted in 1815 was now growing exceedingly well. The carriage came down to Strathtay by Dowally Bridge, and then homeward at a brisk trot along the military road to Dunkeld. Despite the rain, the day's outing had released his mind from tedium. He was glad the Royal Visit was over and done with, and he said as much when he wrote to his London agent the following morning, referring to it as 'the bustle and fatigue of one and twenty daft days'. Winter had sent its first warning to the Highlands. There had been a frost during the night, and at dawn the thermometer stood at 42, very cold. In a month, he said, he must come down to London, where the Radical Press was malevolently abusing him.

His daughter, Lady Elizabeth MacGregor, regretted his abrupt departure from Edinburgh. She had thoroughly enjoyed the King's Jaunt, and the time she had spent with her father. His grandchildren, she told him, were all well, still able to bathe in the sea at Portobello, a practice she intended to continue throughout the winter if possible. Worn out by his exertions, Sir Evan MacGregor had gone to Lanrick for rest. 'The doctors say his constitution has been so much injured by his long residence in India that it will be years before he can recover entirely.' Now contemplating his future, the most colourful figure of the Visit had no reason for optimism. The wars were over, and a soldier's trade had become uncertain. He decided to visit London and there sell his wits or his sword, and he asked his father-in-law for letters of introduction that might secure him a post. 'Anywhere other than hot climates. At my time of life it cannot be consonant to my feelings to be thrown upon the shelf.' At least his right to be recognized and styled chief of the Griogaraich was no longer in serious dispute. With emotions stirred by the Visit, and by the thought of the King surrounded by 'a phalanx of the sons of Alpin', 2650 men of his name had signed an address thanking him for giving them an opportunity to 'taste the delight of expressing as a Tribe, our devoted loyalty to the Chief of the Chiefs of Scotland'.

The fashionable hotels of Edinburgh, the Waterloo, the Royal, Davidson's and others, were all vacated by their noble guests before the Royal Squadron had left the firth. Lord Montagu collected his nephew, the young duke, his own children and several more nephews and nieces from Barrie's Hotel, and took them all back to Dalkeith House. The equally teeming family of Colonel Wemyss of Wemyss left Gibb's Hotel on Friday, as did Lord and Lady Gwydir, the Earl of Aberdeen, Viscount Keith, MacLeod of MacLeod and a dozen more. Accompanying the newspaper reports of this carriage-borne exodus, were announcements by brewers, vinegar-makers, pastry-cooks, lamp-makers, hairdressers, booksellers, butchers and others, all eager to inform their customers that the King had been pleased to appoint them his tradesmen in ordinary.

The Sutherland Men were among the first to take their tartan from the city streets. James Loch wrote to Scott from Dunrobin, congratulating him on his decision to call the clans to Edinburgh. 'I rejoice in it also on account of Lady Stafford, as I am confident the appearance of her men has done more to contradict the lies told in regard to her than anything else could do.' George Gunn brought the

Sutherlanders back to Dornoch, whence they were marched in military order to the green before Dunrobin Castle. Her Ladyship proudly reported their arrival to Scott. Her son, Lord Francis, had received them in Highland dress, and after she had spoken to each man 'they had a *Déjeuner à la Fourchette*, danced reels, and repaired to their homes, some of them dancing by the way'. Their colours and their targes were left at the castle where she intended to hang them above the staircase. She was warmly grateful to Scott for his assistance in securing her family's right to carry the Sceptre, and the fact that good friends had helped her to retain it had doubled its value. Lord Stafford's illness had thrown a shadow over the occasion, of course, but she had never felt happier. Now that the lies were discredited, Mr Loch's great policy could proceed. Her happiness was thus

> . . . increased by the prospect of effecting more improvements in this country introducing several branches which will occupy the people profitably to themselves. I rejoice to think that this visit of the King's to Scotland, that as it has been will do a great deal to excite the [conscience] of the country in every way & to bring the Highlanders forward, who have not been overlooked on this occasion, & we shall all revive our tartans & our badges & our national manners & language with increased satisfaction.

Clearly if clumsily expressed, this was the true value of the Royal Visit to many great landowners in the Highlands. A theatrical display of Gaelic splendour on the part of conscientious chiefs had demonstrated that Garth and other critics were liars, and that the Highland people knew they were being improved for their own good alone. Although some must leave their glens or their country for ever, they could be confident that their dress, their customs, and their language would be safely preserved by their evictors.

Once the pressing obligations of the Royal Visit were lifted, Scott's resilient strength collapsed. He quickly left Castle Street for the calm and comforting environment of Abbotsford, but his melancholy was not easily cured by the familiar sight of the Eildon Hills, now serene in their autumnal plaid, or by the Tweed flowing musically beyond his windows. 'I have not been well,' he would write to Daniel Terry, 'a whoreson thickness of blood, and a depression of spirits arising from the loss of friends.' He feared this condition would be reflected in *Peveril*, and that the book would 'smell of apoplexy'. He had the notion for a new novel, the story of a Scottish archer of the Guard at the court of Louis XI. It is tempting to believe that *Quentin Durward* was born from the recent pageant, conceived by the romantic revival of the moribund Company of Archers. Scott had done much to please his own conscience, to honour his obligations to his King and to his countrymen. Not by the pageantry alone, but by the sanctification of Scotland's few tangible relics of regality. In the coming weeks he would urge the lifting of the attainder that still impoverished and crippled the spirit of some Jacobite families. With the help of Robert Peel he would also secure the return of the great cannon Mons Meg. This monstrous piece of fifteenth-century artillery had been spitefully removed from Edinburgh Castle after the last Jacobite rebellion, and sent in shabby triumph to London. Although few Scots in 1822 may have given much caring thought to where it was and why, its return did seem proper now that a Jacobite King sat in London and that the grief for Culloden could be shared by all.

Scott sometimes laughed at the frailty of his health, saying it was the consequence of 'very hard exercise of body and mind, not to mention too much good living', but he was angry when that persistent rash made it impossible for him to mount a horse. He tried to be philosophical about it. Wiser than his doctors, he was now sure that it had saved him from something worse. 'I believe it was distress of mind,' he told Terry, 'suppressed as much as I could and mingling with the fatigue; certainly I was miserably ill, and am now only got quite better.' The success of the Royal Visit continued to comfort and inspire him. He sincerely believed that in 'moral grandeur' it had been beyond anything else he had witnessed. The hearts of all men, poor and great, had been completely merged. He was particularly proud of having recalled the past so vividly, and he delighted in the response of the clans to his summons. He wrote of this to his admirer Lady Abercorn. 'I wish you could have seen so many plaids and plumes and shields and drawn broadswords, all under banners that had not been seen since 1745.' Such satisfaction was impregnable, resisting reasonable truth or carping criticism, and it is unlikely that he was deeply hurt by any of the sour comments that were now being made. In London *The Times* was contemptuous of his role in the Visit, discounting his importance and deriding 'the Government press which described in glowing terms the intrusion of the titled bard upon his Sovereign on the night of his arrival'.

> It is somewhat ludicrous to observe the pains with which the Edinburgh Government scribes endeavour to press Sir Walter Scott into the front rank of the personages who occupied the proscenium during the arrangements for His Majesty's reception in Scotland ... Why is not Sir Walter Scott contented with having received a gentleman's reception from the King? ... Everybody knows that from first to last Sir Walter Scott permitted himself to be put forward as a director of the most trivial matters connected with arrangements for the Edinburgh pageants. That while meddling in all the details of matters for which his habits and pursuits so ill fitted him, he should, like other men who, moved from their own proper spheres, have committed odd acts, was only what might have been expected, but his friends should not have forced these eccentric aberrations into light.

Although the clansmen were gone from Edinburgh, the city was not allowed to forget them. Aware of the interest aroused by so much swirling tartan and so many fearsome weapons, by the transformation of the 'bare-arsed banditti' once despised by Lowlanders into heroes of tragic mould, several newspapers published a serial account of *The Highland Clans and their History*. At best this was culled from Garth's *Sketches*, at worst it was compounded from legend or clouded fact supplied by chiefs and their families. Many of these no longer spoke Gaelic with any facility, or kept the bards who had once been the repository of such histories, and the reliability of their information was accordingly weak. Its publication provoked rivalry and quarrelsome dispute, which heightened the appeal of the subject to its readers. If there was a common theme, apart from the barbarity and mayhem of constant feuds, it was that all Highlanders, that is to say all Highland gentlemen, could be placed upon the same legendary plane as a Roland, an Oliver or a du Guesclin. Even the Misses Grant of Rothiemurchus, normally level-headed about their race, were worshippers of this myth before the Royal Visit was over. At the Caledonian Hunt Ball a riband at the hem of Jane's dress became loose, and could not be successfully pinned or tied. Describing the resolution of this small problem, she managed to illustrate how gallant a Highland gentleman was, how resourceful, how handsomely yet sensibly dressed, and how chivalrous in his surrender of an honour that could have been his alone. The Highlander so described was MacLeod of MacLeod.

> The gentlemen felt in vain in the pockets of their embroidered waistcoats for knives. At length, a chieftain who was dancing down in full belted plaid and phillibeg, took from the sheath of his dirk his maiden knife, and gave it into the eager hand of a gallant officer who, kneeling down, cut off the offending ribbon, and all was right.

Inevitably the disputes became hot-tempered, and inevitably that conducted by and about Glengarry was the most envenomed. He began it in the *Observer* with a letter so prolix that the newspaper printed the first half of it on the Saturday following the King's departure, and the second on Monday. Characteristically, it began 'I was shocked beyond description . . .', and then described the nature and causes of that shock in forty column inches and four thousand words. The immediate cause was the publication in the *Observer* of some celebratory and florid verses by a Miss MacDonell. She was said to be Alasdair Ranaldson's daughter, which he promptly denied, not because he disliked the poem but because justice had not been done to its true author, the daughter of his kinsman, MacDonell of Scotus. From such trivia, a mere feint, he pressed a forthright attack upon Garth's urban Highlanders.

> I cannot pass over that non-descript convention of anything rather than Highlanders, the Celtic Society; an incongruous assemblage of all ranks, that have no common bond of union among them. They neither speak the language, nor know how to put on correctly the garb of the 'Gael', and yet, *without*

possessing the blood or the manly frame of that interesting race, or any ostensible cause whatever, they barefacedly *masked themselves* in the Highland garb, and trusting to the cloak of this *assumed character*, in their tartan, and with eagle plumes in their bonnets, the *distinctive mark of the chieftain of old!*

An angry response was immediate, from Mackenzie of Gruinard and others who hid their identity behind such pseudonyms as *A Celt* or *A True Celt*. They were dignified and carefully polite and thus no match for Glengarry's continuing abuse. He derided them all for 'imagining themselves, from dreams of Celtic importance, to be something terrific, ha! ha! ha!'. He sneered at MacKenzie's poverty and lowly military rank. He returned again and again to Highland dress, upon which he would submit to no other authority. 'I have been much disgusted, repeatedly, by seeing the belted plaid and the shoulder plaid disfigured and caricatured by members of the Society *in public*.' He bridled at what he took to be insults in the letters from those he had himself offended. As long as he wore the warlike garb of his ancestors, he said, he would not be *herded* by the best man among his enemies. His past record as an impetuous duellist made that a threat to be taken seriously.

The arrogance and vulgarity of Glengarry's continuing abuse, his reference to the *Mulatto* and the *Jew* whom he said he had seen masquerading in the ranks of the Celtic Society, at last persuaded the *Observer* that it might be time to put an end to the correspondence. Before this could be announced, the editors of all Edinburgh newspapers were summoned before Sheriff Duff. He told them that he had read the various letters which had appeared in the *Observer*, written by A. R. MacDonell, A Celt, Mac Mhic Alastair and others, and that in his opinion

> ... they tended to provoke a breach of the peace. That he considered himself entitled to stop any paragraph from appearing in a paper which had any such tendency. He was aware that this might be a very difficult matter for the Editors of Newspapers, but the Editors knew well that if they inserted paragraphs of a provoking tendency from one quarter, they could not easily refuse to receive paragraphs on the same subject from the opposite party.

In publishing this statement, and with heavy-footed irony, the *Observer* thanked Sheriff Duff for his benevolent solicitude. It was always happy to be informed of its errors, it said, and until it received the Sheriff's statement it had been unaware that there was any control over its mistakes save that which arose from its own discretion. It discontinued the publication of such letters for three weeks, and then revived the dispute with a long tirade against Glengarry, written by *A Sober Celt*.

David Stewart of Garth went home to Glenlyon soon after the King's departure. He was saddened and embittered by Alasdair Ranaldson's behaviour. On 9 October he wrote to Scott, hoping that the Celtic Society's petition for the King's patronage would be granted. He had at first opposed this, but had later agreed, because he now believed that Glengarry's hostility to the Society made the King's protection necessary. He had taken no part in the acrimonious newspaper debate, nor ever would, but he told Scott that he could refute every line of Alasdair Ranaldson's attack. Had it not been for that difficult man, the Royal Visit would have passed without an angry word or an unpleasant feeling.

> Glengarry is a conspicuous man and is held up as a model of Highland character, although he stands by himself without another of similar principles, conduct and general behaviour. So far is he from being a model that I know no man like him, and he does infinite injury to his fellow-countrymen in the false and erroneous view he offers to the public of what he is pleased to call a true Highlander.

MacDonell died six years after the King's Visit, fatally injured when leaping from a sinking steamer on Loch Linnhe. His Society of True Highlanders ended with him, but his image was mirrored in the enduring mythology of the Highlands, and his bizarre notions about his 'interesting race', the 'blood and manly frame' of its people were accepted with a confidence equal to his arrogance. Despite their mutual hatred, the differences between him and the members of other Highland societies were a matter of degree only in the culpability of a great deception. Although it is difficult to believe that any man then or since could take Alasdair Ranaldson seriously, Scott did and most affectionately, and therefore it could not have been difficult for others. With the assistance of Raeburn's superb portrait, the chief of Glengarry, or someone like him, soon represented Scotland on the lids of biscuit-boxes, shortbread-tins, on porridge packets, railway posters and postcards, in picture-galleries and children's books. No other nation has cherished so absurd an image, and none perhaps would accept it while knowing it to be a lie. For that monstrous error, the pageantry of Scott and the euphoria of the King's Jaunt were largely responsible.

The Royal Visit cannot be dismissed as Atholl set it aside, no more than twenty-one days of daft play-acting. Scotland could not be the same again once it was over. A bogus tartan caricature of itself had been drawn and accepted, even by those who mocked it, and it would develop in perspective and colour. With the ardent encouragement of an Anglo-Scottish establishment, and under the patronage of successive monarchs who took to kilt and cromach with Germanic thoroughness, Walter Scott's Celtification continued to seduce his countrymen, and thereby prepared them for political and industrial exploitation. It gave them a picturesque national identity where none had been wholly satisfying since the Union, and reminded them, as Scott had hoped, of 'all those peculiarities' which distinguished them as Scots. It also, and pre-eminently, united Lowlander and Borderer as one nation with a diminishing Gaelic minority whose existence had once aroused uneasy guilt or derisive contempt, but whose costume and history might now be honourably assumed by all. Finally the pageant devised by Scott and Murray encouraged Scots to believe that of all the peoples of the United Kingdom they might perhaps consider themselves to be the most favoured by God and the Monarchy (which they, indeed, had supplied).

There was, of course, a grimmer Scotland during that exciting August. However, the scaffold in Stirling was hidden and the fires in Strathnaver were obscured by the illuminations in Edinburgh. The fears aroused by the Radical War had been laid by the sight of three thousand sabres on Portobello Sands. Baird, Hardie, Wilson and their brothers could be condemned by Scott as democratical scoundrels, and their followers contemptuously dismissed as 'the lowest shop-keepers and mechanics'. The lamenting voices of James Cummin, George MacDonald, Angus Sutherland, Annie Mackay and others quoted here, would not be heard until six decades hence, and would not then materially affect the course of the nation. Wherever an anguished and bewildered Gaelic people now resisted the rape of the Highlands and the theft of their self-respect, they were suppressed by soldiers, marines and warships.

When Scotland settled into its nineteenth-century role as the foot-soldier, ironsmith, collier, ship-builder, carter, shepherd, and counter-hand of a flourishing British imperialism it accepted – or at best did not furiously resent – the image created for it by the Plaided Panorama of 1822. Of all the sadness in its history from which it could have chosen a Lost Cause worthy of regret, it accepted – or at best did not strongly reject – the Stuart Prince and the disastrous rebellion that had begun the despoliation of the Highlands and the dispersal of their people. Under the inspiration of Lady Nairne, of Scott, Aytoun and countless others, Scotland sang its Jacobite songs for another hundred years. No laments were heard – or none beyond the bounds of the *Gaidhealtachd* – for the evictions, the burnings and the white-sailed ships that were emptying the glens while the men who profited from this diaspora formed their Highland societies and solemnly debated the correct hang of a kilt and the exact drape of a plaid. Thus a Highland gentleman, one year after the King's Visit, could address a grave letter to the Highland Society in Edinburgh with worrying questions as to the proper form of dress to be worn at a Highland Ball. Was it the belted plaid or the small plaid ... were waistcoats of tartan ... was gold or silver lace worn ... was the broadsword laid aside for dancing ... were bonnets cocked in the form of a horse-shoe ... were buttons covered with tartan or coloured silks ...?

The romantic myth became sober fact when Victoria and her consort adopted the Highlands, but sometimes truth can be laid beside the more acceptable fictions. During the Queen's summer stay at Balmoral in 1855 she asked the artist Kenneth MacLeay to paint a series of portraits of retainers on the estate, and of other familiar Highland figures. He was a draughtsman of skill and a beguiling colourist. The work he produced was brilliantly executed and the portraits faithfully represent the conventional picture of a Highlandman. Each subject is sturdy and erect, sometimes anciently armed and sometimes carrying a rod or a sporting-piece. He is clear-eyed, shoulders broad and calves swelling, his manly frame wearing kilt and plaid with unconsious ease.

William Duff was one of the subjects, an Atholl man who had been a shoe-maker, a game-watcher and a boatman to the Duke, but who was now a fisherman at Dunkeld. He was a literate man, a fine Gaelic singer, and a good fiddler. In MacLeay's portrait he is an impressive figure, well-kilted, with a loose jacket and vest, a bonnet tipped over one eye. His hair is dark, his white beard full, his cheeks ruddy and healthful. He looks as the Queen and his employers thought he should look, a humble Highland *gentleman*, a dignified subordinate within an immutable system of class and race. The illusion is broken by the survival of a photograph from which Macleay worked, or in which Duff was persuaded to pose in imitation of the portrait. He wears the same costume and holds what may be the same tall rod, but an unkempt kilt hangs obliquely below his knees, his diced hose standing like boots about his thin legs. His uncocked bonnet-is set square upon his head, as if the photographer had thrust it there impatiently. His sporran, straggling horse-hair and tassels held in a metal clasp, is the ridiculous military version that replaced the simple leather purse of more practical times. His white hair is long and untidy, merging with his beard to frame a gentle face and weary, deep-set eyes.

There is an irony in the year when MacLeay's flattering portraits were commissioned. Elsewhere in the Highlands the young men of Sutherland were turning from the recruiting officers and from their ducal landlord who wished them to enlist for the Crimean War. 'Since you have preferred sheep to men,' they said, 'let sheep defend you.'

Of course there were sober minds at the time of the King's Jaunt, cautious voices protesting that all was foolish fancy, but common sense has never destroyed a pleasing illusion. Some were content with mockery, and none more impudently than William Cranstone. His slender immortality rests upon the surviving account of his expenses during the Visit. His attendance at all the public events cost him £41, and if this sum was honestly assessed it must follow that he was not a pauper. He copied his 'expences and incidents' in a fine hand, and on 11 November he sent them to the King, whom he cordially addressed as *My Dear Sire*.

I act in no public capacity whatsoever and have therefore no claim for anything of the kind, but as I stand much in need of cash just now, and have no where from whence I can expect it, I thought the best expedient for me to try would be the present scheme of sending you the inclosed account which I was sure would meet with your approbation, and as you had plenty of money could easily comply with my request.

He asked the King to excuse his impoliteness and his familiarity, for he was unaccustomed to addressing Royalty. The amount owing could be remitted in any way convenient to His Majesty, 'but if you would like to see me first, I will wait upon you with the utmost cheerfulness . . . provided you will send me down a few pounds for the purpose of paying my travelling expences coming up'.

The letter was passed to Robert Peel who handed it to his secretary without written comment or directions as to a reply, not even the word *Mad* with which he occasionally dismissed a perverse correspondent. Thus it may be assumed that William Cranstone received no answer, and that his account for the King's Jaunt is still unpaid. So indeed is Scotland's.

PRINCIPAL CHARACTERS

ADAM of Blairadam, William. Lord Chief Commissioner of the
    Scottish Jury Court. An intimate friend of Walter Scott whom
    he invited to form a committee that could devise and
    manage the King's reception in Edinburgh.

ARBUTHNOT, William. Lord Provost of Edinburgh and a member of
    Scott's committee. Knighted by the King during the civic
    banquet.

ATHOLL, John Murray, 4th Duke of. *Am Moireach Mor*, the chief of
    Clan Murray. Active member of the committee for building a
    National Monument. Successfully urged a limit to the
    number of Highlanders admitted to Edinburgh during the
    Royal Visit, which he described as 'one and twenty daft days'.

BAIRD, John. Radical weaver and commandant during the 1820
    insurrection. Hanged and beheaded at Stirling.

BRADFORD, General Sir Thomas. Commander-in-chief in Scotland.
    A Peninsula veteran who suppressed the Radicals.

BREADALBANE, John Campbell, 4th Earl of. Chief of the
    Breadalbane Campbells, a contingent of whom he brought to
    Edinburgh for the Visit.

CASTLEREAGH, Robert Stewart, Viscount, later 2nd Marquis of
    Londonderry. Foreign Secretary in Lord Liverpool's
    administration.

COLLINS, William, artist. Came to Edinburgh to paint the Visit, but
    also to marry.

CONYNGHAM, Elizabeth, Marchioness. The King's last mistress.

CRABBE, George. Poet, botanist, surgeon *inter alia*. A self-taught
    man of many parts. Scott's English guest during the Visit.

FERGUSON, Adam, later Sir. An old soldier for whom Scott secured
    the post of Keeper of the Regalia, and thus a colourful role in
    the ceremonies.

FOX, Henry. Young English visitor. Son of Elizabeth Vassall Fox, Lady Holland, who presided over the Whig circle at Holland House.

GARTH. See Stewart.

GEORGE IV. Leading player.

GLENGARRY. See MacDonell.

GRANT of Rothiemurchus, John Peter. Lawyer and landowner of Speyside who brought his daughters and son to Edinburgh for the Royal Visit.

GRANT, Jane. Second daughter of Rothiemurchus above. Her letters, with those of her sister below, give a vivid picture of Edinburgh during the Visit.

GRANT, Mary Frances. Third daughter of Rothiemurchus. Her letters, with her sister's, were privately published some years later, and have been largely obscured by the brief and inaccurate reference to the Royal Visit in the memoirs of the eldest daughter Elizabeth, who did not go to Edinburgh.

HARDIE, Andrew. Radical leader. Hanged and beheaded at Stirling in September 1820.

HAMILTON, Alexander Douglas, 10th Duke of. Premier peer of Scotland, and thus with a particular role in Scott's pageant. He sometimes claimed to be the true heir to the crown of Scotland.

HOPE, John, 4th Earl of Hopetoun. Veteran soldier and master of Hopetoun House where the King took breakfast on his last day in Scotland.

KEITH of Ravelston, Sir Alexander. A friend and distant cousin of Scott, and a member of his committee. His claim to be the Hereditary Knight Marischal of Scotland was enthusiastically supported by Scott who accordingly gave Keith a role to play in the pageant.

KNIGHTON, Sir William. The *accoucheur*. Private secretary and physician to the King. A shadowy figure, the subject of much gossip and hostility. Accompanied George IV to Edinburgh.

LIEVEN, Dorothea de. Wife of the Russian ambassador to London. One-time mistress of Metternich, for whom she worked to persuade the King to go on 'the Journey' to Vienna.

LIVERPOOL, Robert Banks, 2nd Earl of. First minister of the Tory administration. Opposed the proposal for the King's Journey to Vienna, and probably directed it toward Edinburgh.

LOCH of Drylaw, James. Commissioner of the Marquess of Stafford's estates in England and Scotland. Principal creator of the Policy of Improvement. Hoped that his employers' participation in the Royal Visit would deflect or destroy hostile criticism.

LOCKHART, John Gibson. Son-in-law and biographer of Sir Walter Scott, whose pageantry for the Royal Visit he gently mocked as 'Celtification' and 'a Plaided Panorama'.

MACDONALD of Staffa, Ranald. Highland eccentric, and officer of the Celtic Society and the True Highlanders. As Sheriff of Stirling, he officiated at the execution of Baird and Hardie.

MACDONELL of Glengarry, Alasdair Ranaldson, also referred to here as Glengarry. Self-obsessed, hot-tempered and flamboyant clown of the Visit. Disliked by Stewart of Garth, but admired by Scott as 'a treasure'. Formed the Society of True Highlanders, and invented the Glengarry bonnet.

MACGREGOR of MacGregor, Sir Evan. Chief of the name, and the most colourful figure of the Visit, surpassing even Glengarry. A battle-scarred, brave and considerate man. Atholl's son-in-law.

MACKENZIE of Gruinard, William. An old soldier of modest achievements. Founder of the Celtic Society, and as such the butt of Glengarry's contempt and abuse.

MELVILLE, Robert Saunders Dundas, 2nd Viscount Melville. A powerful member of a great family of Scottish lawyers and statesmen. He was First Lord of the Admiralty at the time of the Visit, but acknowledged as the Tory Administration's manager of Scotland. Welcomed the Royal Visit as a means of countering Radical disaffection.

MONTAGU, Henry James Scott, Lord. Guardian of his young nephew the 5th Duke of Buccleuch, and in that capacity offered the King the use of Dalkeith House during the Visit. A friend of Walter Scott, with whom he corresponded vigorously.

MURRAY, William. Actor-manager of the Theatre Royal in Edinburgh. Advised Scott upon the pageantry, and was himself responsible for dressing Parliament Hall and the Assembly Rooms for banquet and ball. Grandson of the Jacobite turncoat, Sir John Murray of Broughton.

NAIRNE Caroline, Baroness. Jacobite songstress. Published her work anonymously during 1822. Born Caroline Oliphant, of a house passionately attached to the Stuart cause. She was still Mrs Nairne, wife of an old soldier during the Visit, an event which she seems to have studiously ignored.

PEEL, Robert. Britain's new Home Secretary. Came to Edinburgh for the King's Visit, which he does not seem to have enjoyed, but during which he formed a lasting friendship with Scott.

SCOTT, Sir Walter. Pageant-master.

SIDDONS, Mrs Harriet. Actress, sister of William Murray, and the daughter-in-law of the great Mrs Sarah Siddons. Her husband, the actor Henry Siddons, had shared management of the Theatre Royal with Murray until his death in 1815. Mrs Siddons also advised on style and fashion for the Visit, and her daughter Sally later married William Grant of Rothiemurchus.

STAFFORD, Elizabeth Gordon, Marchioness of Stafford. Countess of Sutherland in her own right, and later 1st Duchess of Sutherland upon her husband's elevation. Romantic, and practical, more English than Scots, an enthusiastic supporter of Loch's Policy of Improvement. The object of bitter criticism which she hoped participation in the Royal Visit would counter and destroy.

STAFFORD, George Granville Leveson-Gower, 2nd Marquess of, later 1st Duke of Sutherland. English. Acquired large Highland estate by marriage, and employed James Loch to improve it.

STEWART of Garth, David, Lieutenant-Colonel, later General, also referred to here as Garth. Perthshire laird, recorder and defender of Highlanders and Highland regiments. Fierce critic of landlords and the dispersal of the Gaelic people by eviction. A member of Scott's committee for the Visit and responsible for organizing the Highland contribution.

TURNER, Joseph Mallord William. Came to Edinburgh to paint the Visit. Though his work did not please his patrons, or the

King, it is the most vivid visual record of the occasion, particularly the *March of the Highlanders* and *George IV at St Giles*.

WALKER, Sir Patrick. Self-appointed Usher of the White Rod, and active throughout the Visit in this vaguely defined role. His 'hereditary office' was contemptuously dismissed by Lord Melville. Owner of the *Edinburgh Observer*.

WILKIE, David. Came to Edinburgh with William Collins, both of them having accreditations from Lord Liverpool to paint particular incidents during the Visit. Wilkie's work was the most successful, in popular terms, of all that done by artists in the city for the occasion.

WILSON, James. Hosier, clocksmith and preacher. Hanged in Glasgow for his part in the Radical insurrection of 1820.

WILSON, William. Owner of a Bannockburn weaving firm which he ran with his brother and others of his family. Supplied much of the tartan cloth worn during the Visit, and in the decades following.

ACKNOWLEDGEMENTS

The material for this book has come from many sources, much of it from manuscripts in public and private archives, and I am in debt to those who granted me access to them, and whose courtesy and kindness lightened the burden of my work. I am particularly grateful to the following:

Keith Adam of Blairadam; the Duke of Atholl, for access to the muniments at Blair Castle, and to Mrs Jane Anderson, their keeper; Tristram Clarke of the National Register of Archives (Scotland); George A. Dixon, Archivist of the Central Regional Council, Stirling; Captain Alwyne Farquharson of Invercauld; Clive Goodall; J. R. Ker, for helpful introductions in Scotland; Miss Jane Langton, the Registrar of Archives, Windsor Castle; Brigadier Sir Gregor MacGregor of MacGregor; Dr Atholl L. Murray, Keeper of Records at the Scottish Record Office; Mrs D. M. A. Randall of the Staffordshire Record Office; Mrs Carolyn Rowlinson of the University of Stirling Library; Dr Thomas I. Rae, Keeper of Manuscripts, National Library of Scotland, for his kindly help once more; Basil Skinner; Dr Gordon Teall of the Scottish Tartan Society. I am also grateful for the help given me by the patient staffs of the National Library of Scotland, the Scottish Record Office, the National Register of Archives (Scotland), the Public Record Office, the British Library, and the London Library.

SOURCES

With a few exceptions only, the quotations at the head of the chapters in this book are taken from the evidence given to the Napier Commission in 1883, and from statements gathered by a civil engineer who himself gave evidence. They were made in Gaelic, and the version here used is a literal translation. The engineer's statements were published by John Stuart Blackie in 1885 (see *Bibliography*). Other quotations are taken from the Sutherland Papers, and from newspaper reports etc. of the Radical trials in 1820.

MANUSCRIPT SOURCES

Atholl Charter Room, Blair Castle
Box 68, Section 12

Correspondence of the
4th Duke of Atholl, 1822

Bundle 1026

4th Duke's Journals
Notebooks 34 and 35, 1822

Blairadam, Kinross
Adam of Blairadam
Muniments

Box William Adam 1822A
4/870/40–70

British Library
Add. MSS 38195
Add. MSS 40304

Liverpool Papers
Peel Papers

Castle of Invercauld, Braemar
Farquharson of Invercauld MSS   Box 22, Misc 1

SOURCES

Central Regional Archives (Scotland)
MacGregor of MacGregor MSS   Bundles 31, 64, 68
(Lanrick & Balquhidder)   71, 87, 109

National Library of Scotland
Sutherland Papers   313/779
Abbotsford Collection   867
    909
Letters to Walter Scott   3894
    3695
Grant of Laggan MSS   3813/116–118

Public Record Office
Home Office Papers   HO 28/48 Admiralty Corr.
    1822
    HO 43/31 Entry Book, 1821–22
    HO 44/12 Letter-Book,
    June–Dec, 1822
    HO 102/35 Scotland Corr.
    1822–24
    HO 103/35 Scotland, General
    Letter-Book, 1810–24
Admiralty Papers   ADM 51 Captains' Logs
    ADM 52 Masters' Logs

Scottish Record Office
Barcaldine Papers   GD 170/28/12/1
Buccleuch Papers   GD 224/32/4/9–12
Exchequer Papers   E 215/6
Hopetoun Muniments*   TD 85/117
    Box One, Bundle 218
    Box Two, Bundles 234, 241,
    1237
    MS Volume 385
Seaforth Papers   GD 46/17/61
    GD 46/4/188–9
Scott of Harden MSS   GD 157/2548

(* These papers are not on deposit at the Scottish Record Office. Access through the SRO.)

Scottish Tartan Society, Comrie
   Wilson of Bannockburn
   Letters, Book 2A (typescript)

Staffordshire Record Office
   Stafford-Sutherland Papers   D593/P/18/1
                                        /18/2
                                        /20
                                        /22/1/28

CONTEMPORARY NEWSPAPERS AND JOURNALS

The *Scotsman*
The *Edinburgh Advertiser*
The *Edinburgh Evening Courant*
The *Edinburgh Observer*
The *Edinburgh Star*
The *Weekly Journal*
The *Caledonian Mercury*
The *Stirling Journal*
The *Inverness Journal*
The *Inverness Courier*
The *Perthshire Courier*
The Times
The *London Evening Courier*
The *Morning Chronicle*
The *Gentleman's Magazine*
Blackwood's Magazine

BIBLIOGRAPHY

Adam, R. J. *Papers on Sutherland Estate Management, 1802–16.*
   Scottish History Society. Edinburgh, 1972

Arbuthnot, Harriet *The Journal of Mrs Arbuthnot, 1820–32,* edited by
   Francis Bamford and the Duke of Wellington. London, 1950

Armitage, Gilbert *The History of the Bow Street Runners.* London,
   1932

Aspinall, A. (Ed.) *The Letters of George IV, 1812–1830.* 1938

Atholl, 7th Duke of (Ed.) *Chronicles of the Atholl and Tullibardine
   Families.* Edinburgh, 1908

Barron, James *The Northern Highlands in the Nineteenth Century –
   Newspaper Index and Annals.* Inverness, 1903

Blackie, John Stuart *The Scottish Highlanders and the Land Laws.*
   London, 1885

Buchan, John *Sir Walter Scott.* London, 1932

Collins, Wilkie *Memoirs of the Life of William Collins, Esq., R.A.*
   London, 1848

Crabbe, Rev. George *The Life of George Crabbe, by his Son, introduction
   by Edmund Blunden.* London, 1947

Cunningham, Alan *The life of Sir David Wilkie, with his journals,
   tours, and critical remarks on Art, and a selection of his correspondence.*
   London, 1843

Daiches, David *Scott and Scotland.* Scott Bicentenary Essays, edited
   by Alan Bell. Edinburgh, 1973

Dunbar, John Telfer *History of Highland Dress.* Edinburgh, 1962

Ellis, P. Beresford, and Seumas Mac a' Ghobhainn *The Scottish
   Insurrection of 1820.* London, 1970

Finley, Gerald *Turner and George IV in Edinburgh, 1822.* Edinburgh,
   1981

Fox, Henry *The Journal of the Hon. Henry Edward Fox, 1818–1830,*
   edited by the Earl of Ilchester. London, 1923

Fyfe, W. T. *Edinburgh under Sir Walter Scott*. London, 1906

Gash, Norman *Mr Secretary Peel, the Life of Sir Robert Peel to 1830*. London, 1961

Grant, Mrs Anne (of Laggan) *Letters from the Mountains*. Edinburgh, 1803

Grant, Elizabeth (of Rothiemurchus) *Memoirs of a Highland Lady, 1797–1827*. Edinburgh, 1896

Grant, Jane and Mary (of Rothiemurchus) *Letters from Edinburgh, 1822*. N.d.

Greville, Charles *The Greville Memoirs*, edited by Lytton Strachey and Roger Fulford. London, 1938

Grierson, H. J. C. (Ed.) *The Letters of Sir Walter Scott*. London, 1932–7.

Grimble, Ian *Clans and Chiefs*. London, 1980

Hibbert, Christopher *George IV, Regent and King, 1811–1830*. London, 1973

Huchon, René *George Crabbe and his times, 1754–1832*, trans. Fredk Clarke. London, 1907

Huish, Robert *Memoirs of George the Fourth*, vol. ii. London, 1831

Johnson, Edgar *Sir Walter Scott: The Great Unknown*, vol, ii. London, 1970

Knighton, Lady *Memoirs of Sir William Knighton, Bart*. London, 1938

Lever, Tresham *The Letters of Lady Palmerston*. London, 1957

Lieven, Dorothea de *The Private Letters of Princess Lieven to Prince Metternich, 1820–26*, edited by Peter Quennell assisted in translation by Dilys Powell. London, 1937

—— *Letters of Dorothea, Princess Lieven, during her residence in London, 1812–34*, edited by Lionel G. Robinson. London, 1902

Lockhart, J. G. *Memoirs of the Life of Sir Walter Scott, Bart*. Edinburgh, 1838

—— *Narrative of the Life of Sir Walter Scott, begun by himself and continued by J. G. Lockhart*. Edinburgh, 1848

Macleod, Donald *A History of Destitution in Sutherlandshire*. 1841

—— *Gloomy Memories in the Highlands of Scotland*. 1857

Mudie, Robert *A Historical Account of His Majesty's Visit to Scotland*. Edinburgh, 1822

Oman, Carola *The Wizard of the North, the Life of Sir Walter Scott*. London, 1973

Parker, Charles Stuart *Sir Robert Peel, from his Private Correspondence.* London, 1891

Pope-Hennessy, Una *The Laird of Abbotsford.* London, 1932

Quayle, Eric *The Ruin of Sir Walter Scott.* London, 1968

Rogers, Rev. Charles *The Life and Songs of the Baroness Nairne.* London, 1869

Sage, Rev. Donald *Memorabilia Domestica.* Edinburgh, 1889

Scott, Sir Walter *Hints addressed to the Inhabitants of Edinburgh and Others in Prospect of His Majesty's Visit, by an Old Citizen.* Edinburgh, 1822

Skene, James *The Skene Papers – Memories of Sir Walter Scott,* edited by Basil Thomson. London, 1909

Skinner, Basil *Scott as Pageant-Master – the Royal Visit of 1822.* Scott Bicentenary Essays, edited by Alan Bell. Edinburgh, 1973

Stewart of Garth, David *Sketches of the Character, Manners and Present State of the Highlanders of Scotland, with details of the Military Service of the Highland Regiments.* Edinburgh, 1822

Tullibardine, Marchioness of *A Military History of Perthshire, 1660–1902,* vol. i. Edinburgh, 1908

Crofters' Commission, Baron Napier and Ettrick *praeses Report of Her Majesty's Commissioners of Inquiry into the Condition of the Crofters and Cottars in the Highlands and Islands of Scotland.* Edinburgh, 1884

—— *Evidence taken by Her Majesty's Commissioners of Inquiry into the Condition of the Crofters and Cottars in the Highlands and Islands of Scotland.* Edinburgh, 1884

INDEX

385

INDEX

Perestroika

Mikhail Gorbachev

Updated to include Mikhail Gorbachev's June 1988 Speech to the Party Conference

Perestroika, which means 'restructuring', is Mikhail Gorbachev's own unprecedented account of the revolution he is at present implementing in the USSR: a revolution in attitudes, in ideas and in practice that entails a radical alteration of both domestic and foreign policy. For perestroika is the next stage in socialist history, when greater responsibility, initiative, openness and a spirit of 'emulation' are to be strongly encouraged in the people through a real sense of personal involvement.

Global peace is the fruit for which perestroika is potentially the seed. Frank in his criticisms of the past, trenchant in his recommendations for the present, the General Secretary is unswerving in his conviction that the needs of the world are inseparable from those of his country in the search for 'a nuclear-free, non-violent world'. *Perestroika* is a coherent, inspiring vision for an international political scene as fraught and divided as it has ever been, and must be one of the most important political documents of our times.

'Gorbachev's grand design for the renewal of mankind . . . is breathtaking'   *The Times*

The Real Charles

Alan Hamilton

Outspoken reactionary, meddling in community affairs he knows nothing of? Naive idealist, hijacked by the 'loony green brigade'? Frustrated heir? Shy and irrelevant appendage to Diana's glamour?

Or warm, witty and forthright man of action? A scholar and leader of tremendous moral courage, a sportsman who has pushed himself to the limits of physical endurance, and a worthy successor to the throne of England?

In his hard-hitting, controversial biography, royal watcher and *Times* correspondent Alan Hamilton sweeps aside the gossip to lay bare *The Real Charles*. Tracking the fine achievements of a startlingly varied career, he reveals why Charles's first forty years have proved critical for the future of the King of England.

FONTANA PAPERBACKS

Fontana Paperbacks

Scottish Interest Titles
Non-Fiction

☐ The Clans & Tartans of Scotland (*illus*) **B**	**ROBERT BAIN**	£4.95
☐ The Poems and Songs of Robert Burns	**JAMES BARKE (Ed)**	£3.95
☐ Land of the Scots (*illus*)	**CAROLINE BINGHAM**	£2.75
☐ Benny (*illus*)	**JOHN BURROWES**	£2.95
☐ The Magic of Findhorn	**PAUL HAWKEN**	£2.50
☐ Scotland (*illus*) **LF**	**LORD HOME**	£2.95
☐ The Stuarts (*illus*)	**J.P. KENYON**	£2.50
☐ A Century of the Scottish People, 1830–1950 **B**		
	T.C. SMOUT	£6.95
☐ A History of the Scottish People, 1560–1830 **B**		£6.95
☐ The Life and Death of St Kilda (*illus*) **B**	**TOM STEEL**	£3.95
☐ Scotland's Story (*illus*) **B**		£4.95
☐ Gazetteer of Scottish Ghosts (*illus*) **B**		
	PETER UNDERWOOD	£1.95
☐ A Grain of Truth	**JACK WEBSTER**	£2.95

You can buy Fontana paperbacks at your local bookshop or newsagent. Or you can order them from Fontana Paperbacks, Cash Sales Department, Box 29, Douglas, Isle of Man. Please send a cheque, postal or money order (not currency) worth the purchase price plus 22p per book for postage (maximum postage required is £3).

NAME (Block letters) _____

ADDRESS _____

_____

While every effort is made to keep prices low, it is sometimes necessary to increase them at short notice. Fontana Paperbacks reserve the right to show new retail prices on covers which may differ from those previously advertised in the text or elsewhere.

Tom Steel

The Life and Death of St Kilda

On 29 August 1930 the remaining 36 inhabitants of this bleak but spectacular island off Scotland's western coast took ship for the mainland. A community that had survived alone for centuries finally succumbed to the ravages that resulted from mainland contact. What their lives had been like century after century, why they left, and what happened to them afterwards is the subject of Tom Steel's fascinating book. It is the story of a way of life unlike any other, told here in words and pictures, and of how the impact of twentieth-century civilization led to its death.

This edition contains two new chapters that take account of the lives of those who, for very different reasons and in very different ways, have come to live and work on St Kilda in recent years and have continued the extraordinary story of this most gruelling and spectacularly beautiful island.

'First-rate recreation of a vanished way of life' – *Scotsman*

'Compulsive reading' – *Guardian*

A FONTANA ORIGINAL